Christian Morality & You

Right & Wrong in an Age of Freedom

Christian Morality & You

James Finley
Michael Pennock

Ave Maria Press • Notre Dame, Ind. 46556

Nihil Obstat: Rev. Mark A. DiNardo
                Censor Deputatus

Imprimatur: Most Rev. James A. Hickey, S.T.D.
                Bishop of Cleveland

Library of Congress Catalog Card Number: 76-15218
International Standard Book Number: 0-87793-112-7

Photography: Ronald Brander, cover; Terry Barrett, 96;
                John Howard, 164; Martha Howard, 8, 180;
                Mary E. Kronstein, 18, 56, 66, 102, 112, 117, 122;
                Religious News Service, 46;
                Bruce Roberts, 130, 138, 184-5;
                Patrick Slatery, 30, 84, 146.

Printed in the United States of America

Acknowledgments

We wish to thank the following individuals for their strong support, kind help and constructive criticism. The strengths of the text lie in no small measure to their help.

Msgr. William Novicky and Father Mark DiNardo have given unceasing support in guiding this project to its completion. Father Paul Hritz has greatly helped in forming the theological outlook of the authors and the text. Father Dennis Dillon, S.J., has been an outstanding editorial advisor. Many of his suggestions have been incorporated. Sister Mary Owen, S.N.D., has helped in the technical aspects of the production. Sister Mary Andre, O.S.U., did the original cover for the pilot project.

We are indebted to the following for their suggestions and comments: Father Don Cozzens, Sister Cathy Hilkert, O.P., Sister Caroline Capuano, H.M., Sister Ruth Ann Bruner, H.M., Sister Pat Finn, C.S.J., Sister Marianne Durkin, C.S.A., Steve Schnell, Dr. Fred Schnell, Patrick Riley, Rosey Torrence, Blair Chirdon, Bert Polito, Sister Mary Borgias, S.N.D., Sister Julie Marie, S.N.D., the theology faculty at St. Ignatius High School and the countless students we have taught, both past and present.

Special thanks to our wives, Kaye and Carol, for giving us the needed moral support to bring this project to completion.

James Finley
Michael Pennock

Contents

1   Who Are You? 9

2   Who Are You?—A Christian Response 19

3   Relationship and Responsibility 31

4   The Ethical Teachings of Jesus 47

5   Conscience 67

6   Law and Freedom 85

7   What's This Thing Called Sin? 103

8   Sexual Morality 123

9   Respect for Life 139

10   The Community Dimension in Morality 153

11   Sources of Morality 165

12   Christian Morality—Summary and Problems 181

1

Who Are You?

"Man is an epitome of the world; he is a little world in himself, in which all that is to be found in the great world of the universe is to be found."
—St. Francis de Sales *(Spiritual Conferences, 3)*

It might seem strange to the reader that a book on morality should begin with a chapter entitled "Who Are You?" After all, don't most of us know who we are? What has that got to do with what is right and what is wrong? Hopefully, the answer to that question will become plain in this chapter and the next.

For starters, we might mention that the real value in defining who we are comes when we begin to apply that definition to how we relate to others. It is in knowing ourselves that we can better understand how we ought to act toward others.

Before we actually begin our inquiry into the question "who are you?" let us reflect for a few moments on how we answer that question at this point in our lives. Below you will find six brief descriptions of man as seen by various philosophers in different times and different places. For the sake of this exercise, these descriptions are greatly simplified and contain just a kernel thought which helps to characterize a particular way of looking at who we are. Under each description is a scale on which you are asked to mark whether you strongly agree (7), agree (6), agree somewhat (5), are indifferent to (4), disagree somewhat (3), disagree (2), or strongly disagree (1) with the statements made. Choose as best you can by deciding where you stand in relation to the question "who is man?"

9

PHILOSOPHY #1:   "I cannot live locked up inside myself. I must be open to the world and those around me. I must be meditative so that other people and the forces found in the universe can flow through me so that I can overcome all illusion about myself and the world and thus discover an ultimate reality."

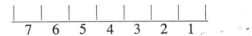

PHILOSOPHY #2:   "I'm here for one purpose: to get as much 'gusto' out of life as I can. Pain and suffering are evils that must be avoided at all costs. The main thing in life is to always feel good."

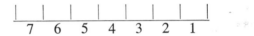

PHILOSOPHY #3:   "My purpose in life is to work for the glorification of the group. The individual has no worth as such. I'm like a cog in a big machine as I submit my efforts to the larger efforts of the state."

PHILOSOPHY #4:   "I must do whatever I can to increase my own 'freedom.' Freedom means doing what I want to do. 'Hell is other people.' What is good is that which furthers my interests."

PHILOSOPHY #5:   "I have worth. I must strive to live a life of loving service for my fellowmen, all of whom in the last analysis are my brothers and sisters. Life has a final meaning which resides outside of me, that is, in God, and in my relationship to Jesus Christ."

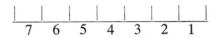

PHILOSOPHY #6: "In the light of death, life has no real meaning. It is a joke—'the tale of an idiot signifying nothing.' "

These rather overdrawn examples illustrate contrasting views of how we can look at life and a person who tries to find some meaning in that life. We will discuss several of these in more detail later in the chapter. But you may be interested to know which major views the above descriptions represent.

Philosophy #1 describes an *Oriental* view of man. Some Buddhists, for example, try to live a life of gentle submissiveness to the cosmic powers flowing in the universe, powers which they try to let control their destiny.

Philosophy #2 corresponds to the *Playboy* theory of life. This is sometimes known as *hedonism* where pleasure, especially of the physical, sensual type, is almost made into a god. You will find this philosophy pushed in many advertisements bombarding the American scene today.

Philosophy #3 delineates a *communistic* view of man. The best-known exponent of this way of life was Karl Marx, who preached that the individual has worth only to the degree that he helps the interests of the state. Over half the world's population is dominated by this view of humanity.

Philosophy #4 depicts an extremely individualistic way of looking at man. It is sometimes called *atheistic existentialism* and its most famous proponent is the French writer Jean-Paul Sartre. Unlike John Donne who wrote that "No man is an island unto himself," Sartre holds that each person is radically alone and separated from all others.

Moving to the next description, one can easily see that Philosophy # 5 best describes a *Christian* way of life. Chapter 2 will develop in some detail the presuppositions of this view of man.

And, finally, Philosophy #6 corresponds to a *nihilistic* world view which maintains that man and his life have no ultimate meaning. This philosophy was especially popular in Europe during the aftermath of the Great Depression.

You may wish to form into small groups of 3-4 for the following exercise.

Please rank in order the above philosophies, from the most to the least desirable to live by. Try to state reasons for your choices.

You might also rank them as you think most Americans would. Try to offer evidences for your ranking.

THE IMPORTANCE OF OUR CONCEPT OF MAN

The preceding exercise was important because it helped us think about our concept of man. There are few things in life more important than our way of thinking about ourselves and others. This is true because our behavior towards others often enough flows from what we think about mankind in general. Even our attitudes towards others are affected by the way we think about humanity. The theory we consciously or unconsciously hold about others strikingly determines our practice towards them.

A couple of examples may help here. Have you ever met a person for the first time and immediately liked him or her? Do you notice how you acted towards the person afterwards? Most probably, you were kind, considerate, and well-disposed towards the person. Or consider a person you do not like even though you cannot quite understand why. You find yourself being rude and short-tempered with him or her for no apparent reason. Perhaps the reason lies in an initial negative impression of the person which has sunk into your unconscious and which helps make you relate negatively to the person.

The first example recalls a famous psychological experiment in the education field. The purpose of the experiment was to test the theory that our general idea of people strongly affects our behavior towards them. In a controlled experiment, a group of teachers were told that their new class of students was a "superior" group. In reality the class was quite "average." But because the students were "billed" as bright students, the teachers expected good results. The teachers' positive attitudes towards the students helped them to achieve beyond their ability.

One thing should be noted: It is impossible to escape a particular concept of man. We are brought up in an environment which works on certain assumptions about man. We naturally, and very often unconsciously, absorb these assumptions and theories without ever really examining them critically to see how valid they are. Environmental factors like advertising, sports, movies, television, business ethics and numerous other social pressures greatly affect the way we view a person and consequently how he should act.

For example, look at modern advertisements. Commercials for deodorants, mouthwashes, skin blemish removers and other cosmetics have a basic assumption that man is a creature who must be physically attractive to have much worth in the eyes of his fellowman. They try to sell the American public the following concept of a person: to have good breath and white teeth is to be a good person; to have bad breath is to be socially undesirable.

Note how this view has affected us in our relationships to others. How many of us judge the value of others on externals such as how they look rather than on what they are internally? The so-called "beautiful people" are not better than the rest of us (and indeed not worse), but notice how advertisements and movies make them out to be the ideal people the rest of us are somehow supposed to emulate and imitate.

"You owe it to yourself." Advertising has another subtle effect on us in that it creates needs. Blaring over the airwaves, hitting us graphically in newspapers and magazines, sophisticated ads and commercials sell us the philosophy of consumerism. Consumerism works on the principle of "buy, buy, buy" even if you cannot afford the product or even if you do not need it. The real dehumanizing effect of consumerism is that it takes place at the expense of others. We Americans get fatter and fatter (literally as well as figuratively) by consuming nonessential items while the poor of the world get poorer and poorer. It is not that our commercialized society tells us not to think about the poor and those exploited by us in our quest for more and more goods. Rather, it sells us on our need to indulge *ourselves*. But it is in indulging ourselves that we often forget others.

A further example comes from the world of business and politics. A silent assumption on which some politicians and businessmen work is "the public be damned." The man who can "get away with something" without getting caught is often presented as an ideal. Thus, prices can be inflated through price-fixing, or secret contributions can be collected in order to influence policies. These unethical practices are seen as o.k. as long as the businessman or the politician can get away with them. And even if one should get caught, we often hear the excuse that "everyone else is doing it." The assumption behind this behavior is that the public is generally too stupid to know of the corruption that is going on or that the mass of people is easily led and will "buy" almost anything that their business and political leaders sell them. This rather callous view of humanity is not much different from the view of advertising that sees a person as just a body to be beautified.

In what way has advertising influenced you to buy something in recent months? What are some of the assumptions about man that were behind those advertisements?

Can you think of other influences in modern society that "push" a certain view of man?

Why do you think people accept these influences so easily?

DIFFERENT PHILOSOPHIES AND HOW ONE SHOULD ACT

Therefore, it is rather easy to see that what we think a person is greatly affects the way we will act towards others. Consider again our exercise. One of the philosophies discussed there was the Playboy philosophy of hedonism. The Playboy views others as objects whose purpose in life is merely to help him attain happiness. In relating to others, the Playboy will tend to frown upon any total commitment to the other which might involve sacrifice or pain because sacrifice and pain will lessen his pleasure. Thus, a total commitment like marriage, which by its nature is permanent, is taboo for the Playboy type. Marriage for the Playboy is only all right as long as it is temporary and he will not be inconvenienced or asked to sacrifice.

The *Marxian-communist* view of man has strong appeal to many people in the world today. In this view of man, the individual is subordinated to the group. Individual rights, therefore, only exist by the whim of the state. The right to worship, to work where one pleases, to speak out freely against injustices will all be curtailed if the larger group, the state, wants them limited. Individual right to life as such does not exist; abortion, murder of political dissidents, suppression of religious practice will take place if the state thinks them useful. All of these practices flow from the basic view of man that is held by the communist.

One final example from our exercise is that of the *atheistic-existentialist*. His philosophy is very individualistic and pragmatic. An atheist like Jean-Paul Sartre believes that a person is born into absurdity and feels nausea as he realizes this. A certain amount of absurdity can be overcome when the individual chooses to be himself, but as he chooses, he feels alone and in despair. Life has no ultimate meaning. No one can help man, not even God. Some existentialists who accept this view of reality (though not Sartre himself) see no reason to help better the condition of humanity. After all, what is the sense of cleaning up a polluted environment or working for peace or distributing better the goods of the world?

Such efforts, in the last analysis, are folly because life itself has no meaning. Since man is fundamentally and radically alone and isolated from others, why be bothered by social concerns?

These various views of man are all competing for the attention of the Christian. They bombard us daily. They come from the world of politics, from the world of the communications media, from the world of everyday life. At times, we are confused as to which of them are correct, which of them are to be accepted or rejected. Is man just a body who is to give in to every pleasure that comes along? Is he just a sheep in a flock which is easily led? Does life have no meaning?

One idea does clearly emerge from this discussion: If we do not formulate for ourselves a proper image of man, we will easily fall into accepting one which is not at its core Christian. For the Christian, *action* is a way of life. He does not easily and unthinkingly accept everything that comes along. He is one who acts, one who has a definite vision of man and acts according to that vision. He is very reluctant to be tossed about by what others in society would like him to be—whether it be just a pleasure machine, a cog in a smooth-functioning operation, or an isolated individual.

The Christian is one who decides his own course of life because he knows that "not to decide is to decide." The Christian relates positively towards others because he has accepted in faith the word of God. It is precisely this vision which we receive from God's word that we will discuss in the next chapter.

ACTIVITIES

    1. Bring to class a series of ads from commercials, magazines, etc. You might also select a contemporary record or two. Taping commercials from the TV or radio will enhance the exercise even more.

        a. Examine each ad for what it is trying to sell on the surface level. For example, Pepsi ads sell "soft drinks."

b. Then, reexamine the ads to note the assumptions they make about man. For example, Pepsi—What is desirable is to be physically attractive and young, a member of the so-called "Pepsi-generation."

2. The following exercise is designed for you to examine your values and to try to understand where you get them.

   a. Write a short essay trying to answer the question, "What do I consider a 'successful' life for me?"

   b. If you want, share your essay with several other members of your class.

   c. Discuss or think about these questions:

      (1) What is *success?*
      (2) In your view of a successful life for you, what has influenced you to make the choice you did?
      (3) Are these good or bad influences?

   d. The purpose of this exercise is to show that your view of your future has a built-in prejudgment about how you view what is good for men in general.

3. Consider this definition of Christian morality by Sertillanges as quoted by Father Marc Oraison's *Morality for Our Times*: Morality is "the science of what man ought to be by reason of what he is."

   a. If morality is a science, and by definition science is an open-ended body of knowledge, then can our application of moral principles change the more we learn about man? For example, can Christians today tolerate slavery or subjugation of women in light of our current understanding of equality?

   b. If morality is based on the search for norms of free human conduct in light of what man is, how important is it to examine one's view of man? Will a Christian have a different view of man than a Buddhist or an atheist? Where does the Christian get his view of man?

2
Who Are You?
--A Christian Response

"All who are led by the Spirit of God are sons of God. You did not receive a spirit of slavery leading you back into fear, but a spirit of adoption through which you cry out, 'Abba!' (that is, 'Father'). The Spirit himself gives witness with our spirit that we are children of God. But if we are children, we are heirs as well: heirs of God, heirs with Christ, if only we suffer with him so as to be glorified with him."

—St. Paul *(Romans 8:14-17)*

In the last chapter, we saw how others viewed who man is. In the present chapter we shall analyze yet another way to answer that question—the Christian response. A Christian vision of who we are is a unique way of answering the question. When this vision is accepted, it helps us to relate to others in such a way that we are truly responding to the call of God.

There are three basic ways by which the Christian knows who man is. The first is from the way things are, that is, *from the nature of things.* Our very makeup reveals something about us. This has been called many things. Among these, the most common terms are "natural law" or "natural revelation."

The second source of our concept of man comes to us from what God has revealed to us throughout the history of the Jews in the Old Testament. Our faith in *salvation history,* which is God's way of working in man's history, has told us something about ourselves that we could not necessarily reason to.

19

The final source of a Christian vision of man comes to us from the word spoken to us by God the Father through his Son, Jesus Christ, who is the *Word of God*. The Father wishes to communicate to us in the best way possible in order to tell us about himself, ourselves and our relationships with others. Thus, he sent his Son to speak to us through word, deed and especially through his suffering, death and resurrection. In this chapter we shall analyze each one of these sources of a Christian concept of man.

NATURAL LAW

In the words of Teilhard de Chardin, because man is the only animal who "knows that he knows," he is able through *reason* to discover many things about himself. He is able to discover the divine plan for things, including himself, in their very makeup, that is, in the way they are.

Rational

One of the first truths we discover about ourselves is that *we can think*. Though this seems pretty obvious to a casual observer of the human scene, it is the power of rationality which enables us to figure out problems, discover laws within nature, improve our lot as men, and the like. It is this ability more than any other which has helped men to progress. Your pet dog is very much like his great ancestors of the past who were domesticated by your great ancestors in the caves. Your dog can do only what his ancestors did; but you have benefited from the collective wisdom and learnings of men and women before you. The mere fact that you can read and learn from the experience of others, probably in a warm, sheltered environment, not worrying where your next meal is coming from, is proof of this great gift of thinking in mankind.

Free

A fundamental human trait, noted by social scientists as well as theologians, is an individual's *ability to choose*. Unlike animals who are totally bound by instinct, man has a certain amount of freedom which enables him to change, to improve his lot, to direct his future. In more traditional terms, this ability is known as *free will* and it certainly is the faculty which enables man to choose between good and evil. Without it, man can hardly be considered capable of doing right or wrong.

Though psychology has shown that a great deal of a person's behavior is determined by his heredity and environment, almost all social scientists admit that a person does have a certain amount of freedom which enables him to choose. True, I cannot control the environment into which I am born; nor do I have much control over the body I am born into, with its various hereditary strengths and weaknesses. But I still have a certain degree of freedom to change my environment and to work with my particular talents.

For example, I may be born into a family and a society which is extremely bigoted towards members of another race. I am taught to be prejudiced and discriminatory toward this other race. But I may very well grow into maturity regarding human relations by remaining open to other ideas as I am exposed to them. Despite the fact that I am brought up as a bigot in a bigoted society, this does not inevitably force me to be a bigot all my life. If I think, read, talk to others, and then use my freedom, even though it is limited, I can to some extent become more tolerant and loving of all peoples.

Love

One of the greatest proofs of man's freedom is that he can willingly desire the good of another person or he can willingly not desire the good of another person. If he does desire the good of another, he loves. *It takes freedom to love.* The human experience of poets, songwriters, young couples, parents, as well as ourselves, tells us that we are capable of loving or not loving. In one sense, love is the highest form of choosing: this is so because it is choosing "for" other people. Choosing "for" others means advancing their well-being, making sure that they grow, creating the atmosphere in which good things happen to them. This ability which is innate in man is denied to animal and plant life as we know it.

Body-person

We are not only thinking beings and persons capable of loving, we are *body-persons* as well. Having a body, which is part of material creation, manifests a person's relationship to the rest of created reality. (See next chapter.) Some intellectuals would like to pretend that we are purely and merely thinkers, but the reality of the situation is that we have bodies. We become ourselves through the bodies we have. We express ourselves and experience reality through our emotions, our desires and drives, our feelings, and our likes and dislikes. All of these help make us who we are.

Unique, though social

One of the real paradoxes of the human condition is that each of us is a unique person unlike any other person past, present, or future. This means we are each distinct like the rarest of gems which has its own particular glimmer. And yet, despite the fact of our uniqueness, we are social beings. Our uniqueness shines forth only in community with others. We individuals can only become who we are in relationship to others. What a great paradox that is! We can only become ourselves when we relate to others as individuals in the great human family.

Historical

Another characteristic of man is his continuity with the past. In this sense man is a historical being. As stated above, your superiority to your dog is not just that you can think but that you can think in continuity with your past. You sum up in your humanity all that has preceded you. If you would develop total and instantaneous amnesia, your first question would be "who am I?" You would not know yourself because you would not know your past. You are your past. In the same way, the human race has a memory. To be an American is to live in openness to those who lived before you, and likewise, your children's children will live on the fruits of what you do today.

The following illustration indicates how you are a unique genetic blend of all those who came before you. You, too, are in process with the flow which is humanity. You add to the progress of the race by handing on your talents, insights, and values to the future. You are within the continuity of humankind and potentially can add significantly to it.

```
FAMILY TREE              SIGNIFICANT EVENTS

xx  xx  xx  xx    (great-grandparents)  Victorian Age
 |   |   |   |                          Mechanized farm
 ↓   ↓   ↓   ↓                             equipment
                                        Factories

 x   x   x   x    (grandparents)        World War I
   ↓       ↓                            radio
                                        automobiles

   x       x      (parents)             World War II
       ↓                                jet flight
                                        television

       x          (you)                 Man on moon
       ↓                                "Future shock"

     xxx          (children)                 ?
       ↓

 xxxxxxxxxx       (grandchildren)            ?
```

Illustration: Each individual is a genetic blend of all those who preceded him. He carries on the flow of humanity. In the three generations before you, 14 people were involved in bringing you into existence. In four generations, 30 people. In five generations, which is about 100 years, 62 people! This simple illustration underscores our continuity with humanity. We are links in a chain. We have been formed by our individual and collective pasts and we shall in turn form the future. But this is not the whole story. On the contrary, as we shall see, the mystery of man is his *freedom.*

To sum up this section, we can see that natural law or man's reason looking at his very makeup reveals that he can think, that he is a body-person, uniquely an individual in community with others.

He is a historical being endowed with free will which enables him to choose. Briefly stated, man is a loving thinker, or described in another way, a thinking lover.

In light of what has been said so far, which of the following do you think are right or wrong? Put a check mark under the appropriate "Right" or "Wrong" column.

	Right	Wrong
Nuclear testing in the atmosphere for "defense purposes"	☐	☐
Undergoing hypnosis for kicks	☐	☐
Having an operation to make one look ten years younger	☐	☐
Going off and living alone in the woods for the rest of one's life	☐	☐
Voluntarily voting in a government which is against "freedom of the press"	☐	☐
Experimenting with drugs in order to expand one's consciousness	☐	☐
Taking one's own life	☐	☐
Running into the street to save a little child knowing that one's life will be taken as a result of the action	☐	☐

Share your responses in small groups. Discuss reasons for your choices.

OLD TESTAMENT REVELATION

The word of God written into the nature of things is not the only way by which man discovers who he is. The written word of God as found in the Old Testament also reveals to us certain things about man.

Image of God

The most striking revelation about the nature of man comes from the book of Genesis. There it is written: "God created man in his image; in the divine image he created them; male and female he created them" (Gn 1:27). What a tremendous thought that is! By being created in the very image of God, a person's very activity of thinking and loving, in fact his or her very being, reflects the beauty, the wisdom, the love of the Creator.

Fundamentally good

Reading further along in Genesis, we note that "God looked at everything he had made, and he found it very good," (Gn 1:31). It is precisely because we are the very image of God that we are fundamentally good. What a refreshing thought this is in contradistinction to those philosophies of life which hold that man is evil and has no worth. Maintaining that we are good at the core of our being should give us hopefulness concerning our destiny.

There is one important implication which flows from an understanding of humanity as image of God which reflects his goodness: The more a person acts according to the way he or she is made, the more he or she reflects the Creator. Man gives glory to God by being man! We are not, as taught in a more pessimistic philosophy of life, mere clods of earth. We are reflections, images of the Creator.

God's partner

In that same first chapter of Genesis we discover that we are God's partners. "God blessed them, saying: 'Be fertile and multiply; fill the earth and subdue it' " (Gn 1:28). We are in a very real sense *cocreators* with God because we have been given dominion over all of creation, a dominion which we must rule, develop and take care of. In the practical order, what this means is that man is to share in the development of the world.

"The fish of the sea, the birds of the air, and all living things that move on the earth" have been given for man's use and betterment. We are like caretakers who are to use the rest of created reality to develop ourselves. In using creation to develop ourselves, we are in fact drawing closer to our Creator. Using creation, of course, does not mean abusing it. We are not meant to rape the environment. Our task is to hold created reality as a trust in order for us to live our lives with others in as fruitful a way as we can. We are to cooperate in the divine plan by developing, expanding and properly using the goods of the earth which have been given to us.

NEW TESTAMENT REVELATION: Jesus Christ

Turning to our third source of a Christian concept of man, the New Testament, we will refer to one insight, perhaps the most important one, that Jesus has given to us.

Our most basic Christian belief is that a certain man named Jesus of Nazareth is God. Or to state it in another way, God poured himself out and became united with his creation through the great and profound mystery of the Incarnation. God, in short, became one of us. He became one with us in the person of his Son, Jesus Christ. We cannot begin to grasp the depth of the mystery which is the Incarnation, but we can note a few startling implications which are relevant to this discussion.

First of all, if God became one of us in order to share, indeed to give his life for us, what tremendous worth we men must have in the eyes of God. Our belief is that because Jesus died, men live. And we live because the Father must love us so much that he was willing to give his Son to us.

But it is in giving himself to us that the great mystery lies. If God became man, then he too entered history and he is part of our world. Jesus continually referred to God as "Abba," which means Father. God is his Father. But notice the profound and humbling truth which Jesus told us about ourselves. When the apostles asked him in Matthew's Gospel how they should pray, Jesus taught them the "Our Father" (Mt 6:9-15). He told his disciples and he tells us that we can dare address God by the same title that he himself used. This revelation of Jesus should change the course of human history. It is true that we are not sons and daughters of God in the same way that Jesus Christ is the Son of God, but we have been adopted into the family, so to speak. We have been adopted and we are in continuity with our brother, the Son of God, Jesus.

Family of Man

What then is the earthshaking reality present in this truth? If indeed we are sons and daughters of the Father by adoption and Jesus is our brother—and our faith tells us this is so—*then we men and women are brothers and sisters.* We are not mere members of a common herd which is humanity, we are not radically isolated from one another, nor are we worthless beings. *We are simply members of the same family under the Fatherhood of God.* And if this is what we are, and there is absolutely no reason to doubt the word of Jesus, then we can easily understand how we ought to relate to one another. Because of the profound insight Jesus has shared with us, we must without hesitation treat one another as brothers and sisters.

The gift of the Holy Spirit given to the Christian at Baptism enables him to accept in truth this common brotherhood. It is the Spirit of Jesus and his Father which binds us together into this family, into the body with Christ as the head. The Spirit enables us to live this reality in joy, peace, patience, charity, gladness and friendliness.

When Jesus taught his disciples about the Last Judgment, he most certainly had in mind the unity of mankind. By becoming one of us, God wants us to treat one another with the greatest of love and respect. Let us now read the words of the Evangelist:

> When the Son of Man comes in his glory, escorted by all the angels of heaven, he will sit upon his royal throne, and all the nations will be assembled before him. Then he will separate them into two groups, as a shepherd separates sheep from goats. The sheep he will place on his right hand, the goats on his left. The king will say to those on his right: *"Come, you have my Father's blessing! Inherit the kingdom prepared for you from the creation of the world. For I was hungry and you gave me food, I was thirsty and you gave me drink, I was a stranger and you welcomed me, naked and you clothed me. I was ill and you comforted me, in prison and you came to visit me."* Then the just will ask him: *"Lord, when did we see you hungry*

and feed you or see you thirsty and give you drink? When did we welcome you away from home or clothe you in your nakedness? When did we visit you when you were ill or in prison?" The king will answer them. *"I assure you, as often as you did it for one of my least brothers, you did it for me."* Then he will say to those on his left: *"Out of my sight, you condemned, into that everlasting fire prepared for the devil and his angels! I was hungry and you gave me no food, I was thirsty and you gave me no drink. I was away from home and you gave me no welcome, naked and you gave me no clothing. I was ill and in prison and you did not come to comfort me."* Then they in turn will ask: *"Lord, when did we see you hungry or thirsty or away from home or naked or ill or in prison and not attend to your needs?"* He will answer them: *"I assure you, as often as you neglected to do it to one of these least ones, you neglected to do it to me."* These will go off to eternal punishment and the eternal fire.
—Matthew 25:31-46

Doing or failing to do to each other is responding or failing to respond to our brother, Christ. Our basic Christian responsibility flows from this new relationship to Christ: Because he is our brother and we are sons and daughters of the Father by adoption, live as though you are members of the same family.

SUMMARY

If it is true that our concept of man helps us to determine how we ought to act towards others, what are some concrete implications for the one who accepts the Christian view of man we have set forth in this chapter?

To reiterate, we have said that for the Christian, a man is a *rational, loving body-person* who realizes who he is as a *unique individual* by living as the *image of God,* the *partner of the Creator,* who is a child of God, in relating to his fellows in community. If these points are true then it follows:

1. In thinking and loving man becomes more of who he is. The more human he becomes the more he reflects the God who created him. To lessen either of these activities is somehow to

dehumanize man. For example, I am acting as a human when I study or earn a living. Studying and working can be very moral actions because they help me develop as a human. In studying I reflect God's image; by working I cocreate with him. On the other hand, immoral action results when I surrender my ability to think by taking harmful drugs for kicks or drinking in excess because by doing so I am giving up part of what it means to be a man.

2. Because we are social beings, we have tremendous responsibilities in regard to others. We should "subdue the earth" for the benefit of all and in so doing, as partners of God, allow God's creative nature to shine forth for all men. Man is not an island; he lives in relationship to others and the rest of his environment and he must do his best to live in harmony with them. For example, it would be wrong for man to pollute the atmosphere by his great misuse of the good clean air necessary for life itself. Pollution is a social sin and an evil because man is God's partner who is to use, not abuse, nature.

3. And, finally, our destiny and movement towards God must be seen as loving and relating to all men, even to the "least of these." Morality is not an individual affair between men and God alone. It ceases to be individual the moment we become members of a family united as brothers and sisters in Christ our Lord. To be a Christian is to be concerned not only for the poor and suffering in our neighborhood, but for the poor and suffering everywhere.

EXERCISE FOR DISCUSSION

List three (3) implications for moral living for each of the following observations concerning man. Share and discuss your observations.

1. Man is a historical being.
   a.
   b.
   c.

2. Man is partner of God.
   a.
   b.
   c.

3. Man lives in community.
   a.
   b.
   c.

3
Relationship and Responsibility

Jesus constantly rebuked the Pharisees for their legalism, that is, their tendency to overemphasize external observance of the law at the price of forgetting the fundamental inner attitude of seeking always to do God's will. The danger of legalism is not a thing of the past. Each of us must constantly try to keep first things first in the realm of morality and this involves, in part, avoiding the notion that morality is nothing more than "keeping the rules."

One way to help us avoid a legalistic attitude in morality is by keeping in mind that ultimately all morality is about love. Jesus tells us this: "As the Father has loved me, so I have loved you. Live on in my love. You will live in my love if you keep my commandments." And a little later in the same text Jesus adds, "You are my friends if you do what I command you" (Jn 15: 9-14). And what is his commandment? He tells us clearly when he says, "This is my commandment: love one another as I have loved you" (Jn 15:12). This chapter is devoted to an examination of morality seen as our free (and hence responsible) response to the love relationship we have with all others as our brothers and sisters in Christ.

Perhaps the best way to begin our discussion of our responsibility for love relationships is by considering for a moment the following incident and what it reveals to us about the kind of responsibility that always accompanies friendship.

Discuss the following incident and answer the questions that follow:

Your best friend has been accused of cheating on a college entrance exam and, as a consequence, is told that he is not eligible for college. In actual fact, you are the one who cheated, yet you say nothing and let him take the severe penalty which you deserve.

1. What was the more seriously immoral act committed here? Was it cheating on the test, or allowing your friend to be hurt?

2. If you said the more serious offense was hurting your friend, what is the reason for your answer? Is it because there is a law which says that you cannot hurt your friends, or is it because there is something in friendship itself that tells you what you did was wrong?

3. Does the wrong committed toward your friend imply some kind of responsibility towards others with whom we have a relationship?

4. Would you say that your failure in friendship was a kind of failure in love? Does all love imply some kind of relationship for which we are responsible?

5. Do you think that what we do to others not only affects our relationship with others but also affects our relationship with God? In other words, can we do anything to hurt our relations with others without at the same time hurting our relationship with God?

RELATIONSHIPS IN THE WORLD OF NATURE

Relationships between two or more people or between people and God are not the only kinds of relationships we know to exist. Indeed, the universe reveals to us a countless number of different kinds of relationships in nature. Examining these relationships briefly can help us better understand human relationships which bring with them moral responsibility.

The world of nature can be seen as a vast network of relationships in which the sum total of living things exists in mutual dependence on one another. Our present awareness of the threat of pollution of the environment has helped to bring out the delicate nature of the relationships that exist among living things, and the devastating results of man's attempt to manipulate the environment in an irresponsible way.

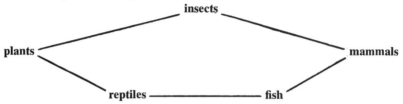

What is to be noted about the relationship that exists between animals is that it is devoid of responsibility, and is so because animals act out of instinct rather than free choice. A lion, for example, is not responsible for killing its prey, nor is the butterfly responsible for taking nectar from the flower. Surely the lion has a relationship to the animal it has just killed, but he did not choose to act toward his victim in the way he did. He killed his prey because he does what lions do. There is no choice in the matter. It would be a waste of time and energy to go out and give a sermon to the lion explaining to him that it is not nice to go around killing other animals the way he does. The reason such an effort would be a waste of time is not merely that animals cannot talk, but also because animals cannot stop being the animals they are. We say that animals act according to their nature or that they act out of instinct. In short, there is no freedom in an animal's relationship to other animals. As we shall see, there is also no valid application of morality to the animal kingdom.

Where there is no freedom, there is no responsibility.
Where there is no responsibility, there is no morality.

INSTINCTUAL LOVE IN THE ANIMAL KINGDOM

There is yet one more characteristic of animal relationships that can help us to understand our own relationship to one another; namely, instinctual love among animals. If we define love in its broadest possible terms, it can be said to be an attraction or desire for something outside ourselves. An example of this among human beings is the common expression of the word "love" whenever we refer to anything we really want to do or have. For example, we often hear expressions such as, "I love apple pie" or "I love to go swimming."

Understanding love in the sense described above, animals can be said to have a certain kind of love for one another and for such things as food and drink. But once again the nature of this love is determined by animal instincts. The mother cat does not choose to love her kittens. In a sense, she cannot not love them. She must love them because her love for them is one with her being a cat. So, even though we can validly show love relationships among animals, the kind of love proper to animals is one with their nature. We cannot, therefore, speak of an animal's obligation or responsibility to love. A cat is no more responsible for loving her kittens than she is for killing a mouse. It is purely a matter of a cat being a cat. There is no freedom here, and so there is likewise no responsibility.

A WORD ABOUT LOVE

Love is a commonly used word today. We see it on bumper stickers and sweatshirts. We hear it on the radio and in poetry. But what is love, really? What does love have to do with morality, personal relationships and responsibility?

Such questions are by no means easy to answer. Love is, in a sense, a mystery and no one will ever be able to fully understand or explain it. For our purposes here, however, we can make a few remarks about love that can help clarify the place of love in our moral response to God.

The most simple and yet one of the most important things to say of love is that it is love that gives us all our personal relationships to one another. Love is that power in us that moves us to go out of ourselves, give of ourselves, and unite ourselves with the one we love. We may experience accidental relationships with others as when we happen to have the same color, or come from the same family, or go to the same school. But we become directly, deeply and personally related to another only when we freely choose to love another and thereby no longer live for our own selfish needs alone but to become concerned about and committed to the happiness of the one we love. Out of such love flow the relationships for which we are morally responsible.

For us as Christians, it is important to note that this personal love for others which gives rise to moral responsibility is not a love that comes primarily from ourselves alone, as though we were free to love or not to love and hence to be responsible for others or not to be responsible as we see fit. Rather, this personal love has existed in God from all eternity, for God is love. And God gives this love to us in Christ for us to accept or reject.

---

1. Below are listed a number of different kinds of love. Briefly indicate the importance and characteristics of each. Also note the painful and destructive results of an abuse of each kind of love. Discuss moral and immoral actions in terms of fidelity to love relationships. What are the unique characteristics of the last form of love given on the list?

   —"Love" for food and pleasure

   —Love of a father for a child

   —Love of a mother for a child

   —Love of son/daughter for father/mother

   —Love for one's self

   —Love for a friend

   —Emotional, sexual love

   —Love of God

2. How does each kind of love constitute a relationship for which we are responsible? What does it mean to say that not to have loved is not to have lived?

3. If you were to list the above kinds of love in order of their importance, in what order would you place them? Give reasons for your choices.

4. Love is a two-way street. In other words, we not only love others, but we are the recipients of others' love as well. Discuss moral responsibility to those who love us.

5. The New Testament tells us that, "Love then consists of this: not that we have loved God, but that he has loved us. He has sent his Son as an offering for our sins" (1 Jn 4:10). What does this tell us concerning our relationship to God? In other words, in what sense are we related to him by love even if we ourselves fail to love him in return?

HUMAN RELATIONSHIPS—THE RESPONSIBILITY TO LOVE IN FREEDOM

The first thing to note about human relationships is that there are many ways in which they resemble animal relationships. This is so because man is an animal. As a mammal, man does more or less what the other members of the animal world do in terms of bodily functions. We are born and we die. We eat, sleep and rear our young. What is more, the science of biology can demonstrate many ways in which our skeletal structure and other bodily traits reveal our membership in the animal world.

This same line of thinking can be carried yet further. Much of our love is also an instinctual type of love. A human mother naturally loves her baby, for example. The mother doesn't have to choose to love it. The love comes spontaneously. We can say the human mother's love is built into her nature much in the same manner as the instinctual love of the cat for her kittens. We are a part of the universe, creatures in nature like all other living things.

The well-known poem *Desiderata* expresses this aspect of human existence:

You are a child of the universe
No less than the trees and the stars
You have a right to be here.
And whether or not it is clear to you,
No doubt the universe is unfolding
As it should.

MAN AS UNIQUE

Now that we have pointed out some salient features of the relationships that exist among animals and gone on to show our close resemblance to the animals, it is now our task to see how we differ from the animals. This is important: It is not enough to say that man is an extremely sophisticated animal, or that he is by far the most developed species of animal on earth. These statements are true in themselves but they become false, from a Christian viewpoint, if they are meant to imply that man is nothing more than this. Christianity holds that man is truly set apart, not because of his biological development, but because he is a person. A person is one who thinks and loves. Both these activities are far beyond the range of animals. Furthermore, man's deepest dignity as a person comes from God in whose image he is made. In the context of Christianity, this is the true meaning of what it means to be a person. If this is what a person is, then morality can be seen to flow from our responsibility to be what we are; namely, reflections of God. But to get to this point we must back up and focus our attention on what it means to say that man is free, and then go on to see how this affects human relationships and eventually calls forth a need for morality.

---

1. Go back to the different philosophies of man listed in Chapter One. Which of the philosophies would tend to stress man's similarity to animals? Which would stress the ways in which man differs from animals? Why?

2. Why do you think Christianity would naturally tend to emphasize man as unique among all creatures?

3. Does the fact that God became a man of flesh and bone call for Christians to be careful that they do not try to deny their bodily life?

4. Look back to the points made in Chapter Two about man's life as being historical. Then discuss how this helps demonstrate human freedom and autonomy from other creatures. Consider: When a fish, for example, is born, it will live out its life in the same way that fish have been doing for millions of years. This is not so with you. You are living out your life in a way that would be vastly different if such men as Christopher Columbus or such events as the Revolutionary War had not made an impact on the course of human events. We not only live a life but we also live a life molded, not by instincts, but by the free acts of others and our own past actions.

5. It was said earlier that a human mother must, in a sense, love her own baby. Discuss the implications involved in pointing out that, unlike the mother cat, the human mother can choose not to love the baby which her instinctual drives as a mother tell her to love.

6. Compare your relationship to your brothers and sisters to the relationship between kittens in a litter. What does it mean to say that you do not choose your brothers and sisters but you must choose whether or not you will love them? Does this chosen love make your bond with them a human one, rather than simply a bond of nature? Does this bond of chosen love also make you responsible for them?

7. Discuss: We are truly part of the animal kingdom, yet, as persons, we are more than animals. It is this "more" that makes us open to moral responsibility.

MAN: Free and Responsible

It is a great dignity to be free. It means that you are not subject to any force outside yourself that controls your behavior. Rather, you stand as the origin of your own actions. This dignity, however, also bears a price tag, and that price tag is responsibility. This is why small children need the guidance of parents. They do not yet possess that freedom that makes them accountable for their actions. Freedom is a prerequisite for responsibility, because if we are not free then we cannot truly choose, and if we cannot truly choose then we cannot be held responsible. The reverse of this is also true. If you try to shirk your responsibility you are at the same time attacking or calling into question your own freedom.

So, then, responsibility is both a dignity and a burden. We want it, yet we fear it at the same time. What high school student, wanting the car for an important date, has not gone to great lengths to convince his parents that he is responsible for his actions and therefore should be allowed to have the car? The same student, however, will, in the event of an accident, try to convince his parents that he is not responsible for what happened.

Discuss the morality of suicide in light of the individual's responsibility for love relationships. Is it true that every self-destructive act in some way destroys those who love us? Apply this to the morality of taking drugs.

There are two well-known stories in the Old Testament which serve very well in demonstrating the tendency in man to shirk the responsibility that comes with his freedom, and then go on to blame his failure on another. The first story is from the opening chapters of the book of Genesis (Gn 3:1-13). As you know, God created Adam and Eve and placed them in the garden of Eden in which they were free to do as they pleased except they were not to eat of the tree of the knowledge of good and evil. The text reads:

> But Yahweh God called to the man . . . "Have you been eating of the tree I forbade you to eat?" The man replied, "It was the woman you put me with; she gave me the fruit, and I ate it." Then Yahweh God asked the woman, "What is this you have done?" The woman replied, "The serpent tempted me and I ate."

The humorous expression, "the devil made me do it" echoes this age-old tendency in us to be quick to dodge the accusing finger and have it pointed elsewhere. What is not so quickly seen is that to dodge one's responsibility is also to dodge one's freedom and so to enter into a dehumanized state resembling the animals.

MAN: Responsible to Love

The second story from the Old Testament goes right to the heart of both morality and the central message of this chapter. The story is also well known and comes from Genesis (Gn 4:1-16). The story is that of Cain and Abel. The scene is similar to that of the Adam and Eve story: Cain has just committed a terrible act, God comes to ask him what he has done. The text reads:

> Cain attacked his brother Abel and killed him. Then the Lord asked Cain, "Where is your brother Abel?" He answered, "I do not know. . . ."

Then Cain asked a question which comes ringing down through the centuries to our own day. Cain asked, "Am I my brother's keeper?" This is the million-dollar question. It is one we must ask ourselves: To what extent are we responsible for the well-being of others?

To answer the question we must stop to think what it means to exist in a relationship to others. There are different ways in which we can speak of relationships. For example, two chairs sitting side by side are in a physical relationship to each other. This lowest type of relationship is simply that of physical proximity.

We saw in animals a higher kind of relationship which arises out of an animal's ability to act upon other beings in its environment. Animals care for, eat, kill, drink, chase and so on. In other words, they directly affect others. This constitutes an active relationship to the world around them. The point is that these active relationships are motivated by instinct. All of an animal's actions proceed from his instincts. Nature then is the ground or atmosphere, as it were, in which animals carry out their relationships.

We also pointed out that man shares in this world of nature. But, he goes beyond the realm of nature in that he is a person, as Chapter Two expressed it, a knowing lover and a loving knower.

An animal can simply live out its life doing whatever it is that its instincts motivate it to do. But you, as a person, cannot simply live out your life. You must choose what you will do. Your life doesn't run under its own steam. You can become a saint or a sinner, a king or a pauper, good or evil. In short, to rise above the moorings of nature is to possess the power to direct your own life in active relationships with others. The question is, if you cannot depend on nature to support the way in which you actively relate to others, then what is to be the atmosphere, the underlying foundation that binds human beings together in truly human relationships?

The answer is love. Love is the be-all and end-all of human

relationships. It is for love that people find a reason to live in the face of unbelievable obstacles. And without love people find other pleasures and goals empty and useless. This love in its highest form must not be restricted to the instinctual love proper to animals. Rather, it must be a chosen love, for chosen love is the ground we walk on. It is chosen love that gives human existence its ultimate dignity and meaning. If the chair you are now sitting on should suddenly give way, you could end up with a broken back. But if those whom you love should suddenly fail to be responsible for their love relationships with you, the result is a broken heart. A broken back is troublesome enough, but a broken heart is destructive of the very fabric that holds human life together and gives it meaning.

The saying, "It's my party, I'll cry if I want to," expresses an attitude that reflects wanting to be free from obligations toward others. Contrast this saying with "When we cry, others taste salt."

Is it "our" party or is it "my" party? In other words, the more deeply you have entered into a love relationship with another, the more deeply your actions affect his or her life. Your life is lived out in an active relationship with the one you are bound to in love. What does this say about your responsibility for this relationship? In these terms, can the freedom that comes in love rule out the freedom of "doing your own thing"? Does freedom become "doing our own thing"?

Consider the pain experienced in a broken home. Does this say something about the immorality of a family member failing to be responsible for the love relationships in the family?

ACTIVE-PASSIVE RELATIONSHIPS

As you look back on your childhood, it is easy to see the deep influence that parents and others have on forming the personality of a child. This illustrates the point that not only do you affect others but others affect you as well. Many of the influences we receive from others are positive ones that help us grow into responsible adults. Yet, hardly anyone escapes negative influences that can leave psychological scars that hinder freedom. This means that many actions that are unkind or in other ways immoral are not actions freely chosen but rather actions motivated by the fears and insecurities of childhood.

This means that human freedom is not absolute but relative to the forces that affect our actions. Growth into adulthood must also be growth into freedom. We must not let ourselves be forever subject to drives and needs that are unworthy of human dignity. This growth in freedom is a lifelong process calling for both patience and determined effort. We discover in this struggle that freedom has a price, that it is not easy to fully act in freedom. But the price of freedom does not equal the price of not being free, for not to be free means not to be human.

Once we realize our own frailty, it helps us to understand the frailty of others, including those people who have hurt us in various ways. Often it is the people who have hurt us that need our forgiveness the most, especially if they are loved ones who have hurt us out of human frailty. When we forgive those who have hurt us, we set them free from their guilt and, at the same time, reach a higher degree of freedom ourselves in deep relationships of freely given forgiveness. It is in this forgiveness that love grows, and we become more fully human.

CHRIST: Relationship and Responsibility

This chapter concludes with a very important question. What difference does Jesus make in our understanding of relationship and responsibility? The conclusion we will be searching for is that in giving us the Holy Spirit, Jesus gives us a new relationship to God and others. This new relationship brings with it the responsibility to love others the way Jesus loved us.

The most obvious way to interpret what it means to love others the way Jesus loved us is to look to Jesus as a model on which to base one's life. St. John clearly confirms the importance of the Christian doing just that. St. John writes, "The way in which we can be sure we are in union with him (Christ) is for the man who claims to abide in him to conduct himself as he did" (1 Jn 2:5-6).

The ideal offered to us in Jesus is that of loving everyone, even our enemies. We see this most clearly in his own death on the cross when instead of hating his executioners he prayed for them saying, "Father, forgive them: they know not what they are doing" (Lk 23:34).

Jesus not only lived out the ideal of unlimited love for others but he went on to tell us to do the same, "My command to you is: love your enemies, pray for your persecutors. This will prove you are sons of your heavenly Father, for his sun rises on the bad and the good. . . In a word, you must be made perfect as your heavenly Father is perfect" (Mt 5:43-48).

Imagine you are walking with a friend, when you suddenly come upon a group of men beating up a young person your own age. Both you and your friend begin shouting for help, but do nothing to try to stop what is going on out of fear of what could happen to yourselves. Suddenly you realize that the young person being beaten up is your own younger brother. In an instant, an automatic reaction causes you to forget what could happen to you, and you rush into the group of men trying to stop them from hurting your brother.

1. What did your sudden recognition of your relationship to the one being beaten up have to do with affecting your responsibility towards him?

2. Discuss the moral teaching of Jesus in terms of helping us to see everyone as our brother. Now what does this say of those who were beating up your brother? Are they your brothers, too? What is your responsibility to them?

3. Discuss: The Christian can hate the evil that is done but he can never hate the one who commits it.

JESUS GIVES US THE SPIRIT

We have seen that Jesus calls us to a new responsibility to love others. What must be realized is that this new responsibility springs from a new relationship to God and others that results from Jesus sending us the Holy Spirit.

The Holy Spirit is the spirit of love that makes the Father and Son to be one in the Trinity. To be given the Holy Spirit is to be given the love that Jesus has for his Father and for us.

The seed of this Christian love, or charity, is given to us in Baptism. Its fulfillment is a lifelong process that takes place as in the Spirit we try more and more to be open to Christ in our lives. In possessing his Spirit we are united to all those he loves, and we are responsible to become his presence on earth. This is the full meaning of a Christian relationship and responsibility to God and others.

In speaking of the central importance of the love we have by possessing the Spirit given to us by Jesus, St. Paul gives us one of the most beautiful and most frequently quoted passages of Scripture:

> Love is patient; love is kind. Love is not jealous, it does not put on airs, it is not snobbish. Love is never rude, it is not self-seeking, it is not prone to anger; neither does it brood over injuries. Love does not rejoice in what is wrong but rejoices in the truth. There is no limit to love's forbearance, to its trust, its hope, its power to endure.
> —1 Cor 13:4-7

None of us measures up to this kind of love. But it is the Spirit of Love given to us by Jesus that draws us toward an ever greater degree of this kind of Christlike love. It is through the eyes of this love that we see others to be truly our brothers and sisters, that we grow to seek the good of others as much as we do our own, and that we find it possible to love even our enemy.

SUMMARY

The material in this chapter can be summarized as follows:

1. All living things exist in a relationship to one another. Mankind is bound together in the union of chosen love.

2. Moral actions are actions that deepen love relationships. Immoral actions fail to respond to the demands of love.

3. Our freedom is never absolute, but we must constantly strive for an ever-increasing degree of freedom with which we can give our love to others.

4. Jesus gives us the Holy Spirit which is the spirit of love with which he loves the Father and us. To be a Christian is to be called to love others with the love of Christ.

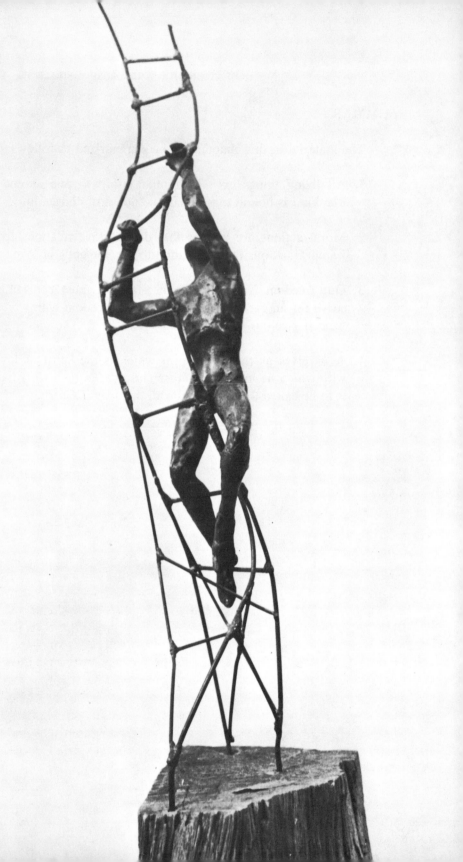

4

The Ethical Teachings of Jesus

To dream the impossible dream,
To fight the unbeatable foe,
To bear with unbearable sorrow,
To run where the brave dare not go.

To right the unrightable wrong,
To love, pure and chaste, from afar,
To try, when your arms are too weary,
To reach the unreachable star!

This is my Quest, to follow that star,
. . .

And the world will be better for this,
That one man, scorned and covered with scars,
Still strove, with his last ounce of courage,
To reach the unreachable stars!
              —from *Man of La Mancha*

Many readers will recognize the words quoted above. They are from the highly successful Broadway musical, later a movie, *Man of La Mancha*. *La Mancha* tells the story of the famed idealist and visionary from literature, Don Quixote. Quixote is one of those rare individuals who met the trials of life with a positive, self-sacrificing attitude of service for others. His story is inspirational because in it he meets the challenges of life head-on. Never once does he let pessimism or a negative attitude permeate his thinking. As a result, he comes across as a Christ-figure who somehow seems very relevant in a world where Christian virtue is sometimes laughed at.

In many ways, we Christians are like Quixote. The message we are called to live by our Lord seems in the eyes of the world to be an "impossible dream." But it is precisely in following him that the "impossible" can become possible. In this chapter, we will investigate more closely the message, the ideal with which Jesus challenges each of his followers.

But before we examine this message, it is rather important to state the following: Much of Christian morality flows from its founder. How seriously we take his message depends pretty much on what we think of him. Perhaps more than any other founder of a religion, *Jesus is his message.* As he himself said, "I am the way, the truth, and the life." He either is the way to eternal life, or he is not. He cannot be both simultaneously.

As we begin this chapter on the living words of Jesus regarding our moral life, it might be interesting to think about our own relationship to him. One of the key questions Jesus asked his apostles was "Who do you say that I am?" This question is as relevant to us today as it was to Peter, James, Thomas, or any of the other apostles. The following questions are difficult ones, but in honestly thinking about our own response to them, we might better appreciate the importance Jesus and his message have in our lives.

Where did you first hear the name *Jesus?*
Who taught you the most about him?
Do you believe that he existed?
Did he ever help you?
Did you ever ask for his help?
What does he mean to you now?
What do you want him to mean?
Where can you find him today?
Do you look for him?
Do you believe his claims and the claims of the Church about him?
Do you want to believe those claims? Why or why not?

These questions, of course, are difficult ones! But in a way they are no more difficult than the question Jesus asked of his weary and confused followers on the seashores of Galilee or on the dusty roads of Judah. Like the ones posed by our Lord, they have as their purpose the focusing of our attention on our beliefs concerning the one person who has most affected human history. Certainly, the more we understand Jesus Christ and the closer we get to him, the more we will be able to make sense of his teaching. In this chapter, then, we shall try to see a little better those words of his upon which Christians for centuries have tried to model their lives.

JESUS AS THE MESSAGE

See what the Father has bestowed on us in letting us be called children of God! Yet that is what we are. The reason the world does not recognize us is that it never recognized the Son. Dearly beloved, we are God's children now; what shall later be has not yet come to light. We know that when it comes to light we shall be like him, for we shall see him as he is. Everyone who has this hope based on him keeps himself pure, as he is pure.

This, remember, is the message you heard from the beginning: we should love one another. We should not follow the example of Cain who belonged to the evil one and killed his brother. Why did he kill him? Because his own deeds were wicked while his brother's were just. No need, then, brothers, to be surprised if the world hates you. That we have passed from death to life we know because we love the brothers. The man who does not love is among the living dead. Anyone who hates his brother is a murderer, and you know that eternal life abides in no murderer's heart. The way we came to understand love was that he laid down his life for us; we too must lay down our lives for our brothers. I ask you, how can God's love survive in a man who has enough of this world's goods yet closes his heart to his brother when he sees him in need? Little children, let us love in deed and in truth and not merely talk about it.

—1 John 3:13; 11-18

The above lengthy quote from St. John's Epistle is an excellent faith-summary for the Christian. It talks of the reality of love as a central reality for the Christian. The reality of a love-response stems from who Jesus is and what he did for us.

As we have already seen reiterated in a couple of chapters, an essential Christian insight into the human condition is that we are the children of God and the brothers and sisters of his Son, Jesus. We should live that reality of adopted children by living a life of love directed towards our brothers and sisters.

Implied in the reality we have been discussing is the Incarnation. For us Christians, the Incarnation is a profound and glorious mystery because in it we profess that God became man in order to draw us to himself. This mystery, as we know from the New Testament, was a stumbling block to faith for both Jew and Gentile. It professes an apparent contradiction, namely, that the infinite, all-powerful God would care to become limited by joining himself with one of his creatures.

Even in his own day, Jesus seemed so ordinary, so like other men, that men and women found it difficult to believe the truth they saw occurring in their midst. For example, Nathanael gave a flippant response to Phillip when he heard that Jesus was the long-awaited prophet: "Can anything good come from Nazareth?" (Jn 1:46). Or note the unwillingness of Jesus to work miracles in his own hometown of Nazareth when his townsfolk scoffed at him: "He could work no miracle there, apart from curing a few who were sick by laying hands on them, so much did their lack of faith distress him" (Mk 6:5).

But it is precisely in and through the humanity of Jesus that God the Father spoke to us men. As St. John so aptly describes the reality of Jesus in his gospel, Jesus is the Word of God spoken so that men may live. His whole life, not only what he taught and spoke, but his every action—his miracles, his loving presence at meals and among the sick in pressing crowds, and especially his suffering, death and resurrection—these all speak to us about fundamental reality.

And what is reality but truth? Note how many people were reluctant or unwilling to hear the truth in his day. (How true is this statement even today!) One of the most significant questions in all the New Testament is asked by Pilate at the trial of Jesus. Recall how Pilate responded to the challenge of Jesus: "Anyone committed to the truth hears my voice." "Truth!" said Pilate, "What does this mean?" (Jn 18:37-38). Here, Pilate was looking Truth himself in the face and, like many today, could not or would not recognize him.

For Jesus, truth was doing the will of his Father. He sums up in his very being the really real—he shows what it means to live, what it means to love. He taught us in human words and with human gestures that his Father intends us for loving union with him and all men, and Jesus actually showed us the greatest form of human love—that of giving one's life for another.

Jesus' message was real, then. By dying on the cross, he put into action the message he had spent three years preaching.

One summary of Jesus' *action-message* can be found in the Sermon on the Mount. It is known as the Golden Rule: "Treat others the way you would have them treat you: this sums up the law and the prophets" (Mt 7:12).

"Do unto others as you would have them do to you." This message is concerned with action, with positive effort on behalf of others. Contrast this with the teaching of a famous Jewish rabbi of Jesus' day. When asked to sum up the teaching of the law and the prophets, the rabbi responded: "Avoid doing to others what you do not wish them to do to you." Whereas the message of Jesus is "to get involved" as the Father has gotten involved with humanity, the rabbi cautions a more conservative approach. The rabbi wants us merely to keep from harming others. Jesus wants us to act, not just react.

Beloved, let us love one another because love is of God; everyone who loves is begotten of God and has knowledge of God. The man without love has known nothing of God, for God is love. God's love was revealed in our midst in this way: he sent his only Son to the world that we might have life through him. Love consists in this: not that we have loved God but that he has loved us and has sent his Son as an offering for our sins. Beloved, if God has loved us so, we must have the same love for one another. No one has seen God. Yet if we love one another God dwells in us. The way we know we remain in him and he in us is that he has given us his Spirit. We have seen for ourselves, and can testify, that the Father has sent the Son as savior of the world. When anyone acknowledges that Jesus is the Son of God, God dwells in him and he in God. We have come to know and to believe in the love God has for us. God is love, and he who abides in love abides in God, and God in him. Our love is brought to perfection in this, that we should have confidence on the day of judgment; for our relation to this world is just like his. Love has no room for fear; rather, perfect love casts out all fear. And since fear has to do with punishment, love is not yet perfect in the one who is afraid. We, for our part, love because he first loved us. If anyone says, "My love is fixed on God," yet hates his brother, he is a liar. One who has no love for the brother he has seen cannot love the God he has not seen. The commandment we have from him is this: whoever loves God must also love his brother.

—1 John 4:7-21

---

1. List and discuss 3 implications of a morality based on "Avoid doing to others what you do not want them to do to you."

2. List and discuss 3 implications of a morality based on "Treat others the way you would have them treat you."

THE LAW OF JESUS: People-Centered

One of the major problems in discussing the "moral teaching" of Jesus is the difficulty in citing specific "laws" he handed down. At times, moralists would like to refer to scripture and cite specific teachings of Jesus on issues such as abortion, euthanasia, cloning and the like, but unfortunately Jesus did not address himself to those specific problems. Rather, many of Jesus' moral decisions were made in concrete circumstances. His so-called "law" is very much people-centered.

As St. John repeatedly points out in his First Epistle, much of Christian morality revolves around the concept of love. For Jesus, love was always situated in a very concrete life situation of interaction among people. For example, in Luke's Gospel (Lk 7:36-50), the notorious sinning woman who anointed his feet was forgiven her sins because of her great love. Indeed, she was even seen as more hospitable than the hypocritical Simon the Pharisee who had invited Jesus to dinner.

Jesus' "law of love" often got him into trouble with the official priestly and scribal interpretation of the Law. One example of this concerned the Law's prohibition of healing on the Sabbath. In Luke's Gospel, we see that Jesus cured a woman possessed for 18 years; he considered his loving action more important than an interpretation of the old Mosaic Law about keeping the Sabbath holy (Lk 13:10-17).

For Jesus, love was never just a concept to be swooned over or sung about. It was always a reality which of its nature must incarnate itself in concrete human deeds like pardoning, lending money without expecting repayment, showing compassion and refraining from judging and condemning others. (Lk 6:27-38).

St. Paul elaborates on the centrality of love in his famous First Letter to the Corinthians. Here, perhaps better than anywhere else in all the literature of the world, we find the truest nature of the love taught by Jesus. Paul teaches that love is patient, kind, not jealous, not pretentious, never snobbish, rude, self-seeking, or prone to anger. Love rejoices in truth and never fails (1 Cor 13:4-8).

THE PARADOX IN JESUS' TEACHING

The more closely a person begins to look at the moral teaching of Jesus, the more he or she begins to see its paradoxical nature. A paradox is a statement which appears to contradict itself. Let us consider a few examples.

> You know how among the Gentiles those who seem to exercise authority lord it over them; their great ones make their importance felt. It cannot be like that with you. Anyone among you who aspires to greatness must serve the rest; whoever wants to rank first among you must serve the needs of all. The Son of Man has not come to be served but to serve—to give his life in ransom for the many.
>
> —Mk 10:42-45

By the standards of the world, this code of living for the Christian seems ridiculous. The world would ask: "How can you be great and powerful if you go around serving others?" But for Jesus, the real Christian is one who imitates him. True greatness lies in serving others, not being served by them.

In John's Gospel, this same teaching appears when Jesus goes around and washes the feet of the apostles. This action of Jesus occurred after a dispute among the disciples as to which one would sit at the place of honor in the kingdom he would establish. Here, in their last moments with Jesus, the apostles were arguing over a place of importance. They seemed to miss the whole thrust of what he had been teaching for his three years with them. To teach them that places of honor, that greatness in the eyes of the world were not part of his message, he got up from his place at the head of the table and went around washing their feet. This task was very humiliating and reserved only for the servant or slave. But Jesus performed it to indicate the wisdom of his paradoxical saying that the first among you shall be last, and the last first. In a way, every Christian is a foot-washer, a person who serves others without thinking about himself.

"Every Christian is a foot-washer." Discuss the implications of this paradox for:

a. a student council leader,
b. a parent,
c. the oldest brother or sister in a family,
d. the president of the United States.

A second paradox of Jesus occurred when he told the Pharisee Nicodemus that Nicodemus had to be reborn in order to live. Of course, Jesus was talking about death to sin and about spiritual rebirth through one's acceptance of Jesus in baptism.

But behind this wise teaching of Jesus stands the paradox "to live one must die to self." This saying makes little sense when measured against the standards of the world. These standards often tell us to indulge and gorge ourselves on the goods of the world. They rarely, if ever, tell us to deny ourselves, to die to self.

Yet, in the reality which is Jesus, this saying makes all the sense in the world. To the degree that we die to self, to that degree we love and in effect live. I can only love when I give up my own self-interest (die to self) and go out to the other. But when I go out to the other, that is, when I love, I really become more of who I am; I really live. Love is the one "commodity" that the more we "spend" of it, the more we receive in return. Not only is this true from our own experience, but we even have it on the promise of Jesus himself.

> Peter was moved to say to him, "We have put aside everything to follow you!" Jesus answered: "I give you my word, there is no one who has given up home, brothers or sisters, mother or father, children or property, for me and for the gospel who will not receive in this present age a hundred times as many homes, brothers and sisters, mothers, children and property—and persecution besides—and in the age to come, everlasting life. Many who are first shall come last, and the last shall come first."
> —Mk 10:28-31

THE TEACHING OF THE SERMON ON THE MOUNT

More than any other place in the New Testament, we find the moral teaching of Jesus best summarized in Matthew's Gospel in the famed Sermon on the Mount. The Sermon is found in chapters five through seven of Matthew's Gospel. Every Christian should read and study it often. It is to the New Testament what the Ten Commandments are to the Old Testament.

One of the basic points of the Sermon is that it is addressed to those who wish to aspire to Jesus. These are those individuals who have accepted the Good News and have made a basic conversion, a basic turning to Jesus. Understood, of course, is that this conversion is a lifelong process. We Christians are men and women of weakness, subject to sin, but our fundamental direction is for Christ; we are continually pulled towards him through his help and grace.

The Sermon on the Mount captures the joyfulness of the person who makes a basic decision for Christ. Consequently, it begins with the inaugural statements of the Beatitudes, which proclaim a new order for those who hunger and thirst for God. Our hunger and thirst will be satisfied and quenched through Jesus—and beyond our expectations. So Jesus concludes his beatitudes with this joyful note: "Be glad and rejoice, for your reward is great in heaven" (Mt 5:12). One who accepts Jesus and his teaching has every right to rejoice for having found the truth.

The next section of the Sermon briefly discusses the Christian as the salt of the earth and light of the world. (These two images will be treated in some detail in Chapter 10 of this book.) Matthew then mentions how Jesus came to fulfill the Old Law, not to overthrow it. This point is elaborated in the next verses by a comparison of the teaching of Moses with the new, fuller teaching of Jesus in moral matters. Note below how Jesus intensifies the Old Law by asking a higher standard for his followers:

OLD LAW	NEW LAW
a. You must not kill and if you do, settle at court.	a. You must not even be angry with your brother. And if you are, settle your dispute before worshiping.
b. You must not commit adultery.	b. Even if a man looks lustfully at a woman, he has committed adultery.
c. If you divorce, give your wife a writ of divorce.	c. You must not divorce.
d. You must not break your oath.	d. There is no need for oaths because a Christian always says what he means.
e. "An eye for an eye and a tooth for a tooth" morality.	e. Offer the wicked man no resistance. Turn the other cheek, give your extra cloak, walk the extra mile.
f. Love your neighbor and hate your enemy.	f. Love your enemies and pray for those who persecute you.

These six teachings contrasted to the Mosaic Law show the intense kind of love Jesus requires of his followers. It is the kind of love he himself showed to his disciples day in and day out. It is the kind of love that led him to Calvary where he offered up his life so that all men could achieve eternal life.

In other sections of the Sermon, Jesus called for purity of intention. He asks that money be given to the poor in a way that a person does not show off in front of others. He requests that prayers be recited simply and gives the perfect Christian prayer, the Our Father. He forbids his followers from displaying the fact that they are fasting. The point of all of these is that Jesus desires his followers to do good works but not in a way to show off. He requires of his followers that they be satisfied with the knowledge that God the Father sees and blesses their good works and prayers.

Reading through the Sermon on the Mount causes many problems for the Christian today. Many of us do not really know how we should take what Jesus taught. Does he really mean that we should "offer the wicked man no resistance?" Or is this his manner of speaking in exaggerated ways to get us to see the importance of loving? Christians for centuries have been wrestling with the question of how literally we should take the directives of the Sermon on the Mount.

A common Catholic interpretation of the Sermon current among moral theologians is that the teachings in the Sermon are "directional norms," norms which point to the kind of life we Christians must live if we wish to be identified with Jesus. Father Charles Curran suggests that these are goal commandments of Jesus that every Christian must take very seriously and try with God's loving grace to live up to. What is needed is continual conversion —a deepening relationship with Jesus whereby we can better live the words of life that Jesus has given to us.

Such an interpretation of the Sermon on the Mount should make us Christians uncomfortable and help us realize that to be Christian means to live in tension. This is a healthy tension which prompts us to be concerned and involved with our brothers and sisters, which prompts us always to do more than we are doing at any given moment. What we are promised if we try to implement these goals in our own lives is a sense of peace which comes from the Spirit of Jesus. What greater good can there be?

OTHER NEW TESTAMENT TEACHINGS

Although the bulk of Jesus' moral teaching does occur in the Sermon on the Mount, we can glean the following five general directions for Christian living from the other teachings of Jesus in the New Testament:

1. We should keep material goods in their proper perspective. We should not be enslaved by them; rather, they should serve us.

2. We should be "relative pacifists." What is meant by this is that we should with the greatest of energy try to solve our problems with others in a peaceful way. As Jesus himself states, "Those who use the sword are sooner or later destroyed by it" (Mt 26:52).

3. To follow Christ, to walk in his footsteps means we have to be willing to suffer. As in the song "The Impossible Dream" quoted at the beginning of the chapter, any quest worth striving for is worth suffering for, is worth denying ourselves. Redemption and healing come through suffering.

4. Others, even our families, cannot be allowed to impede our progress in spiritual matters. Human respect and standards cannot get in the way of following Christ.

5. In the way we pray, in the way we do good works, in the way we serve others, our attitude should be one of humility. We should not show off but be content with the thought that God the Father knows and appreciates the good we do. We should not always expect the praise of other men.

THE TEN COMMANDMENTS

In light of Jesus' moral teaching, the ethical wisdom of the Old Testament is seen in its full glory. The Old Testament summary of man's response to God is, of course, the Ten Commandments. These commandments are fully understood only in the context of covenant.

The Jew understood his special relationship to Yahweh in terms of covenant. A covenant implied certain rights and duties. On Yahweh's part, he specially blessed the Jewish people. He delivered them from Egypt, gave them a land and nationhood. In brief, he created them as a people and sustained them through his abundant blessing whenever they were undergoing trials, hardships, sufferings and persecutions. Indeed, he sustained them despite their unfaithfulness. For their part, the Jews were to live a certain quality of life which would help them maintain their identity as God's Chosen People and help them be a sign to all nations of the oneness, majesty and glory of their God—the one true God. In sum, the Jews were to live the Law, summarized in the Ten Commandments, as an affirmation of Yahweh's gracious calling and his act of creating them as his chosen people.

Today, the Christian also lives the Ten Commandments, not as a burdensome list of obligations, but as a willing response to God's loving call to be his people. In responding, that is, living in the spirit of the Ten Commandments, the Christian is saying "yes" to his identity, his vocation. That vocation is to witness in the Spirit to the Father of Jesus the Lord. The first three of these commandments emphasize our need "to love God above all things"; the last seven indicate our obligation "to love our neighbor as ourselves." In analyzing the Ten Commandments, try to focus on how each is a *response* in love to a loving God. (The version of the Commandments given is from Dt 5:6-21.)

In response to God:

> 1. *I, the Lord, am your God, who brought you out of the land of Egypt, that place of slavery. You shall not have other gods besides me.*
>
> This commandment points out the need to set priorities. Our problem today is not that we worship golden calves but that we make a good thing more important than the Creator of the good thing. Sex, money, power, prestige—these are all good in their place—but when we make our whole life revolve around them we no longer have things in proper perspective. We are unfaithful to God when we substitute one of these other things for him.

2. *You shall not take the name of the Lord, your God, in vain.*

The second commandment emphasizes the need to recognize that some things are sacred. Our speech reflects who we are. Respectful attitudes toward the holiness of God manifest our recognition that we are creatures and God is the Creator. This commandment also applies to the way we worship God. Our attitude should be one of confident humility asking that God's will be done. It is not pagan worship where one demands God to do his will.

3. *Take care to keep holy the sabbath day as the Lord, your God, commanded you.*

Faithfulness to God demands that we adore him. His will manifests that we do so with others. Our salvation is not something we work at alone, rather, we in the Christian community realize the extreme importance of presenting ourselves to the Father joined with others in the Spirit with our Savior, Jesus Christ. Sunday, the day of the Lord's resurrection, is a day to set priorities.

Responding to God through others:

4. *Honor your father and your mother.*

Covenant love extends to our families. Children owe their parents love; they show love to parents through respect, obedience, courtesy and gratitude. Parents, too, have an obligation to love their children by caring for them, educating them and respecting their dignity as individuals. Finally, brothers and sisters owe each other courtesy, respect, patience and kindness so that the family is a reflection of the kind of loving community that all Christian communities aspire to be.

5. *You shall not kill.*

This commandment stresses the importance of holding as a sacred trust the gift of life God has given us. We have a serious obligation to watch out for the life and safety of others by curbing reckless behavior such as bad driving and the like. But we must also care for our own bodies. We do this by eating good food, avoiding harmful substances such as drugs and getting proper rest and relaxation.

6. *You shall not commit adultery.*

Unfaithfulness to the marriage covenant—as in adultery—is unfaithfulness to the covenant of unity to which God calls each married couple. Likewise, an improper use of our procreative faculties distorts the divine plan of creative love. Responsible use of sex manifests deep concern for others.

7. *You shall not steal.*

Stealing breaks down trust. Trust is needed for smooth human relationships. Shoplifting and cheating are two forms of stealing prevalent in contemporary America, both of which destroy trust. In a way, not using God-given talents and abilities is a form of theft. By not developing our gifts we keep others from sharing something good given to us to enrich not only ourselves but others as well.

8. *You shall not bear dishonest witness against your neighbor.*

Revenge, gossip, scandal, and lies all destroy the covenant love between individuals. The touchstone of one's character is honesty; to be dishonest is to distort our mission of witness to the truth. Love of neighbor means witnessing to the truth because the truth will set us free.

9. *You shall not covet your neighbor's wife.*

10. *You shall not covet your neighbor's house or field . . . nor anything that belongs to him.*

> Obsessively desiring or lusting out of motives of jealousy or materialism or selfishness destroys love between neighbors because internal desires can breed hate and rivalry. These two commandments show the importance of pure intention and decent motives when dealing with others. They demonstrate that destruction of relationships comes from within.

SUMMARY

The ethical teachings of Jesus make sense if we accept the fundamental reality that Jesus is God. He has shown us the best way to live as human beings. To live the Christian moral ethic means very much to let Jesus live in us. Jesus has promised his Spirit to those who believe in him. It is the Holy Spirit who gives us the strength to do the work of our Lord in the world today. In a very real way, he depends on us to do that work—we are his hands, his feet, his loving touch present to men.

Once again, much of the Christian moral ethic makes sense in connection with the Christian concept of man. Jesus' ethical demands boil down to "be who you are." We are sons of God and brothers of Jesus—let us live that reality, let us live as a family united to him. The Church—which is the family of believers, the People of God—has the duty to be leaven to the rest of the world. We are light to the world; we are salt of the earth.

ACTIVITIES

1. Divide the class up into four groups. Each group is to investigate one of the gospels and try to come up with moral teachings of Jesus not discussed in this chapter. Discuss these questions in relation to the teachings found:

   a. In what way are these sayings "people-centered"?

   b. How might these teachings be applied today in:

      —your school,
      —your home,
      —our government?

2. Imagine you were transported to another world where the people on that planet had never heard about Jesus or his teaching. If you were allowed to preach to those people only three moral teachings of Jesus Christ, which three would you choose?

      —Compare your choices with those of your classmates.

      —Try to decide which are the most important ones.

5

Conscience

"Conscience is condensed character."
—Anonymous

Many small children are familiar with the story of Jimminy Cricket who tells Pinocchio always to let his conscience be his guide. The wisdom of this advice hits people as they grow older. But many are painfully aware of the problem presented by this advice: namely, "What is your conscience?"

Conscience is sometimes called the "subjective norm of morality." This means that conscience is the final arbiter in the making of moral decisions. A person's conscience takes into consideration all the available data when confronted with a decision. It helps a person make the final judgment to act or not to act in a given situation. Along with the objective norm of morality—law—conscience helps a person determine whether he is doing right or wrong. This chapter will try to define and describe "conscience," and the next chapter will discuss the role of law.

In an attempt to answer the question "What is your conscience?" we present below several situations which call for a "conscience response." Please read and study each of the situations and then try to decide how you would help resolve the problems presented.

SITUATION A:

You go to a school where there is a lot of pressure to achieve a high grade. This situation is further complicated by your demanding parents who expect you to do well. You have a pretty good average over your four years in high school, averaging around a high B. You are now in your senior year in a sociology class. The teacher is not the best in the school and, as a matter of fact, is a little unfair. He has planned a difficult test for you and your classmates. You know from past experience that 50 percent of the students cheat on his exams, thus ruining any chance for a curve. You have studied pretty hard, but you know that unless you cheat, many others will get a higher grade than you. What would you do?

Reasons to cheat:	*Reasons to remain honest*:
1.	1.
2.	2.
3.	3.
4.	4.

My decision: On a scale from 1 (most inclined to cheat) to 5 (I will remain honest), I would decide:

SITUATION B:

A good friend of yours offers you some drugs in order for you "to get high." You show an initial unwillingness to take them. He tries to talk you into it by saying that his experience with drugs is that they are fun. Besides, he says, you cannot really hurt anyone but yourself. He further adds that it is nobody's business but yours whether you take the drug or not. The law and parents should not prevent you from enjoying yourself. Would you take the drug?

Reasons for taking it:　　　*Reasons for not taking it*:

1.　　　　　　　　　　　1.
2.　　　　　　　　　　　2.
3.　　　　　　　　　　　3.
4.　　　　　　　　　　　4.

My decision: On a scale from 1 (most inclined to take it) to 5 (I will not take the drug), I would decide:

SITUATION C:

Your post high school career has taken you into the Air Force. Unfortunately, your country is at war with a small nation which may go communist. You respect law and believe very much in the values of your own country. On a particular day, you are ordered to bomb and totally destroy a small village. The village is *suspected* of containing a pocket of terrorists, but it is *known* that many old people and small children live in the village. The villagers are not participants in the war. Should you bomb?

Reasons to bomb:　　　　*Reasons not to bomb*:

1.　　　　　　　　　　　1.
2.　　　　　　　　　　　2.
3.　　　　　　　　　　　3.
4.　　　　　　　　　　　4.

My decision: On a scale from 1 (most inclined to bomb) to 5 (I refuse to obey the command), I would decide:

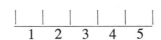

Divide into groups of four and discuss the following questions:

1. Is cheating ever right? Does the argument "because everyone else is doing it" make it right? Can you think of some consequences for society if morality were based on that argument?

2. Would your decision concerning the drugs have made a difference if the drug were marijuana? LSD? Do parents and society have a right to limit your "fun"?

3. In the third situation, are we always obliged to follow authority? Where do we draw the line between disobedience to law and conscience?

WHAT IS CONSCIENCE?

It is important to know what conscience is in order to respond better to others and to God. It is often described as an "inner voice" which tells one what is right and what is wrong.

Perhaps a better way to describe conscience is in terms of self-awareness. Conscience can be defined as an awareness of oneself which helps an individual act and thus become the kind of person he or she is capable of becoming. In other words, conscience judges whether an action I am about to engage in or an attitude which I hold will help me grow as a person or whether such an action or attitude will stifle, or even kill, my growth.

As Christians, we know that our growth or nongrowth does not take place in a vacuum. Our actions and attitudes are not directed solely to other people or ourselves. A religious notion of conscience sees it this way: Conscience is a *person's inner dialogue with God who calls each one to act like the man/woman he or she is.* It is a judgment of an individual in the center of his or her being. This judgment helps one become what he or she is. For the Christian, then, conscience is God's invitation to each individual to live as his child.

Conscience helps tune a person in to what God wants for that person in a given situation. It works at three separate points in every decision and action. An example may help here to show the three levels in which conscience is operative:

> Bob used the family car last night. While backing out of the parking lot on his way home from a dance, he damaged another car to the tune of about $300. He did about $100 worth of damage to the family car. Realizing that his insurance rates would skyrocket if he admitted the accident, Bob failed to leave a note on the damaged car, nor did he try to locate its owner. Today, Bob feels uneasy over his decision.

Clearly, in the above example, Bob dishonestly left the scene of the accident without reporting it. His conscience was at work:

> a. *Before he acted,* when he was trying to judge what to do or what not to do. Conscience helps a person to sort the data before a decision is made. It helps in examining the right or wrong thing to do by reflecting on the teaching of our Lord and his Church, the rights of others, the helpfulness to one's growth, and the like.

> b. *As he acted,* by enabling him to make a judgment after considering the relevant data. Conscience ultimately makes it possible for a person to act or not to act, to hold an attitude or not to hold one. It is that depth of our being which says "Yes, I am going to act," or "No, I refuse to act."

> c. *After he acted,* through any afterthoughts he may have about his action the previous night. The third function of conscience is to help a person judge after the action whether his judgment was right. As in Bob's case, maybe fear the night before helped make him act the way he did. If he is "conscientious" today, he will regret his action and try to make amends.

CONSCIENCE SURVEY

Below are listed three statements which are different ways of looking at conscience. There is provided a scale which ranks from (5) strongly agree with the statement made to a (1) for strongly disagree. (3) represents an "I don't know" response. Check the scale at the point which represents your thinking on the issue.

a. Something is right for me if I think it is right.

b. In making moral decisions, sincerity is all that matters.

c. No one has the right to judge my actions to be right or wrong.

After you have ranked these, gather into small groups to discuss the following questions.

If sincerity is what matters, then was it all right for Hitler to kill the Jews? for war resisters to burn draft board records?

If some action is all right if "I think it is all right," what is the role of law? How should others affect my decisions?

Do ends justify means? For example, may a poor man with a family rob a bank for money to feed his family? Or may a teenager get an abortion to protect her reputation?

What happens when my conscience conflicts with Church authority? What must I do?

Though a Catholic Christian believes that sincerity and personal freedom are important in the making of conscience decisions, they are not supreme. For the Christian, individual decisions are always made with others in mind. For example, in the case of Bob who wrecked the car, it is very important for him *sincerely* to arrive at a decision and to do so with *freedom*. But his sincerity and freedom do not make his action right! He must take into consideration the rights of the owner of the damaged car. Further, he should consider the consequences of his action for society as a whole. What if everyone were dishonest in dealings with others? Surely, then, society could hardly exist. And without a society which judges behavior as sometimes good and sometimes bad, Bob would not even have the right to drive in the first place.

KINDS OF CONSCIENCE

Please consider the following case:

Tom, Sally and Jack were with a group of friends the other evening celebrating the end of the school year. They had a good time at one of the local spots. One of the members of the group thought it would be great fun to get into a car and recklessly drive onto the fairways of one of the suburban country clubs. The purpose of the joyride would be to wreck one of the greens with deep tire marks. Several members of the group decided to engage in the destruction, but Tom, Sally and Jack declined to do so.

By investigating the reasons Tom, Sally and Jack did not engage in the destructiveness, one can discover the three basic types of conscience.

Type 1—Fear Conscience:

Tom arrived at his decision not to join the group for one simple reason—he was afraid of being caught. In many ways, he really wanted to be with the others, but his fear of the long reach of the law kept him from doing so. Tom is like those who see God, Church, parents and other authority as "cops" who are out to get a person for slipping up. They conform not so much because it is the right thing to do, but because they fear the consequences. This rather immature conscience-type is summed up well in the following poem:

> *"Conscience is that still, small voice*
> *That quells a wicked thought*
> *Then adds this sequence*
> *'Besides, you might get caught.' "*

Type 2—Person-centered Conscience:

Sally also declined the invitation to joyride. But her decision was made on a much more mature basis than Tom's. Her conscience easily detected the folly of destroying someone else's property. She knew the reason for "no trespassing" was to protect the rights of others. Her conscience made her sensitive to the needs of others: the owners of the golf course and the players. This type of conscience is quite an advance over Tom's fear mentality.

Type 3—Christian Conscience:

In arriving at his decision not to destroy the golf course, Jack demonstrated the highest level of conscience development. Like Sally's, his was a mature conscience. But his conscience acted as a guide, or judge, of his behavior in response to the promptings of God speaking to him in the innermost part of his being. His decision respected the rights of others; so his conscience is person-centered. But he saw the issue in a wider context. By doing the right thing, Jack's conscience aided him in acting as a child of God who treats others as brothers and sisters, not merely as other human beings with rights. His decision reflected his Christian concern of responding to others as he would like them to respond to him. His decision was a conscious response to the Holy Spirit inviting him to love the other as Jesus Christ would have him love. Jack's norm was neither fear nor merely human respect for others, though these at times are worthwhile responses, his norm was none other than Jesus himself.

The goal of every Christian should be to get beyond fear as a motivation for action. Rather, responding to people as persons related to us as brothers and sisters in Christ is the ideal in Christian behavior. Living our lives as though we are children of God with a destiny of final union with him is the norm for Christian living. And the conscience that prompts us to act in this way is the mature conscience for which one should strive.

PRINCIPLES IN CONSCIENCE FORMATION

But how does one form a conscience as described in Type 3 above? How does one make decisions based on conscience? The following two principles should help answer these questions.

PRINCIPLE #1: Yes, as Jimminy Cricket says, one must follow his or her conscience. *Conscience is supreme.* In moral decisions, you must follow your conscience, even if it is wrong.

Two points should be emphasized here:

   a. Because a person has no higher court of appeal before acting than his conscience, he or she is ultimately responsible for his or her actions. Nobody else can be blamed for them. In Bob's case, he could not blame anyone for his wrong action of leaving the scene of the accident. It was his decision; he is responsible for it.

   b. But by saying that conscience is supreme, *it does not mean that an individual man is superior to God, the Church or his fellowmen.* True, a person is responsible for his or her actions, but these are not done in isolation from others. For example, a person always has the duty to examine the consequences of actions to see what effect they will have on others, the environment, and in the final analysis on a relationship with God. Being "responsible" means being able to respond in an authentic way to God who calls us to him through our everyday living. We can either answer his call as his children, ignore his call, or answer "irresponsibly."

PRINCIPLE #2: Though a person must always follow his or her conscience, *he or she has the duty to develop continuously an informed conscience.* Father Gerard Sloyan, in his classic *How Do I Know I Am Doing Right?* lists several checkpoints which help a person arrive at an informed conscience that enables one to act correctly and morally. You might think of an important decision you have made recently and think back to see which of these you followed.

☐ *Have a pure intention.* Sincerity is important. A person who wants to do something simply "to get away with it" hardly has what one might consider a pure intention. The following questions help one determine a "pure intention": Why do I want to do this action? Is my motivation selfish? Is it for the sake of others? Will this action benefit me, that is, help me grow? Have I considered all the data? Or am I acting on impulse?

☐ *Consult the teaching of Jesus in the New Testament, the Prophets, Moses and Paul.* If one really wants to be a Christian, that is, a follower of Jesus Christ, he or she must know what he said and seriously reflect on its meaning as well as one can. Am I aware, for example, of the "ethical teachings of Jesus"? the Ten Commandments? the position of the Church?

☐ *Ask the question: "How does this action of mine measure up to the yardstick of love?"* For the Christian, every authentic response to God and neighbor is a response in love. And love is not something watered down but a real self-sacrificing attempt to meet others and God. Is my concept of love more than just "feeling"? Do I realize that love consists in giving as well as receiving?

☐ *Consult the people of God wherein Christ and his Spirit reside.* What is the teaching and belief of the bishops, theologians, holy and learned men, the brotherhood of believers? Do I even care what this teaching is? Do I consult it? Do I bother asking other Christians for an opinion?

☐ *Follow the current debate on the great moral issues.* For example, what are the pros and cons in regards to abortion, mercy-killing, premarital sex? Especially, what is the position of the Catholic community on these issues?

☐ *Pray for God's graceful guidance in all my actions.* Ask God's Spirit to make me a creature of love. If we sincerely want to do the right thing, follow the above directives, and ask for God's help, he won't mislead us. Doing the right thing with God's help brings us a calmness and peacefulness.

☐ *Be sorrowful for my sinfulness, not just my sins, confessing them fully and humbly, asking for the help of God.* Sure, there are times when we are going to fail. At times, we forget who we are, that we are God's children. There are times when immediate gratification, when what others think, when laziness help influence us to make a wrong decision. But God understands that. He simply wants us to admit that we have failed to live as his children. Like the father in the parable of the "Prodigal Son," he is always willing to claim us as his own and shower his abundant love on us. All we need do is turn back to him and ask for his help.

☐ *Follow "my" conscience.* When all is said and done, I must follow my conscience.

Of course, it would be the rare person who accomplishes all of the above in any given moral decision. These are goals for which we strive. Conscience development is a growth, a maturing process. Our duty as Christians is to remain open to God's Spirit who leads us on to a deeper relationship with Jesus Christ and his Father.

SIMULATION: JURY

Scenario: The following simulation casts you as a member of a jury which is to decide what kinds of crimes and sins are most reprehensible, that is, outrageous to you and your fellow jurors. Your opinion, thought and reflection are highly valued in this attempt to set priorities on the issue of crime and to help you apply the concepts of the last two chapters.

Part 1:

1. On the following pages are described 13 situations, all of which are potentially destructive of human relationships. After each situation is a key word which will help you remember the details of the story.

2. Read each situation in turn. After reading each story, transcribe the key word under the column entitled "Key Words" on the following page. Mark in the space to the right a number from 1 to 7 to measure your *emotional* reaction to each situation. 1 represents the weakest emotional reaction; 7 the strongest. 2 through 6 represent progressively stronger reactions. You may use the same number as often as you like. You may change your reactions as you go along. But remember, measure your *emotional* reaction.

3. After you have read and reacted to all the situations in turn, please rank the four which evoked your strongest emotional response, and the two which brought about your weakest reaction. Transcribe the key words in the column marked "E."

---

1. It has come to your attention that a religion teacher at your school, married and the father of five children, was picked up last week by the police. Apparently, he had accepted the solicitation of a so-called "lady of the evening" and was about to take her to a motel room when they were caught by two members of a vice squad. TEACHER

2. A little boy, a neighborhood pest and brat, hates a certain old lady in the neighborhood for constantly yelling at him for playing on her lawn. To get even with her, one day he fills a milk bottle with urine, props it up against her front door, and rings the bell.

When she opens the door, the bottle falls into her living room soiling the rug. BOTTLE

3. The woman in the previous story seeks to get revenge on the neighborhood brat. On Halloween she inserts a fresh razor blade into a shiny apple and gives it to the boy when he comes to the door. Later, the boy bites into the apple and cuts his lips rather badly. RAZOR BLADE

4. A big news item in Sunday's paper reveals that there is a strong Army lobby urging Congress to allow a prominent South Vietnamese general to emigrate to America. The news item also reports that the general was responsible for selling a million dollars worth of heroin to American soldiers. HEROIN

5. A close friend of yours confides to you that he stayed home from school the other day. He disguised his voice and called in "sick" by claiming he was his father. Since both of his parents were at work, he was free to use the family car. He did so and tells you he was involved in a near-fatal, hit-skip accident. Thus far, neither the police nor his parents know of the crime. ACCIDENT

6. You recently have found out that a neighborhood boy who got his girlfriend in trouble paid for an abortion. The reason he gave was that her parents were ready to disown her and that he was not financially ready to marry her. ABORTION

7. A TV news item reveals that during the Watergate crisis a high-level government official plotted to assassinate a well-known columnist because of the columnist's revelations of so-called sensitive government secrets. Luckily for the freedom of the press, the threat was never carried out. PLOT

8. The following situation is told to you by a close friend. On his annual Easter jaunt to Florida, your friend and his companion intended to play golf at a rather posh country club. Unfortunately, when your friend went to pay his greens fee, he was told that the course was semiprivate. What this meant, in effect, was that he could not play because he was black. FRIEND

9. A neighbor girl who is in the third grade came home from school yesterday and told the family that her teacher, who is a man, kept her after school and, once they were alone, made sexual advances. NEIGHBOR GIRL

10. A factory owner of a large industrial chemical plant is losing money by using his antipollution equipment. So, at night when no one is watching, he opens the pollution control valves and allows the liquid pollutant by-products to be disposed of in a nearby stream. POLLUTANTS

11. It has come to your attention that a drunken motorist fell asleep at the wheel yesterday, lost control of his car, and caused an accident when the car ran up on the sidewalk injuring, luckily not killing, two passersby. DRUNK

12. A car for which you have personally saved for a number of years has been maliciously destroyed by some vandals before you have been able to insure it. CAR

13. A widow and her two young children have just returned from the funeral of her husband and their father to discover that some hoodlums have broken into their home and stolen most of their prized possessions. WIDOW

Part 2:

1. Form into small groups of six.

2. Compare your initial rankings.

3. Now, let the group rerank the top four and bottom two. This time react as though you could remove all emotion from your consideration. Judge on a *rational* basis alone. In other words, on a rational (reasonable) basis, which of these situations *should* evoke the strongest reactions; the weakest? Recopy these key words in the column marked "R."

4. Your group should arrive at a consensus in 15 minutes.

KEY WORDS   **E**

1. ——————— ——   1. ————————————

2. ——————— ——   2. ————————————

3. ——————— ——   3. ————————————

4. ——————— ——   4. ————————————

5. ——————— ——   12. ————————————

6. ——————— ——   13. ————————————

7. ——————— ——   **R**

8. ——————— ——   1. ————————————

9. ——————— ——   2. ————————————

10. ——————— ——   3. ————————————

11. ——————— ——   4. ————————————

12. ——————— ——   12. ————————————

13. ——————— ——   13. ————————————

Part 3:

1. The entire class should form in a circle, if possible.

2. Each group in turn should share its rankings from column "R" with the rest of the class. A brief statement of reasons for the choices made should be given at this time.

3. After each group has reported, *discuss* the following questions:

   a. Did your small group come to any different conclusions using *reason* alone than you did using *emotion?* If so, why? If not, why not?

   b. Was this a difficult task to do? Is it difficult for a human being to judge any situation without emotional consideration?

   c. What made one situation more serious than another? (the number of people? the kind of people? the kind of crime? the role of the individual? etc.).

   d. What priorities did your group set in coming to consensus? Were they different than those of another group?

   e. How much did the *intention* of the characters in the story affect your decisions? the *circumstances?* the *action* itself?

   f. What assumptions did you make about each story? Did these change any of your choices?

   g. How do you think Jesus would rank these? Do you have any evidence to support your choice?

   h. Can you find evidence in the New Testament which shows that Jesus was quite upset with the following:

   —hypocrisy;
   —downgrading of human life;
   —failure to identify all men as neighbor;
   —harm performed to the outcast and defenseless victim, such as women and children.

EXERCISE:

Apply to the following situation what you have learned in this chapter.

A friend, who is Catholic, comes to you for advice. She and her boyfriend have had sexual relations. As a result, she is pregnant. Her parents do not know yet. Her boyfriend has enough money for her to get an abortion. He is pushing hard for the abortion idea. The girl wants to do the right thing. Factors bothering her in the decision include:

a. Her parents are very strict and might disown her if they find out she is pregnant;

b. She has an excellent reputation—if she goes through with the pregnancy, others will look down on her;

c. If she has the baby, she wants to keep it, but she knows her boyfriend does not want to get married.

What would you advise?

6

Law and Freedom

"Love, and do what you will."
—Saint Augustine

Imagine yourself rummaging through the attic and coming across an old, faded photograph of your grandmother taken when she was a young girl. As you blow the dust off the oval frame and gaze at the picture, many thoughts cross your mind, one of which is the realization of how much things have changed since grandmother's day.

In terms of morality, it seems fair to say that we have come from the comparatively strict attitudes of the Victorian era into the more liberal, "do your own thing" attitudes of today. The stuffy parlors and tight corsets of yesteryear reflect what we consider to be the stuffy and uptight moral prudishness that we have so obviously rejected in becoming the "turned-on generation."

Needless to say, the Catholic Church appears to many to be as old-fashioned as grandmother's picture. In fact, many young people are turned off by the Church precisely because they are unable to reconcile Christian moral standards with today's free, easygoing standards of morality.

It would be false to say the moral standards of the Church are not challenging, or that they do not call for the courage to stand up and be different. But it is equally false to see Christian moral standards in terms of outdated laws that destroy freedom.

Gather into two groups, each with a good supply of daily newspapers:

One group should try to find as many articles as it can which illustrate that broken laws often involve an infringement of others' basic rights (for example, murder which denies another the basic right to life).

The second group should look for examples of laws which help set people free of different forms of injustice.

Both groups can then discuss the problem of unjust laws, that is, laws which jeopardize the value of human life instead of safeguarding it (for example, abortion laws or laws that do or did exist by different forms of dictatorship).

FREEDOM

The purpose of this chapter is to discuss what is meant by Christian freedom and how law relates to that freedom. The main objective is to show how the law of Christ is a law that gives us the freedom to love in the deepest way possible. But first we must back up and begin by asking ourselves, "What is freedom?"

For the sake of simplicity, we will divide freedom up into two main types; namely, inner freedom and external freedom. Inner freedom refers to the freedom to be all we can possibly be. And external freedom refers to freedom of action, the freedom to do all we can possibly do. We will discuss inner freedom first.

Inner Freedom

Inner freedom, the freedom to be all we can possibly be, is a state of fulfilled being rather than a way of acting. Inner freedom means freedom from such things as isolation, suffering and death, in short, from all that prevents us from being fully alive. Because all of us must die, none of us can attain total inner freedom while on earth. However, we can attain various degrees of inner freedom, and, by means of religion, the hope of perfect inner freedom after death.

An example of a kind of inner freedom is found in the experience of two people who fall deeply in love, and in their love are set free in an experience of unlimited happiness.

The inner freedom of this love, for all its power and wonder, is obviously not total and final. A bride, for example, cannot promise her spouse freedom from all suffering, much less can she promise him freedom from death. In short, her love does not have the power to make him all he can possibly be.

Nevertheless, the inner freedom found in human love is real. Furthermore, it brings out two important truths about inner freedom. The first is that inner freedom is found in a love relationship. It is love that makes us all we can possibly be.

The second point is that the couple in love achieve inner freedom by means of external freedom. In other words, their daily actions toward each other are the means by which they maintain the inner freedom of love. If a husband, for example, "freely" chooses to be unfaithful to his wife, his freedom of action becomes the means of destroying his inner freedom to be all he can possibly be in love. Ultimately, his action is a kind of antifreedom force. No matter how "freely" he chose to be unfaithful, he nevertheless freely chose not to be free. What is seen here is that in a love relationship one is free to do what he or she must do in order to be faithful to love.

Human love, as we know it on this earth, eventually ends in death, but God's love does not. The Church's celebration of Easter is a constant reminder that the focus of faith in Christ is not grounded in his high moral values or his great wisdom. Rather, Jesus offers to us a participation in his own total victory over death. It is the Christian hope that in Christ we will become all we can possibly be. The alleluias sung on Easter morning are grounded in Jesus' promise that "whoever believes in me, though he should die, will come to life; and whoever is alive and believes in me will never die" (Jn 11:26), and in the realization that his promise will be fulfilled because he has given us the Spirit. It is St. Paul who said, "If the Spirit of him who raised Jesus from the dead dwells in you, he who raised Christ from the dead will bring your mortal bodies to life also through his Spirit dwelling in you" (Rm 8:11).

We will, of course, reach our goal of total inner freedom only in heaven. The point is, however, that we will achieve total inner freedom only by means of external freedom. It is at this juncture that we see the importance of Christian morality. Our moral actions are the means to achieving the inner freedom of perfect fulfillment in God. An immoral act is an act freely performed against one's own ultimate freedom. As with all people in a love relationship, the Christian is free to do what he or she must do in order to be faithful to love. Freedom without this fidelity to love is not freedom but license.

This point is brought out in the story of Adam and Eve in the Garden of Eden. In freely choosing to disobey God, they freely chose to undermine their own inner freedom. Just as a husband or wife is free to love his or her spouse, he or she is also bound by that love. We can see there the paradoxical truth that moral obligations are in the last analysis obligations to our own freedom.

Lastly, it is worth pointing out that, just as inner freedom is not found in the possession of any external object, so too the hindrances to inner freedom come ultimately from within ourselves, in our free choice not to be true to love. We become, in short, our own obstacle to our own freedom, prisoners locked within ourselves.

1. Read the story of St. John the Baptist, especially his imprisonment and beheading by Herod (Mt 14:1-12). In what sense was Herod the one who was the prisoner, and John the one who was free?

2. Compare Shakespeare's Romeo in the play *Romeo and Juliet* to the character of Scrooge in Dickens' *The Christmas Carol.* Romeo was hopelessly in love with Juliet. Scrooge, on the other hand, was in love with no one. Scrooge was his own man, yet, was he more imprisoned within himself than was Romeo? In other words, does a love relationship take us out of ourselves and give us a taste of inner freedom? Do we need commitment to another to be free? Does love have its own inner laws that bind and yet set free?

3. Discuss the paradoxical statement that in all love relationships we are free to do what we must do.

External Freedom

External freedom is not the freedom to be all we can possibly be, but rather the freedom to do all we can possibly do. This is what most people think of when they hear the word "freedom." External freedom, in a Christian context, is a means to an end. We attain to inner freedom by responding to God's love in our daily actions. Thus morality can be seen as a free response to God's call to perfect freedom. There is then a paradox in human freedom. The paradox is that the free choice not to respond to God's call is a free choice not to be free, because it is a free choice not to fully be. We bear within us not only the seeds of our own fulfillment but also the seeds of our own destruction. This is the meaning of sin.

Consider a small child. Its parents take away a knife it is playing with. Then they take away a bottle of poisonous cleaning fluid the child is trying to open. The child begins to cry because it cannot do what it wants to do.

Discuss the parents' actions in terms of safeguarding the child's deeper freedom to be over his now-misguided freedom to do.

THREATS TO FREEDOM

Once we realize the importance of freedom in our lives, it is easy to see why any threat to our freedom is an attack on human dignity. Just as with our discussion of freedom, we will divide the threats to freedom into inner and external types.

External Threats to Freedom

External threats to freedom are forces in society which directly or indirectly endanger our quest for inner freedom. This includes such things as oppression, injustice and prejudice.

Events such as the Revolutionary and Civil wars, people such as Martin Luther King and Ralph Nader, or movements such as the lettuce and grape boycotts and women's liberation, are all examples of the constant need to struggle against the forces of oppression in any form.

Certainly, Christians must be in the forefront with those working for a free society. The Fathers of the Second Vatican Council state:

> Whatever insults human dignity, such as subhuman living conditions, arbitrary imprisonment . . . disgraceful working conditions, where men are treated as mere tools for profit . . . all these things and others of their like are infamies indeed. . . . Moreover, they are a supreme dishonor to the Creator (*Constitution on the Church in the Modern World,* No. 27).

The bishops go on to point out that Jesus does not simply call us to heaven as individuals, but he also calls us as a people to the kingdom of God. We are bound by the love of Christ to work toward the perfection of society in preparation for the kingdom. Put in other terms, a Christian never goes to heaven alone. Our call from God comes in and through the society in which we live. We are committed to work toward the perfection of society so that all people may find the means to become all they can possibly be. This may often involve reaching out and helping those whose freedom is being abused.

Internal Threats to Freedom

Internal threats to freedom are, as the term implies, the threats to freedom which come from within ourselves. The internal threats to freedom which we will discuss are ignorance, passions and habits. Within each of these is an element for which we are not responsible because we do not have total control of all our thoughts, emotions and life experiences. At the same time there is an element for which we are responsible. It is, of course, the responsible aspects of these hindrances to freedom that are the concern of moral theology.

IGNORANCE

Ignorance is a threat to freedom because in ignorance we can hurt ourselves as well as others. Consider, for example, that you have a close friend who is very sensitive about a particular aspect of his or her personality. You, however, find this trait of your friend to be amusing and never miss an opportunity to mention it. Months later your friend tells you about his or her feelings on this matter. You then suddenly realize that in ignorance you have been hurting your relationship with your friend. The same holds true with our relationship with God. We must always make an honest effort to properly inform our conscience. It is morally wrong to deliberately remain in ignorance about what is morally wrong.

Another aspect of ignorance as a hindrance to freedom is seen in light of the mysterious nature of our own minds. So many of our deepest needs have their roots in the depths of the subconscious where we do not have access to them. This means that we may be doing a certain thing when we suddenly become aware that our deepest motives may be unworthy ones. Perhaps jealousy, revenge, or even hatred is motivating us to do what we are doing under the cover of friendship or perhaps our obligation to correct another. In conclusion, we are not responsible for that of which we are ignorant. But we are responsible not to remain ignorant to the extent we are able to do so. We must constantly work toward an ever greater understanding of ourselves and of our relationship to God.

Imagine you find a large sum of money in a plain envelope. If you do not know to whom the money belongs, it is obvious that you are not morally responsible to return it. Would it be morally permissible to make no effort to find out to whom it belongs? Would this deliberate ignorance of the money's owner be a form of stealing?

PASSIONS

The passions or the emotions are those inner forces that affect us both spiritually and physically in moving us to act in a certain way. These passions, such as joy, love, fear and sorrow, are in themselves good, and they form an important dimension in our lives. But it is important to see that while under their influence we are restricted in our freedom. This restricting power on our freedom is where the passions are potential sources of immorality.

Some actions have no moral significance and so giving way to our emotions in such circumstances is also without moral significance. For example, the wild enthusiasm at a football game is neither moral nor immoral in itself.

Some actions are directly immoral and so the giving way to the emotions that move us to do such things increases our involvement in the action. What is more, the emotions such as fear, hate, sorrow can do more than move us to intensify our involvement in destructive acts to ourselves and others. The emotions can become overpowering and, under their influence, we temporarily lose our use of free will and so become dehumanized.

While under the full impact of these emotions we are not responsible for our actions to the extent they have taken over. We are responsible, however, not to let ourselves become so dominated by these emotions. For example, one who has a violent temper is not fully responsible for his actions while he or she is acting in a rage. This person is, however, to see to it that he or she checks these emotions before they get out of hand. We can see here how the threats to freedom can act upon one another in terms of moral responsibility. For example, a person who continually loses his temper has an obligation to do his best not to become dominated by his destructive feelings. He must also try to overcome his ignorance concerning why he is so prone to behave the way that he does.

Once again, it should be made clear that the passions are in themselves good. They become evil only when directed toward an evil action that dehumanizes us. The passions involved in sexual love in marriage, for example, are directed toward a good end; namely, the deepening of love and the procreation of children. The same thing can be said about the strong emotions of joy that are often experienced at celebrations or at the meeting of close friends who have been separated for a long period of time. A stoic rejection of the passions is not the goal of Christian morality.

HABITS

If you have ever watched a baby trying to learn how to use a spoon for the first time, you were probably struck by the humorous sight of someone trying to find his or her own mouth! If you try to think of how it is you are able to find yours, you come to some understanding of the importance of habits. Habits are a form of second nature to us. Habits are things we do spontaneously, effortlessly, without thinking. It is easy to see why habits are invaluable in our lives. Imagine how it would be if every time you sat down to eat you had to begin all over again to learn how to find your own mouth in order to feed yourself!

Habits are very significant in our moral life as well. As with the passions, when involving actions such as driving a car, that is, actions which are neither moral nor immoral, we can say that habits themselves are neither moral nor immoral. When the habit is a good habit we say that it is a virtue. This means that we can develop the virtue of going out of our way to help others, for example. A virtuous person is one who spontaneously does what is good because he or she has developed good habits. Here good living becomes a way of life.

Habits that are directed toward immoral actions are called vices. Bad habits form us to do spontaneously that which in the beginning called for a deliberate act of the will. For example, the first time a person steals something, he or she may feel a great degree of guilt in the awareness they have done something wrong. But after repeatedly stealing, the act becomes effortless. In stealing long enough the person takes on the identity of a thief. In lying long enough the person takes on the identity of a liar.

To determine the degree of responsibility in actions involving habits, we can use the same principle we applied to the passions. In other words, to the extent a person has been taken over by a particular habit, that person has a decreased amount of responsibility for what he or she is doing. By the same token, the individual is bound to avoid becoming entrenched in bad habits, and is obligated to try to replace them with good habits.

---

1. Imagine a sailor who becomes an alcoholic while stationed on a remote island thousands of miles from home. Discuss the different external and internal threats to freedom that would lessen his moral responsibility for what he is doing.

2. Discuss what it means to say that not only must we work at trying to do what is right, but we must also work at holding on to the freedom that enables us to choose in the first place. Bring both external and internal threats into your answer.

We can summarize this section on freedom with the following statements:

Our day-to-day actions are the means to the inner freedom of being all we can possibly be.

Inner freedom is found in love relationships which bring with them the obligations of love.

Moral actions are actions that deepen our love relationship with God in whom alone we find ultimate inner freedom.

Human freedom is very real but is always relative to the external and internal threats to freedom.

WHAT IS LAW?

In a sense, freedom is related to law in the same way a lake is related to the shore that contains it. Just as the shore gives the lake shape, holds it in its boundaries, so law gives shape to our freedom and marks off its boundaries. Law is then a binding rule of conduct which serves to give shape and direction to our freedom.

Another preliminary observation about law would be that in the last analysis, our conscience is the final lawgiver. Our conscience, however, must be properly formed and work in conjunction with reality outside ourselves, especially with regard to the obligations that arise in our relationships with God and others. The concern here is not to investigate further the material found in the chapter on conscience, but rather to supplement that material with an investigation into law as more commonly understood, that is, as a binding rule of conduct which we receive from outside ourselves. Law will be divided into the following categories: natural, civil, divine, and church law.

Natural Law

Natural law refers to the laws that are built into the nature of life itself, and thus are knowable to all people in all societies. Murder, for example, is universally condemned in all societies, because it is known to reason that murder is a direct attack on the value of human life. This universality of natural law holds true in spite of the fact that different societies give very different interpretations to what it means to murder. For example, in our society, we hold that killing out of vengeance is murder. Other societies permit killing another out of vengeance, and no more consider it murder than we do in judging the morality of killing in self-defense.

Discuss the Catholic Church's condemnation of abortion from the standpoint of natural law.

Civil Law

The laws that come to us from civil authorities are basically the particular applications of the natural law, and as such are binding rules of conduct to protect the common good.

The Christian response to civil law is that we are bound in conscience to obey all valid civil laws. We see this in Jesus' command to "give unto Caesar the things that are Caesar's." We see it, too, in St. Paul's words to "Let everyone obey the authorities that are over him, for there is no authority except from God, and all authority that exists is established by God" (Rm 13:3).

The moral obligation to obey civil authority is in direct proportion to the seriousness of the law in terms of its effect on our well-being and the well-being of others. For example, the law requiring all bicycles to have license plates has little moral significance compared to the laws prohibiting drug companies from selling dangerous drugs, or the laws forbidding the shooting of guns in city streets.

Divine Law

Divine law is the law that comes to us from God in revelation. It is divided up into three periods. First, there is the divine law received by the Jewish people before the time of Moses. Secondly, there is the Mosaic law which was initiated in the giving of the Ten Commandments to Moses on Mount Sinai. And, finally, there is the law given to us by Christ.

The natural law is binding on all men. Civil law is binding on all the members of the society in which it is made. Divine law is binding on all those in a faith relationship with God. Divine law is unique in that it calls for us to respond not to the blind forces and laws of nature, nor to the collective legislative body of the society, but rather to God's personal command.

Many people look upon the Ten Commandments as cold, impersonal rules of conduct. This is just the opposite of what the Jews of the Old Testament saw them to be. The Ten Commandments are the high point of a covenant relationship which is a two-way commitment between God and man. God promised the chosen people his love and protection, and in return he asked them to respond to his invitation by living out their lives according to his will. It is love not legalism that binds the commandments to the chosen people's hearts. Notice that the commandments are, for the most part, a formulation of natural law known to all men (Ex 20:1-17, Dt 5:7-10). But now, coming from God, they are given a new meaning; they become the revelation of how we are to obtain that inner freedom spoken of at the beginning of this chapter. This becomes clearer in considering that we are made in God's image. Keeping the commandments is acting out in daily life what we are in our inmost selves. Since we are made in his image, we are called to act in conformity to his will.

---

1. Discuss: Your parents tell you that they do not want you drinking, especially if you are going to be driving the car. Discuss your obligations to obey them with regard to the natural law, to the civil law, and to the divine law. Compare this to your obligations to obey your parents if they tell you to mow the lawn.

2. Imagine a married couple writing out what they feel to be the other's obligations in being faithful to their marriage relationship. How would this list be comparable to the Ten Commandments? How would it differ? Imagine a stranger being told that he or she had to keep the same set of rules. Why would he or she feel his or her freedom was being abused? Compare this to the person who has no personal relationship to God being told he is supposed to keep the Ten Commandments.

3. Do all love relationships presuppose some kind of obligation to be faithful to the relationship? Does this supply a deeper insight into the meaning of the Ten Commandments?

Church Law

Church laws are the expression of divine law as it is applied to particular circumstances of Christian life. For example, the divine law to keep holy the Lord's day is made specific in the Church's law that we must attend Sunday Mass. Church laws can change as the Church faces new circumstances to which Christians have to adapt. The moral obligation to observe church laws is relative to the seriousness of the law insofar as it affects our relationship with God and others. As with civil laws, church laws throw light on the social dimension of our moral life and also on our need to respond to God and others in the concrete details of daily life.

The Church has presently come out of a period when she laid greater stress on the importance of observing church laws, but this should not distract us from their importance. The main thing is to get away from a childish dependence on others to tell you what to do while at the same time realizing that to be in any community involves the keeping of certain laws held by the community.

Furthermore, the laws of the Church must be seen as flowing from a reality deeper than the law itself; namely, from the divine law. When the Church changed her laws on fasting, the pope made it clear that the Christian is still obligated to deny himself in order to follow Christ. He went on to add that fasting has been a traditional means of expressing our desire to deny ourselves in order to follow Christ. Yet, when the fasting laws for Lent were dropped, many Catholics simply quit fasting. Their fasting was not being done out of a personal response to Christ but out of a legalistic attitude that Catholics should fast simply because they are told to do so. Freedom is found not in throwing off laws but in making them part of our own personal response and commitment to Christ.

Jesus and the Law of the Spirit

The chapter on the ethical teaching of Jesus provides a thorough treatment of this subject. Here we will make but a few observations that directly apply to law and freedom as related to Christ.

First of all, the fact that Jesus was a Jew, acted like a Jew, and thought like a Jew makes it obvious that he had a deep respect for the written law of the Old Testament. What is more, he saw himself as the fulfillment of that law, and we find numerous examples of his respect for and identification with God's covenant with men.

At the time of Jesus, the Pharisees were a dominant group in the Jewish community who failed to stress the personal relationship aspect of the law, but instead said the response to the law should be a detailed fidelity to the oral traditions that developed out of the Old Testament. Their legalistic attitude and their self-righteousness clashed with Jesus' message of freedom and his call to renew our hearts from within.

Compare the attitude of the Pharisees with that of Catholics who have little or no Christian value in their lives, yet insist on the observance of external obligations such as attendance at Sunday Mass.

The Sermon on the Mount (Mt 5-7) is the high point of Jesus' ethical teaching. Here he makes clear that we are called to live a life of love for all people, regardless of what they have done to injure us. He asked not so much for observance of laws but a new heart given over wholly to love.

Jesus said at the Last Supper that "He who obeys the commandments he has from me is the man who loves me" (Jn 14:21). The point is that observance of Jesus' command to love liberates us from a legalistic attitude but at the same time it binds us even more than before, because it calls us to a greater love and hence to a greater fidelity. St. Paul reflects this same idea in his condemnation of the idea that keeping the law alone will give us salvation. He insisted that salvation is in Jesus Christ, who has saved us from the weight of the law. But he then goes on to assert that in the love of Christ we will strive even more to keep the commandments, not out of fear of breaking the law, but out of love of Christ. The com-

LAW AND FREEDOM 101

mandments' call for a good life is echoed by Jesus' command that we "be made perfect as our heavenly Father is perfect" (Mt 5:48). Our call to perfection presupposes a careful observance of the commandments as guidelines to inner freedom.

---

1. Discuss attendance at Sunday Mass in terms of fidelity to our union with Christ.

2. Discuss the role of an all-embracing relationship to Christ in terms of its effect on our relationship to our other obligations at school, at home, etc.

3. Discuss St. Augustine's saying, "Love and do what you will."

4. Discuss the Ten Commandments from the standpoint of external freedom. Then discuss the Ten Commandments from the standpoint of the covenant and internal freedom.

5. Discuss the eight Beatitudes in relationship to inner freedom. Why would a person with a legalistic attitude toward morality find the eight Beatitudes frustrating when considered as a norm for moral behavior?

We can summarize this section on law with the following statements:

Natural law is the universal law found in the structure of life itself.

Civil law is the particular application of natural law and the means of assuring the common good.

Divine law is the law given to us by God in revelation.

Church law is the particular application of the divine law as lived out in the community of the Church.

Law is intended to protect and assure inner freedom.

Jesus gave the law of the Old Testament a new significance with the new covenant he established between God and ourselves. The law of Christ is that we seek perfection by loving all men, even our enemies, as Christ loved us.

7
What's This Thing Called Sin?

It is precisely in this that God proves his love for us: that while we were still sinners, Christ died for us. —Romans 5:8

A discussion on Christian morality will eventually lead to a consideration of sin. Certainly, if we admit that Jesus Christ came to save sinners, then it becomes very important for us to discuss the nature of sin and its relationship to Christian living. But before we venture into this topic, please consider the following exercise. It is designed to get you to think about some basic attitudes toward sin and morality. Please check on the lines those statements that you pretty much agree with.

—— 1. Sin has to do with the breaking of rules and regulations, especially those set up by the Church.

—— 2. What's wrong is what I think is wrong.

—— 3. Some actions are wrong even if I don't think they are wrong. They may be wrong in themselves and for others, but not necessarily for me.

—— 4. The problem with evil and sin today is that it seems to be tolerated by so many in society: the violence and pornography, war, cheating and lying in government circles, and the like.

—— 5. What I don't like is someone telling me it's wrong to smoke marijuana, for example, while he himself drinks alcohol. This is phoniness to me, and phoniness is the worst sin of all.

—— 6. I can't see going to church if it is nothing but a big bore. To me, it is just as good to take a walk in the woods and worship God in my own way.

—— 7. I see sin primarily in terms of relationship. Any time I do something to harm my relationship to God or neighbor, I sin. This includes attitudes I have toward them.

—— 8. Morality and sin are quite confusing to me. When I was in grade school, things were much more "cut and dried." Mental sickness and circumstances were not used as excuses as they seem to be so much today.

After you have responded to the above statements, assemble in small groups and examine the attitudes toward sin and morality which are reflected in each comment. Try to state in a few words a description of the attitude contained in each statement. Then try to state in your own words what *your* attitude toward sin is.

WHY ALL THIS TALK ABOUT SIN?

One of the problems with the topic of sin is merely trying to talk about it. As a matter of fact, one of the major charges leveled against Christians is that they tend to overemphasize sin. Some people strongly maintain that too much talk about sin results in a "fire-and-brimstone" approach to religion where fear of hell and eternal damnation are taught as the primary emphasis. Consequently, these same people see Christianity as a joyless religion, too negative in its approach to the problems of the world.

Can you remember the last time a "fire-and-brimstone" sermon was preached to you?

What was your reaction to it?

The above criticism raised about Christianity is not really a fair one. As we shall see in this chapter, Christianity is a joyful religion precisely because the claim it makes for mankind is that sin and its consequences can be overcome. Rather than taking an unrealistic view of man, Christianity is fundamentally realistic in that it recognizes what the condition of man is as it tries to articulate what has been, what should be, and what can be done about it.

Then, why this disaffection with talk about sin? Father Eugene Maly in his book *Sin: Biblical Perspectives* offers three reasons. The first reason suggests that the word "sin" is too personal. Sin implies the description of a relationship with a personal being we call God. Maybe some people today believe in the existence of evil or personal fault but without reference to the traditional concept of a living God. To have no faith in a personal, loving God means not to believe in sin.

A second reason sin may not be popular today is because of nit-picking juridical or legalistic distinctions presented about it in the past. Fine arguments about "material" and "formal" sin, mortal and venial sin, and exhaustive listings of categories of sin have tended to bore the ordinary Christian who seeks to live a vital, though stumbling response to a living God.

The final possible explanation for contemporary dislike of sin offered by Father Maly is the belief that man is fundamentally incapable of failure. This utopian view of man sees him progressing to a more glorious future than his past and that certainly his nature is improving all the time. To say that man lives in a sinful condition does not set well with this view of man.

CHRISTIANITY HOLDS THAT MAN IS CAPABLE OF PROGRESS

To a certain extent, Christianity does agree that man has progressed and grown considerably since he emerged from the caves. Man is a great builder; he contributes much to the development of the world. Note some of the achievements of man over the past few centuries which would lead a person to conclude that man is indeed incapable of failure.

Science. Our grandparents had trouble coping with the so-called "horseless" carriage. But who would have believed that in the 1960's man would be walking on the moon? And in our lifetimes there will undoubtedly be colonies of "earthlings" populating space stations and maybe even other planets.

Science has also brought about a communications revolution. We in the United States can easily communicate with any people almost anywhere via telephone, telegraph, or television. Never in man's history has there been the potential for world unity due in no small measure to our ability to exchange ideas almost instantaneously.

Along with the communications revolution there has been a revolution in transportation. Goods and people are closer to each other than ever in man's history.

A third revolution brought about by science is a "leisure" revolution. Machines, tools, computers, and the like have lessened our work load such that it will not be uncommon for the next generation to work a maximum of 20 hours a week. With so much free time, people will have the opportunity to develop really human lives by pursuing—if they wish—studies, cultural and artistic achievements, and play.

Medicine. The average life span of Americans has doubled in the past 75 years or so due to man's achievements in medicine. He has found a cure for polio, diphtheria, and many other killer diseases. He is capable of transplanting body parts to extend his life. We are living better and longer lives due to the painstaking work of our doctors and researchers in the field of medicine.

Social science. We have made strides in this field, too. Man has developed some sophisticated forms of self-rule where individuals have a say in the choice of their leaders and in the development of programs that affect their welfare. Some governments have programs of universal education, health benefits for all their citizens, social security benefits such as old-age pensions and unemployment insurance.

CHRISTIANITY MAINTAINS THAT MAN IS CAPABLE OF EVIL AND SIN

While admitting these tremendous advances in the above and other fields, Christianity recognizes—on the other hand—certain destructive tendencies in man. We are both builders and destroyers; we are living paradoxes. Evidences of evil and sin in the world are present all around us. Note the following examples:

War. World War I was labeled the "war that would end all wars." Yet 20 short years after the completion of that war, the nations of the world were using their tremendous scientific know-how for destructive purposes. Our own country will not long forget the Vietnam War that resulted in internal strife in our country, loss of respect abroad, and a widespread economic recession.

Prejudice. Job and housing discrimination based on one's religion or race is rampant in this country and abroad. Prejudice reached its natural conclusion with Hitler's attempted genocide of the Jewish people in the Second World War.

Corruption. Young people are almost cynical about the greed and corruption and lying in top governmental offices. Daily we read stories about price-fixing in big business or bribe-taking by our police forces. Widespread thievery takes the form of income-tax cheating and shoplifting.

Cosmic evil. If the above is not enough to convince the "utopian" of man's evil tendencies, he still has to contend with so-called "cosmic evil." Tornadoes kill innocent people. Earthquakes destroy men, property and fortunes. Daily, people—through no fault of their own—are born lame, retarded, impoverished, and the like.

Much evil afoot in the world results from man's inhumanity to man, his failure to live a constructive kind of life. To the degree that a person is responsible for his/her own evil attitudes and actions, to that degree he/she is sinning. Of course, there is much evil in the world for which mankind does not seem directly responsible. For example, natural disasters bring about much human suffering which is not the apparent responsibility of human evil. Cosmic calamities are part of the great mystery of evil.

The following exercise is designed to get you to think about your own image of sin. After you have finished the exercise, you may wish to gather in small groups to share your reasons for a particular choice.

Please circle the phrase you think sin is more like in the following pairs.

Sin is more like . . .

a. crashing a stop sign;
b. not going to the wake of a friend's father.

a. failing to help with the chores at home;
b. staying out three hours later than when you are supposed to be in.

a. reading a pornographic book;
b. backbiting a classmate whom you don't like.

a. fighting with a younger brother;
b. hitting a car in a parking lot ($50 damage) and skipping out.

a. doing against someone;
b. not doing for someone.

Consider the following:

John has just returned from a weekend "spiritual renewal" with the youth group of his parish. It was an especially worthwhile experience for him. His one resolution made on the retreat was to break his bad habit of cheating. He does well for a while but he soon finds himself "borrowing" his friend's homework and test answers on the several occasions he did not study. Despite his firm resolve, John has found himself cheating again.

Many of us, no doubt, have found ourselves in similar situations. We try to break a bad pattern of behavior just to find ourselves falling back into it again. This tells us something about the nature of sin. Even the great St. Paul recognized the problem. Paraphrasing him, he summed up the problem this way: "The things I don't want to do, I do; the things I do want to do, I don't do." We are sinners; we have a predisposition to do the wrong thing.

BIBLICAL PERSPECTIVES ON SIN

Any Christian consideration of sin must first look to the bible. It is in the bible where we find the history of a people struggling to live a life of obedience to their loving God. It is in the bible where we find some of the greatest psychological insights into sin.

One fact clearly emerges from the reading of the Old Testament and that is that God is very much interested in his people. He calls them to life and gives them a land to live on. All he asked for in return was for men to recognize the living, personal relationship he called them into. The Old Testament describes sin as any breaking or lessening of this living, personal relationship (Is 1:2).

Pride is often seen as the reason for man's stiff-necked refusal to love his God or other men. It is in the Genesis story of "original sin" where we see the pride and stubbornness of Adam (man) and Eve (woman) which led to disobedience of God's command. Pride cut off the living relationship between God and man and led to death.

In the Old Testament, this living relationship was expressed in terms of a covenant, an agreement of love between God and his people to be faithful to one another. God was always loyal to the Jews. But recorded in the Old Testament were many expressions that belied the chosen people's supposed attitude of love toward him: terms like "stiff-necked" and "hardhearted people"; "missing the mark" and "stubborn" (Is 29:13).

> But these people have a stubborn and rebellious heart; they have turned aside and gone away.
> —Jeremiah 5:23

The New Testament also talks of sin in terms of relationship. Jesus affirmed that the greatest commandment had to do with a loving relationship: "You must love God above all things and your neighbor as yourself." This commandment drives home the importance of loving and worshiping God—this is our primary duty. Many of our sins of lack of love flow from idolatry of other things—making things or self more worthy of worship than God.

Discuss how the following are sins once they become worshiped, that is, made into a kind of god:

    a. sex
    b. money
    c. alcohol and drugs
    d. human praise for one's efforts
    e. another person
    f. power

SOCIAL DIMENSION OF SIN

What was stressed in the Old Testament concerning the covenant notion was that a failure to relate to God was a *community* failure. Because one person was not loving, the whole community in its relationship to one another and to God suffered. The prophet Amos was especially sensitive to the failure to love in the Jewish social injustices to the poor and downtrodden (Am 2:6-16).

A similar community idea is expressed by St. Paul in the New Testament in the Body of Christ imagery. In the Spirit of Jesus and his Father we are one; through the blood of Christ we are related to one another. As a result, because there flows from a Christian concept of man the idea that we are children of God, there must be a social concern for all. For example, the argument used in some circles to justify abortion is false: namely, that a woman has a "right to her own body." Rather, the new life in her body belongs to the whole community, the family of mankind, not just to the individual mother.

In what way are the following "community sins"?

—endangering my life while skiing recklessly?
—an evil sexual thought consented to?

SIN AS ACTION OR NONACTION FLOWING FROM ATTITUDE:

Today, theologians add to this biblical understanding of sin as a personal affront to a living God having communal dimensions. They also talk about it in terms of the so-called "fundamental option." Father Maly states the "fundamental option" this way:

Modern moral theologians stress more the basic attitudes that motivate man in his daily living. These are called fundamental options, and they refer to those underlying attitudes towards God and man that affect moral decisions. Thus, if man has chosen to direct his whole life completely to self, without regard for God or others, then his state of life can be said to be that of "mortal" sin. All his actions will be affected by this choice. If his basic choice is for God and others, then his wrong actions will be judged as morally venial or serious to the extent that they fail to be in accord with his basic choice.
—*Sin: Biblical Perspectives,* p. 33.

The familiar story of the Good Samaritan illustrates well the notion of fundamental option. The sin of the priest and the Levite was that of *omitting* to love the injured victim of injustice. Their basic attitude was not to get involved with the foreigner, so they decided not to act. But Jesus taught that love of neighbor exists in positive action in his favor. Further, he taught that one's neighbor includes the foreigner, even the enemy. Those who fail to act do so because of a fundamental *attitude* of indifference.

A fundamental attitude can lead to sins of *commission* too. Many of these sins are catalogued in the Ten Commandments: sins such as idolatry, blasphemy, disobedience, killing, adultery, theft, and the like. These, too, flow from basic attitudes. Disobedience from a prideful disposition or sexual abuses from a self-centered perverted attitude towards a created good are only two examples of acts which come from basic attitudes.

How do *attitudes* of hate lead to acts of:

—killing
—jealousy
—discrimination
—backbiting

How do *attitudes* of love lead to acts of:

—sharing
—caring
—getting involved

WHEN IS A SIN A SIN FOR ME?

This section of the chapter will attempt to answer the question, "When is a sin a sin for me?" Before directly trying to answer that question, we should distinguish between two concepts: "being responsible for" and "being blameworthy for" particular actions.

A person is "responsible," meaning "answerable," for his or her actions and attitudes. For example:

a. Did I crash the red light? Yes.
b. Did I make a mistake on my income tax? Yes.
c. Did I hit you with a golf ball? Yes.

The above were *my* actions. I am answerable for them. I have to admit that they flow from me.

On the other hand, I am "blameworthy," morally speaking, only if I have moral guilt for my actions. For example:

a. Yes, I crashed the red light, but only to avoid hitting a child who ran into the intersection. I am responsible for my action, but not blameworthy.

b. Yes, I made a mistake on my income tax, but simply because I accidentally and inadvertently failed to carry over a "0" in the "exemptions column." I am responsible for my action, but since I did not intend it, my blameworthiness is lessened. Perhaps, though, I should have been more careful.

c. Yes, I hit you with a golf ball because I intended to do so. I am *both* responsible and blameworthy for my action.

In traditional terms, a sin is a serious sin for me under the following circumstances:

1. IS IT WRONG? Do I have an attitude or have I performed an action which does indeed alienate my living relationship between myself and God or between me and my neighbor? Clearly, a nasty word spoken to a classmate does not help my relationship with him or her. In fact, it may very well harm it. But the nasty word ordinarily is not so serious as to totally destroy the person, my relationship to him or her, or my relationship to God. On the other hand, my continuously held attitude of hate towards the mem-

ber of another race which culminates in an act of violence and murder certainly is of its nature quite serious and has as its outcome the destruction of a relationship. Such an act has been called "mortal sin."

2. DO I KNOW IT IS WRONG? Certainly, I am not blameworthy for something I did not know or realize to be a destructive attitude or action because of my age or inexperience. For example, a person may claim that he or she did not realize that getting drunk to the point of losing self-control was serious. But when a person finds out that whenever he or she surrenders (through drinking or drugs) one's ability to think or judge and consequently is destroying part of what it means to be human—and this is a serious matter—then he or she has the duty to avoid doing likewise again. A person is not blameworthy for actions committed in the past due to ignorance which was not one's fault. But everyone should try to remain open to new knowledge in growth to a deeper and fuller relationship to God.

3. DO I FREELY ENGAGE IN THE EVIL? Not only must my action or nonaction be wrong in itself, not only must I know what it is that I am doing or not doing, but I must choose to do it freely and willingly. For example, I may steal something—which is wrong—because I am being forced under the threat of death to do so. I am not blameworthy for the action. Likewise, I may have a very bad habit which lessens my freedom to act right in a certain situation. But I must try my best to resist and overcome the habit by asking for God's help.

How are the following properly called *serious* attitudes and actions which tend to kill relationships between God and man? man and man?

—apostasy (proclaiming Christ, then denying him)

—marital infidelity

—war

—racial prejudice

JESUS AND SIN

How does Jesus Christ fit into this discussion on sin? He came that men may have life and have it more abundantly. In his earthly ministry, Jesus forgave sin. Since only God can forgive sin, Jesus demonstrated how God's power had broken through to eradicate evil and its effects. As detailed in Mk 2:5-7, the religious leaders of Jesus' day did not want to believe the good news that sin was forgiven in Jesus. But Jesus vindicated his power to forgive sin when he healed the man's sickness.

"Which is easier, to say to the paralytic, 'Your sins are forgiven,' or to say, 'Stand up, pick up your mat, and walk again'? That you may know that the Son of Man has authority on earth to forgive sins" (he said to the paralyzed man), "I command you: Stand up! Pick up your mat and go home." The man stood and picked up his mat and went outside in the sight of everyone. They were awestruck; all gave praise to God, saying, "We have never seen anything like this!"

By his death, Jesus allowed the ultimate effect of sin to destroy him as it destroys us. But by his resurrection from the dead, he manifested that sin has been conquered because death has been conquered. It is precisely because of the resurrection and the assertion that sin has been overcome through Jesus that Christians are fundamentally joyful and hopeful in the face of their own sinfulness.

Furthermore, the Christian maintains that Jesus gave the power to forgive sin to the community of believers, the Church. As we see in Mt 18:18 and Jn 20:23, the community of Christians has the duty to forgive sin in the name of Jesus.

The joy over the reality of the forgiveness of sin prompts the Christian to extend this forgiveness to others. If we expect God to forgive our sins, then we must stand ready to forgive those who have offended us. In the teaching of the great Christian prayer of the Our Father, Jesus included as one of the petitions: "forgive us the wrong we have done as we forgive those who wrong us" (Mt 6:12). God's forgiveness is always there and available to us—but it does not reach the heart of the man who harbors enmity towards his brother. "If you bring your gift to the altar and there recall that your brother has anything against you, leave your gift at the altar, go first and be reconciled with your brother, and then come and offer your gift" (Mt 5:23-24).

God's forgiveness given to us in the person of Jesus leads to healing—a making whole. So, too, our extension of God's forgiveness into the world helps heal enmities between men. Just imagine the consequences for the following situations if a generous dose of forgiveness were present:

- on both sides of this country's race issue

- in management and labor disputes

- in the Middle East conflict

- on the issue of Women's Liberation

SIN AND RECONCILIATION

The Catholic has the opportunity to confess his sins in order to be healed of them and be reconciled to the community. This takes place in the Sacrament of Reconciliation—Penance. For those who receive the sacrament with the correct attitude, Penance is seen as a joyful time because in it individuals meet Jesus in a special way. In this sacrament, Jesus the healer, Jesus the forgiving brother, meets the penitent and helps him or her overcome the sinful attitudes and actions that keep the individual from growing into a deeper and more loving relationship with God and others.

Religious pollsters tell us, though, that many Catholics are not going to confession the way they used to in the past. If the sacrament is one of a joyful meeting with the Lord, it becomes difficult to understand the falling off in the reception of this sacrament. One of the most common reasons given is that confession is too routine. People find themselves confessing the same thing time after time and they note little growth in their spiritual lives.

The recently revised ritual of the Sacrament of Reconciliation is an attempt to make the external actions of the sacrament more meaningfully express our need for healing. One of the prime needs which is met in the new ritual is the need to experience community. Obviously, there is no sense talking about confession if people do not see the need of *church,* or indeed if they do not perceive themselves as *church.* If the Church is that visible group of people which makes the love of Christ visible to one another and the world, then it stands to reason that my failures to love involve not only me and God but also they involve my brothers and sisters. The new rite helps us deepen our understanding of church, that is, community, so that I not only experience the reality of reconciliation with the whole community but I feel in a deep, moving way the healing love of Jesus Christ as it is presented to me in that community.

This sense of community coupled with a renewed sensitivity by the confessors to "receive the penitent kindly" as a real sign of the personal, forgiving Christ and the new emphasis on preparing for the sacrament through personal prayer should go a long way towards renewing the sacrament in the Church. Personal prayer especially will help the penitent examine his life with God's strength and grace and identify those basic *underlying attitudes* which are at the root of so many *actions* or *failures to act*.

Examination of Conscience

This exercise is designed to enable a person to think about basic attitudes so that he or she can identify the areas in his or her life that need growth. Since it is beneficial to concentrate on *specific problems* which are at the root of much sinful behavior, we have listed below characteristic attitudes, different in different people, which tend to stifle growth in a relationship between a person and God and between a person and others.

Any one of the following examples could be the basis for a complete confession, assuming there is no (other) mortal sinfulness.

> "I get so angry with my failures that at times I am quite sarcastic to my parents, brothers and sisters, and classmates."
>
> "I take a certain satisfaction in learning and spreading the faults of those whose ideas about ———— I do not like."
>
> "I refuse to take responsibility for my mistakes either as a student or a child. I always find someone else to blame."
>
> "I continually broadcast my abilities and make myself the center of every conversation."

"I cause inconvenience to others by a haphazard way of doing things, making them wait, spoiling their plans, ignoring their needs."

"I am very stubborn and domineering. If I don't immediately get my way, I lose my temper and seek to get revenge."

"I almost never pray."

"I begrudgingly go to Mass and have a negative attitude towards others who go but don't live up to my level of spirituality."

"I tend to take a selfish view of the opposite sex as a way to satisfy my lust instead of seeing them as unique persons made in the image and likeness of God."

"I am prejudiced against black persons (Jews, police, teachers, etc.) and I see everything about them through a filter of prejudice and emotion."

"I rarely watch my language and frequently find myself using God's name frivolously."

"I cause pain unnecessarily to my parents by being secretive about my activities and friends."

"I think nothing of cheating on exams and, when caught, lying to get out of it."

"I reluctantly forgive the faults of others though I expect them to forgive me readily."

"I generally have a closed mind about new ideas, especially when they conflict with my own convictions."

"I let my weakness for liquor lead me to drink too much, which in turn leads to loose talk, lying, reckless driving and endangering the lives of others, and the like."*

---

* The above examination is modeled on one given in Fr. Leonard Foley's *What's Happened to Confession?* Cincinnati: St. Anthony Messenger Press, 1970, pp. 113-117.

SUMMARY

Christians do not accept the charge leveled by some that theirs is a "fire-and-brimstone" religion of fear in order to get people to conform to a certain set formula of behavior. True, they admit there is sin. They see men as living paradoxes—both builders and destroyers. They claim that sin is a failure to grow in a living relationship with God and others. They know that sin has its social consequences. But they are convinced, in faith, that through Jesus Christ we can be rescued from sin. They believe that through his death and resurrection the ultimate effect of sin has been conquered. They know in hope and in joy that through God's loving forgiveness the sinful attitudes they have can be healed by the loving touch of Jesus. Furthermore, they are aware of their duty to extend this forgiving touch in the world in order to show to mankind what God has done for us in the person of his Son.

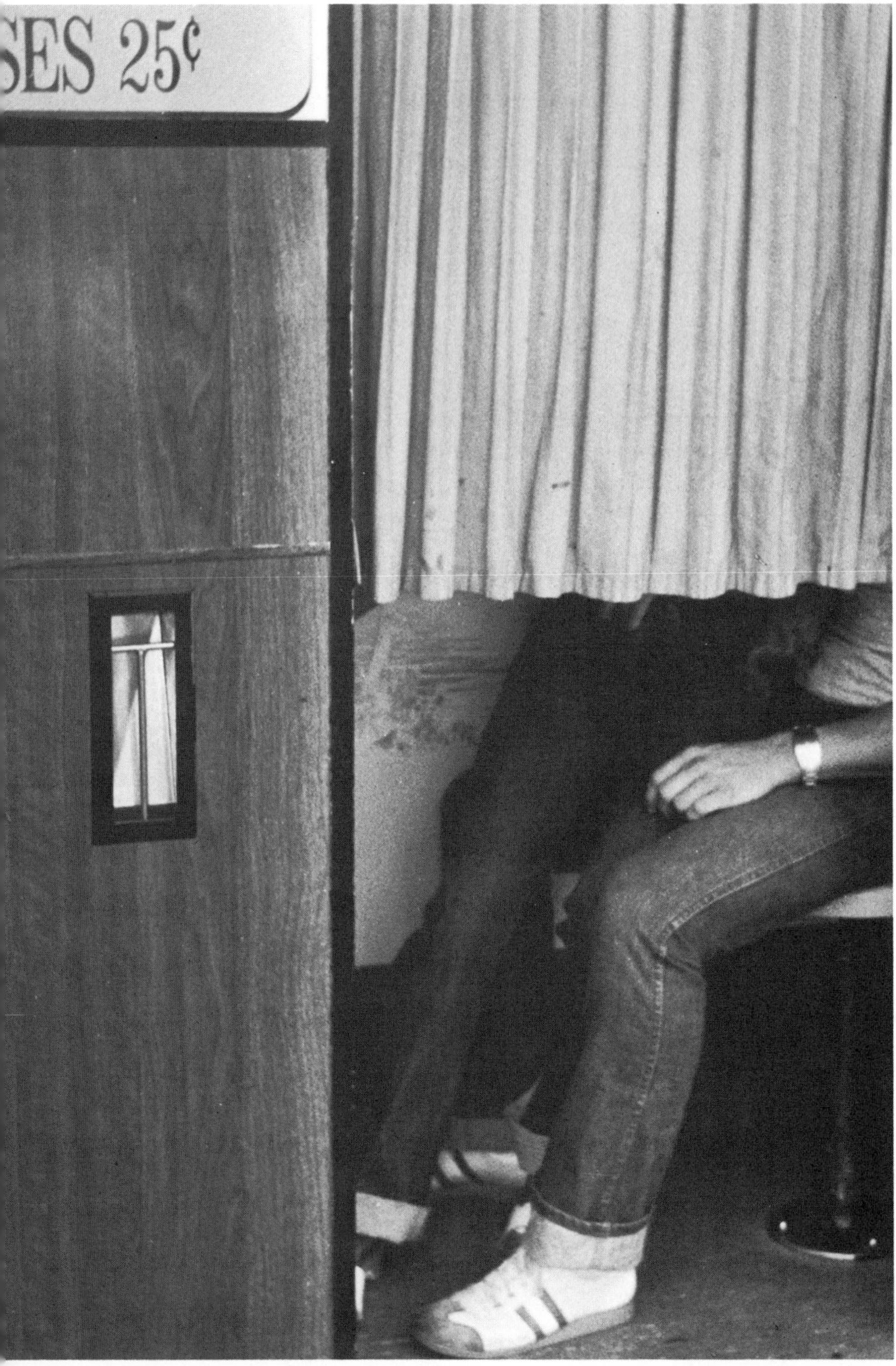
SES 25¢

8
Sexual Morality

"Be (of love) a little more careful than of everything."
—e. e. cummings

A high school student once remarked that he first started liking girls the moment he discovered that they weren't boys. He may have been exaggerating, but it is certainly no exaggeration to say that male-female relationships play an important part in a teenager's life. In fact, such relationships are often experienced as the most alluring and exciting mysteries of life.

All is not fun and games, however. Social awkwardness, rejection and misunderstandings make for tears instead of laughter. One of the most troublesome kinds of problems is in the area of sexual morality. "How far can you go without doing wrong?" expresses this commonly felt dilemma. In trying to decide just when kissing becomes sinful, or in trying to answer why premarital intercourse is sinful, the individual finds himself or herself faced with questions that have no easy answers.

This chapter attempts to help answer these questions by placing sexuality in the broader context of the Christian vision of man, our society today, the ethical teaching of Jesus, the nature of human relationships, and other critical areas that give a perspective to sexual morality. This broadening of the horizon and seeing sexuality in relation to other areas of life will help to focus more realistically on the key questions that many teenagers wonder about as they try to formulate and live up to authentic Christian values.

SEXUALITY AND BEING HUMAN

The broadest base on which sexuality can be examined is that of human nature itself. To be human is to be either male or female. In other words, to be human is to be sexual in one's very being. Our sexuality in terms of our femininity or masculinity affects many, if not all, of our day-to-day actions.

Consider the following characteristics, then discuss the differences between the way females react or act in these circumstances as compared to males. Discuss whether these characteristics are learned from the society or if they are inherited.

	Male	Female
Ability to bear pain	————	————
Cries easily	————	————
Parenthood (Is being a father the same experience to a man as being a mother is to the woman?)	————	————
Aggressiveness	————	————
Independence	————	————
Sensitivity to the feelings of others	————	————

Men and women in our society are expected to act in certain ways. For example, women are expected to cry at movies and be passive, and men are expected to like sports and be aggressive. These commonly expressed notions about the differences between the sexes are often the source of disputes over whether such characteristics are inherited or learned from the society. Regardless of how these characteristics come about, one thing is clear—our sexuality includes much more than the narrow category of actions most people think of as being sexual. Rather, sexuality reaches into many areas of human experience and daily life.

Discuss the claim of women's liberation that female passivity is a learned pattern of behavior rather than an inherited characteristic proper to femininity as such.

SEXUALITY AND HUMAN RELATIONSHIPS

Because of the far-reaching influence of sexuality in our orientation to daily life experiences, it is little wonder that sexuality also influences human relationships. It seems almost too obvious to mention, for example, that if your mother were not a woman, she could not be your mother!

Consider the relationships charted below.

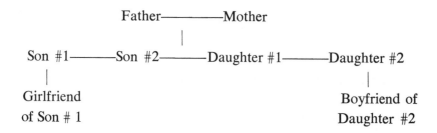

The masculinity or femininity of the above individuals obviously affects the way in which they relate to one another. The mother and father could hardly be the mother and father if both were of the same sex. Also, there is a basic difference between a father-son and a father-daughter relationship, just as there is a difference between a mother-son and a mother-daughter relationship.

Furthermore, the way in which sexuality is expressed also determines the nature of the relationship. For example, son #1 surely doesn't feel the same way about his girlfriend as he does about his sister. Also, son #2 may be a very good friend to his brother's girlfriend but the girlfriend doesn't feel the same toward both of them (or at least son #1 hopes she doesn't!).

SEXUALITY AND LOVE

It is at this point that the relationship between the mother and father can be seen to be unique. They are the only two who have made a commitment unto death to be faithful to each other. Likewise, they are the only two who can morally engage in sexual relations. Placing their sexual activity in the context of a family is critical to understanding the basis of Christian sexual morality.

Their sexual union not only was the source of life of their children, it is also an outward bodily expression of their total gift of themselves to each other. Sexual intercourse implies a revealing and giving of one's inmost self. This self-surrender and giving is the very basis of love, and it is thus that having intercourse is often spoken of as "making love." As we saw in an earlier chapter, relationship with another implies responsibility for that relationship, and the deeper the relationship, the deeper the responsibility.

Sexual love is a mysterious thing, but one thing that can be said about it without much dispute is that it comes from the depths of the heart. Sexual intimacy implies a deep-felt union that brings with it tremendous potential to develop and strengthen the two involved or to hurt and dehumanize them. To "go all the way" physically is proper only between two people who have gone all the way in the broader context of a commitment to share the responsibility that goes with such a deep relationship. This is why sexual intercourse in marriage is such a meaningful act in continuity with the married couple's whole life together. It is also why sexual intercourse outside marriage is unworthy of the name of love in its deepest dimensions.

The greater the dignity of the human race, the greater the dignity of human sexuality. Christianity gives man the greatest possible dignity and hence gives his sexuality the greatest possible dignity. We must constantly strive to see the power and beauty of sexuality if we are to see it in a Christian context, and so come to understand the basis of Christian sexual morality. This understanding begins in seeing sexuality in terms of committed love and family relationships.

Sometimes books addressed to teenagers trying to show why premarital sex is undesirable will focus on all the negative consequences that can result from it, such as venereal disease, unwanted pregnancy, broken family relationships, and so forth. Certainly the young person must be aware that such dangers are very real and they may well serve as a deterrent to premarital sex, but they fail to build foundations on which a young person can build a positive concept of sexuality. We must base our sexual morality not on what is wrong in immoral sexual acts, but rather upon what is good in moral sexual acts.

---

1. The following excerpt is from a book called *The Velveteen Rabbit*, by Margery Williams Bianco. The discussion is between two stuffed animals who are discussing what it means to be real. Compare the Skin Horse's answer to the married love relationship described above.

   "Does it happen all at once, like being wound up," he asked, "or bit by bit?"

   "It doesn't happen all at once," said the Skin Horse. "You become. It takes a long time. That's why it often doesn't happen to people who break easily, or have sharp edges, or who have to be carefully kept. Generally, by the time you are real, most of your hair has been rubbed off, and your eyes drop out, and you get loose in the joints and very shabby. But these things don't matter at all, because once you are real, you can't be ugly, except to people who don't understand."

2. What is the difference between having fun and being happy? Apply the distinction between fun and happiness to the difference between a Playboy philosophy of sex and the approach suggested in the above quote.

All of this idealistic talk about the meaning of sex in marriage may seem a bit removed from the more practical moral problems facing the adolescent. In a sense, this is true. Yet, it must be remembered that we can fully understand something only by seeing it in terms of what it is at its best. For example, the art of cooking is not appreciated in eating nothing but burned food. Likewise, athletics are not appreciated in seeing only sandlot baseball, but rather in watching professional athletes at their best.

The same holds true in trying to understand sexual morality. An adolescent must face moral questions in light of what sex is in the fullness of married love. In acknowledging the trials, the depth, the beauty and the fulfillment of married love, the young person can come to see that sex is not a toy, that to abuse the power of sex is to abuse a deep expression of love that gives birth to new love and to new human life. In short, the young person can come to approach the problem of sexual morality with the beginnings of a mature Christian conscience.

THE DIFFICULT STRUGGLE

The teenager who tries to live up to the standards of Christian sexual morality is in for a difficult struggle. First of all, a struggle is involved because, put simply, sex is a problem. Sex is rarely neat and clearly defined like problems in a math book. Rather, the sex drive is strong, mysterious and sometimes tries to act as though it had a mind of its own. And it is strongest during the years of adolescence.

There are also social reasons why a young person's search for high sexual ideals is difficult. The first social difficulty is the matter of delayed marriage. In almost all past cultures, and still in some today, people married at the age of puberty. Not so in our culture. Due to factors such as educational requirements, marriage is delayed until the late teens or early twenties for women, and as late as the late twenties for the men. This means that all sexual activity is immoral during the very years it is the strongest. This is bound to cause problems, especially between young people who feel strongly about each other, and who have been dating for some time, or may be engaged, yet know they have several years to wait before getting married.

Another social element adding to the problem is today's widespread sensuality and permissiveness which puts pressure on the young person to conform. Who can but smile to the old song lyrics: "A rooty toot toot, A rooty toot toot, we're the boys from the institute. We don't smoke, and we don't chew, and we don't go with girls that do." Such Victorian sentiments went out with nickel Cokes and high button shoes. To a great extent, it is truly a blessing we have emerged from the prudish ways of bygone days. But the problem is that the pendulum has swung so far in the opposite direction that for a boy in high school to admit that he doesn't have "experience" is like admitting he sleeps with a teddy bear or uses a Mickey Mouse toothbrush. The double standard of morality still calls for girls to maintain some semblance of propriety, but they, too, are expected to join in on the "You've come a long way, baby" bandwagon. This is not to imply that our society has become one huge orgiastic Sodom and Gomorrah. Studies show that the sexual practices of Americans have not changed drastically in recent years. The point is that the attitudes have changed. What was formerly done in secret is now done openly, and the vast majority of mass media and public opinion condone such action by their lack of criticism. To the adolescent, so dependent on peer acceptance, the Christian has all the appearances of one swimming against the tide of public opinion. For most people, this does not present a very appealing ideal. A Christian has to be one who can dare to be different. This may be inspiring or idealistic, but it is rarely easy.

Discussion: List the magazines, films, television shows and records that promote a permissive attitude toward sex. Compare this attitude to the one implied in the material on married love presented at the beginning of this chapter.

CULTURAL ASPECTS OF THE CHURCH'S ATTITUDE TOWARD SEX

A little later in this chapter we will discuss the Church's teaching on sexual morality in light of the scriptures. This will be done to stress the fact that, at bottom, the Church's teaching on sexual morality is grounded in the goodness of sex as a creation of God.

The Church, however, is human as well as divine. It is not only founded upon divine revelation but is also a pilgrim community bearing all the weakness of the human condition. This also applies to the Church's attitudes towards sexuality, which often appear to be negative and, at times, almost antisexual.

Before examining some of the historical and cultural influences that have contributed to negative attitudes towards sexuality in the Church, it is well to keep two things in mind. First we must be careful not to let the pleasure-seeking and materialistic influences in today's society so influence our thinking that we fail to see the dignity of sex and the wisdom in the Church's teaching. Secondly, the Church's weaknesses never undo the promises of Christ that he would be with the Church until the end of time. We must in faith try to see the underlying truth in the Church's teaching.

The following are some of the historical and cultural causes of the Church's negative attitude towards sexuality:

1. The very first Christians thought that the second coming of Jesus was to occur within a very short period of time. This apocalyptic attitude is frequently expressed in the Gospel of Mark and in the early writing of St. Paul. Within this context, marriage has little or no value because there is not going to be enough time to settle down and raise a family. This attitude continued for several centuries and found expression in such things as men going out into the deserts of Egypt to be hermits. On a longer term basis, it put an emphasis on celibacy as being superior to marriage.

2. The writings of the philosopher Plato speak of the soul of man being in the body like a prisoner in a cage. The goal of the wise man, said Plato, is to free one's self from the shackles of physical pleasures. This thinking found its way into the Church in the writings of St. Augustine, who was also influenced by the Manichaean idea that the body was evil. It would be difficult to overestimate the power and greatness of Augustine's contributions to the theology of the Church. But it is also hard to overestimate the influence of his negative bias toward sex on the monks of the Middle Ages who were to write the Church's moral theology manuals.

3. The Middle Ages themselves were strongly otherworldly. In other words, the whole thrust of Christian life was placed in a concern to save one's soul and get to heaven. The religious life became termed "the way of perfection," and there was little appreciation of the holiness of marriage as a vocation. In fact, there was an attitude that sexual love even in marriage was to be engaged in to the extent necessary for the procreation of children and the release of passion. Opinions were such that one finds popular old wives' tales of the period saying that each time a married couple had sexual intercourse, it removed one day from the end of their lives as a punishment. Once a friend of St. Francis was asked if a man could sin by enjoying sex with his own wife, and the reply was, "Can a man get drunk on the wine in his own glass?"

These attitudes led to a frame of mind in which sexual sins were not only sins but they became *the* sins, sins worse than all others. Great concern was given for the slightest sexual desire, thought or action, any one of which could damn a person to hell forever. At the same time, however, there was little or no concern for social sins such as exploitation of the poor or cruelty in war. Not that such things weren't seen to be sinful but rather that they didn't make one "dirty" the way sexual sins did.

Ideas such as those expressed above totally turn many young people off who assume that such ideas represent the Church's teaching. As said before, we must be careful about jumping to easy conclusions. We must keep in mind the sensual bias of today's society, the fact that in many ways the Church is deeply influenced by the historical period of the day, and, lastly, we must remember that there is a kernel of truth in these attitudes—namely, that sex can easily dehumanize us and make us self-centered.

The friend of St. Francis was, in a sense, right in that a man can get drunk on the wine in his own glass. The point is that a Christian must be careful not to set his heart on anything material in a way that excludes God and the giving of one's self to others. It goes without saying that the exploitation of sex can easily do just that.

We can say more in favor of the Church's overall teaching on sexual morality. The Church's teachings are grounded in revelation which itself offers the highest possible dignity to human sexuality, and also to the underlying need for sexual morality. It is in this sense that the Church rises above the shortcomings of every age and of the weaknesses of human nature to teach us a sexual morality based on our dignity as children of God.

PRINCIPLES OF CHRISTIAN MORALITY
BASED ON SCRIPTURE

Old Testament. The fact that God is the creator of all things, and the fact that he looks upon all things as being very good (Genesis 1) say something about the deepest reality of sex; namely, that sex is very good. More than this, because sex is such a powerful expression of love, and because God is love (1 John 4:7), sex can be said to be very, very good.

The conclusion to this would be that sexual sins are not sins because sex is so bad, but rather because it is so good. Sexual sins are a form of irresponsibility for the depth of love implied in sexual relationships. The idea is that the sex organs, sexual acts, feelings and thoughts, can, in themselves, be nothing but good. We can deny our own sexuality only at the price of a self-destructive denial of our own humanity as created by God.

Sexual actions become morally wrong in the abuse of sexual power by using sex outside of God's will. The story of Adam and

Eve and the doctrine of original sin both point to the mystery that the human heart so easily becomes self-centered. Out of weakness, we can so easily let sex be a way of selfishly exploiting the other instead of giving to the other in a context of committed love.

New Testament. It is interesting to note that Jesus rarely refers to sexual sins at all, and when he does it is in the context of forgiving them. This is in sharp contrast to his frequent and sometimes severe condemnation of the hypocrisy and pride of the Pharisees. In fact, one of the Pharisees' chief criticisms of Jesus was that he associated with sinners such as prostitutes.

This helps give us a sense of balance in judging the weight of sexual sins and also in trying to evaluate ourselves. It seems valid to say that the most grievous sins in the eyes of Jesus are those sins committed in strength and not those committed out of the weakness of human nature. He was unmitigated in condemning those who tried to make themselves morally superior to others. He condemned an attitude that did not let one's love reach out and include everyone, even one's enemies. Most of all he called for that total inner renewal where a person turns from a self-centered to an other-centered life. It is for this reason that sexual sins, insofar as they proceed from man's inner weakness, are not the focal point of morality as far as Jesus is concerned. In the light of the gospels, our touchstone with God is our hearts, not our genitals.

The point is, however, that the total conversion which Jesus asked of his disciples involves the whole person. It is a conversion that changes not only the outside of a person and his actions, but more, it changes the person inside. Jesus once said, "You have heard the commandment, 'You shall not commit adultery'; what I say to you is: Anyone who looks lustfully at a woman has already committed adultery with her in his thoughts." Jesus calls not for a list of rules the Christian is not to break, but rather for an attitude towards others. It is an attitude of responsible love in which the abuse of sex is totally out of place.

The high divorce rate in our country today clearly indicates that a happy, lasting marriage is not something that is automatically assured with the pronouncing of marriage vows. What do you think are the main causes for a love relationship leading toward a marriage becoming bitter and ending in divorce? What attitudes toward sexuality strengthen a marriage? Which will threaten that relationship?

Imagine two people getting married who are trying to base their life on a total inner commitment to be Christlike to each other and their children. In other words, what role should our faith have in supporting and helping to bring about a lasting love relationship?

SUMMARY

Rather than attempt to answer specific questions about sexual morality, it has been the intention of this chapter to make clear the Christian attitude towards sex which the reader can then apply to each individual question. One theme of the chapter has been the idea that what is called for is a realistic acceptance of human nature, on the one hand, and a fidelity to the message of Christ, on the other.

In an effort to further clarify this balance between accepting the actual while never losing sight of the ideal, the following set of points is offered for consideration. First of all, we will examine those points which call for the realistic acceptance of human nature.

1. God loves you and in this love you are called upon to love yourself. There is never a situation where failings in sexual morality are to be an occasion for self-hatred or belittlement. Such an attitude is not true guilt but only neurotic self-destruction. We must be patient with ourselves and learn that a wholesome grasp of one's own sexuality comes with maturity and a lifelong growth in Christ.

2. Most sins in the area of sexuality do not result from an isolated

and deliberate act of the will. A person does not get out of bed in the morning and say, "Well, guess I'll go out and commit fornication this morning." Rather, strong emotions, physical desires, deeply felt affection and other similar forces often dominate one's consciousness and lessen the ability to make free and responsible choices. It is good to remember in such circumstances that the extent to which one does not have full control of the will is the extent to which there is no sin.

3. The pressures to go along with the crowd in a materialistic society make it all the more difficult to maintain one's moral integrity as a Christian.

4. According to the gospel, it is not sexual sins but rather sins of unkindness, pride and hypocrisy which most separate us from the love of God. We must avoid confusing an antisexual attitude with Christian morality.

The above points emphasized the importance of self-acceptance and realism in evaluating sexual morality. The following points stress the fact that we must not let realism become infidelity to the challenge of living up to the high ideals of Christian life.

1. It is true that unkindness and pride are among the most serious sins in the light of the gospels. The point is that sexual sins are often the expression of unkindness and pride.

2. It is true that forces such as emotions can greatly lessen the use of free will and hence also lessen moral responsibility. What must be remembered is that the individual must avoid those places and people that are the cause of losing one's freedom. To deliberately lose one's ability to think clearly is itself a sign of insincerity, and can bring with it moral guilt. Drinking, parking, drive-in movies, petting are danger signs that a sincere person will regard with due caution. Human weakness is one thing; indifference and insincerity are another.

3. Each partner must remember that what may cause no temptation to one person may cause strong temptation to the other. A mature, sincere couple will be honest with each other in this regard.

4. A good general rule to go by in trying to decide the morality of a sexual act is to ask yourself the question, "Will this act make

my partner more of a person before God, before himself and his loved ones?"

5. Sex, wrongly used, can hurt others. Not only is this so in the obvious ways of venereal disease and pregnancy, but also in the broader context of a person's moral, psychological and social development.

6. There is no getting around the painful fact that to be a Christian involves the willingness to be different from the crowd. The fact that "everyone is doing it" is not the issue. The issue is that, for the Christian, sexual intercourse, and all acts directly leading to sexual intercourse, are to be reserved to the total commitment of married love. Sexual morality for the unmarried young adult is not founded on the idea that sex is bad, on the contrary, that it is so good.

DISCUSSION

1. Is sex just like any other physical sensation? Why or why not?

2. In what ways is Christian sexual morality both beautiful and difficult at the same time?

3. Why is it hard to live up to a Christian sexual morality in today's society?

4. Should a boy resent it when a girl "draws the line" on a date?

5. How much of the responsibility for drawing the line do you think the boy should have? How much should the girl have?

6. What are the differences between infatuation, desire, and love?

7. What does it mean to distinguish the cultural influences on the Church's attitudes towards sex from the inner reality of her teaching which is based on scripture?

8. Discuss celibacy as a unique form of witness to the dignity of sexuality. Why is it especially hard for someone raised in and influenced by our present society to understand or appreciate the value of celibacy?

9. Discuss sexual morality as flowing from the dignity of the human person.

10. In what sense is one's sexuality a kind of secret? What is implied in the revealing of this secret?

9
Respect for Life

"Life is a book in which we never get beyond the first syllable."
—Dag Hammarskjold

Respect for another means we have a sense of the other's worth. We have a sense of honor and esteem for all that involves the well-being of the other. We begin to appreciate the importance of this quality of respect the moment we feel ourselves being treated in a way that is in any way disrespectful—being laughed at, taken lightly, or in any way mistreated are painful experiences known to all of us. This chapter focuses in on the moral obligation of the Christian to respect all reality and especially all human life as created by God the Father and redeemed by Christ.

KINDS OF RESPECT

The following exercise will help introduce the topic of respect for life. Letting 1 represent the least amount of respect and 5 the most, indicate on a scale of 1 to 5 the amount of respect you would tend to have for each of the following.

1. a president of student council
   | | | | | | |
   1 2 3 4 5

139

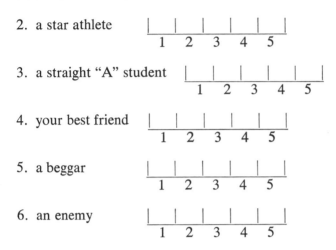

2. a star athlete

3. a straight "A" student

4. your best friend

5. a beggar

6. an enemy

Respect for Positions of Leadership

The first kind of respect to be discussed is referred to by the first example in the above exercise. Respect for those in positions of leadership flows from a natural tendency found among all peoples to respect the leaders of the community. This is one reason the Watergate scandal involving President Nixon was so devastating to the country. The president's office warrants such high respect that any scandal involving the president is overwhelmingly destructive to the nation's sense of security. The pomp and ceremony that surround all kings, queens and other world leaders can serve to further illustrate this kind of respect.

One characteristic of this kind of respect is worth noting; namely, the respect is focused not so much on the person as on the person's position. In other words, the respect is directed towards the person's power and influence rather than on the actual person holding the office.

Respect Based on Personal Qualities

Numbers two and three in the above exercise, respect for a star athlete or exceptional student, refer to respect for others based on their personal qualities. A gifted artist, student, cook, or athlete, are examples of the kind of people we respect because of what they can do better than the average person. This kind of respect often goes hand in hand with respect for positions of leadership because of the simple fact that gifted people are often chosen as the leaders in a community. The point is that in this kind of respect the focus is not on the person's position but on his or her personal qualities.

Respect Based on Friendship

The fourth example in the opening exercise, respect for a close friend, refers to yet another kind of respect for others that is, in a sense, very different from respect based on either position or personal qualities. This kind of respect is the respect given to someone you love. It is the respect found between friends, lovers, brothers, sisters; in other words, between any two people united in a bond of love.

Jesus once said: "treat others the way you would have them treat you" (Mt 7:12). This can be restated to say that you should respect others in the same way you respect yourself. In terms of love relationships, this is the natural thing to do in light of the nature of love. In love we extend ourselves into the one loved. We share the person's sorrows and joys, just as they share ours.

It is very significant that the respect we have for loved ones transcends both the person's position in the society and individual talents. The loved one may be a scrubwoman or a queen, a street sweeper or a congressperson, but the love between the two individuals makes these things irrelevant. By loving another we are able to respect the person just because of the person he or she is. A friend does not have to perform to win our admiration. Just being who he or she is fulfills the basis for the respect. And the deeper the love, the more true this becomes.

This last point can be taken yet further by the following example. When John Kennedy was assassinated there were widespread and immediate feelings of hatred against Lee Harvey

Oswald, the accused assassin. In the midst of all this anti-Oswald commotion, a reporter asked Oswald's mother what she thought of the incident. During the interview she said a surprising thing. She said, "He's really such a good boy!" There is a sense in which she was right. She was still able to respect her son. Because of her love for him, she was able to distinguish the person she loved from the terrible act he committed.

Respect for others can be divided up into the following types:

1. respect based on a person's position in the community

2. respect based on a person's individual qualities

3. respect based on love

Selective Respect

Respect for others based on position, qualities or love is a good and essential aspect of human life. It would be a sad day when we no longer respected our leaders or our friends.

But there is a shortcoming to respect based on such things; namely, it tends to be a selective respect. It tends easily to show us why we should respect certain people but it fails to show us why we should respect all people.

The fifth example in the opening exercise, that of the beggar, presents a problem because we have not yet hit upon a basis for which we can respect those who apparently deserve no respect. The beggar is certainly not a leader in the society. He doesn't seem to exhibit any personal qualities that deserve respect. And certainly, he is not someone we go up to and throw our arms around as our dearest friend. In our selective respect we tend to shun such people or even demonstrate the opposite of respect in attitudes of open disgust or ridicule.

Discuss the problem of prejudice, and of racism in our country in particular, in terms of selective respect. Consider how the Africans were brought to this country like animals without names, social dignity, religion, or culture. They ceased to be persons and became things or objects. Do you think all prejudice tends to make us unable to see the other as someone to respect? This idea can also be applied to what the Nazi soldiers did to six million Jews, or what the settlers of early America did to the American Indians.

RELIGION AND UNIVERSAL RESPECT FOR LIFE

"THE RABBIT HUNTER"*

Careless and still
The hunter lurks
With gun depressed,
Facing alone
The alder swamps
Ghastly snow-white
And his hound works
In the offing there
Like one possessed,
And yelps delight
And sings and romps,
Bringing him on
The shadowy hare
For him to rend
And deal a death
That he nor it
(Nor I) have wit
To comprehend.
—Robert Frost

The last lines of the above poem by Robert Frost speak of man's awareness that life is a mystery. Man is more than a very sophisticated monkey or an elaborate electrical, chemical factory.

All living things, and man in particular, share in the profound mystery we call life. The quote by Dag Hammarskjold used at the beginning of this chapter, "Life is a book in which we will never get beyond the first syllable" is also expressive of this idea.

The great religions of the world have all expressed this sense of awe and wonder before the mystery of life. Man's religious sense calls forth a response of respect for all life wherever it exists, from the smallest flower to man himself.

In the Eastern religions this respect for life goes to lengths which seem strange to us. For example, Jainism, which is a religion in India, holds that its followers should not walk out at night for fear they might step on an insect. Similarly, certain Buddhists strain their drinking water for fear of swallowing an insect.

Of course, it goes without saying that these religious groups are against violence in any form to higher animals and so are opposed to eating meat. Likewise, of course, they usually oppose all violence to human beings in any form whatsoever, even in self-defense. All these customs flow from the conviction that life is sacred.

CHRISTIANITY AND RESPECT FOR LIFE

The Judeo-Christian tradition of our own Catholic faith is in its own way no less insistent upon the sacredness of all life, especially human life. In the context of the scriptures, the sacredness of life is posited in the opening verses of the Book of Genesis wherein we see that all life is created by God and man is created in God's own image and likeness.

More significant yet is Christianity's belief that God himself became human in the person of Jesus Christ. Because of Christ, we can say that to be fully human is to be Godlike because God has made himself to be like us. Jesus identified with all of human life, except sin. In his life and death he has united himself to humanity to the extent that he told us that what we do to others we also do to him.

Towards the end of St. Matthew's Gospel we hear Jesus describing the last judgment at the end of the world. He says that on Judgment Day he will say to those who are damned:

"I was hungry and you gave me no food. I was thirsty and you gave me no drink. I was away from home and you gave me no welcome, naked and you gave me no clothing. I was ill and in prison and you did not comfort me."

Then they in turn will ask:

"Lord, when did we see you hungry or thirsty or away from home or naked, or ill or in prison and not attend to your needs?"

He will answer them:

"I assure you, as often as you neglected to do it to one of these least ones, you neglected to do it to me."

The well-known legend of St. Francis kissing a leper covered with sores is a statement of St. Francis' ability to see Jesus in the poor and the sick. We are called upon to do the same. All human life is a gift of God, made in his image. Furthermore, Jesus has radically united himself with all human life, especially with the poor and the lowly. Because of this, we, as Christians, are bound to respect all life no matter how lowly, weak or unbecoming its form may be. It is in Christ that we find the deepest foundation for respecting a beggar or any stranger.

Abortion

In light of the sacredness of life described above, it is easier to understand why the Church has been so opposed to abortion. The unborn child shares in the mystery of human life. Because human life is a gift from God, it is not ours to dispose of as we please. Ultimately, we do not belong to ourselves but to God who created us from nothing.

It is true that the unborn child has but begun to develop, but this is no justification for abortion. The unborn child is not fully

developed but neither is anyone on earth. Each of us is in a different stage of growth and development on a journey toward final perfection. It is not for us to say that just because the unborn child has barely started on the journey of life, we have the right to fail to respect his or her life.

Here we see how critical faith is in answering the crucial question about the inmost reality of human life. If human life is nothing more than well-developed animal life, or if the only real concern of human life is that which we can experience with our senses, then the proabortionists certainly have many strong points on their behalf. The critical issue arises as soon as we say that human life comes from God as a sacred gift that transcends what we can control or understand. It is in the light of faith that taking the life of the unborn child becomes a serious moral problem.

Suicide

It becomes clear why suicide is an attack against a basic respect for life when we examine the effects of suicide on human relationships. In other words, if you were to commit suicide, you would not only be killing yourself but also causing deep pain to those who love you. We cannot destroy ourselves without also partially destroying those who have extended themselves into us by giving us their love.

In light of Christian faith, this understanding of the immorality of suicide is certainly valid. Yet, it is not enough because it fails to show why suicide is immoral for the person who has no family or loved ones. In others words, why couldn't a totally isolated person commit suicide morally?

The answer, of course, is found in turning to the same principles applied in the problem of abortion. In the religious sense, life is never a commodity, a thing that can be disposed of when we see fit. Each of us is ultimately sacred not because we are loved by others but rather because we are loved by God who creates us from nothing to share in his love.

Euthanasia

There are many factors that make euthanasia, or mercy killing, a complex moral question. Technology today can produce machines and medicines that can artificially prolong life almost indefinitely. This raises the complex question about determining the point at which these extraordinary means can be morally withdrawn from a dying patient. Of course, there are no pat answers, but one thing is certain. Mercy killing becomes immoral at that moment in which human life is treated as a commodity that can be preserved or continued according to what seems the least painful or most practical course of action. The dignity of human life as coming from God demands of us the highest possible respect for life and a careful concern that we do not slip into easy answers or courses of action that provide an easy way out.

War

The issue of the morality of war also touches upon the problem of respect for life. Traditionally, the Catholic Church has accepted the just war theory, which holds that a country may morally engage in war as long as certain requirements are met, such as trying every possible peaceful means of settlement first and engaging in war only to the extent necessary to gain victory over the unjust aggressor. The standards of just war make all acts of malicious aggression clearly immoral. Likewise, it seems obvious that it must be considered moral to engage in war in certain circumstances. For example, the face of the Western world would be very different today had no one battled against the forces of Hitler.

Yet, war too presents moral problems. The unbelievable power of atomic warfare to destroy whole civilizations in a matter of minutes has caused the bishops of the Catholic Church to publicly state that atomic warfare is immoral. And the long and bitter struggle in Vietnam has caused many people to question the validity of war in any form. Again, as with mercy killing, there are no easy answers to the questions about the morality of war. What is essential is to see that warfare becomes immoral at the moment those involved begin to intentionally ignore the dignity of human life.

Some examples of attacks against human dignity in war would be the killing of women and children or the wounded and aged, the torture of prisoners or such actions as cutting off food and water supplies to entire cities allowing the inhabitants to die of starvation.

War presents moral problems because it appears almost impossible to engage in war without also taking part in activities as those described above. Also, as mentioned earlier, new atomic weapons have increased war's power to undermine the dignity of human life.

The pacifist or the conscientious objector can never stand up and demand that all who profess to be Christian must follow in his or her footsteps. But in light of Jesus' command that you should "Love your enemies and pray for those who persecute you" (Mt 5:43), the pacifist is a constant reminder that war is at best a necessary evil. Human life flourishes where there is peace both interiorly and in the society at large.

A Christian love and respect for life calls for a concern for anyone anywhere who suffers injustice and pain. This fact helps stress that our faith is essentially social and can therefore not be restricted solely to a private affair of religious practices. Also made evident is the Christian's call to actively take part in the society in which we live.

Discuss some of the problems in trying to work toward a moral solution to abortion, suicide, euthanasia and war.

The following issues are examples of areas in which respect for life is a central theme. Discuss each in light of the above material:

prison reform	aid to starving nations
care for the retarded	racial equality
care for the aged	women's rights

JESUS AND LOVE FOR ONE'S ENEMIES

Earlier in this chapter we saw that Jesus has united himself to all mankind to the extent that what we do to others we also do to him. This is the basis for a Christian respect for life, the implications of which were discussed above.

It must be noted that loving the poor and lowly is still not a wide enough circle to embrace the love to which Christ calls us.

In his hour of death on the cross, Jesus cried out, "Father, forgive them; they do not know what they are doing" (Lk 23:34). His plea on behalf of his own executioners is a dramatic assertion of Jesus' insistence that we must forgive those who have harmed us.

The message of Jesus is that God turns towards mankind and says, in effect, "You cannot make me stop loving you." Jesus can be seen as God's eternal and faithful love to a humanity that so often fails to respond to his love. Peter once asked Jesus, "Lord, when my brother wrongs me, how often must I forgive him? Seven times?" "No," Jesus replied, "not seven times; I say, seventy times seven times" (Mt 18:21). Christ asks us to strive to give our love not only to the poor and needy but to our enemies as well.

Many people have read or heard about *The Diary of Anne Frank.* One of the reasons why it is such a moving book is that it helps us realize that each of the six million Jews who died in the gas chambers was also an Anne Frank. In other words, each one was a unique, sacred individual. The radical demand of Christ that we love our enemies calls for us to see that Hitler, too, was an Anne Frank! He, too, was a sacred, unique individual loved by God. This does not mean we must not abhor the evil deeds which hurt others. What is meant is that, no matter how hateful the act, the one who commits it must never be excluded from our love. We must not let our respect for life stop short of those who have wronged us. To intentionally do this is to put one's self outside the Church as that community which professes to be Christ's forgiving presence through history.

Not only must we avoid excluding others from our love because of the wrong they have done, we must also not exclude ourselves because of the wrongs we have committed. The great sin of Judas was not his betraying of Christ. Peter also denied Christ but became a great leader in the early Church and is a saint today. Judas' great sin was in failing to accept Jesus' forgiveness. If he would have approached Jesus nailed to the cross and asked for forgiveness, Jesus would have instantly forgiven him. Jesus is forgiveness. In the moment of forgiving his betrayer he, Jesus, would have been at one of the peak moments in which he could have acted out what he was, God's infinite and saving forgiveness to mankind. We must hate the evil deed and never the one who commits it, and this includes ourselves. Suicide as well as lesser forms of self-destruction, such as drug addiction or alcoholism, are all attacks on the dignity of human life. Self-hatred is also opposed to human dignity. We must always be ready to accept the guilt of our wrong-doings but this is not to be confused with attitudes which attack our own essential goodness in the eyes of God as we stand redeemed in Christ's love. A Christian's respect for life must know no limit because God is the author of life and loves all life infinitely.

At the close of the American bishops' pastoral letter titled *Human Life in Our Day* we find the following words which are a fitting summary of this chapter.

> Christians believe God to be the "source of life" (Jn 5:26) and of love since "Love comes from God" (1 Jn 4:7). "God is love" (1 Jn 4:8) and man has been made "in his image and likeness" (Gn 1:26). Thus, man is most himself when he honors life and lives by love. Then he is most like to God.

> In her defense of human life the Church in our day makes her own, as did Moses, the words in which God himself reduces our perplexities to a clear, inescapable choice:

> "I call heaven and earth to witness against you this day, that I have set before you life and death . . . therefore, choose life that you and your descendants may live. . ." (Deut 30:19).

10
The Community Dimension in Morality

> *The community of believers were of one heart and one mind. None of them ever claimed anything as his own; rather, everything was held in common. With power the apostles bore witness to the resurrection of the Lord Jesus, and great respect was paid to them all; nor was there anyone needy among them, for all who owned property or houses sold them and donated the proceeds.*
> —*Acts 4:32-35*

Word association games are interesting for a psychological reason. They tend to reveal a person's true thoughts on a given topic. The following chapter deals with an elusive dimension in a discussion of morality—the dimension of Christian community. The exercise below is designed to help elicit initial, true feelings about certain concepts. When you see a word, jot down the first thought that comes to mind. For example, when some people see the word "pope" their first thought might be "authority." Please honestly react to the following words.

Church ————————————————————

Jesus ————————————————————

Christian ————————————————————

Morality ————————————————————

Community ————————————————————

Catholic ————————————————————

When finished with this exercise, please gather into groups of 3-5 and compare responses. How many of your initial reactions were "people-centered"? How many were "institution-oriented"? In what way might all the words be saying the same thing?

MORALITY DOES HAVE TO DO WITH COMMUNITY

As we saw quite graphically in Chapter 3—"Relationship and Responsibility"—the very definition of morality of necessity indicates the community dimension involved. Sertillanges, as quoted in Oraison's *Morality for Our Times,* defines morality as "the science of what man ought to be by reason of what he is" (p. 22). "What man is" from a Christian perspective was discussed in Chapter 2—each person is a child of God and thus brother and sister to our Lord and to each other. Hence, our moral response to God involves others. A "community dimension" is involved.

Another view of morality which naturally flows from the one above holds that authentic morality involves responding to the demands others make on us. In this view of morality, others are involved at the core of being a moral person. We are moral to the degree that we make an authentic response (answer) to those who call to us. In this sense, then, our responding to others in community determines how well we are living as children of God.

A third way to look at the community dimension in morality is to carefully examine 1 Cor 12:12-13:13. This would be a good time to put down the text you are reading, open your New Testament to these chapters of Paul's First Letter to the Corinthians, and prayerfully reflect on the message contained there. In brief, Paul emphasizes that the Spirit of Jesus and his Father, that is, our helper and paraclete, unites us into one body, the members of which are intimately related to each other. Each member needs the other in order that the body be whole. If one member suffers, the entire body is affected. In other words, because we have come together in a union (community) by the power of the Holy Spirit, our response to God is *always* going to involve others. The heart of Christian morality is that it is communal.

All of these definitions of morality and indeed the thrust of this book are that of a Christian view of morality. But if the demands of this stance toward morality have not troubled the reader by now, perhaps the question should be asked at this point. "Why should I follow a *Christian* morality? Can I not be saved simply by living a good life of love like many others who have never heard of Christ?"

Consider the following:

> Most probably you have read in the newspaper about a heroic effort to save someone's life. Perhaps it was a story something like this: A little girl was playing ball with her brother. The ball rolled into the street. The little girl went after it. A bystander, a teenager, saw the girl running into the street. He also saw a car approaching her at some considerable speed. His moment of instant decision was that the only way the girl could be saved would be if he dashed into the street into the path of the car and pushed the girl out of the way of its onrushing speed. Without hesitation or fear for his own life, he proceeded to do so. The happy-sad story ended only too predictably: The girl is saved; the teenager is killed in his successful effort to rescue her.

Discuss the following questions in relation to the above story:

1. What if the teenager in the story were Bob who did not believe in God. What might his heroic action mean?

2. What if the hero were Tom, a practicing Catholic. Might his rescue mean something different than Bob's?

3. If we might grant that Bob and Tom were acting morally in this situation, then what difference did it make that Tom was a Catholic?

WHY SHOULD WE LIVE A CHRISTIAN MORALITY?

The question posed above is a good one and one that almost every young person must be able to answer for himself or herself. One way to examine the question is to look at our own backgrounds.

Because we as individuals have a history and belong to certain groups, we of necessity will assimilate the values we have been exposed to. A sense of being a certain kind of person comes from our past influences—one influence of which is our Catholic heritage.

Parents, friends, relatives, teachers, and others have been raised as Christians in the Catholic tradition and have wished to pass on their values. This is not only natural, it is good. Our individual histories, though they have their differences, have this in common: We have learned about Jesus and his teaching through others. These others are his Church—a group of people with Jesus Christ as the head, bound in unity in the Holy Spirit, who in faith desire to live the message of Jesus Christ.

Included in this background of ours is our association with the *Catholic* Church. Many Catholic young people today do not mind being called "Christian," but they balk at the idea of being termed "Catholic." It is difficult to understand at times this hesitation to be identified with one's past. Although sometimes motivated by the worthy desire to remove barriers between Catholics and Protestants, this hesitancy is more often due to today's hang-up about authority systems, or hypocrisy on the part of some believers, or some bad experiences with "Church people."

But whatever the reason for the disaffection with the word *Catholic,* none should lose sight of two points concerning it. For one thing, the adjective "catholic" in its root meaning denotes universality. The Church which is being described is for all men at all places in all times. Being part of such a community of the people of God is in no way something to be ashamed of. Secondly, *Catholic* used as a noun is a person who identifies himself or herself with a particular tradition, a particular way of looking at Christ and responding to him.

Likewise, the word "church" has its problems today. Many, no doubt, thought of "church" in the word-association game as primarily a building or a place of some sort where people worship. But in its root meaning, church is the assembly of the community of believers. Church is people; church is a community of like-minded people bound together in Christ.

Thus, being a member of the Catholic Church means being a member of a particular community which in faith accepts Jesus as Lord and attempts to live out the implications of that faith.

Another way to approach an answer to the question is to review the story of Tom and Bob. Bob, you might recall, did not believe in God. But he was, humanly speaking, a good person. He tried to live up to his abilities. He lived a moderate life. He tried his best to help others. After all, he gave up his life for another person. Surely, he was a good person.

Did Bob have to be a Christian or a Catholic to be saved? The answer to this question is "no." In all probability Bob attained eternal life—and people like him do, too—because Jesus came to save all men. In the words of Vatican Council II:

> Those also can attain to everlasting salvation who through no fault of their own do not know the gospel of Christ or his Church, yet sincerely seek God, and, moved by grace, strive by their deeds to do his will as it is known to them through the dictates of conscience. Nor does divine Providence deny the help necessary for salvation to those who, without blame on their part, have not yet arrived at an explicit knowledge of God, but who strive to live a good life, thanks to his grace. Whatever goodness or truth is found among them is looked upon by the Church as a preparation for the gospel. She regards such qualities as given by him who enlightens all men so that they may finally have life.
> (Chapter 2, Section 16 of the *Dogmatic Constitution of the Church*)

Because God in his own wisdom extended his loving grace to Bob, he was saved even though he was not a Catholic or a Christian. His good life, his response to others, reflected his moral life—but a life lived without knowledge in an explicit sense of Jesus.

Tom, on the other hand, was a Catholic. He, too, lived a good life—a life directed more to others and to God rather than a self-centered one. Tom's life was culminated in the way he died. He knew who he was—a son of God—and by his action of saving the little girl he concretized, he enfleshed the reality of Jesus Christ alive in the world today. His response to the little girl's plight was a living out of the life-love he was committed to as a Christian. Indeed, his death manifested the greatest kind of love recommended by his Lord: laying down his life.

Tom made a profound witness to the world in which he lived by giving up his life for another. He witnessed to the fact that Jesus lives today. Externally, both Tom and Bob performed the same extremely generous act of self-sacrifice. But Tom and other Christians like him are not "better" people than non-Christians. We are not "better" because all men are equally the children of God. Bob and Tom are both good; they are both saved. But once again we are left with the question: "Why be a Christian? Why live our lives under the banner of Jesus Christ?"

Let us finally attempt to answer that question! To be a Christian is both a privilege and a challenge. *By gratefully accepting the privilege and eagerly living out the challenge, being a Christian should make a difference.*

Being a Christian is a privilege in the sense that we have been given an explicit awareness of God's total self-communication to mankind—in the person of his Son, Jesus Christ. This knowledge, this faith, is a gift. God has chosen us because he has a task for us to perform. The fact that he has chosen us does not make us better than anyone else.

This privileged knowledge we have of Jesus Christ gives us hope, hope that the human condition is ultimately redeemable. Our community of believers knows in faith that the evils, the frustrations, the hates of this world will eventually pass away. Our community knows that these have been overcome by the suffering, death, and resurrection of our Savior, Jesus Christ.

Our community of believers has it on the word of one no less than the Son of God that death does not end it all—that even death and apparent annihilation are meaningless in light of Jesus' resurrection. This hope borne of faith in our Lord makes life more meaningful for today in light of what has already taken place in Jesus and will take place in each believer who accepts his loving salvation and friendship.

But this privilege is a real challenge. We are not given our knowledge of Jesus just to keep him to ourselves and rest satisfied that we are saved. Rather, we are challenged by Jesus himself to go out into the world and preach in word and deed the good news of our redemption.

In this way, we are Jesus people. Our community of believers are the hands, the feet, the caring and sharing of Jesus in the world today. In a certain sense, he needs us—his Church—to do his continuing work of healing and loving in the world today. To love as Jesus did is a real challenge—in a sense, a burden.

Besides being Jesus people, we are resurrection people. Our Christian living should point in a joyous and glad way to the ultimate victory of goodness in our eventual union with God.

Three images sum up well the duties of a Christian for being afforded the privilege of his or her faith. All three denote challenge. All three teach us that to live as Christians has meaning because it offers something to others that no other religion can.

LEAVEN. Jesus spoke of the kingdom of God as the case of leaven (yeast) pervading the dough and causing it to rise. So, too, the Christian is like leaven whose effect in the world is to change it, to raise its awareness of ultimate meaning in life. The image of leaven does not bespeak numbers or quantity, rather quality. By the quality of our lives lived in response to God and others, we help through word and deed to show others who they are and what their destiny is.

LIGHT. Jesus called his followers the light of the world. Jesus is the true guiding light and we are his followers who have the task of letting his light reflect off us. We help others discover real meaning in life by letting Christ and his life shine forth in the way we live.

SALT. Jesus also called his followers the "salt of the earth." This image connotes two different meanings. Salt has a preservative quality. By salting meat, it could be saved for future consumption in a day when electric freezers were not invented. So, too, the Christian by his deeds participates in the saving actions of Jesus and helps make these actions come alive in the contemporary world. Salt is also a seasoning. By living a Christian life, a person brings a certain flavor into the world. His life should change it for the better.

Why be a Christian? Why live a Christian moral life? The answer lies in our willingness to participate in spreading the good news of Jesus. It is a challenge to live our lives as Christians, but it is a challenge—when lived—which helps the rest of mankind know that there is a God, a God who cares for us very much and wants us eventually to be reunited with him in eternity. By joyfully living as Jesus would have us live we make believable the claim that we are saved and that God has wondrous things in store for us and all mankind.

What difference does being a Catholic make in your life?

Can you think of some individuals, famous or otherwise, who were in a true sense like leaven, light or salt?

Is it more difficult to be a Catholic than a member of some other religion? If not, why not? If yes, in what way more difficult?

BEING A CATHOLIC CHRISTIAN GIVES US THE OPPORTUNITY TO MEET JESUS IN A SPECIAL WAY:

There are two important beliefs of Catholics that help distinguish their tradition from that of other Christians. In the words of Father Richard McBrien in his book, *Who Is a Catholic?* we note the first essential difference:

> Whereas the specific difference between Christian and non-Christian lies in the fact of baptism and the explicit confession of faith in the Lordship of Jesus Christ, the basic difference between Roman Catholicism and every other form of Christianity is in its understanding of ecclesiastical office, and, more specifically, the office of the pope (p. 20).

It is the belief of the Catholic that Jesus handed on his teaching authority to his Church and that the Church has not only the right, but the duty, to instruct Christians in the area of faith and morals. This authority resides in the *magisterium* of the Church, that is, in the bishops and the pope as their head. It is this belief in the teaching authority of our bishops and our pope that makes Catholics consider very seriously in all of their moral decisions the noninfallible teachings made and to accept in faith all infallible teachings. These teachings, we believe, are under the guidance of the Holy Spirit and stem from our serious acceptance of Jesus' presence in his Church and his promise not to mislead it.

A second most important distinguishing factor of the Catholic is his belief in the sacramental presence of Jesus. By this is meant that Jesus presents himself really and totally in his Church through special moments and signs. We have already seen that Jesus is present in his Church, that is, in the community of believers who are united to him as their head. He is also present some way in each Christian who lets Jesus Christ live in him or her. But a third presence of Jesus is in his sacraments.

The key sacrament to which all the others build is the Eucharist. The Eucharist is often called a celebration because through this sacrament we celebrate who we are in union with our Lord. Unfortunately, for too many young people, and if we are to believe pollsters some older people, too, this celebration has lost its meaning. But perhaps part of the decline in Mass attendance is due to a failure to understand what it is all about.

The celebration of the Eucharist is about being with others who believe as we do. This coming together is quite special because we do it to worship God and recognize that we, as Christians, can go to the Father only with one another because the Father has sent his Son Jesus to be our brother and show us the way.

There is something psychologically sound about communal worship, too. Because we are social beings, we need the support and help of our fellow believers. This is especially true in a society which has values quite antipathetic to Christianity. Liturgy is a special time to remember who we are, what our destiny is, and that we need the help of the Son of God to live out that destiny in community.

Coming to Mass also gives us the opportunity to practice charity to all assembled there. Even if we would rather not be there for whatever reason, going and participating and worshiping with other Christians shows that we take seriously the faith that has been entrusted to us.

It is in the Eucharist that the Catholic is nourished by the word of God. He derives nourishment not only from the Word—the Son —when he receives Jesus in Communion, but he derives nourishment from the written word which is proclaimed in the Mass. The word of God proclaimed, thought about and prayed over becomes a living word that helps us become who we are. As sons and daughters of the Father we need constant reminders of our dignity. The liturgy of the Mass gives us the community of strength in unity to live out the implications of who we are.

The Eucharistic celebration becomes a symbol, a sign, for the larger community, especially when celebrated on Sunday, the day of the Lord. On Sunday, the Catholic worships on the first day of the week—the day our Lord was raised from the dead. Our community sign of unity is another example of light, of hope, given to the world that there is an ultimate meaning to life outside the ordinary humdrum existence we apparently live in. If we Catholics fail to see the value of Sunday Mass maybe it is because we fail to see God in our lives and thus worship has become meaningless for us. Or perhaps the reason resides in our failure to see Jesus in whom love for God becomes inseparably one with love for the brother.

SUMMARY

Morality has much to do with community. It is within the context of other people that we live out our lives. Christians are today in the same situation of the Church of the Acts of the Apostles. We very strongly need one another and our Lord to help make it possible for us to live a life of love directed to all men. By experiencing the love of God in Christian community—and this is done in a unique way at the Eucharist—we can better share this love with others not only in the community, but outside it as well.

EXERCISES

1. A friend comes to you and says she has stopped going to Mass at her parish because she "doesn't get anything out of it." What would you tell her to help her see that she's looking at it from the wrong angle? It is not "what we get out of it" but rather "what we put into it." Is there anything concrete that you or your classmates can "put into" your parish liturgies to make them more meaningful for you and others in the community? (It might be an interesting challenge to take those recommendations to your parish council or pastor and request how you might help implement them.)

2. Write a short reaction to these:

   a. For me, to be a Christian means—

   b. For me, to be a Catholic means—

   Share these with your classmates.

11

Sources of Morality

"You are the salt of the earth. But what if the salt goes flat? How can you restore its flavor?"
—Jesus *(Mt 5:13)*

A pluralistic society is one in which the members of the society are offered more than one norm of moral behavior. Such a situation presents the individual with the problem of not merely trying to do what is right, but of having to decide what is right in the first place. Expressing the same thing in the form of a question—which source of morality is the right one to follow? The following incident should help illustrate the nature of the problem.

> Tom is a senior in high school. He wants the family car for the evening, and asks his mother for the keys. She gives him the keys and tells him to have a good time. But, just as he is leaving the house, Tom's father comes downstairs and tells Tom that he cannot have the car because of his low grades on his last report card. Tom's mother totally disagrees. She gets angry and tells Tom to ignore his father and go ahead and leave.

Tom is faced with the predicament often described as "damned if you do, and damned if you don't." His problem arises from his parents, as two sources of morality, telling him to do two contradictory things at the same time. On a much broader scale, this is the plight of modern-day Americans who are often besieged with not two but many contradictory answers as to what is the right thing to do in any given situation. It is not as though the proabortionists, for example, came out and said they realized they were wrong, but were pushing abortion all the same. On the contrary, they strongly assert that Catholics are wrong and they are right. It is not hard to see why such a situation is the cause of moral confusion and uncertainty.

The following exercise will hopefully help to further clarify this point. The following positions are held and fostered by different groups in our country today. Each of the positions listed is considered to be immoral by the Church. State briefly why the Church opposes the position (a help on this would be to refer to Chapter 2, "Who Are You?—A Christian Response").

1. Marriage should be abolished so people could move on to another partner when they wished.

2. A woman should be allowed to have an abortion on demand.

3. We should painlessly kill the very old and the retarded because they are no longer useful to the society.

4. It is a waste of time to go to church. Besides, religion is no more than a superstitious hangover from the past.

5. The only worthwhile goal in life is to amass as much material wealth as possible. Nothing else matters.

The sharp contrast between the Church's teaching and the ideas expressed above is but a small indication of the widely divergent and often contradictory answers given for moral questions. The question that automatically emerges is: "Whom are you to believe?" When your faith comes up against the thinking of others, how are you to arrive at the right answer to the problem? Surely the Church isn't saying that everyone is wrong except those who follow the Church's way of seeing things. Surely the Church does not ask you not to think for yourself. The picture presented is a confusing one. It seems at times as though everyone were walking on Jell-O, and the only certain thing that can be said about any moral question is that the answer will always be uncertain. In this day and age, even the simplest statement is followed by a question mark. We appear to have lost our compass in a world that constantly offers new answers to new problems.

THREE GUIDELINES TO REMEMBER:

Now that we have made clear some of the moral problems that arise from living in a pluralistic society, we can begin by stating a few principles that may help to clarify things.

The first point is that each person and idea with which you come in contact is only a possible source of morality. Nothing is an actual source of morality until you internalize it by believing in it. As soon as we believe in someone or something, we let that idea into ourselves and are changed in the process. We see this in a child's growth and development. A child spontaneously believes, that is internalizes, all that it is taught by its parents. This deep faith in the parents is what makes the parents such an overwhelmingly significant force in a child's life.

But as we grow into adulthood, we should no longer blindly believe everything we are told. We are not meant to be sponges that spontaneously absorb every idea that is presented to us. Rather, we have both the power and the responsibility to judge for ourselves what we will believe or not believe. The following example will illustrate what is being said here. Imagine two students who are studying communism. The first student gains much knowledge about communism but his study in no way directly affects his thinking. The second student, however, actually becomes a communist. He, in other words, makes an act of faith in the principles of communism and this act becomes the source that changes his whole life. So, too, with any other reality of life. They remain only possible sources of morality as long as we do not believe in them. They do not become actual sources of morality until we internalize them in an act of faith. It is one thing to learn about abortion. It is something else to believe in it. One can *know* about atheism and remain a Catholic. But one cannot *believe* in atheism and be a Catholic. One of the problems of living in a pluralistic society is that we often internalize values we see on television and elsewhere without realizing we have done so. Living in a pluralistic society calls for clear thinking and an awareness of ourselves.

> "Sticks and stones can break my bones, but words can never hurt me" are the lines of a well-known children's lyric. The statement is true only so long as you do not believe such words. If you begin to believe them or those around you begin to believe them, words can hurt just as badly as sticks and stones. This same idea is expressed in the words, "The pen is mightier than the sword."
>
> The same holds true with unchristian moral values. They are harmless to the Christian unless the Christian begins to believe in them and acts by them.

The second point to keep in mind is that we must be very careful to distinguish between "the world" and "evil in the world." In other words, we must recognize that the Church has no monopoly on goodness. It is obvious that there is much good in the world, even though it is in no way associated with the visible Church. For example, research projects that try to overcome diseases such as cancer, or the CARE or Red Cross programs that help poor and underdeveloped nations. Being a good Catholic in a pluralistic society does not mean shutting one's eyes to the goodness in the world. On the contrary, a Catholic should be willing and ready to take an active part in all activities that work toward the betterment of mankind.

The third point is that the world is not only a place of goodness but also of evil actions and ideas that lead people away from their dignity as children of God. Here the Catholic must be able to rely on his or her own convictions that flow from faith in Jesus Christ and the teachings of the Church.

One well-known thinker once said, "Distinguish in order to unite." That is, just as the pieces of a jigsaw puzzle must each be perfectly shaped in order to fit together into a whole, so, too, the different groups in a pluralistic society must each try to be true to their own convictions if they are to truly unite and form a living society. Catholics must take their active place in the community by being true to Christ. This cannot be done if Catholics yield to every force in society, so that they become invisible by becoming no different from those who are not Christians.

Discuss the following:
  1. Gandhi once said, "If you Christians were more like your Christ, the whole world would be Christian."

  2. If being a Christian were a federal offense, would there be enough evidence against you to convict you?

CLOSED SOCIETIES

Before moving on in our discussion, it is worthwhile to stop and realize that not all cultures are pluralistic like ours. Most primitive cultures, medieval Europe, as well as present-day Red China and the Soviet Union, are examples of relatively closed societies. In a closed society there is but one acceptable norm of behavior. This does not mean that opposing norms of moral behavior are nonexistent. What is meant is that whenever opposing norms of behavior appear they are more easily recognized as "foreign," "immoral," or otherwise undesirable, thus greatly reducing the degree of moral ambiguity that is often found in a pluralistic society.

Discuss the advantages and disadvantages of both pluralistic and closed societies. Do you think that too much moral freedom results in moral confusion? Are closed societies a threat to freedom? Is it possible to have the best of both kinds of society?

TWO POSSIBLE SOURCES OF MORALITY

Before continuing in our investigation of the problem of being a Catholic in a pluralistic society, we will shift for a moment from the social dimensions of pluralism to the more personal, psychological level of daily life. It seems fair to say that two of the most commonly referred to sources of morality for the adolescent are one's own friends and emotions. We will briefly discuss each, beginning first with friends as a possible source of morality.

Friends as a Possible Source of Morality

It is a good and necessary part of friendship that we let our friends affect us by seriously considering their attitudes and opinions. This is especially true in adolescence, when peer relationships play such an important role in growth and development. In order to make an important point, however, we will examine a situation in which a person uses friends as a source of morality in a bad sense. That is, friends are used as the only source of morality. In other words, the person purposely avoids referring to his or her parents, to a priest or counselor as people who could help them make moral decisions.

The following diagram should help you visualize the problem being discussed. Note in the diagram that your only two accepted sources of morality are your two friends. Note, too, that all other possible sources of morality are rejected. Lastly, take note of the fact that "friend A" gives you a "no" reply to your question because of the sources of morality he or she has accepted. It is for the same reason that "friend B" gives you a "yes" reply.

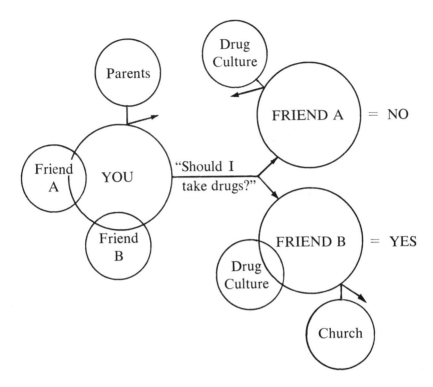

The above example brings out the point that, although you can and should be open to the judgments of your friends, you, at the same time, must know your own convictions. Perhaps your friend has rejected a source of morality which you yourself strongly believe in. For a person to blindly follow the will of another in this way is not to be that person's friend but rather a mindless puppet. True friendship always respects differences, and helps each partner to feel more secure with his or her own convictions. Jesus' warning that if the blind lead the blind, both will fall into the ditch is easily applied in turning solely to friends as your source of morality.

Emotions as a Possible Source of Morality

Young people also frequently depend on their emotions or feelings in trying to make a moral decision. With regard to the emotions, two extremes are to be avoided:

First, we must avoid a stoic denial of the emotions as though cold, hard logic was the only worthwhile measuring stick of life's decisions. We are not computers, nor are moral decisions made in an abstract vacuum. Feelings of love, sympathy or concern are often powerful forces to move us to good actions.

The second extreme is to conclude an action is morally right simply because it feels right. The first extreme is wrong because it isn't human enough. This second extreme is wrong because it isn't realistic. It fails to take into account the mysterious and often irrational force with which our emotions can express themselves.

Our feelings can be compared to clouds overhead: They may be bright and cheery, or dark and foreboding. They are a real part of our world, yet you would not want to try to ride home on one. Ignoring our feelings can make us inhuman, yet letting ourselves be led by our feelings alone is like trying to walk on smoke. In short, we must both master and respect our feelings at the same time. They may often indicate what is the right thing to do, but they must never be our only guide in the face of serious moral questions.

If you should happen to wake up tomorrow morning feeling sad and depressed, that doesn't mean that life itself is sad and depressing. Your course of action would hopefully not be to go out and shoot yourself, but rather to do something positive to get back in a good mood. The same with moral problems: Simply because you feel a certain act is right does not mean it is actually right. You will hopefully try to find out if your feelings are valid or not.

Imagine a girl in high school who discovers that she is pregnant and is considering having an abortion. Discuss the reactions she will have to face when she tells her parents, friends, boyfriend, teachers, and so on. Discuss the emotions involved in this ordeal: such as shame, guilt, despair, or fear. Why would she be wrong to let these emotions become her only guide?

THE CATHOLIC IN A PLURALISTIC SOCIETY

Earlier in this chapter we began to discuss the problems involved in being a Catholic in a pluralistic society. We can now conclude this discussion by focusing in on the problem in greater detail.

We can begin by pointing out that the totally uncommitted person in a pluralistic society appears to have a certain kind of freedom in being able to choose any set of moral values he or she wishes. Many people today choose to do just this; they choose not to choose so as to be able to do as they please.

Speaking in the terms of the chapter "Law and Freedom," we would say that the uncommitted person possesses an external freedom but can never have inner freedom as long as he or she refuses to commit himself or herself to another. Inner freedom, the freedom to be all we can possibly be, comes only in the commitment of a love relationship. In love we become set free from sterile isolation and self-centeredness. At the same time, however, we are bound and committed to the loved one who has set us free. This commitment to the will of a loved one makes the loved one an important source of morality in our lives. Hurting or in any way offending the loved one is immediately seen to be wrong and in some sense, immoral. A Catholic certainly should be someone who has found some degree of inner freedom in his or her love relationship with Jesus Christ in the community that is the Church.

Furthermore, a Catholic Christian's relationship to Jesus is not simply a relationship among others. Rather, it is unique, and for this reason fidelity to the will of Christ is also unique. It transcends the fidelity of a disciple to a great moral teacher, or the fidelity proper to deep friendship.

The uniqueness of a Christian's relationship to Jesus consists in the following truths of our faith:

1. God created us from nothing in an act of infinite love. All that we are and have we owe to him. We are related to God as children to a Father.

2. The mystery of sin is that we have fallen away from a true relationship with God. We have become, in a sense, wounded and unable to heal ourselves.

3. God sent his only Son who healed us in his death on the cross. We are related to Jesus as the sick are to the physician who heals them.

4. Through belief in Jesus we gain access to the power of his resurrection, so that we too can share in his victory over death and sin.

5. It is not enough simply to believe in Jesus. We must then live out that faith in our daily actions. This daily fidelity to Jesus in day-to-day life is the root reality of Christian morality. Jesus once said that, "If you love me, you will keep my commandments." Being moral is, for the Christian, being true to God's love which comes to us in Christ.

The Catholic as Active in Society

The Second Vatican Council has expressed a renewed awareness in the Church of the goodness and worth of all people everywhere. A Christian is called upon not only to recognize the goodness in the world, but to work actively in and with all those elements in society which foster the dignity of mankind and which work towards overcoming such things as disease and poverty. The document of the Second Vatican Council titled *The Church in the Modern World* states it this way:

"The Church recognizes that worthy elements are found in today's social movements, especially in evolution toward unity . . ."

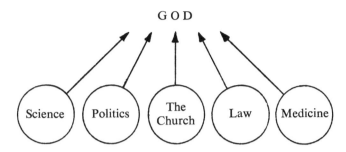

The Christian sees that all those who are working for the betterment of human life are working for God's cause. The Christian is unique among all these groups in that the Christian believes and proclaims that Jesus Christ is the fulness of all that mankind is striving for, and that the world will eventually overcome all suffering in him alone.

Discuss ways in which the Church has actively worked in your community to help others. What are some things that the Church has not done so far yet which need to be done in your community?

The Catholic as Prophet in Society

The above discussion has been limited to the role of the Catholic Christian in a society working for the betterment of the human family. Here the Catholic can be compared to a man trying to reach the top of a steep and densely wooded hill. The traveler does not know exactly where each of the paths lead, but he feels confident in following any path which continues to lead him farther up the hillside. So, too, with the Catholic working in the society. The Catholic does not know, for example, where advances in technology will lead the human family, but he feels confident in actively taking part in all activities which promote the good of mankind.

It is a fact of life, however, that not all paths lead up the hill. In fact, many paths lead directly down the hill. In other words, there are forces of evil in the society as well as forces of good. In a pluralistic society, this is all the more a problem because forces of evil may present themselves as forces of good.

The measuring stick used by the Catholic in determining the morality of any act is not the convictions of those promoting the act, but rather the teachings of Jesus as made known in the gospels and the Church.

This means that the Catholic is called upon to refrain from actions which are clearly against the teachings of Jesus. What is more, the Catholic may be called upon to play the role of a prophet and speak out against the wrong being done. Here the term "prophet" does not refer to predicting the future, but rather refers to the biblical notion of a prophet—one who calls down God's judgment on the world. Here, too, the Catholic is not shunning the world. On the contrary, the Catholic is criticizing the world out of love for the world. The Catholic is saying that in performing the particular act in question the world is shortchanging human dignity. The following exercise should help explain this point.

Explain why each of the situations listed below would be activities with which the Catholic could and should be concerned. What element in each would force the Catholic to withdraw from the group or even to speak out against it?

1. A group working for prison reform begins a program to examine the possibilities of brain surgery on hardened criminals to take away their power to think or function as human beings.

2. A research team tests new drugs to find a cure for cancer. Part of their program involves experimenting with live human fetuses, then killing them.

SECULARISM, MATERIALISM AND PRAGMATISM

The Catholic in our society is not only up against dehumanizing activities, such as those cited in the above exercise, he or she is often surrounded by an attitude or an understanding of life itself that has little or no use for religious thought. This antireligious attitude toward life can take many forms. The first one which we will briefly examine here is that of secularism.

Secularism must be distinguished from secularization. Secularization is the praiseworthy contribution of modern man which avoids the primitive temptation to explain all mysterious and unknown forces in terms of spirits, gods, or some other supernatural power. Due to secularization, modern man is aware of his mastery over life and of the fact that the future of the world is, in a very real sense, in his hands.

Secularism is something quite different. Secularism is an attitude or philosophy of life which holds that only secular values are real and that all religious values are nothing more than superstition. The sincere Catholic, or any religious person for that matter, appears as a round peg in a square hole. Religion becomes an isolated act on Sunday mornings. And morality becomes "doing your own thing." This attitude is antireligious not by attacking religion head-on, but simply by making religion irrelevant.

How many TV series can you name in which the characters seriously and openly speak of the place of God in their lives?

Materialism holds not that material things have value, but rather that only material things have value. More money, a bigger car, a nicer home: These are the only values worth living for. Because religious values cannot directly add to your material gains, they are a hindrance.

Pragmatism holds that a thing is worthwhile only if it is useful. Since God cannot build a computer or give you a better complexion, he is not real, or at least he is unnecessary.

Although it is true that a possible source of morality is not an actual source of morality until we internalize it by believing in it, it is also true that, if we are not careful, we can subconsciously internalize values without being aware of them. Values in a society are like the air we breathe. We take it in without being aware of it. So, too, television, movies, songs, friends, advertisements, all continually and subtly form our scale of values which, as we saw in Chapter 1, determines our morality. This fact of human psychology stresses the importance of mature and serious reflection regarding our own scale of values in light of our relationship to Christ. Our moral values flow directly from our notion of what it means to be human. For the Christian, it means to be God's child. It means to be Christ's presence in the world.

The world today desperately needs the peace of Bethlehem, the patient labor of Nazareth, the strength of Good Friday and, most of all, the hope of Easter. In short, the world needs Christians who will stand up and be Christians not by preaching sermons but by living Christlike lives.

True, we must let our moral values be affected by friends and emotions, by the world in which we live. But, most of all, our morals must be affected by Christ. This is what makes a Christian a Christian. In this way we will not be acted upon by the world, but rather we will be the active force of Christ's love in the world. Only by being true to Christ can we heal both the world and ourselves.

The Christian is called upon to be a leaven, a light and salt to the world. Apply these images from the gospel to modern times.

SUMMARY

This chapter can be summarized by the following points:

In a pluralistic society we are often confronted with conflicting moral values.

A possible source of morality is made an actual source of morality by our believing in it.

Such things as friends and our emotions should be among our

sources of morality. We must, however, not let ourselves be guided by them in a way that undermines our own convictions.

A Catholic Christian forms his or her morality basically on the teachings of Jesus as made known by the gospels and the Church.

The teachings of Jesus prompt the Catholic to support and aid all activities that promote the good of mankind.

The teachings of Jesus also prompt the Catholic to withdraw from or counteract all activities that attack the true dignity of man as a child of God.

Secularism, materialism and pragmatism create an atmosphere in which it is often difficult to live up to Christian ideals.

Only by being true to Christ can we be true to ourselves and to others.

12

Christian Morality
--Summary and Problems

"Morality does not make a Christian, yet no man can be a Christian without it." —Daniel Wilson

The present chapter is an attempt to summarize the major points of the other 11. It further will present several "problems" or situations which will enable the reader to apply some of the principal points of Christian morality discussed in this book.

Among others, the following are offered as summary points of Christian morality:

1. The way we view who man is is often determinative of how we react towards him. Christians are daily bombarded with unchristian views of man. These can affect us and help us act towards others in unchristian ways.

2. Based on the natural law and divine revelation, Christianity offers a refreshingly optimistic view about the nature of man. Christianity maintains that each person is fundamentally good, redeemable, and loved by God. It holds that each man and woman, whether he or she knows it, is potentially a child of God, and brother or sister of Jesus Christ and of each other.

3. A basic principle of Christian morality is that each person ought to have attitudes and act in accord with the dignity of his or her own nature. This dignity includes not only adopted sonship but also the dignity to think and choose. It includes the reality of individual uniqueness in social contact with others. It maintains that man is an image of God and his copartner in the further development of creation.

4. Man is a free creature who is responsible for his freedom. He is able to respond in love to the demands his brothers and sisters place on him. He is intimately related to Christ and shows his love of God by responding to the teachings of Jesus under the guidance of the Holy Spirit.

5. The message of Jesus is summed up in the word "love." Love involves an active concern for the other. It involves trusting in God and a willingness to serve others. It involves doing more than the expected. It involves forgiveness. It means a willingness to suffer. It means prayer and good works done in a spirit of humility. It denotes a putting of the world's goods in perspective, using them, not becoming their slave.

6. The subjective norm of morality is one's conscience. A person has to follow his or her conscience, but he or she has the duty to develop a properly formed conscience. Conscience is an inner dialogue with God which enables a person to discover responsible behavior. A Christian conscience manifests purity of intention, evidence of consulting the teaching of Jesus and his Church, and a prayerful openness to the action of the Holy Spirit.

7. Laws are guidelines to help us control our external actions for the sake of our inner freedom to be all we can possibly be. Natural law, such as the law against murder, is universally known to all men. Civil law is each society's particular interpretation of the natural law. Divine law is known in faith as coming from God in revelation. Church law is the particular application of divine law for the Christian community.

8. Divine law is best understood in terms of a covenant relationship of love between God and man. In all love relationships, we are free to do what we have to do in order to be true to love. Thus, for the Christian, laws are important but only because fidelity to love is important. It is Christ and not laws who saves us.

9. Sin is an alienation from a living relationship with God and others. It always has social implications. It often flows from basic attitudes of pride and self-centeredness and manifests itself in actions as well as in failures to act. A person is morally guilty of sin if the matter is sinful and he acts with knowledge and freedom.

10. Christian belief holds that through the saving power of Jesus, sin is forgiven and its ultimate effect of death has been overcome. The Catholic has the sacrament of reconciliation wherein he or she can encounter the forgiving love of Jesus.

11. Sex, as created by God, and as an expression of love and the means of bringing about new life, is essentially good. Sexual sins are actions which abuse the goodness of sex by using it outside of God's will as made known to us in revelation.

12. Christian sexual morality focuses not so much on specific actions but on an overall attitude toward sexuality. This overall Christian attitude calls upon us to seek the highest possible ideals in sexual morality. At the same time we must accept ourselves for what we are in our weakness. We must distinguish between sexual sins committed out of weakness and sins committed to deliberately hurt or degrade ourselves or others, or in open indifference to our relationship to God.

13. All people automatically respect the lives of loved ones. A Christian is called upon to see everyone in light of God's love which embraces all people everywhere. This respect for the lives of others must extend even to our enemies. A Christian is to hate the evil deed but is never to hate the one who commits it.

14. Living a life of Christian morality in the Catholic tradition is a community job. A Catholic Christian should and does make a difference. He or she is light, leaven, and salt for the world. He or she celebrates who he or she is as a child of God in the Eucharist, the sacrament of unity.

15. A pluralistic society often presents contradictory moral values. A Catholic's moral sense is guided primarily not by whether or not the crowd is doing it, but rather whether or not the act in question is in conformity with the will of Christ as made known in revelation and the Church.

16. A Christian view of man calls for a Catholic's active participation in all activities in the society which promote the betterment of the human family. By the same token,

the Catholic is called upon to witness against all activities which degrade or ignore the sacredness of human life.

17. The forces of materialism, secularism and pragmatism create an atmosphere in which it is difficult for people to find God or to see why it is even worth asking about him in the first place. These attitudes bring about such things as abortion and euthanasia which so easily reduce human life to the level of a commodity.

MORAL PROBLEMS FOR ANALYSIS

The following are offered to test the reader's understanding of some of the principles elaborated in this book of Christian morality. The answers and solutions to the problems are not necessarily simple. Many responses to God in the modern world are difficult and, consequently, men and women of intelligence must utilize their God-given gifts to discern his will in the world. A problem is briefly stated. After each problem, there is space to write out reasons pro or con for the stated action. Finally, there is space for the reader to write out a rationale for his or her own solution to the problem.

The reader should try to test the principles of morality presented in this book by asking the questions: What is the Christian thing to do? What is the teaching of Jesus? of the Church? What are the consequences of the action for the individual? for others? Is performing or not performing the action consistent with being a child of God? Etc.

PROBLEM #1:

Joan is a junior in high school. She works a part-time job to help her mother with the expenses of raising her family. Her father is dead. Joan is a good student who does not fear hard work. She is taking a rather difficult chemistry course this semester. Her teacher is one of the toughest in the school and is quite demanding. The course calls for the writing of two ten-page term papers. In simple terms, Joan does not have the time to write one of the papers. Science is not her academic strength, nor does her planned career as a secretary demand that she have an extensive knowledge of science. A friend offers to do her paper for $2 a page. The friend is a "science whiz" and is sure to do an "A" job. Joan is seriously considering taking her up on the offer. Based on Christian principles, what is the moral thing to do?

Reasons for:	Reasons against:
1.	1.
2.	2.
3.	3.
4.	4.

In your opinion, what should be done and why?

PROBLEM #2:

Gary has just finished a course in Christian morality. He has studied quite well the Sermon on the Mount and is convinced that war is immoral. He believes that the military, with its armaments, its support of regimes abroad which are sometimes dictatorial and its whole attitude toward war are immoral. Through several part-time jobs this past year, he has earned $3,000. No tax was taken out of his paychecks because of the nature of his several jobs. But now at income tax time, he realizes that because he earned over the minimum amount nontaxed for a person his age, he owes the government about $300. He realizes that a substantial portion of his federal tax goes to the military. He is seriously considering only paying a portion of the $300 for nonmilitary purposes. Based on Christian principles, what should be done?

Reasons for:	Reasons against:
1.	1.
2.	2.
3.	3.
4.	4.

In your opinion, what should be done and why?

PROBLEM #3:

You are caught in a dilemma. Your parish priest has asked you and other members of the parish youth group to picket a so-called "adult bookstore" which carries pornographic reading materials and "art movies." The bookstore has moved into the business district of your town. It strictly limits its visitors to those 21 years of age and older. A person has to show an I.D. to gain entrance to the store. You have been reading a lot lately about censorship and individual freedoms. Your general feeling is against censorship. The parish priest is trying to exert pressure to close the store and is enlisting your aid. What would you do? Based on Christian principles, what should be done?

Reasons for:	Reasons against:
1.	1.
2.	2.
3.	3.
4.	4.

In your opinion, what should be done and why?

PROBLEM #4:

*Linda failed to return home from a dance Friday night. On Saturday she admitted she had spent the night with an Air Force lieutenant.

Her parents decided on a punishment that would "wake Linda up." They ordered her to shoot the dog she had owned for about two years.

On Sunday, the parents and Linda drove the dog into the desert near their home. They had the girl dig a shallow grave. Then her mother grasped the dog's head between her hands and her father gave his daughter a .22 caliber pistol and told her to shoot the dog.

Instead the girl put the pistol to her right temple and shot herself. The police said there were no charges that could be filed against the parents except possibly cruelty to animals.

On the basis of Christian morality, what immoral act was committed by each person involved.

1. Linda   3. The Lieutenant

2. Her parents   4. The police

On the basis of your opinion, which of the people involved committed the most serious sin?

---

*The story is quoted from Jeffrey Schrank's *Teaching Human Beings: 101 Subversive Activities for the Classroom,* Boston: Beacon Press, 1972, pp. 66-68. Schrank excerpted this from *Search for a New Land,* by Julius Lester, Dial Press, New York, 1968.

PROBLEM #5:

Susan is a senior in high school. She has gone out of her way to make friends with a new girl in the school who has a very difficult time making new friends. The new girl's family is rather poor, and she has to work part time to help her parents pay bills. One day Susan discovers that her new friend is selling hard drugs at a nearby grade school. She (Susan) cannot decide whether or not she should turn her friend in to the police. Based on Christian principles, what should she do?

Reasons for:	Reasons against:
1.	1.
2.	2.
3.	3.
4.	4.

In your opinion, what should be done and why?

PROBLEM #6:

Tom has just gotten a new job working at a large record store near his home. He discovers that the manager obtains some of his records by illegal means. Tom also discovers that the other employees at the store habitually steal records, and they urge him to do the same. They point out to him that the records do not rightfully belong to the manager anyway. Tom cannot decide whether or not to take the records. Based on Christian principles, what should he do?

Reasons for:	Reasons against:
1.	1.
2.	2.
3.	3.
4.	4.

In your opinion, what should be done and why?

John Marston, Satirist

ANTHONY CAPUTI

OCTAGON BOOKS

A DIVISION OF FARRAR, STRAUS AND GIROUX

New York   1976

Reprinted 1976
by special arrangement with Cornell University Press

OCTAGON BOOKS
A DIVISION OF FARRAR, STRAUS & GIROUX, INC.
19 Union Square West
New York, N.Y. 10003

Library of Congress Cataloging in Publication Data

Caputi, Anthony Francis, 1924-
    John Marston, satirist.

    Reprint of the ed. published by Cornell University Press, Ithaca,
    N.Y.

    Bibliography: p.
    Includes index.
    1. Marston, John, 1575-1634.   I. Title.
[PR2696.C3   1976]   822'.3   75-38929
ISBN 0-374-91286-6

Manufactured by Braun-Brumfield, Inc.
Ann Arbor, Michigan
Printed in the United States of America

TO MARJEIN

Preface

AN important part of John Marston's value to Renaissance studies derives from the unusual integrity of his canon. It is rare to find among the Elizabethans and Jacobeans a writer who produced all his work in a single decade, and rarer still to find one who restricted himself as rigorously as Marston did to satire and satiri-comic expression. Yet it is largely because of this concentration that Marston's work has so high a degree of internal consistency and largely because of this consistency that it so effectively sums up the literary scene at the turn of the century. However narrow its range, we shall be hard put to find a more illuminating introduction to the shifting currents of thought and taste or a better-documented artistic biography in that period.

The key to the unusual integrity of Marston's work is, I am convinced, his seriocomic view of the Renaissance world. In important respects all his poems and plays are variant expressions of this view and of the separate attitudes that make it up. The problem, accordingly, is how best to get at this view, how best to penetrate to the unity of Marston's separate efforts without distorting their individual character. The problem would be relatively simple if this world view or its constitutive attitudes were dominantly intellectual, that is, if the view were substantially an intellectual position that could be fairly described in terms of ideas alone. But it is not. Although a certain philosophical orientation is crucial in everything Marston wrote, it is no more important to his world view than certain matters of tone, gesture, and manner. Marston's seriocomic view is, in fact, as much a stance or a way of apprehending and dealing with his world as it is a way of thinking about it, as much a state of thought and feeling as it is a philosophy.

For this reason I have subordinated my study of Marston's ideas to a formal study of his work as a continuous experiment in satiricomic forms. I have chosen to focus on individual works and on the structure by which they induce particular states of thought and feeling because only by this approach, I feel, can we do justice both to the individual works and to the dynamic character of the view governing them. To gain emphasis and clarity, I have treated some works at greater length than others. The tragedies and occasional pieces, however interesting and important in their own right, are seldom indispensable to the story I am trying to tell, though they are eminently useful in clarifying certain aspects of Marston's career. Accordingly, I have not treated them so fully as I have the satirical comedies, where the seriocomic view is met in all its amplitude. Where I have found, moreover, that biographical details, literary sources, and literary, intellectual, and theatrical history can shed light, I have used them. But my main purpose has been to relate this kind of evidence to the picture of Marston's development as a satirist and as a spokesman for an influential point of view in his time.

If in what follows I have succeeded in showing something more than is presently known of Marston's importance in his age, as well as something more of the undoubted literary value of his best work, much of the credit goes to my teachers and friends. I should like especially to thank Messrs. William Rea Keast,

David Novarr, Walter J. Slatoff, and Hal H. Smith of Cornell University; Mr. John Senior of the University of Wyoming; Mr. Edward B. Partridge of Bucknell University; Mr. R. C. Bald of the University of Chicago; and Mr. F. P. Wilson, formerly of Merton College, Oxford. They were, I know, more helpful than they know. I should also like to thank the Committee for the Grant-in-Aid Fund of the Department of English at Cornell for its generous financial assistance.

ANTHONY CAPUTI

Cornell University
November 1960

Contents

	Abbreviations	xiii
I	The Orphan Poet	1
II	Sharp-fanged Satirist	23
III	The Neo-Stoic	52
IV	Playwright for the Child Actors	80
V	Lovers-in-Distress Burlesques and *Antonio's Revenge*	117
VI	The Disguise-Plot Plays	157
VII	Final Experiments	217
Appendix A:	Problems of Date and Authorship in the Plays	251
Appendix B:	The Occasional Pieces	276
	Selected Bibliography	279
	Index	285

Abbreviations

CS: *Certain Satires.*

H & S: C. H. Herford and Percy and Evelyn Simpson, eds., *Ben Jonson* (Oxford, 1925–1952), 11 vols. Since this edition does not represent act and scene divisions at the top of the page, I have referred to volume and page numbers.

"Life":   Ford Elmore Curtis, "John Marston: His Life and Works" (Ph.D. dissertation, Cornell University, 1932).

Plays: H. Harvey Wood, ed., *The Plays of John Marston* (London, 1934–1939), 3 vols. I have used Volume III for *Histriomastix* and *Jack Drum's Entertainment,* and, since the edition gives neither act or scene divisions nor line numbers, I have referred to page numbers.

SR: Edward Arber, ed., *A Transcript of the Registers of the Company of Stationers of London, 1544–1640* (London, 1876), 6 vols.

SV: *The Scourge of Villainy.*

Works: A. H. Bullen, ed., *The Works of John Marston* (London, 1887), 3 vols. I have used this edition as a reference text.

Chapter I

The Orphan Poet

JOHN MARSTON has long been the chief victim of his notorious obstreperousness. When with the publication in 1598 of *Pygmalion's Image and Certain Satires* he deliberately turned his back on recent literary models to bring to English letters a new voice, he introduced a voice by any standard startling and highly individualistic. Here was a poet who snarled and growled, who trembled with exasperated indignation, who shrieked to make himself heard:

> Ambitious Gorgons, wide-mouth'd Lamians,
> Shape-changing Proteans, damn'd Briarians,
> Is Minos dead, is Rhadamanth asleep,
> That ye thus dare unto Jove's palace creep.[1]

His was, indeed, a new kind of poetic utterance. What Marston could not have anticipated is that it is also so sensational that it

[1] *Works*, III, 287, ll. 1–4. All the poems have been reprinted in Volume III of *Works*. Henceforth, I shall simply indicate line numbers, when possible.

has always called undue attention to itself. As society has gradually lost touch with the context of these poems, readers of them
have quite understandably been drawn to their most striking
surface qualities and particularly to the poet's voice to explain
them. Small wonder that many critics have tried to explain them
in terms of what they imagine to have been Marston's personal
perversity or that Marston the man has been lost in such explanations.

Unfortunately, to identify Marston with the sometimes hys-
terical satirist of his poems is to rule out the possibility that he
was self-consciously cultivating a pose and, if this were so, to set
aside all inquiry into why he might have chosen so outlandish a
pose. In fact, to fail to distinguish between the pose and the
poseur is to reduce the poems to one—at best to two or three—
of their most obvious features and, accordingly, to distort them.
Yet critics of Marston, except for the most recent, have taken
the identification for granted. Beginning with the expressed personality of the satirist, they have sought confirmation for it in
the scanty information on Marston's life and have evolved from
the combined evidence of life and work profiles of his character
grotesque enough to explain anything. Of course the profiles have
covered a considerable range. Although all critics have agreed that
Marston was violent and unstable, some have charged him with
obscenity, clumsiness, and insincerity, while others have admired
his originality, skill, and moral fervor.[2] Such disparate judgments

[2] For a fair sample of traditional opinion see the following: the anonymous
article in the *Gentleman's Magazine*, CCI (1856), 306–313; William Hazlitt,
"On Marston, Chapman, Dekker, and Webster," *Lectures on the Literature
of the Age of Elizabeth* (London, 1870), pp. 72–81; William Minto,
Characteristics of English Poets from Chaucer to Shirley (Edinburgh, 1874),
pp. 434–440; A. W. Ward, *A History of English Dramatic Literature* (Lon-
don, 1875), II, 66; A. C. Swinburne, "John Marston," *Nineteenth Century*,
XXIV (1888), 531–547; George Saintsbury, *A History of Elizabethan Litera-
ture* (London, 1887), pp. 195–199; H. J. C. Grierson, *The First Half of the
Seventeenth Century* (New York, 1906), pp. 104–106; J. Le Gay Brereton,
Elizabethan Drama: Notes and Studies (Sydney, 1909), pp. 113–115; and
T. S. Eliot, *Elizabethan Essays* (London, 1934), pp. 177–195.

were inevitable, however, as long as critics assumed that Marston's work required little more ancillary knowledge to be understood than Kipling's does. The confusion between the man and the mask has persisted, at any rate, with the general consequence that Marston has long been a fascinating anti-Shakespeare in Renaissance studies—as Garnett and Gosse would have him, "a screech owl among the singing birds."

Only recently have critics begun to admit that Marston is a complex figure with profound affiliations to key literary and intellectual movements in his time. Yet even this criticism has yielded limited results. Most of it has centered on the satiric movement at the turn of the century and on the theory and practice of Marston's verse satires. It has, it is true, contributed a great deal to our understanding of Renaissance satire and to our appreciation of Marston's self-consciousness as a writer. But if it has isolated certain of the Renaissance assumptions about formal satire and has clarified Marston's indebtedness to literary trends, it has done so by limiting its view to the verse satires and by limiting its search to a search for literary causes alone.[3]

The results have been beguiling. We have recovered a number of the reading skills necessary to approach Renaissance satire fairly, but we have not recovered enough to see more than superficial continuities between Marston's verse satires and the plays of the next half-dozen years. At the same time we have assembled detailed accounts of Marston's technical performance but very

[3] See especially the work of Oscar James Campbell, *Comicall Satyre and Shakespeare's "Troilus and Cressida"* (San Marino, Calif., 1937); M. C. Randolph, "The Medical Concept in English Renaissance Satiric Theory," *SP*, XXXVIII (1941), 127–157, and "The Structural Design of the Formal Verse Satire," *PQ*, XXI (1942), 368–384; Hallett Smith, *Elizabethan Poetry, A Study of Convention, Meaning, and Expression* (Cambridge, Mass., 1952); Eugene M. Waith, *The Pattern of Tragicomedy in Beaumont and Fletcher* (New Haven, 1952); Lila H. Freedman, "Satiric Personae: A Study of Point of View in Formal Verse Satire . . ." (Ph.D. diss., University of Wisconsin, 1955); John Peter, *Complaint and Satire in Early English Literature* (Oxford, 1956); and Alvin Kernan, *The Cankered Muse* (New Haven, 1959).

little that does him any real credit as a writer or helps to explain his prominence among his contemporaries.

The whole question of Marston's reputation in his time is central, perhaps, to gauging accurately his importance as a Renaissance writer. We need not agree with Francis Meres, John Weever, and Charles Fitzgeoffrey when they rank him among those best for satire;[4] nor need we take seriously the fact that practically every list of important playwrights named him, as William Camden's did in 1605, with Jonson, Shakespeare, and "other pregnant wits."[5] But whether we agree or not, we must take seriously that these men felt as they did about Marston and must attempt to account for the prevailing judgment so neatly summarized later by Anthony à Wood "that he was in great renown for his wit and ingenuity in sixteen hundred and six."[6] That we have failed to understand Marston's popularity is probably the result of our having looked chiefly at the literary causes of his work, of our having assumed that he was important in his time for the manner of his satires and plays rather than for anything he expressed in them. To clarify the assumpton is, of course, to clarify its limitations. Surely it is more reasonable to believe that Marston was esteemed not only because he wrote well in a style then in vogue but also because he embodied something that his audience thought important.

It is but a short step from this conclusion to the hypothesis that any attempt to understand Marston as a literary figure of consequence in his time, as well as any attempt to discover the integrity of his tightly knit canon, must use as many approaches

[4] Francis Meres, *Palladis Tamia*, in *Elizabethan Critical Essays*, ed. G. Gregory Smith (Oxford, 1904), II, 320, and *Works*, I, xxiv.

[5] The pertinent quotation from Camden's *Remains Concerning Britain* (1605) is to be found in *The Jonson Allusion-Book* compiled by Jesse Franklin Bradley and Joseph Quincy Adams (New Haven, 1922), p. 33. For similar quotations from John Taylor's *The Praise of Hempseed* (1620) and Edmund Howe's *Annals* (1631), see the same work, pp. 120 and 165.

[6] *Athenae Oxoniensis*, ed. Philip Bliss (London, 1813), I, 764.

to him as possible. To recover the reading skills, the ethical and literary assumptions, and the peculiar conditions that prompted his contemporaries to value him highly, it will be necessary to assemble the lines of influence between his works and the environment in which they were produced—between the works and the literary group of which he was a member, between the works and the theatres and acting companies for which he wrote, and between the works and the writers whom he studied. Since the beginning of any career so often implies the end, and particularly since the beginning of this one is so close to its end, it will be reasonable to begin by observing Marston as he takes up the satirist's scourge. Rather early we shall have to go beyond the prevalent notion that Marston never did more than this; but this early gesture deserves detailed examination because it remained one of his most important.

John Marston was born early in the autumn of 1576 and was christened at the Wardington Parish Church in Oxfordshire on October 7.[7] His father, John, was a prominent landowner in the Cropredy district of Oxfordshire and, later, a successful lawyer in Coventry and London. His mother, Mary Guarsi, was the daughter of an eminent Italian physician who had settled in England. Thus favored by birth with prosperous and influential connections, the young Marston was educated at Oxford and prepared for a career in the law. He matriculated at Brasenose College on February 4, 1591/2 and took his B.A. on February 5, 1593/4. As early as 1592 his father, who was by this time a Reader at the Middle Temple, secured his admission at that institution; in November of 1595

[7] Ford Elmore Curtis' work on Marston's life in "John Marston: His Life and Works" (Ph.D. diss., Cornell University, 1932) assimilates that done by R. E. Brettle and published by him in a series of articles: "John Marston, Dramatist, Some New Facts about His Life," *MLR*, XXII (1927), 7–14; "Marston Born in Oxfordshire," *MLR*, XXII (1927), 317–319; "John Marston, Dramatist, at Oxford," *RES*, III (1927), 398–405; and "The 'poet Marston' Letter to G. Clifton, 1607," *RES*, IV (1928), 212–214.

young John took up residence with him. There he was to live, off and on, through the early years of his brief adventure in literature.

John Marston's entrance into the brilliant life of the Inns of Court seems to have been an event of cardinal importance in his life. As Herford and Simpson have so justly observed of the Inns at that time, they "were the nucleus of a society never before so numerous or so accomplished, of wits and men about town— lawyers, courtiers, young graduates from the universities—who thronged the aisles of Paul's, indited Senecan blank verse in City garrets, or disconcerted the middle classes by their free living and free talk." [8] Apparently, Marston had been exposed to this life at a very impressionable age: his father had retained rooms at the Middle Temple as early as 1577; [9] and though we have no tangible evidence that his son occasionally stayed with him, that he did is highly probable.[10] In any event, at the age of nineteen Marston was lodged close to the fountainhead of taste and fashion in late sixteenth-century England. In two short years he had forsaken the law and joined the literary movement fostered by his fashionable confreres.

With the leaders of this movement Marston had almost everything in common. After decades of ferment, the intellectual climate at the universities had at last reached a state that put the Thomist-Aristotelian orthodoxy seriously in question. Students of Marston's generation saw authority challenged on all sides: they saw Aristotle's logic under attack; they saw Cicero and Isocrates yield as models of imitation to Seneca, Tacitus, Lucan, and others as the suspicion grew that elaborateness of style was a hindrance to thought; they saw various attempts to reconstitute within a broad Christian framework the theoretical foundations of a new

---

[8] H & S, I, 10. See also Louise Brown Osborn (ed.), *The Life, Letters, and Writings of John Hoskyns* (New Haven, 1937), pp. 6–14, 20–22.

[9] "Life," p. 18.

[10] "Life," p. 46. This probability is heightened by the fact that Marston's actual installation in 1595 went unnoticed by the Inn's record-keepers.

moral philosophy. The intellectual freedom that led to the highly divergent, though essentially Christian, revivals of Platonism, Stoicism, and occult philosophy, and that, with a different emphasis, led to the skepticism of a Montaigne was the proudest possession of the wits, scholars, and men about town who peopled the Inns of Court world. John Marston was inflamed by it as much as any.

A more detailed examination of the intellectual side of Marston's commitment to literature can be safely postponed, however, in favor of looking first at certain of the more obvious motives propelling the group he joined. The English scene in the 1590's has been sufficiently studied to clarify what was available for satire in the way of political, economic, and social dislocations,[11] and the clear indebtedness of this group to Juvenal, Persius, Horace, and Martial accounts to some extent for the form its attacks took.[12] But none of this explains to complete satisfaction why these writers felt it their peculiar mission to attack. After all, why were they not content to write sonnets, pastorals, and narrative poems, as their predecessors had done? The answer to this question is by no means easy, for the impulses that threw these writers against their society in the 1590's were strangely mixed. Certainly not the least important of these—and, perhaps, the one that should be isolated first—is that this group was disposed not only by intellectual inclination but also by the simple fact of its juniority to embrace rebellion.

When Marston took up residence at the Middle Temple in 1595, the Inns of Court were peopled by men like Sir John Davies, John

[11] See especially Helen C. White, *Social Criticism in Popular Religious Literature in the Sixteenth Century* (New York, 1944); L. C. Knights, *Drama and Society in the Age of Jonson* (London, 1937); Lewis Einstein, *The Italian Renaissance in England* (New York, 1902), pp. 155–173; and Robert S. Brustein, "Italianate Court Satire and the Plays of John Marston" (Ph.D. diss., Columbia University, 1957).

[12] R. M. Alden, *The Rise of Formal Satire in England under the Classical Influence* (Philadelphia, 1899), and T. K. Whipple, *Martial and the English Epigram* (Berkeley, Calif., 1925).

Donne, Richard Barnfield, John Hoskyns, Richard Martin, and Christopher Brooke, and their circle included men like Ben Jonson, Everard Guilpin, and John Weever, who did not reside at the Inns. It would be too facile to say that this group constituted a new and quite distinct generation of writers. But, in fact, these men were all rather younger than the writers then dominating English letters. While Spenser, Lyly, Sidney, Greene, and Peele had been born in the fifties, and Drayton, Daniel, Shakespeare, and Marlowe had been born in the sixties, most of the members of the new group were born in the seventies. Although this fact could easily be overworked, when it is taken with other things, it accounts for much that they did. Eager, as young men have always been, to flex their muscles and start a revolution, they were above all eager to make their marks quickly and decisively, even if at the expense of their predecessors. Confronted by the monumental accomplishments of their elders—the work of Spenser, of the sonneteers, and of the writers of romance—they turned to innovation. The actual difference in age is finally, perhaps, not so important as other differences I shall take up, but it serves as a useful point of departure because it is relevant to so much the group did. If John Weever's remarks about "yong mens Rhetoricke" can be taken as typical, moreover, it was a difference of which they were aware.[13]

Roughly between 1595 and 1605 these men and others like them were unified by similar motives and the purpose of charting new directions for English letters. Almost none of them published before 1595, and most of them produced the work that best clari-

[13] *Epigrammes in the Oldest Cut and Newest Fashion* (1599), ed. R. B. McKerrow (London, 1911), p. 54. The complete epigram reads:

> Say you that I am obscure?
> Why this is yong mens Rhetoricke,
> Owles must not iudge of *Coruus* sure,
> For he speakes nought but Rhetoricke:
> Either too high, or els too plaine,
> And this is now a schollers vaine.

fies their aims between 1595 and 1600. Preliminary to all else was their rejection of the immediate literary past—of the Petrarchan love tradition, of the tradition of the sonnet and the romance, and of the sweet, musical poetry that these traditions had nurtured.[14] Samuel Rowlands summed up this impulse in his insistence that poets should

> Leaue *Cupids* cut, Womens face flatt'ring prayse,
> Loues subiect growes too threed-bare now adayes
> Change *Venus* Swannes, to write of *Vulcans* Geese,
> And you shall merite Golden Pens apeece.[15]

And John Weever's claim that he could not follow the lead of the past was typical:

> I cannot shew then in a sugred vaine,
> Wit, iudgement, learning, or inuention:
> I cannot reach vp to a *Delians* straine,
> Whose songs deserue for euer your attention:
> Nor *Draytons* stile, whose hony words are meete
> For these your mouths, far more than hony sweete.[16]

This self-conscious break with the past prompted such characteristic gestures as Hall's dismissal in the first two satires of *Virgidemiarum* of the genres popular among his elders. In addition, it prompted a number of literary strategies calculated to prejudice or to circumvent altogether comparison with the immediate past. To minimize the accomplishments of their elders, the new writers

[14] Exceptions can be found to this statement, of course. One of the grounds on which Marston attacked Hall in *Certain Satires* ("Reactio") was Hall's rejection of the literature of the past; yet even Hall was respectful of Spenser. On the other hand, anyone wishing to attack Hall's satires would have been nigh forced into Marston's position because Hall dealt so prominently with the literature of the past. As a general rule, the statement holds.

[15] *Letting of Humours Blood in the Heade-Vaine* (1600) (Hunterian Club ed.; London, 1880), I, 5.

[16] *Epigrammes*, p. 11.

wrote parodies and burlesques of the genres that Sidney, Daniel, and their peers had excelled in, or they put these genres to fresh uses. To elude comparison, they exploited genres neglected by their elders and deliberately cultivated a tougher, more realistic, more ingenious, and, in their minds, more serious and sophisticated poetic style. Out of all this came the rash of satires and epigrams at the end of the century, the revolution in prose and verse style, and the dramatic experimentation that resulted in Jonson's and Marston's contributions to the theatre.

In 1595 the first clear signs of the emergence of this group appeared in the work of two men who were probably not closer to it than its periphery. Both Thomas Lodge and George Chapman were distinctly members of the older generation. Yet both had obvious affiliations with the new group: Lodge resided at Lincoln's Inn and in the course of his long career attempted at one time or another most of the current literary fashions, while Chapman was always a poet of the intelligentsia. Although neither seems to have taken a persistent interest in the group, in 1595 Lodge provided a statement of its aims, if only a partial one, as clear as any we are likely to find. In the letter "To the Gentleman Readers whatsoever," prefatory to *A Fig for Momus*, he discussed the genres represented in the work:

Under this title I haue thought good to include Satyres, Eclogues, *and* Epistles: *first by reason that I studie to delight with varietie, next because I would write in that forme, wherein no man might chalenge me with seruile imitation, (wherewith heretofore I haue beene uniustlie taxed.) My* Satyres *(to speake truth) are by pleasures, rather placed here to prepare, and trie the eare, then to feede it. . . . For my* Epistles, *they are in that kind, wherein no Englishman of our time hath publiquely written.*[17]

In the same year Chapman brought out his *Ovid's Banquet of Sense,* a work which, if it did not introduce a new genre, at least introduced an old one with a difference. The prefatory letter to

[17] *Works of Thomas Lodge* (Hunterian Club ed.; London, 1878), III, 6, 7.

Mathew Royden in itself offers interesting evidence of the literary standards and the haughty exclusiveness of the emergent group. The title poem is the child of what Chapman calls his "new pen" in that it is a "new" use of the Ovidian love poem.[18] Although clearly modeled on the erotic poems that had had a vogue in the past few years and that were still in vogue in 1595, *Ovid's Banquet* mixes the sensuous, indeed sensual, extravagance of the conventional Ovidian love poem with an alloy of sober philosophy and scholarship—footnotes and all—apparently for the purpose of dignifying the genre. What is more, even the sonnet sequence published with *Ovid's Banquet,* "A Coronet for his Mistress Philosophy," represents an unusual use of the sonnet form. Accordingly, this book, too, is important as an early product of the motives that soon prompted Ben Jonson to recommend *Cynthia's Revels* as a novelty:

> In this alone, his MUSE her sweetnesse hath,
> Shee shunnes the print of any beaten path;
> And proues new wayes to come to learned eares:
> Pied ignorance she neither loues nor feares.
> [H & S, IV, 43]

Although Lodge and Chapman apparently only flirted with the movement, they anticipated what the younger writers were to do in the years that immediately followed. Richard Barnfield, for example, published most of his work between 1594 and 1598. Much of this work is fairly conventional; some of it is decidedly unconventional; but all of it is marked by qualities that prompted Edward Arber to point out its "constant strain after novelty; either through unusual subjects or by an unusual treatment of ordinary subjects."[19] Even Barnfield's first book of poems, the

---

[18] In the prefatory letter Chapman is clearly eager that the newness of his work be appreciated. See *The Poems of George Chapman,* ed. Phyllis Brooks Bartlett (New York, 1941), pp. 49, 50.

[19] *Poems 1594–1598* by Richard Barnfield in *English Scholar's Library* (Birmingham, 1882), III, xxiii.

Affectionate Shepherd (1594), exhibited this penchant when he appended to a series of complaints in the conventional manner a mock complaint entitled "Helen's Rape, or A Light Lantern for Light Ladies." With much the same intention to work from odd angles he wrote *The Encomium of Lady Pecunia, or The Praise of Money* (1598) as a mock encomium designed to turn the conventional rhetoric of praise to a satiric use. Of this poem Barnfield himself said, "At length I bethought my selfe of a Subject, both new (as having never beene written upon before) and pleasing." [20]

Barnfield was hardly alone in his search for novelty, moreover, and certainly not unique in his attempts to achieve it by turning the conventional genres upside down. It is almost too commonplace to rehearse what John Donne was doing with the innocent Elizabethan song forms during these years, and now we are fairly confident that *Epithalamium Made at Lincoln's Inn* is a mock epithalamium, written perhaps for an entertainment at the Inns of Court.[21] During these same years Sir John Davies wrote his *Gulling Sonnets,* the purpose of which he stated in the dedicatory sonnet "To His Good Freinde Sr Anth. Cooke":

> Here my Camelion Muse her selfe doth chaunge
> to divers shapes of gross absurdities,
> and like the Antick mocks with fashion straunge
> the fond admirers of lewde gulleries.[22]

And in 1600 John Weever brought out his *Faunus and Melliflora,* a curious medley from a formal point of view, but a work that, whatever else it may do, unquestionably mocks the tradition of the Ovidian love poem, indeed pokes particular fun at *Hero and Leander* and *Venus and Adonis* by burlesquing famous scenes and parodying their language.

---

[20] "To the Gentleman Readers," letter prefatory to "The Encomium of Lady Pecunia," Barnfield, *Poems,* p. 83.

[21] David Novarr, "Donne's 'Epithalamion Made at Lincolnes Inne': Context and Date," *RES,* VII (1956), 250–263.

[22] *The Complete Poems of Sir John Davies* (London, 1876), II, 55.

Concurrent with these attempts to treat the conventional genres in unusual ways and to establish for each type an antitype were, of course, the related efforts to strike out in new directions. T. K. Whipple has said, "There was no more striking and significant phenomenon in the world of letters than the sudden appearance and popularity of the classical satire . . . and the classical epigram, modelled on Martial." [23] Previous writers had occasionally written in both genres, but the last five years of the sixteenth century saw the new writers take these genres as their own, formulate for them what came to be their laws, and impose on them what came to be their prevailing character. Sir John Davies, Sir John Harington, Everard Guilpin, Thomas Bastard, John Weever, Francis Davison, Joshua Sylvester, Ben Jonson, and John Donne, all wrote epigrams; Joseph Hall, John Marston, John Donne, Everard Guilpin, Thomas Bastard, John Weever, and Richard Barnfield, all wrote satires. That members of an exceedingly energetic intelligentsia should seize upon genres that they, at least, viewed as peculiarly classical is not surprising. But this coincidence was probably less important than that these genres had the special merits of having been relatively untouched by previous writers and of offering clear opportunities to reject the past and attack the present. Everard Guilpin came close to making this point when in "Satyre praeludium" he set the satirist and epigrammatist off from contemporary frivolity:

> The Satyre onely and Epigramatist . . .
> Keepe diet from this surfet of excesse. . . .
> The bitter censures of their Critticke spleenes,
> Are Antidotes to pestilentiall sinnes. . . .
> They are Philosophicke true *Cantharides*
> To vanities dead flesh. An Epigrame
> . . . is not afraid
> To speake the truth, but calls a iade, a iade.[24]

[23] *Martial*, p. 329.
[24] *Skialetheia* (1598), Shakespeare Association Facsimiles, No. 2, ed. G. B. Harrison (Oxford, 1931), C1–C1ᵛ.

However narrowly prejudiced Guilpin may seem here, and however far we still are from explaining his total attitude satisfactorily, he is conspicuously attuned in this passage to the pervasive ambition amòng his fellows to find new worlds to conquer and, in doing so, to enfold himself in a mantle of exclusiveness.

It is in the context of this movement that Marston's early work is best understood and particularly in the context of the numerous attempts to write parodies, burlesques, and variations on the conventional genres that what seems to have been his first work, "Pygmalion's Image," is most satisfactorily read.[25] Toward the end of the dedicatory poems in *The Metamorphosis of Pygmalion's Image and Certain Satires* Marston calls upon "The World's Mighty Monarch, Good Opinion" to "Protect an orphan poet's infancy." His use of the phrase "orphan poet" is significant. Since both his parents were living at this time, he clearly did not think himself an orphan in the usual sense. He seems to have meant, on the contrary, that he was an orphan in that he had no protector or patron other than "Good Opinion." But the specific meaning of the term "Opinion" in Neo-Stoic thought and, as we shall see, in Marston's work makes such a statement wildly ironical: Marston's calling upon Opinion amounts to his summoning as his patron one of the chief sources (in his view) of error and corruption. The statement, nonetheless, is not out of key in this dedication. It is perfectly probably that Marston was at this time proud of his lack of patronage and anxious to broadcast the fact. Certainly he echoed this pride later in this dedication to "Nobody, . . . [his] most respected Patron" at the beginning of *Antonio and Mellida* (1602). Furthermore, he was never one to falter before the complexity of the kind of irony involved in his calling on "Good Opinion" to protect him.

---

[25] "Pygmalion's Image" is the first work in Marston's first publication, *The Metamorphosis of Pygmalion's Image and Certain Satires*. In the prefatory poem "To His Mistress" he refers to it as "the first blooms of [his] poesy" (l. 6), and in the "Satira Nova," added to *The Scourge of Villainy* in 1599, he refers to it as "old Pygmalion" (l. 38).

But it is also likely that he meant something more by the phrase "orphan poet" than simply that he was a young poet without a patron. Seen in the context of his fellows' efforts at innovation, the phrase could easily have meant a poet without a conventional muse to invoke and without predecessors or models. Marston frequently took pride in this feature of his work—in *The Scourge of Villainy*, for example, when he boasted in "Ad rhythmum" that his "liberty / Scorns rhyming laws," when in "To Detraction" he insisted "I am myself, so is my poesy," and when in Satire VI, he defended his "respectless, free-bred poesy" (l. 100) against charges of derivativeness. It is this sentiment, moreover, that is clearly reflected in Guilpin, who calls his poems "orphants" and who concludes his satires with a line reminiscent of Marston's: "My lines are still themselves, and so am I." [26]

The phrase "orphan poet" is useful, then, for relating Marston to the vogue for innovation and change animating the poets of the intelligentsia. It epitomizes the impulse so crucial and so widespread in the group to be free of patrons, predecessors, and models, to be known as originators and pioneers. It sums up one of several attitudes that must be recognized before the poetry and drama that lie beyond "Pygmalion's Image" can be approached fairly.

"Pygmalion's Image" has been a source of disagreement from the time of its first publication in 1598. We know nothing of the poem's history before that time, but we cannot ignore Marston's insistence in print that it was not a conventional erotic poem. In "The Author in praise of his precedent Poem," which follows "Pygmalion's Image" in the original volume, he calls upon Rufus and Luxurio with heavy-handed sarcasm to crown him for his display of "the Salaminian titillations, / Which tickle up our lewd Priapians," insisting with mock pride that he has in every respect imitated the procedure of the successful writers in this

[26] *Skialetheia,* E3ᵛ.

genre (ll. 1–17). A little later in the same poem he changes direction by bluntly asserting that the "voluntaries and mercenarians" who metaphorically represent the stanzas marching to his command are

> Faint and white-liver'd, as our gallants bin;
> Patch'd like a beggar's cloak, and run as sweet
> As doth a tumbril [dung cart] in the pavèd street. [ll. 24–26]

In the second and final verse paragraph he speaks of his "dissembling shifts" and then proceeds to censure himself before others do for an inadequate performance. Finally, in Satire VI of *The Scourge of Villainy* he attacks the Curios, Mutos, and Friscuses who have stupidly misinterpreted the poem, vociferously insisting that he

> wrot
> Those idle rhymes to note the odious spot
> And blemish that deforms the lineaments
> Of modern poesy's habiliments

and lamenting,

> Oh that the beauties of invention,
> For want of judgment's disposition,
> Should all be soil'd! O that such treasury,
> Such strains of well-conceited poesy,
> Should moulded be in such a shapeless form,
> That want of art should make such wit a scorn! [27]

---

[27] Lines 23–32. In lines 29 and 30 I have retained the readings of the texts of 1598 and 1599: "soil'd" instead of "spoil'd" and "strains" instead of "strain." Although Bullen points out in a footnote that "spoil'd" appeared in the "corrected" edition of 1599, I have found no evidence of it. See G. B. Harrison's reprint of the edition of 1599 (London: The Bodily Head Quartos, XIII, 1925), p. 60.

Only his brief reference to the poems in the opening lines of Satire II of *Certain Satires* leaves the slightest doubt about his general intention; and even here, when he admits that he has "lisp'd like an amorist," his use of the term "lisp'd" suggests that he was not imitating the amorists respectfully.

But Marston's protestations have hardly prevented critics from disagreeing about the poem. Many have felt that the Curios, Mutos, and Friscuses were probably correct: that it is a conventional Ovidian love poem and that Marston's satiric claims for it represent no more than an afterthought—a decision taken when he was faced with the prospect of publishing the poem with *Certain Satires*. H. Harvey Wood's view is fairly typical; he says that "there is no doubt that in *Pigmalions Image* Marston was trying his 'prentice hand at the licentious narrative poem. . . . One can hardly blame the Elizabethan reader who failed to detect the moral and satirical purpose of the poem: it is, indeed, as hard to find today as it was then." [28] Many critics, on the other hand, have agreed with Marston's claims, but have talked about the poem in terms too general to make clear what kind of parody, burlesque, or satire it is.[29] And even those few who have dealt with the poem in some detail have failed to clarify its structure and neglected the basic problem of reconciling the erotic elements that have so long troubled critics of Wood's persuasion with the satiric elements. Ford Elmore Curtis, for example, perceptively points out that the poem's brevity and the novelty of a commentator are sufficient causes for suspecting the poem's seriousness, but he does not demonstrate how a satiric purpose operates beyond the explicit satiric comments of the commentator.[30]

If "Pygmalion's Image" is read in the light of the efforts of

[28] *Plays*, I, xix. But see also Nathan Drake, *Shakespeare and His Times* (London, 1817), I, 636; Ward, *History*, II, 53; and *Works*, I, xvi, xviii.

[29] J. P. Collier, perhaps the first critic to support this view, advanced the typical account; see *The Poetical Decameron* (Edinburgh, 1820), I, 230, 231.

[30] "Life," pp. 60–68.

Marston's fellows to burlesque the genres in which their elders
had distinguished themselves and to introduce into these genres
greater ingenuity and sophistication than their elders had shown,
it reveals the structure of a coherent, extremely ingenious, if not
altogether satisfactory, burlesque. It is a very complicated structure, admittedly, because Marston is both ridiculing the manner of the class of writers and gallants whom he called amorists
and at the same time setting off the superiority of his poet-
commentator. Moreover, it is a structure that Marston does not
control as well as we might wish. But as a structure it provides
an interesting introduction to the literary mind that is our immediate concern.

On the simplest level Marston burlesques the conventional
poses and parodies the language of the amorists much as he was
to continue to do in his plays. His mocking attitude first appears
in the tongue-in-cheek extravagances of the mock dedication to
"Good Opinion":

Sole regent of affection, perpetual ruler of judgment, most famous
justice of censures, only giver of honour, great procurer of advance-
ment, the world's chief balance, the all of all, and all in all, by whom
all things are that that they are, I humbly offer this my poem.

This tone of mock seriousness continues in the prefatory poem
"To His Mistress," in which the poet-commentator calls upon his
"beauteous angel"

> To grace the first blooms of [his] poesy.
> Thy favours, like Promethean sacred fire,
> In dead and dull conceit can life inspire;
> Or, like that rare and rich elixir stone,
> Can turn to gold leaden invention.

In the body of the poem the ridicule of the amorists proceeds
largely from Pygmalion's behavior—from his absurd attempts to
caress and fondle the statue, from his extravagant prayer to Venus,

and from his distracted plea to the "Sweet happy sheets" to take him in.

Against the behavior and language of Pygmalion is set the poet-commentator, whose remarks serve both to heighten Pygmalion's absurdity and to set himself off as a lover of a different and superior kind. At one point, for example, he compares Pygmalion's timid reluctance to view the statue's privates to the embarrassment of the "subtile city-dame" who, when she thinks unchaste thoughts in church, covers her eyes but peers through her fingers; at another he compares Pygmalion's adoration of the statue to the foolishness of the "peevish Papists" who crouch and kneel before their dumb idols. At still another point, however, he shifts his attention from the shortcomings of Pygmalion to the obvious superiority of his own tactics in love:

> I oft have smiled to see the foolery
> Of some sweet youths, who seriously protest
> That love respects not actual luxury,
> But only joys to dally, sport, and jest;
>
> .   .   .   .   .
>
> And therefore, ladies, think that they ne'er love you,
> Who do not unto more than kissing move you. [ll. 109–120]

Marston's commentator is, accordingly, the poet-lover then fashionable among his fellows—the sophisticated man about town who wooed with a jest, who mocked his own seriousness, and who frankly admitted that his intentions were carnal. Though far simpler, he is the spiritual kin of Jack Donne of the *Songs and Sonnets*.

But Marston's ridicule of the amorists involves still more than this. Critics have paid insufficient attention to the fact that when he argued his satiric purpose in *The Scourge of Villainy*, Satire VI, he denied two charges: first, that he had written a conventional erotic narrative poem and, secondly, that he had seriously intended "some female soul to move." The first denial presents no

difficulty for we have every reason to believe him; but the second
is rather unexpected and requires some explanation. That Marston
was thought by some to have wished to move "some female soul"
is startling, particularly since such a purpose was no part of the
conventional Ovidian love poem. Such a purpose begins to make
sense only when we recall that seduction was, of course, the constant labor of the amorists and that ridicule of their ineptness at
it would not have been amiss in a poem with the satiric purpose
that Marston claims for this. Apparently, we should construe
Marston's defense of himself as meaning that he had framed the
poem along the lines of a seduction poem, as well as along the
lines of a parody and burlesque, not "some female soul to move,"
but to heap additional ridicule on the amorists.

By looking carefully at the poem we can find, it is true, a structural dimension that mocks the amorists by underscoring the commentator's superiority in the sophistries of love. At the same time
we must admit that Marston's ingenuity in plying this strategy is
sometimes drawn so thin as to be hardly visible. By treating the
narrative of the Pygmalion story so that it supports the commentator's direct appeals to his mistress, Marston has made of the
poem, among other things, a tenuous and excessively witty argument for sexual surrender. In general, this argument is framed to
persuade the poet's mistress to profit by the lessons couched in
Pygmalion's tale and, accordingly, to yield herself to him. The
main line of the persuasion emerges from the parallelism between
the poet's mistress and the statue that complements the parallelism between the commentator and Pygmalion. The parallelism is
set up in the closing lines of the prefatory poem "To His Mistress"
when the commentator says,

> And as thou read'st (fair) take compassion—
> Force me not envy my Pygmalion:
> Then when thy kindness grants me such sweet bliss,
> I'll gladly write thy Metamorphosis.

In the body of the poem the parallelism is chiefly sustained by the narrative, which is fashioned to emphasize the similarities between the commentator's mistress and the statue, and by the commentator's remarks. But it is also supported by such minor devices as his practice of explicitly comparing his lady's beauty to the statue's and even by the calculated slip of the tongue in stanza eight, where he absurdly compares the ivory statue's breasts to ivory as his eye wanders from the statue to the woman. Finally, in stanza thirty-two he underscores both the parallelism and its implications in the argument:

> O wonder not to hear me thus relate
> And say to flesh transformèd was a stone!
> Had I my love in such a wishèd state
> As was afforded to Pygmalion,
> Though flinty-hard, of her you soon should see
> As strange a transformation wrought by me. [ll. 187–192]

The poet-commentator is merely expressing, accordingly, in terms somewhat fresher and more ingenious than those of the amorists the standard arguments for sexual surrender. His mistress, like the statue, is dead, cold, stony, and heartless until she yields; indeed chastity is a state equivalent to lifelessness. Love, on the other hand, is a power capable of almost supernatural transformations, a power, therefore, that everyone should want to participate in. His argument is, I confess, almost too subtle for its own good; but it is very probably a deliberate facet of Marston's design here.

On the whole, accordingly, the evidence favors our accepting Marston's claim that "Pygmalion's Image" was from the beginning satiric in intention—a poem designed to disintegrate the amorists as self-respecting writers and lovers, designed to support the suggestion that they are not only childish, cowardly, and dishonest, but also (most disgraceful of all) ineffective. Yet it is not surprising that the poem has often been misinterpreted. The very quali-

ties that make it a rather typical product of the literary movement
that dominated intellectual circles at the end of the sixteenth
century—its novelty, its often strained ingenuity, its fragile and
complex irony—are precisely the qualities that obscure Marston's
intention. It is one thing to see the poem as an orphan poet's
first offering when it is placed alongside Davies' *Gulling Sonnets*
or Barnfield's *Encomium of Lady Pecunia;* it is quite another to
identify the type when the poem is taken alone. Marston was still
too new at this role to control so witty a conception effectively,
and even he seems to have been aware of the inadequacy of his
performance.[31]

Despite the poem's difficulties, however, its general lines are
sufficiently clear to reveal Marston in the act of casting his lot
with the fashionable poets and of doing so with a talent of some
promise. It is a poem that clarifies how he won his reputation as
a "Gentleman that wrote divers things of great Ingenuity"[32] by
underscoring the ambition so important to him and his fellows
to give the world something new. It gives us a first glimpse, moreover, of the highly ironic attitude at the core of all his work in
satire.

[31] See the last stanza of "The Author in praise of his precedent Poem."
[32] The quotation is from Anthony à Wood, *Athenae,* I, 762.

Chapter II

Sharp-fanged Satirist

JOHN MARSTON'S work in verse satire is, perhaps, as exemplary as anything he was ever to do of the purposes that unified the fashionable poets at the end of the sixteenth century. In taking up the "Satyre's knottie rod" in 1598, he assumed a stance, a voice, and a state of mind ideally suited to a vociferous declaration of his individuality. This gesture was to exert a permanent influence on his literary career. Although he was soon prevented from publishing verse satires by the Order of Conflagration of 1599 and although his literary efforts after that year were almost wholly dramatic, once he had turned to satire he never abandoned it. It will be increasingly clear, indeed, that his work in verse satire constituted an apprenticeship in the literary methods and techniques that were to be the foundation of his efforts in the drama.

Unfortunately, the task of clarifying and assessing Marston's accomplishment in verse satire is fraught with problems. Renaissance satire is in many respects the most difficult of the Renaissance genres for modern readers. Frequently it is highly topical and allusive. What is often more perplexing, however, is that it it based on a set of assumptions with which modern readers have almost wholly lost touch. Since the days of Hall, Marston, and Donne, English literature has been enriched by the satire of Dryden, Pope, and Byron, whose work is very different and so much more important that modern readers have been educated to judge satire by the standards implicit in it. Too often, accordingly, Hall, Marston, and Donne fare worse in the hands of critics than they ought to fare largely because they fail to manifest the qualities that Dryden, Pope, and Byron display so abundantly. J. P. Collier, who was rather sympathetic to Marston on the whole, says of him, for example, that "in all there is a great deal of strength and fire; some heavy blows, but nothing exquisitely keen, indicating a real talent for satire of the best kind." [1] And even a critic as sensitive to Marston's value as Ford Elmore Curtis seems to rely on eighteenth-century criteria when he quotes epigrammatic lines as examples of Marston's best work.[2]

Recently, numerous attempts have been made to recover the assumptions necessary to read Renaissance satire as it was intended to be read, to rehabilitate what M. C. Randolph calls "Renaissance satiric theory." [3] Taken as a unit, these studies have enabled us to see over the peaks of Dryden, Pope, and Byron to the smaller range beyond. Yet they have also proved a little disquieting in that they have shown—what is so often true— that Renaissance satire was no single thing, no single, tidy coherent entity, but a shaggy cluster of things, a cluster held together by obvious and important similarities, yet a cluster nonetheless. Disentangling Marston from this cluster will require some care.

The multiplicity of Renaissance satire is met most conspicuously, perhaps, in the diversity of Renaissance attempts to explain its origins—not to mention modern attempts to explain these explanations. A useful paradigm for this confusion is Thomas

---

[1] *Poetical Dec.*, I, 253. See also Ward, *History*, II, 53.
[2] "Life," p. 75.   [3] See Chapter I, note 3.

Drant's prefatory poem to *A Medicinable Moral . . . Two Books of Horace's Satires, Englished* (1566), in which Drant derives the word "satyre" from four distinct sources.[4] Moreover, reasonable explanations for this diversity have not been wanting: Lila Freedman has been thorough in clarifying the differences among the Renaissance authorities drawn on, and John Peter persuasive in arguing a varying medieval residue.[5] In emphasizing these differences, of course, we should avoid the implication that the efforts to write satire at the end of the sixteenth century were anything like anarchic; that would be hopelessly wide of the mark. Despite all the theoretical differences, poets and critics found substantial areas of agreement. Whether Marston and his fellows believed satire derived from the rude satyr figure, as the influential Aelius Donatus, Diomedes, and Puttenham had argued, or from the Latin *satura*, as others opined, or from the classical figure of Saturn, their differences apparently did not prevent them from general unanimity on so crucial a matter as the authentic satiric style since all these derivations were perfectly consistent with the conviction that satire was characteristically harsh and obscure. Furthermore, their universal acceptance of a coarse, conversational, often elliptical, sometimes scurrile speech for satire rested firmly on the precedent of Juvenal and Persius, their avowed models. A John Marston might quarrel mildly about the degree to which harshness and obscurity were proper, but he did not deny their authenticity. It is only within this area of general agreement that the diversity in theory becomes important. There it led to differences in practice from poet to poet, and there it begins to be of help in the task of setting Marston off.

This diversity is most important in questions concerning satire's

---

[4] The poem has been reprinted by M. C. Randolph, "Thomas Drant's Definition of Satire," *NQ*, CLXXX (1941), 416–418. Briefly, the four sources mentioned are (1) an Arabic term, meaning glaive or sharp cutting instrument, (2) the mythological woodland Satyr, (3) Saturne, the old god of sullen and melancholy disposition, and (4) the Latin term *satura*, meaning full or satiated.

[5] Freedman, "Satiric Personae," and Peter, *Complaint*.

function and the persona proper to the satirist. It was universally assumed, of course, that satire was corrective. But it was not clear precisely how it was corrective. When Puttenham described the satirist as one who assailed "common abuses and vice . . . in rough and bitter speeches," he did not go on to say that the satirist also provided positive exhortations to virtue. Yet there was some precedent for such exhortation in the classical satirists and abundant evidence of it in the complaint tradition that so deviously conditioned Renaissance satire. The Renaissance satirists, accordingly, were far from agreed on the point: some of them contented themselves with invective; some quite self-consciously tried to balance the railing by arguing constructive moral standards.

The confusion was still greater in the related matter of the persona proper to the satirist. Perhaps nothing has given modern readers more trouble than this element in Renaissance satire. To be sure, their difficulty proceeds frequently from their failure to recognize that Renaissance satirists deliberately assumed a persona; [6] but it proceeds also—after a satiric pose has been acknowledged—from their failure to apprehend the full complexity of the persona and to grasp firmly the fact that this persona differed from satirist to satirist. The speaker in Hall's *Virgidemiarum* is by no means the speaker in Marston's *Scourge of Villainy* or Donne's *Satires*. To understand their differences as well as their similarities, we must consider not only the various precedents followed, but also certain of the aims animating these poets—aims that they shared as young poets writing under the special conditions of their decade, as well as aims that seem to have been peculiar to them as individuals.

All the Renaissance satirists had before them the precedents of Horace, Juvenal, and Persius, and Lila Freedman has done an

[6] In his recent *The Cankered Muse*, Alvin Kernan has both argued the need to distinguish between the satiric persona and the poet (pp. 1–6, 28) and explained at length the emergence of the standard satiric persona in the Renaissance (pp. 39–80).

admirable job of showing their indebtedness to the personae of these Latin writers and their preference for Juvenal's "angry man." [7] All, moreover, fell heir to the rather recent but common tradition that the satirist was a kind of barber-surgeon who administered bitter medicine, let blood, lanced sores, and flayed away infected flesh, a tradition perhaps first set forth only as recently as Minturno's *De Poeta* . . . (1559), but certainly commonplace by the end of the century.[8] And all, of course, were aware of the preacher-persona of the complaint tradition, though, fashionable young sophisticates that they were, they took pains to avoid comparison with the complainant's contemporaneous equivalent, the Puritan zealot, as often as they tried to emulate his moral sincerity. The problem of apprehending the personae of Renaissance satire, at any rate, consists in determining the precise proportions in which these precedents mingle in individual satirists. What is more, in a satirist as ambitious as John Marston, it consists in determining how these precedents mingle with at least one other that has not been sufficiently noticed, that of the Stoic teacher-philosopher as met in Epictetus and others.

In general, the fusion of these strains in Marston's verse satires produced a speaker who is by turns haughty and exclusive, furious to the point of hysteria, amused in the manner of Democritus, grimly hardened to the task of whipping and flaying, and then serious with the earnestness of a dedicated healer of souls. It is useful to think of this persona as a cartoonlike extension of Marston the man, culminating at the outer extremity in the satyr's mask. It is in this mask, of course, that we meet the savage indignation and rude accents of outrage—those features of the persona that are most clearly matters of artifice. At the other extreme, in the voice of the Stoic teacher-philosopher, we meet a voice apparently indistinguishable from Marston's own. For the

---

[7] "Satiric Personae," pp. 24–70.

[8] On this tradition see Randolph, "Medical Concept." Bernard Bernstein quotes the crucial passage from Minturno, "The Poetic Theories of Minturno," *Studies in Honour of Frederick W. Shipley* (St. Louis, 1942), p. 105.

sake of clarity these multiple attitudes might be seen as parts of a process of extension and recession. At moments Marston speaks noisily through the personality of the mask; at others he retreats along the line of extension to speak much as he would in his own person. Once we grant his right as a poet to move back and forth in this way, to complicate his point of view by this device, we shall have no trouble, I think, with the plural attitudes worked with. Each is perfectly consistent with something that Marston the young poet as satirist was trying to do. Despite the presence of artifice, moreover, each is an integral part of Marston's serio-comic view of the world.

Marston runs the gamut of these attitudes with an ease that has often prompted his critics to accuse him of insincerity. But his shifts are perfectly clear once we recognize that they are shifts. In *Certain Satires*, which, as we shall see, is conceived structurally to deepen progressively in seriousness, he moves gradually from the irritated but rather jaunty sophisticate who twice invokes Democritus, the laughing philosopher, in Satire I to the raging satirist of Satire III:

> Now, Grim Reproof, swell in my rough-hued rhyme,
> That thou mayst vex the guilty of our time. [ll. 1–2]

For the most part he holds to this exasperation through Satires IV and V to relinquish it toward the end of V for a tone more suitable to the name "Epictetus," with which he signs the work.

In *The Scourge of Villainy* his shifts are more numerous and complex, but also clear. The prefatory pieces abound in the haughty exclusiveness of the fashionable poets: the speaker is disdainful of detractors, grudging to expose "to their all-tainting breath, / The issue of his brain," yet confident that however little he is understood by his average reader, he will be understood and appreciated by the "diviner wits," those "free-born minds no kennel-thought controls." There is little beyond a certain exaggeration to distinguish this voice from Marston's own.

But the transition marked at the beginning of "Proemium in Librum Primum" is perfectly clear: when he opens with

> I bear the scourge of just Rhamnusia,
> Lashing the lewdness of Britannia,

he has patently assumed the satyr's mask. Here we meet all the notorious scorn, contempt, and abhorrence. The poet leaves his ivory tower to scourge the infected multitude because nothing short of scourging—and not very dignified scourging at that— will suffice. Marston's most extreme cultivation of this attitude follows immediately in the tortured obscurity of Satire I. But he retreats slightly from this extreme in Satire II (he had said in the prefatory letter that the harshness and obscurity of Satire I were excessive), where he adopts the tone that dominates the work.

> I cannot hold, I cannot, I, endure . . . :
> Let custards quake, my rage must freely run. . . .
> My soul is vex'd; what power will resist,
> Or dares to stop a sharp-fang'd satirist? [ll. 1–8]
>
> . . . . .
>
> Who would not shake a satire's knotty rod,
> When to defile the sacred seat of God
> Is but accounted gentlemen's disport? [ll. 38–40]
>
> . . . . .
>
> Who can abstain? What modest brain can hold,
> But he must make his shame-faced muse a scold?
> [ll. 142–143]

He departs from this outrage frequently in the poems that follow: toward the end of Satire IV, for example, where as teacher-philosopher he argues abstract matters of ethical theory; in the "Proemium in Librum Secundum" and "Ad rhythmum," where as fashionable poet-satirist he pronounces on matters of form; or at the beginning of the last satire, where he explicitly bids Grim

Reproof to sleep and invokes "sporting merriment." And his departures are sometimes sudden and brief, as, for example, in Satire VIII, where he punctuates passages of denunciation with abstract reflections on sensuality. But however numerous and abruptly introduced, his shifts are always clear, if you are ready for them; indeed, sometimes ("I am too mild. Reach me my scourge again." IX, 364) they are explicit.

Taken together, these attitudes constitute Marston's satiric persona, surely his central device for controlling and directing thought and feeling in the satires. It is a persona quite distinct from Hall's, or Donne's, or even Guilpin's, whose most resembles it. Yet it is only one of several important features of Marston's satires that set them off from his contemporaries'; and it is only a symptom of the wider diversity to be met in the genre.

For the present purpose Marston's distinctness among the Renaissance satirists can be adequately illustrated by comparing him with that contemporary with whom he most frequently crossed swords, Joseph Hall. Both began writing verse satire at roughly the same time (Hall preceded Marston by about a year), and the obvious similarities in their work need hardly be reaffirmed. Despite their similarities and the common assumptions about satire that these similarities reflect, however, they were by no means agreed on all matters. They did not agree, for example, and there was no general agreement, about the precise position of satire in the hierarchy of genres. Sidney had given it a medial position, above "Iambic" and "Comic," but Puttenham had put it at the bottom, below the pastoral. Marston claimed a high place for it, while Hall consistently referred to it as "lowly." [9]

Fortunately, Hall was fairly outspoken about his views. In addition to his random remarks about satire in the *Virgidemiarum*, he dealt with it at some length in "A Postscript to the Reader," appended to the sixth book. In general, he accepted the stock

[9] Sidney, *An Apologie for Poetrie* (1583), in G. G. Smith, *Elizabethan Essays*, I, 159. Puttenham, *The Arte of English Poesie*, eds. G. D. Willcock and Alice Walker (Cambridge, 1936), pp. 25–27. *The Collected Poems of Joseph Hall*, ed. Arnold Davenport (Liverpool, 1949), p. 11.

assumptions about satire's harshness and obscurity. He described the satirist as a porcupine

> That shoots sharpe quils out in each angry line,
> And wounds the blushing cheeke, and fiery eye,
> Of him that heares, and readeth guiltily.[10]

And in the "Postscript" he described satire as "both hard of conceipt, and harsh of stile." [11] But even while recognizing harshness and obscurity as qualities characteristic of satire, he did so with serious reservations. For one thing he suggests at some points that surface roughness was not accidental in authentic satiric utterance. He was nowhere perfectly clear on the point; but in the Prologue of Book III, where he summarized the complaints already made about his satires (apparently circulated in manuscript), he implies that, theoretically, harshness and obscurity should be expressive of "gall," a term that in this context seems to mean angry contempt. He then goes on in the same passage, however, to admit that, whatever their theoretical functions, he was unable to achieve these qualities in his satires:

> Some say my Satyrs over-loosely flow,
> Nor hide their gall inough from open show:
> Not ridle-like, obscuring their intent:
> But packe-staffe plaine uttring what thing they ment:
> Contrarie to the Roman ancients,
> Whose wordes were short, & darkesome was their sence;
> Who reads one line of their harsh poesies,
> Thrise must he take his winde, & breath him thrise.
> My muse would follow them that have forgone,
> But cannot with an English pineon.[12]

Both this passage and the "Postscript" show that Hall recognized a true satiric style and admired it but that he felt it irretrievably lost to English writers. Although he tried to imitate it, he openly

[10] *Collected Poems*, p. 83.   [11] *Collected Poems*, p. 97.
[12] *Collected Poems*, p. 33.

admitted that his was for the most part a "quiet stile." [13] His fullest discussion of this loss occurs in the "Postscript," where, after introducing his subject with the haughty superiority typical of the fashionable poets,[14] he discursively assembled three reasons for the loss: the ignorance of the age, the age's preference for musical verse, and, most interesting of all, the unsuitability of English for imitating the effects achieved by the Latin satirists.[15]

Marston's refusal to impose any such limitations on satire furnishes us with a valuable index to his behavior as a writer. In this genre, too, he apparently thought of himself as the orphan poet. Of course his feigned contempt for the persons and institutions satirized suggests that he was writing in the genre almost against his will. In the second of the prefatory pieces to *The Scourge of Villainy*, "In Lectores prorsus indignos," he scorned his public and recoiled from the hand-dirtying that comes from dealing with vice; and at the end of the book he committed it in a manner true to his Stoic convictions about worldly vanity to "Everlasting Oblivion." But these speeches are merely parts of the satiric pose; they tell us little about Marston's serious convictions about satire. The conclusion of "In Lectores" far more accurately represents his considered view of the genre. Here, after deciding to submit to the "dunghill pesants," the Castilios and the Gnatos who would abuse his work, he dedicated it to the "diviner wits" who would understand and appreciate what he was about (ll. 80–97). Here, as well as elsewhere, his premise is that satire is an important, though a difficult genre. Earlier in Certain Satires he had with assumed humility expressed a fear that he could not attain to the high estate of satirist:

> O title, which my judgment doth adore!
> But I, dull-sprited fat Boeotian boor,
> Do far off honour that censorian seat. [II, 3–5]

[13] *Collected Poems*, p. 83.

[14] "It is not for every one to rellish a true and naturall Satyre. . . ." *Collected Poems*, p. 97.

[15] *Collected Poems*, pp. 97–99.

In *The Scourge* he was not only confident that he had attained
to the role but also confident that he was taking the genre to
new heights:

> O how on tip-toes proudly mounts my muse!
> Stalking a loftier gait than satires use.
> Methinks some sacred rage warms all my veins,
> Making my sprite mount up to higher strains
> Than well beseems a rough-tongu'd satire's part.
>
> [IX, 5–9]

As we shall see, this ambition is clearly traceable in the differences between Marston's satires and those of his contemporaries.

But Marston's differences with Hall did not end with the question of the dignity of the genre; he also took a slightly different
view of the authentic satiric style. To begin with, Marston held
reservations even more serious than Hall's about the popular assumptions concerning satire's harshness and obscurity. Although
he frequently described his satires as "sharp-fang'd," "rude," and
"rough-hew'd," and although he admitted in the letter prefatory
to *The Scourge* that "there is a seemly decorum to be observed,
and peculiar kind of speech for a satire's lips," he argued in the
same letter that satire was not as harsh and obscure as his contemporaries claimed. Those who held that it was extremely harsh
and obscure, he reasoned, had inferred these qualities from the
ancient satirists whom, in fact, they were unable to read properly.
For them, he added, he had written the "first satire," [16] "in some
places too obscure, in all places misliking me." The authentic
satiric style, he apparently thought, was more moderate: "sharp-
fang'd," "rude," and "rough-hew'd" to some extent, but not as

---

[16] There is a slight possibility that by "first satire" Marston meant *Certain
Satires*, the first group of satires he published. But since *Certain Satires*
is nowhere excessively harsh and obscure, and since Satire I (SV) is by all
odds his most harsh and obscure satire, we may conclude that he was referring to it. That the prefatory letter is referring forward need not, I think,
give us any trouble.

harsh and obscure as Hall and the others contended. Moreover, at no point did Marston suggest that he felt, as Hall did, that English was unsuitable for the authentic satiric style in either his or Hall's conception of that style.

On the other hand, Marston seems to have shared Hall's view that the best satire should express its gall or angry contempt to a large extent through style,[17] but he differed with him on the question of the extent to which satire should express contempt. Despite the apparent unfairness to Hall, Marston constantly accused him of devoting his satires exclusively to railing. The following passage from "Reactio," an attack on Hall included in *Certain Satires,* offers a typical example of the accusation:

> Speak, ye that never heard him ought but rail,
> Do not his poems bear a glorious sail? . . .
> Who cannot rail, and with a blasting breath
> Scorch even the whitest lilies of the earth?
> Who cannot stumble in a stuttering style,
> And shallow heads with seeming shades beguile? [18]

As his practice reveals, Marston was not content to restrict satire to railing, to derision, or even to reasoned criticism of a destructive sort. One of the specific means by which he sought to elevate the genre was by combining satire with fairly elaborate moral exhortation, and in this he is unique in the gallery of Renaissance satirists.

In view of the critical differences between Marston and Hall,

[17] Like Hall, he was not perfectly clear on the point. At the end of Satire III (*CS*) he upbraided himself for "display[ing] / These open nags, which purblind eyes bewray" and urged himself to "Come, come, and snarl more dark at secret sin," but at no other point did he make clear reference to the idea. The point is, perhaps, worth making only as a possible explanation of one of the qualities that the satirists haughtily assumed beyond the appreciative powers of their readers.

[18] Lines 149–158. In renumbering the satires included in *Certain Satires* Bullen numbered the poem entitled "Reactio" in the original "Satire IV" and moved the term "Reactio" to the position of epigraph. I shall refer to the satire as "Reactio."

therefore, it is not surprising that they engaged in a literary quarrel, especially since Marston seems to have been anxious to have a whipping boy. Actually, we have no assurance that either these differences or their critical differences concerning the literature of the past caused the quarrel. Ford Elmore Curtis and Morse Allen have argued that they did.[19] But other critics have argued for other causes, equally reasonable and equally conjectural. Arnold Davenport, for example, has tried not implausibly to link the quarrel with the earlier Harvey-Nashe controversy.[20] And Arnold Stein has argued still more reasonably that the cause of the quarrel was probably a combination of causes.[21] Marston probably resented, he contends, that Hall had published first and had achieved popularity before he had broken into print. Then, making the most of the disparity in their temperaments, he had exploited the possibilities for a quarrel, if only to have someone to disintegrate. Indeed, despite the contention of the older critics Grosart and Bullen that Hall fomented the quarrel by attacking the unprinted "Pymalion's Image" in his *Virgidemiarum*,[22] the one conclusion favored by the known facts is that the quarrel was extremely one-sided, most of the vituperation having come from Marston. As Curtis has pointed out, "there is in Hall no unmistakable reference to Marston." [23] We have only the epigram that Hall supposedly *"caused to be pasted to the latter page of every* Pygmalion *that came to the Stationers of Cambridge"* and that Marston reprinted in "Satira Nova," the satire added to the second edition of *The Scourge*,[24] to represent Hall's contribution to the

[19] "Life," pp. 89–93; Morse S. Allen, *The Satire of John Marston* (Columbus, Ohio, 1920), p. 12.

[20] "An Elizabethan Controversy: Harvey and Nashe," *NQ*, CLXXXII (1942), 116–119.

[21] "The Second English Satirist," *MLR*, XXXVIII (1943), 273–275.

[22] See A. B. Grosart (ed.), *The Complete Poems of Joseph Hall* (Manchester, 1875), pp. xxii–xxvi; and *Works*, I, ixx, xx.

[23] "Life," p. 87.

[24] The lines quoted appear in the satire, *Works*, III, 369. This was the "corrected" edition of 1599. It contained one new satire, the "Satira Nova," which, after Bullen had renumbered the poems, he called "Satire X." I shall

quarrel; and even the epigram's authenticity has been questioned.[25] Marston, on the other hand, twice attacked Hall at length in *Certain Satires*, devoting one whole satire of the five to the purpose, and then continued to attack him in *The Scourge*.[26] In other words, he behaved like a man prompted by resentment and jealousy and determined to make the most of an opportunity for a literary quarrel. All in all, the quarrel was probably not important enough to justify the attention that scholars have given to it; but it does dramatize Marston's distinctness as a young writer of satire. Certainly it had a place among his thoughts when he sat down to work on *Certain Satires* in 1598.

On March 30, 1598 the second part of Hall's *Virgidemiarum*, the three books of "Biting Satires," was entered in the Stationers' Register, the first three books of "Toothless Satires" having been entered in March of 1597.[27] Since Marston referred to the "Biting Satires" in his *Certain Satires*,[28] we may conclude that he did some of the work on *Certain Satires* between March of 1598 and

---

refer to the poem as the "Satira Nova" for the purpose of distinguishing it clearly. I shall keep Bullen's numbering, however, and refer to the final poem as "Satire XI."

[25] "Life," pp. 88, 89.

[26] See Satire I, 5–7, for a possible attack; Satire III, 111–120; Satire IX, 21–43; "Satira Nova" *passim;* and Satire XI, 104–121, 132–136.

[27] For these entries see *SR*, III, 82, 109.

[28] In ll. 13 and 14 of Satire II Marston alluded to the "biting rhymes" of "our modern Satire's sharpest lines," and in ll. 111–114 of the "Reactio" he may have had the following lines from the "Biting Satires" in mind:

> Ventrous *Fortunio* his farme hath sold,
> And gads to *Guiane* land to fish for gold. [IV, iii, 28, 29]

Marston's lines are:

> *Euge!* some gallant spirit, some resolvèd blood,
> Will hazard all to work his country's good,
> And to enrich his soul and raise his name,
> Will boldly sail unto the rich Guiane.

May 27, 1598, when *The Metamorphosis of Pygmalion's Image and Certain Satires* was entered in the Stationers' Register.[29] Of course he may have written large parts of *Certain Satires* before March of 1598 and may have simply added the sections alluding to the "Biting Satires" after their appearance. But if we take March 30, 1598 as the date after which Marston did at least some of the work on *Certain Satires* and take September 8, 1598, the date on which *The Scourge* was entered,[30] as a terminal date, we must conclude it likely that Marston did most of his work in verse satire, perhaps all of it (excepting the satire added to the second edition of *The Scourge* in 1599) during the five months between the end of March and the beginning of September. This work includes the ten satires from the first edition of *The Scourge* and part, if not all, of the five satires of *Certain Satires*. In all, this work runs to more than 2,600 lines.

In view of the probable volume of Marston's work during this period, the care and seriousness with which he executed it are significant. At first glance the contents and organization of *The Metamorphosis of Pygmalion's Image and Certain Satires* suggest that the volume was assembled hastily. Not only is "Pygmalion's Image" different in genre and style from the satires, but the satires themselves do not appear to cohere as a unit beyond the first three. These three satires trace an unmistakable line of development, beginning with the follies described in the epigraph, *Quaedam videntur, et non sunt* ("Certain things seem to be but are not"), continuing with the more serious offenses of *Quaedam sunt, et non videntur* ("Certain things are but do not seem to be"), and concluding with the vices of *Quaedam et sunt, et videntur* ("Certain things both are and seem to be"). Actually, the distinctions declared by these epigraphs are little more than quibbles, though the poems gradually deepen in tone as the speaker works himself into the role of the raging satirist. The

---

[29] *SR*, III, 116.   [30] *SR*, III, 125.

fourth poem, however, the "Reactio," is a personal attack on Hall that is only vaguely relevant to the first three; and the final poem, *Parva magna, magna nulla* ("Petty things are great, great things are nothing"), is hardly a satire at all. It is, instead, a didactic poem in which the thesis set forth in its title is expounded through illustrations from classical story. This heterogeneity has prompted critics to conclude that Marston threw together what he had on hand for the purpose of hurrying into print.[31] The point cannot be settled, of course, with any finality. To the extent that "Pygmalion's Image" and the satires of *Certain Satires* are dissimilar works, their dissimilarity can be used to support the claim. But the claim accounts for almost nothing; if a more compelling explanation of the structure of *Certain Satires* can be found, it must take precedence.

Certain features of the structure of *Certain Satires* suggest that it is neither simple nor carelessly planned. For one thing, the fact that the component poems are different in kind does not necessarily mean that the work lacks design. On the surface, it consists of three easily recognizable types of poems: Satires I through III are general satires; "Reactio" is a personal satire; and the last poem is a didactic poem. As we shall see, these types correspond precisely to the types constituting *The Scourge*. If by comparing *Certain Satires* and *The Scourge* we can infer good reasons for the specific placement of these poems within them, perhaps we shall discern a structural design where none has been suspected.

The Scourge consists of ten satires (eleven in the edition of 1599) and opens with a panoramic survey of satiric types like those found in Juvenal, Satire I, and in Donne, Satire I. This first poem is designed to illustrate its motto *Fronti nulla fides* ("There is no trusting to appearances"). Rapidly the poet's wrath mounts until he rejects philosophy, promises to tell the whole truth, and protests that humor is now impossible. In Satire II his theme is again the whole of society, but this time he surveys the subjects available to satire, illustrating the motto *Difficile est*

[31] Curtis' view is typical; see "Life," pp. 71–73.

Satyram non scribere ("It is hard not to write satire"). And in Satire III he completes his justification for writing satire by again surveying the satiric types to support the implication of the motto *Redde, age, quae deinceps risisti* ("Come tell me what did you laugh at next"), that the state of society is no laughing matter. Satire IV, *Cras* ("Tomorrow"), which completes the first of the three books, advances the moral intention of the work by documenting through *exempla* the thesis stated at the end of the straightforward harangue of the latter half of the satire, that tomorrow is too late to reform.

The remaining satires in *The Scourge*, excluding Satire VI, "Satira Nova," which was added in 1599, and Satire XI, which is another panoramic survey of types calculated to parallel Satire I, represent fuller developments of the major vices treated in the surveys of I, II, III. Satire V, *Totum in Toto* ("All in All"), illustrates the thesis that villainy dominates everything while virtue counts for nothing. Satire VII, "A Cynic Satire," answers the opening cry, "A man, a man, a kingdom for a man," by showing that there is none, that man has lost his distinguishing feature, reason. Satire VIII, *Inamorato Curio*, first illustrates through the usual *exempla* the descent of man to sensuality, then in straight exposition describes the loss of reason to sensuality, closing with an appeal to Synderesis, the spark of divinity and reason that once united man with the godhead. And Satire IX, "A Toy to mock an ape indeed," documents the implied thesis that society is a collection of foolish imitators or apes. Satire XI (Satire X in the original) completes the circle and the scourge by summarizing the wickedness of the age in a survey like that of Satire I and by closing on an appeal to young men to rejuvenate their souls, to recall reason, and to recover Synderesis.

Only Satire VI, *Hem Nosti'n* ("Ha! Do you know me?"), and "Satira Nova," both of which are personal satires like the "Reactio" of *Certain Satires*, seem to depart from this scheme of combining systematic scourging with moral exhortation; but even they, perhaps, were once integral in a way that modern readers find difficult to appreciate. Although in Satire VI the poet turns momentarily to personal injustices, a subject only loosely related to the central concern of the work, its placement at the mid-point in the discourse suggests that it was probably not just an extra poem that somehow had to be worked in but more likely a functional part.

Of all the possible functional parts defined by Renaissance rhetoricians, Satire VI most clearly resembles the structural digression. Quintilian, the source of so much critical theory at this time, had maintained "that this sort of excursion may be advantageously introduced, not only after the statement of the case, but after the different questions in it, all together or sometimes severally, when the speech is by such means greatly set off and embellished; providing that the dissertation aptly follows and adheres to what precedes, and is not forced in like a wedge, separating what was naturally united." [32] In *The Foundation of Rhetoric* (1563) Richard Rainolde incorporated this principle into his discussion of the oration called a "Commonplace," an oration that, with its purpose to exasperate the hearers against the accused and its characteristic "exaggeracion of reason," is not unlike a Renaissance satire. Rainolde's analysis of the twelve parts of this oration designated part seven as the digression.[33] In *The Garden of Eloquence* (1577) Henry Peacham repeated Quintilian: "The digressyon oughte alwayes to pertayne and agree to those matters that wee handle, and not to be straunge or farre distaunte from the purpose, also we muste haue a perfecte waye prouyded aforehande, that we maye goe forth aptelye, and making no longe taryaunce out, retourne in agayne cunninglye." [34] And in 1589 Puttenham confirmed that "it is wisdome for a perswader to tarrie conveniently and make his aboad as long as he may without tediousnes to the hearer." [35] Despite the inherent imprecision of

[32] Quintilian's *Institutes of Oratory*, trans. John Selby Watson (London, 1907), I, 301.

[33] (London), Fol. xxxiii^v–xxxvi^v.   [34] (London), Sig. U4.

[35] *Arte*, p. 233.

this device, it is not improbable that Marston had it in mind here. Clearly Satire VI deals with a subject on which he could "tarrie without tediousnes" and yet which is a sufficiently relevant "excursion" to cohere to what precedes and what follows. And although no such claims of calculation can be made for the "Satira Nova," since when added in 1599 it seems to have been an afterthought, even this addition was not merely tacked on. Instead, it was placed before Satire XI and, according to the technique usual for digressions, at a convenient distance from Satire VI.

If we can assume, then, that Satire VI and, later, the "Satira Nova" were calculated digressions, the structure of *The Scourge* becomes clear. The constituent poems divide themselves into three sustained attacks, culminating in didactic passages at the end of Satires IV, VIII, and XI. The first of the attacks, from I to III, is general, taking a panoramic view of society and its evils; the second, from V (omitting VI, a digression) to VIII, is more specific, dealing with the weightiest evils; and the third, from IX (omitting the "Satira Nova," another digression) to XI, is again general.

Moreover, if we go back to *Certain Satires* and assume that the "Reactio" was designed as a digression there, we find that a similar pattern asserts itself: the three satires represent the attack, "Reactio" the digression, and the final poem the didactic peroration. It is clear that these patterns do not perfectly correspond, and obviously they leave much to explain about these poems. But their outlines are sufficiently clear to indicate what Marston was about and to identify one of the ways in which he attempted to vest satire with what he felt to be its appropriate dignity. As satiric structures these poems were unique in his day.

In outline Marston's verse satires established the structural pattern that he was to experiment with in all his subsequent work in the satiric mode. In the main these poems are fashioned to arouse anger, a sense of incongruity, disproportion, and deformity, and a fear of moral chaos—or feelings that I shall designate collectively by the term "moral distress." The pattern of attack and exposure followed by reflection and moral exhortation traces a movement from moral distress to righteous contempt and resolution. Here this movement is roughhewn and relatively simple, and the passages of reflection and moral exhortation do not so much purge or resolve the feelings of moral distress as direct them to righteous indignation. But Marston apparently saw more in this structural pattern than at first glance meets the eye. In his plays he continued to experiment with it, polishing and enriching it as he acquired skill and sophistication, until in his best plays he achieved with a modified version of it a satiric expression that is impressive by any standards.

But Marston's performance in the verse satires and its relevance to his later work can be traced in even greater detail in the techniques that operate within the structural frames of these works. Like everyone else, Marston reveals himself in little as well as in important things. And in matters of artistic method, frequently the little things tell us as much as the important ones can of the artist that is to be.

The verbal style of the verse satires is, of course, as prominent as the satiric persona. In fact, so intricately are the two related that it is difficult not to see the style as a consequence of the persona's shifting moods. Yet when Marston talked about style, he restricted his remarks entirely—as did his fellow-satirists—to the harshness and obscurity of his persona's most violent speeches; he had nothing to say directly about the style of his philosophic passages. Since recent criticism has done the same, it is necessary, accordingly, to recall that the speaker in the satires is not always violent and that the language is not always harsh and obscure. It is important to recall this, not so that we may argue, finally, the presence of several styles in the satires, but so that we may recognize the considerable range of the style that at one extreme is conspicuously harsh and obscure.

In any of its modulations Marston's verbal style is well calculated to remind us that he was one of a group of young poets in revolt against the sweet, musical, but, in their opinion, vapid poetry of an older generation. Morris Croll has written extensively of this revolt in prose writing to show how its basic intellectual impulse to break out of tradition expressed itself in stylistic departures from the Ciceronian elaborateness so emphatically held a deterrent to thought.[36] In poetry as in prose its most common form is characterized by a striking concentration of language, by statements packed with action and meaning, by the "strong lines" and the masculinity of which Thomas Carew was so appreciative in his poem on Donne.[37] It was a style that stressed, as Bacon put it, matter over *copie* and that demanded intelligence and cultivation in its readers.[38] Of it Chapman had said, "In my opinion, that which being with a little endevour serched, ads a kinde of maiestie to Poesie; is better then that which euery Cobler may sing to his patch."[39] It is this common form of the style that we meet when Marston's persona is, momentarily, a fashionable young poet or a teacher-philosopher, a style not so harsh and obscure as concentrated, tight, and heavily accented. This example from "Cras" is typical:

[36] " 'Attic Prose' in the Seventeenth Century," *SP*, XVIII (1921), 79–128, and "Muret and the History of 'Attic' Prose," *PMLA*, XXXIX (1924), 254–309. See also George Williamson, *The Senecan Amble: A Study in Prose from Bacon to Collier* (London, 1948).

[37] *The Poems of John Donne*, ed. H. J. C. Grierson (London, 1912), I, 378–380. The pertinent passage reads:

> Thou hast redeem'd, and open'd Us a Mine
> Of rich and pregnant phansie, drawne a line
> Of masculine expression. . . .
> Our stubborne language bends, made only fit
> With her tough-thick-rib'd hoopes to gird about
> Thy Giant phansie, which had prov'd to stout
> For their soft melting Phrases. [ll. 37–53]

See also Arnold Stein's articles, "Donne's Harshness and the Elizabethan Tradition," *SP*, XLI (1944), 390–409, and "Donne's Obscurity and the Elizabethan Tradition," *ELH*, XIII (1946), 98–118, and George Williamson, "Strong Lines," *ES*, XVIII (1936), 152–159.

[38] Cf. Bacon's discussion of this distinction, *The Works of Francis Bacon*, ed. James Spedding (New York, 1864), VI, 120ff.

[39] "To Master Royden," *Poems*, p. 49.

If not today (quoth that Nasonian),
Much less to-morrow. "Yes," saith Fabian,
"For ingrain'd habits, dyed with often dips,
Are not so soon discoloured. Young slips,
New set, are easily mov'd and pluck'd away;
But elder roots clip faster in the clay." [*SV*, IV, 93–98]

In its extreme form (and satire provided the occasion for that extreme) it is a style that would be called harsh and obscure by any standard. Marston cultivated these qualities in a number of ways. To produce harshness he used long compound nouns, abrupt phrases, catalogues of epithets, elisions, combinations of plosive consonants, and extreme dislocations in the metric pattern. These techniques serve chiefly to pile up accented syllables and juxtapose tortuous combinations of sound. To blur the dramatic surface and the lines of exposition in such a way that they tend to obscurity, he frequently suppressed transitions, shifted from one speaker to another without clearly designating the shift, and used obscure mythological allusions, archaisms, and technical expressions borrowed from alchemy, casuistry, and scholasticism. Of course his conversational idiom justified in part his inconclusiveness and abruptness; but his apparent aim was not so much realism as a style expressive of "gall" and appropriate to the satiric persona at his most violent.

This is the style most widely met in the verse satires. An extreme example of it can be found in *The Scourge* in Satire I, the satire that Marston admittedly wrote to satisfy those of his readers who thought that satire should be very harsh and obscure:

Marry, God forefend! Martius swears he'll stab:
Phrygio, fear not, thou art no lying drab.
What though dagger-hack'd mouths of his blade swears
It slew as many as figures of years
Aquafortis eat in't, or as many more
As methodist Musus kill'd with hellebore
In autumn last; yet he bears that male lie
With as smooth calm as Mecho rivalry. [ll. 1–8]

But an example more typical of Marston's style throughout the satires can be chosen at random from the other poems. Satire VII, for example, begins

A man, a man, a kingdom for a man!
Why, how now, currish, mad Athenian?
Thou Cynic dog, see'st not the streets do swarm
With troops of men? No, no: for Circe's charm
Hath turn'd them all to swine. I never shall
Think those same Samian saws authentical:
But rather, I dare swear, the souls of swine
Do live in men. For that same radiant shine—
That lustre wherewith Nature's nature decked
Our intellectual part—that gloss is soiled
With staining spots of vile impiety,
And muddy dirt of sensuality.
These are no men, but apparitions
Ignes fatui, glowworms, fictions,
Meteors, rats of Nilus, fantasies,
Colosses, pictures, shades, resemblances. [ll. 1–16]

This passage offers a typical expression of the vexation and contempt at the heart of Marston's style. It illustrates how his indignation, however clearly stated, is also implied in the peculiar contortions and exertions of his language. It is this inner animosity that ultimately gives Marston's style at its best its undeniable authority.

To achieve packed, tightly knotted lines capable of ranging from cacophonous snarling to thundering argument he used even the more conventional elements of his verse in an unconventional way. Like his colleagues, he was suspicious of rhyme, if only because intricate rhyme schemes had been so popular with his predecessors. In "Ad rhythmum," a poem preceding Book II of *The Scourge,* he invites it to take a part in his poem, then characteristically threatens to expel it if it hampers his expression, for, as he says, "know my liberty / Scorns rhyming laws." His use of the decasyllabic couplet, accordingly, is distinctly free. Most of his lines are rhymed; some of them are not; and some of them achieve slightly discordant effects through consonantal or approximate vowel rhymes. His couplets, moreover, are not the basic units of his discourse. They are usually open couplets, at any point in which he begins and ends statements that often run on for several lines. It is not strange, then, that Marston's use of the couplet does not approach in complexity, polish, and subtlety the use to which Dryden and Pope later put it. His aim, clearly, was to sing a very different song. Nor is it strange, on the other hand, that he chose the decasyllabic couplet for his verse satires: even by his time it was a standard feature of satire. Chaucer, Spenser, Donne, Lodge, and Hall had used it before him.

In other respects, too, the originality of Marston's technical performance is sometimes difficult to pin down: frequently it consists in an innovative use of techniques with some kind of precedent in earlier satirists; sometimes it consists in a distinctly new technical strategy. Perhaps no feature of the satires tells us more about this originality than his aim to exalt the genre and the battery of devices by which he sought to do so. Before him, for example, Donne and Hall had been content to unify their individual satires by organizing them according to a single subject. Marston went after a much tighter unity by organizing each poem in terms of a controlling thesis. Usually, he stated or implied his thesis in the epigraph.[40] Such, for example, is clearly true of *The Scourge*, Satire I, where the thesis, *Fronti nulla fides*, is stated, and equally true of Satire III, where the thesis is implied in the epigraph *Redde, age, quae deinceps risisti*. But often, even after he had introduced the thesis in the epigraph, he restated it at some point in the poem, as he does, for example, in Satire V, *Totum in Toto*, when he says, "Well plainly thus, *Sleight, Force, are mighty things, / From which, much, (if not most) earths*

---

[40] See Satires I, II, III, and V (*CS*) and Satires I and II (*SV*), in all of which the thesis is stated in the epigraph. See Satires III, IV, V, VI, and XI (*SV*), in all of which the thesis is implied in the epigraph.

glory springs." [41] And when he did not state or imply the thesis in the epigraph, he usually stated it within the poem.[42] Among his satires, only the personal satires and Satire XI depart from the rule of organization by thesis. The material treated in the personal satires was obviously unsuited to such a method of organization, and the function of Satire XI as the concluding poem of the work, serving to draw together its separate strands, favored a unity of another kind.

The techniques by which Marston illustrated these theses, on the other hand, usually had precedents in the work of Gascoigne, Donne, Lodge, and Hall, and his originality consisted in combining them in satires governed by theses and in using them far more extensively than they had been used by his predecessors. Of all the satires written at the end of the sixteenth century, Marston's are easily the most dramatic, and much of their drama and vitality is traceable to his methods of illustrating a thesis through character sketches and *exempla.*

The more important of these two techniques is that of using character sketches to illustrate the thesis. In its simplest form this did not involve character sketches of any length: frequently he simply referred briefly, as Hall had done, to such known character types as Roscius or Grillus.[43] Sometimes, on the other hand,

---

[41] I have reverted here to the original, since Bullen did not print the italics. See Harrison's reprint, p. 54. For other examples of the restatement of the thesis see Satire V (*CS*), 138–148, and Satire IV (*SV*), 163–166.

[42] See Satire VII (*SV*), 7–16, and Satire VIII (*SV*), 110–117.

[43] This kind of reference is exemplified in Satire I (*SV*), where in a passage from Juvenal (II, 25–28), he alludes to several such figures:

> Mistagogus, what means this prodigy?
> When Hiadolgo speaks 'gainst usury,
> When Verres rails 'gainst thieves, Milo doth hate
> Murder, Clodius cuckolds, Marius the gate
> Of squinting Janus shuts? [ll. 24–28]

Marston and his fellow-satirists probably derived their knowledge of these figures not only from general classical studies, but more particularly from the copiously annotated Renaissance editions of the classical satirists. See,

he followed the example of his predecessors by caricaturing in a few quick strokes types like Sylenus, the old lecher who whispers he'll reform tomorrow (SV, IV, 33–38). The satires are peopled with such figures, many of them merely names with historical associations, many of them crudely drawn monstrosities. No doubt much of the difficulty that modern readers have with Marston results from their inability to assimilate them quickly.

In its more elaborate form this method of illustrating a thesis involved character sketches like those of the epigrammatists— sketches of considerable complexity. These sketches vary in manner of treatment: sometimes the characters are drawn in one fairly long passage; sometimes they are drawn bit by bit as they dart in and out of the poem. Martia, for example, the fashionable lady who wears a mask, a painted face, and a loose gown, who rides in a coach with a coat of arms, and who affects an angelic look, but who is no more than clothes and simpering affectation, is fully drawn in Satire VII (SV, 160–179). Martius, the man of war, on the other hand, accumulates characteristics with each appearance in the work. In Satire I (SV, 1–3) we learn that he is always threatening people and that he has a hacked sword attesting to many battles. In Satire IV (SV, 2–8) we learn that he steals from his soldiers' pay and keeps a prostitute in Whitefriars. And in Satire XI (SV, 52–73) we learn that he speaks constantly in the idiom of fencing, even when he is seducing his reluctant sweethearts. In addition to Martia and Martius, there are Castilio the courtier, Tubrio the braggart, Curio the dancing page, Luxurio the sensualist, and Mecho the cuckold, not including the various characters playing the roles of the grave official, the lecherous wife, the Puritan, the debauchee, and the amorist. Taken together, they constitute the dramatis personae dominating the foreground of the satirist's created world and offering him the most conspicuous targets for his criticism.

----

for example, *Junii Juvenalis Aquinatis Satyrographi opus*, ed. Joanne Britannico (Venice, 1548), and *Q. Horatii Flacci poetae venusini* (Venice, 1562).

It is this cast of satiric types, more than any other single feature of the satires, that vests the poems with their dramatic vitality. Marston's cast of satiric types is not just larger than those of his contemporaries; he has moved the types through the satires with narrative and semidramatic techniques that do much to animate them. Anticipating in many ways his later practice in the drama, he frequently employed the frame device of observing the types in action from some undefined point of vantage. Thus situated, the satirist shouts to them, "Come, Briscus, by the soul of compliment" (*CS*, I, 19), or talks to them as he talks to Tubrio in Satire I (*CS*) when Tubrio lies to him about just having come from the wars in the Netherlands, when actually he has just come from a brothel. Frequently, too, he used the device of observing the types and talking them over with Lynceus, the keen-sighted Argonaut, or one of his other confidants.[44] Indeed, he even gave speeches to Lynceus and to the satiric types from time to time.[45] The primary effect of all this interplay among characters is to animate poems, otherwise fairly strictly controlled by a thesis, with energy and movement rare in the satires of Marston's time.

Although less important than his use of satiric types, Marston's use of *exempla* to illustrate his theses is also symptomatic of the vitality of his satires. For the most part he drew the *exempla* from contemporary life, using such tales as his visit to the rooms of "inamorato Lucian" (*CS*, III, 51–74), the heartsick sonneteer, or his account of the backsliding of Luscus (*SV*, III, 34–52), the debauchee who has forsaken whores at his father's request but taken a Ganymede. But in Satire V (*CS*), as well as elsewhere, he drew *exempla* from classical story. In Satire V (*CS*) he illustrated the chaos of his age in a series of pictures reflecting the chaos on Olympus. Like the satiric types, these vignettes serve to enliven

---

[44] See Satire III (*SV*), 31, and Satire VII (*SV*), 17.

[45] See Satire VII (*SV*), 28–39, for a speech by Lynceus; Satire II (*CS*), 133–138, for a speech by Bruto the traveler; Satire III (*SV*), 11, for a short speech by Luxurio; and Satire VII (*SV*), 106, 110, for short speeches by Mavortian.

the discourse. Viewed more generally, they exemplify the purpose Marston never abandoned of integrating drama with didacticism, the texture of experience with reflection.

All in all, Marston's efforts in the verse satires are most profitably seen in the context of an almost pretentious aim to elevate and dignify this "new" genre. His multifaceted persona, his chameleon-like language, his battery of devices for exposing and ridiculing deformity, and his careful articulation of a constructive attitude toward it—all this is subsumed by the purpose of setting forth what Marston believed to be a mature response to the contemporary world. This response is extremely complex, as we shall see when Marston has improved on his means of communicating it. But even here, despite a strikingly roughhewn quality, we must conclude that he knew what he was about. The pieces fit, though they may rattle a bit: the parts cohere, though the coherence is undeniably difficult to grasp and difficult to hold.

At the center of this coherence, of course, is the constructive attitude so frequently developed explicitly in passages of straightforward exposition. Here Marston's ambition is most in evidence. Clearly, he wanted to combine the rigors of satire with the inspiration of moral philosophy, to balance the storm and stress of his destructive criticism with a sane view of it all.[46] To do this, he occasionally modulated his voice from the savage accents permitted by the satyr's mask to the calmer tones of the teacher-philosopher. In *The Scourge* he interrupted the flow of invective in this fashion at three points: in the latter half of Satire IV and at the end of Satires VIII and XI. At such times he is in every respect the moral philosopher, if a rather impatient one: he cites authorities, he refutes them, and he advances his own views. And, at the same time, he maintains the dominant dramatic character

---

[46] Marston may have derived the idea of using passages of moral exhortation from Persius or, even, Donne. See G. G. Ramsay (ed.), *Juvenal and Persius* (Loeb Classical Library; London, 1950), Satire II, 61ff., and Satire V; and *Poems* of Donne, I, 157, 158, ll. 69–110. But neither Persius nor Donne uses such passages widely.

of the work by permitting his opponents to speak for themselves and by refuting them as if they were standing before him.[47]

Curiously enough, he had a recent precedent for this didacticism in Lodge, who in Satire III of *A Fig for Momus* discoursed at length on the example that fathers should set for their sons.[48] But where Lodge's plea is practical, Marston's is rigorously theoretical; and the difference is significant. Marston's preference for theoretical argument is perfectly consistent with his view of the exalted function of the satirist. His purpose in all his work in satire was not simply to arouse to action but to represent fully what he and his admirers considered a mature, sophisticated attitude toward their world, an attitude typified by its satirical perspective on the world yet based on a solid theoretical foundation.

It is this purpose, finally, that explains the greater impressiveness of his literary task over those set by his fellow satirists. Literary causes alone cannot give an adequate picture of it. However necessary a study of precedents, decorums, and stylistic debts, such study can only illuminate aspects of this work; it cannot illuminate its coherence. In the same way, the combined roles of orphan poet and sharp-fanged satirist cannot explain all the activity of Marston as satirist. To do justice to the total role he was playing, we must now recognize that these poems, as well as the plays written later, were profoundly influenced by his philosophical convictions. The poems and plays as expressions of a complex way of confronting the world of his time cannot be grasped until we understand his personal version of Neo-Stoicism and its place in the total picture.

[47] See Satire IV (*SV*), 92–170.   [48] *Works of Lodge*, III, 34–38.

Chapter III

The Neo-Stoic

THE popularity of Neo-Stoicism among English intellectuals at the end of the sixteenth century is but a small part of the long and intricate chapter in intellectual history that traces the subversion of scholastic authority and the founding of modern rationalism. Throughout the sixteenth century the Aristotelian-Thomist orthodoxy had been under steady fire both in England and on the Continent. Its chief antagonists were the Puritans, with their insistence on simple criteria for truth, and the followers of Peter Ramus, with their disapproval of scholastic subtlety. But even this opposition was only a symptom of a wider, if less concerted, suspicion and insecurity. The revival of such older systems of thought as Platonism, occult philosophy, and Stoicism testified dramatically to the flux and instability of intellectual life. And if the skepticism of a Raleigh or a Montaigne marked out the path of greatest subversion, the way that soon led to the science of Francis Bacon, it was but one of the paths taken. The chief result of all this activity was that scholastic authority tottered, though of course it did not fall. Despite the intellectual unrest, Hooker could still write his *Laws of Ecclesiastical Polity* in the last two decades of the century, and more or less eclectic expressions of orthodox thought continued to emerge from all sides.[1]

In some quarters, however, the effects of the cumulative criticism of orthodox thought were severe. For a Raleigh, a Fulke Greville, a Montaigne, or a Bacon the whole question of truth— of what it is and of how it can be known—was reopened and variously resolved. From the modern point of view their libertinism was undoubtedly the most fertile of the intellectual positions adopted. But it was certainly not the only position, and it was probably not the most popular in their time. Despite crucial differences, libertinism was in many respects similar to the Neo-Stoicism that was more widely cultivated under a less distinguished leadership. Both movements embraced the stylistic aims of anti-Ciceronianism; both encouraged the literary realism that F. P. Wilson has called "an attempt to express and enhance elapsing moments of an everchanging Nature rather than the idea of Nature as a perennial reality";[2] and both ended with private philosophies rather than a single system of thought. Often in particular men, indeed, especially when, like Montaigne, they are not given to systematic thought, it is exceedingly difficult to disentangle the Neo-Stoic from the libertine strain. That Neo-Stoicism was the more popular is probably best explained by the great need for a practical moral philosophy among those most sensitive to the intellectual unrest. Of all the systems of thought and intellectual disciplines then in vogue, it was the best constituted to fill that need easily.

Moral philosophy had been the dominant intellectual interest of the sixteenth century, just as it was to be of the seventeenth— despite the new science. For this reason and others, when the

[1] This phase in intellectual history has been widely discussed. For an excellent, relatively brief discussion of it see Meyrick H. Carré, *Phases of Thought in England* (Oxford, 1949), pp. 178–279. Croll's "Muret" is also very useful.

[2] *Elizabethan and Jacobean* (Oxford, 1945), p. 26.

John Marston, Satirist

need for a fresh approach to ethics developed, Stoicism was the ripest of the classical moral philosophies for revival. Indirectly, it had long been a part of classical studies. Such Stoic writers as Seneca and Plutarch were always widely read, and even Cicero, the parade ground for so much of Latin study, was steeped in the spirit, if not in the letter, of the Stoic system. Renaissance England did not have, it is true, an Antoine Muret or a Justus Lipsius, scholars who worked actively to rehabilitate the Roman Stoics in Continental universities, but the effects of this rehabilitation were felt in England and are still traceable in the list of classical and contemporary Stoic works published there in the sixteenth century.[3] Stoicism, moreover, was by its very nature ideally adapted to fill the void left in many quarters by the subversion of scholastic authority. It offered a simple, tough-minded ethic and a rigorous, privately derived discipline. And despite its inner coherence and self-sufficiency, it was of all classical moral systems the closest and most adaptable to Christianity. Thomas James, the Curator at the Bodleian at the end of the century and the translator of Guillaume du Vair's *The Moral Philosophie of the Stoicks* (1598), said: "No kinde of philosophie is more profitable and neerer approching unto Christianitie . . . then the philosophie of the Stoicks," and this sentiment was shared by virtually all the Neo-Stoics of the time.[4] Classical Stoicism offered the advantages, accordingly, of independent thought along lines that avoided the taint of heresy and of a mode of private salvation that was readily adaptable to the great public commonplaces. With these recommendations it became the nucleus of the variant forms of the Neo-Stoic thought in the late Renaissance.

Classical Stoicism rests solidly on the premise that existence is

[3] In a prefatory section to his edition of Sir John Stradling's translation of Lipsius' *Two Bookes of Constancie, 1594* (New Brunswick, N.J., 1939), pp. 13–32, Rudolph Kirk has surveyed the interest in Stoic writers old and new in terms of translations of the ancient and modern Stoics in the Renaissance, particularly in the sixteenth century.

[4] Edited by Rudolph Kirk (New Brunswick, N.J., 1951), p. 3. Stradling makes essentially the same point, *Constancie*, p. 67.

governed by a rational design. The highest and the best life for human beings—creatures uniquely endowed with a rational faculty—is a life in accordance with that design, or a life in accordance with nature. This concept of the best life was variously understood by the earliest formulators of the philosophy, Zeno, Cleanthes, and Chrysippus, as well as by later Stoics, and it was variously adjusted to a metaphysical foundation. But in general it meant a life directed by right reason, a life reconciled to the end of all life. Right reason, they held, could be taught or cultivated. At its best it is wisdom, and in its progress toward wisdom it manifests itself in the individual's ability to discriminate between those matters that affect the good life, for good or bad, and those that are irrelevant to it. This capacity to distinguish and, subsequently, to choose consists in recognizing first that the rational creature can operate rationally only in those matters over which he has control. War, famine, death in the family, treachery in others—these are matters over which the philosopher has no control and toward which he, accordingly, cultivates a humane indifference. But when choice can frustrate or contribute to the perfection of the individual as rational creature, here the philosopher disciplines himself in desire and aversion, acceptance and rejection. The sign of perfection is the rational control that can be rationally achieved. It begins with the ability to receive impressions (*phantasiae*) rightly, to order the external world in terms of its relevance to perfection. It ends in the triumph of private serenity.

The Renaissance derived this doctrine from many sources, but chiefly from Seneca and Epictetus. From Seneca it derived the intellectual temper, the style, and the copious illustrations of his moral essays and plays. From Epictetus it derived, in addition to these, the theoretical system. Neither, it is significant, can be called a systematic philosopher. Seneca's discursive explorations of anger, providence, clemency, and the like, are often heedless of consistency. And Epictetus, though he focused constantly on the basic tenets of Stoic ethics, paid very little attention to its metaphysical foundations. Both are pre-eminently moral philosophers, practical to the core, with whom the Renaissance had few occasions to be at variance on metaphysical questions, if only because they had neglected them. Epictetus' ideas, moreover, were especially compatible with Christian thought. More than any other Stoic thinker, Epictetus emphasized the divinity at the heart of the universal design. For him existence was governed, not simply by a rational plan, but by a rational plan expressive of an all-wise Providence; in his view the achievement of personal perfection consisted in recognizing the divine will in the rational design and in reconciling the private will to it. In the discourse prefaced by the question, "How must we struggle against our external impressions?" for example, he is nigh indistinguishable from a gifted Christian preacher:

Make it your wish finally to satisfy your own self, make it your wish to appear beautiful in the sight of God. Set your desire upon becoming pure in the presence of your pure self and of God.[5]

No less than his creed, then, Epictetus' way of formulating Stoic ideas undoubtedly had a distinctive appeal for the Renaissance Christian in search of a private ethic. It is not surprising that his *Discourses* and especially his *Manual* furnished the theoretical core of Neo-Stoicism.

In accommodating pagan Stoic thought to Christianity, of course, the Renaissance predictably adapted and modified it, with the consequence that no two of the several versions of Neo-Stoicism that resulted were identical. Justus Lipsius and Guillaume du Vair, its two most important expositors, were clearly in agreement on basic matters, yet clearly different on such subjects as suicide or in the attention given to logic and physics, on which matters Lipsius was far more thorough. In general, the Renaissance assimilation of pagan Stoicism involved a characteristic dissociation of the elements of Stoic thought, a tendency to emphasize ethical theory and to ignore metaphysics.[6] Lipsius is the glaring exception to this generalization, but even he was hard pressed to identify the divine fire of Stoic metaphysics with God and to set aside the Stoic concept of a pantheistic or immanent deity. With much sifting, sorting, and juggling of pagan and early Christian authorities he succeeded, it is true, though not without reserving for himself the right to set aside, categorically, anything hopelessly at variance with Christian ideas. Most Neo-Stoic writers did not attempt so difficult an undertaking; most simply restricted themselves to ethical theory and modified the pagan legacy in the light of Christian values. The Neo-Stoicism that emerged in any of the several slightly different forms was, in Zanta's phrase, *"un stoïcisme très adouci."* As a moral philosophy it was far less austere and severe than its pagan progenitor. Certain passions—like the love of God and pity—were, it allowed, not only utterly consistent with God's word and our nature but indispensable to human perfection in the Christian view of it.

In England this thought seems for the most part to have been imported from the Continent. Although Stoic writers had a considerable vogue at court and in educated circles and although it is possible to see the dim outlines of a Neo-Stoic group in the 1580's and 1590's in the activities of Sir John Stradling and Thomas James at Oxford, England produced no Neo-Stoic theorist of note. The significant accomplishments of Stradling and James were their translations of Lipsius and Du Vair. These translations were key events against a backdrop of activity that also produced translations of Conrad Lycosthène, Pierre de la Primaudaye, Pierre Boaistuau, and Montaigne, as well as numerous translations of Seneca and at least one of Epictetus.[7] But the translations

---

[6] Léontine Zanta, *La Renaissance du Stoïcisme au XVIe siècle* (Paris, 1914), pp. 29–31.

[7] A brief list of these translations would include: by Seneca, *The Forme and Rule of Honest lyuynge,* trans. Robert Whyttyngton (London, 1546),

are probably only a symptom of the activity and interest that
doubtless embraced as well the far more numerous untranslated
Continental works and Latin editions of the classical works.[8]
When Marston entered Oxford in February of 1591/2, the university world seems to have been rife with opportunities to learn
what the Neo-Stoics were about. Certainly by the time Marston
had committed himself to the fashionable literati of the Inns of
Court, he had evolved a personal version of Neo-Stoicism in every
respect congruent with the literary and intellectual aims of that
group.

It is the tempering and directing influence of Neo-Stoicism in
almost every facet of Marston's work that justifies our attention
to it. Marston was neither an original nor a particularly forceful
thinker. But he seems to have been widely read among the Stoics
and Neo-Stoics; and his personal synthesis of Stoic and Christian
ideas, however diversely derived, was integral to his practice as a
writer. His considerable debt to Seneca and Montaigne has long
been recognized. One of the most striking features of the plays is
that before 1603 they are freighted with quotations and parallel
passages from Seneca, while after 1603 they are full of allusions
to Florio's Montaigne. But his debt to Epictetus and to others,
though far more elusive, is probably more profound. He does not,
as far as I know, quote Epictetus anywhere; in fact he only briefly
acknowledged having read him by signing *Certain Satires* with
the name "Epictetus" and by twice alluding to him in such a way
as to suggest that Epictetus was for him something of a model or

---

A frutefull worke . . . Called the Myrrour or Glasse of Maners, trans.
Robert Whyttyngton (London, 1547), *The Remedyes agaynst all casuall
chaunces*, trans. Robert Whyttyngton (London, 1547), *Seven Books of
Benefyting*, trans. Arthur Golding (London, 1578); by Epictetus, *The
Manual*, trans. J. Sanford (London, 1567); by Lipsius, *Constancie* and
Six bookes of politickes or civil doctrine, trans. William Jones (London,
1594); and by Du Vair, *The Moral Philosophie*. . . .

   [8] For the many translations of Stoic and Neo-Stoic works into French,
see Zanta, *Stoïcisme*, pp. 129–147.

guide.[9] The conformation of his thought, however, suggests a heavy intellectual debt, not just to Epictetus, but to several such guides to whom he never alluded.

Like Lipsius and Du Vair, Marston probably looked first to Epictetus on matters of theory, though he could hardly have stopped there. Of course Marston at no point offered a carefully reasoned, step-by-step exposition of his philosophy; but his extremely precise, indeed for a poet highly technical, treatment of basic concepts strongly implies that he was familiar with contemporary as well as classical theorists. It was doubtless from his contemporaries that he derived the conceptual machinery for his personal adjustment of Stoic and Christian ideas. Actually, we have no concrete proof that he knew even the work of Lipsius and Du Vair. Since they were so highly influential, so readily accessible, and so very authoritative on both the concepts and the terminology that form the nucleus of Marston's thought, however, it is highly likely that he did, and highly likely that he also knew others about whom speculation at this point would lead us too far into detail.

Certainly Marston's wider debt declares itself immediately in any systematic account of his thought. He accepted entirely the classic Stoic postulates that nature is governed by a rational design and that human fulfillment consists in the perfection of the rational faculty for the purposes of conformity to that design. His personal view of the rational faculty and of its relations to the divine plan, however, owed much to Christian concepts and to Neo-Stoic modifications of classical Stoicism. Central to his thought was the concept of synteresis, or the doctrine of the spark. In Neo-Platonic and Christian mystical tradition, as well as in

[9] *SV*, "Proemium in Librum Secundum":

> O Epictetus, I do honour thee,
> To think how rich thou wert in poverty!

The Fawn, "To the Equal Reader": "My bosom friend, good Epictetus, makes me easily to contemn all such men's malice: since other men's tongues are not within my teeth, why should I hope to govern them?"

the Stoics and Neo-Stoics who troubled to examine metaphysical foundations, God is defined as a fire that was variously equated with spirit, soul, mind, and reason. In his *Physiologia* Lipsius puts it this way:

God is a craftsmanlike Fire proceeding methodically to create the world, and containing within itself all the seminal reasons; then in accordance with these, everything is constructed by Fate.[10]

The concept of synteresis, a term derived by Marston from the Christian mystics, though it also occurs in Aquinas with a different meaning, posits that some vestige of this fire or divinity resides in man in the form of a spark. This spark was described by the mystics as the "apex of the soul," the "natural will toward God," or "the remnant of the sinless state before the fall." [11] For them it was not just reason, but the best form of it—the highest reason. In Lipsius and Marston it was more loosely the rational faculty at its best, that faculty in man that is divine, that can be identified in spirit, soul, mind, and reason. Marston variously describes it, collapsing characteristically all distinction between mind and soul, as the "intellectual / Compact of fire all celestial, / Invisible, immortal, and divine" (*SV*, VIII, 189–191), the "spark of intellectual" (*SV*, VIII, 81), the "Boundless, discursive apprehension" (*SV*, IX, 209), the "cognisance" (*SV*, VII, 202), and the rational soul (*SV*, VII, 66, 67). To this faculty he refers in his appeals to synteresis ("Return, return, sacred Synderesis"). Through this faculty man achieves perfection and communion with God.

To some the suggestion that Marston held a firm faith in human perfection may seem wildly improbable. Surely his frequently sordid dramatic surfaces seem unsuitable for the expression of such a faith. But as a Neo-Stoic, Marston was in an emphatically

[10] Quoted by Jason Lewis Saunders, *Justus Lipsius, The Philosophy of Renaissance Stoicism* (New York, 1955), p. 127.

[11] Dean Inge has a full discussion of the term's history: William Ralph Inge, *Christian Mysticism* (London, 1899), pp. 359, 360. The term is usually spelled "synteresis," though Marston spells it "Synderesis."

idealist tradition. Epictetus wrote of "the invincible man, he whom nothing outside the sphere of his moral purpose can dismay." [12] Guillaume du Vair wrote of a nature that

hath prouided a rich storehouse of all good things, and inclosed it in our minds: let vs then but stretch forth the hands of our will, and we shall take as much as we will. For if the will of man bee well guided and ordered, it will turne all things to her good.[13]

To understand Marston's aims and to appreciate fully the nature of his violence, we must recognize that he, too, called men "disguised gods" (SV, II, 25), that, even as he polished devices to intensify his expression of fury, he believed in the supremacy of the mind. The verse satires are laced with direct and indirect expressions of this idealism; the plays, particularly *Antonio's Revenge* and *Sophonisba* set it forth even more prominently. But the four short poems that Marston wrote for Sir Robert Chester's *Love's Martyr* (1601), that curious work for which Shakespeare, Jonson, and Chapman also wrote poems, best represent his faith in the potential of man. These poems comprise "A Narration and Description of a most exact wondrous Creature, arising out of the Phoenix and the Turtle Dove's ashes," a "Description of this Perfection," a sonnet "To Perfection," and a hymn on perfection. In the first poem the wondrous creature, "th' extracture of Divinest essence, / The soul of Heaven's laboured quintessence," emerges from the fire to prompt the poet to attempt a description. In the second the poet falters before the task of defining "Perfection blessed." In the third he turns to the reality of imperfection and justifies it as a foil to "this Rareness." [14] And in

---

[12] *Discourses*, I, 127. See also I, 49, 283, 355.

[13] *Moral Philosophie*, p. 59.

[14] The whole poem deserves to be quoted, if only to support the claim that Marston could treat "deformity" and "monstrous issues" with moderation when he chose not to operate within the decorums of Renaissance satire.

> Oft have I gazèd with astonish'd eye
>   At monstrous issues of ill-shapèd birth,
>   When I have seen the midwife to old Earth,
> Nature, produce most strange deformity.   [*cont. on p. 62*]

the last he acknowledges the impossibility of his task by recognizing that perfection is essentially intangible: it is not a creature at all, but a state of mind or soul that is achieved only when the mind or soul has, in Marston's phrase, "No suburbs," when "all is mind." The passionate concern of these poems with perfection is no freak. It was perfectly consistent with, indeed indispensable to, every important conviction Marston held. As a rule Marston was not, it is true, a rhapsodic idealist, though he again approached this intensity in *Sophonisba,* and he duplicated it with less conviction for the occasion of *The Ashby Entertainment.* But his idealism operates continuously in his work to temper and direct not only his didactic purpose but also his derision and contempt.

Far more prominent in his satires, of course, is Marston's concern with imperfection—with the evidences of it and the reasons and remedies for it. Following the classical Stoics, he traced man's failure primarily to that abuse of the mind that reveals itself characteristically in mishandling external impressions or mishandling sense data. Typically, this failure involves, first, neglecting to distinguish between what can and cannot be controlled by

---

So have I marvell'd to observe of late
  Hard-favor'd feminines so scant of fair,
  That masks so choicely shelter'd of the air,
As if their beauties were not theirs by fate.

But who so weak of observation,
  Hath not discern'd long since how virtues wanted,
  How parsimoniously the Heavens have scanted
Our chiefest part of adoration?

But now I cease to wonder, now I find
  The cause of all our monstrous penny-shows;
  Now I conceit from whence wit's scarcety grows,
Hard favor'd features, and defects of mind.

  Nature long time hath stor'd up virtue, fairness,
  Shaping the rest as foils unto this Rareness.

reason and, second, neglecting to attribute values with the aim of life, the perfection of rationality, clearly in view. In general, it consists in man's bondage of what Marston calls "seemings," "resemblances," "Protean forms."

In Marston's England all discussion of this view of corruption was dominated by certain technical terms and figurative expressions to which Marston fell a willing heir and which significantly conditioned his discourse. Of the technical terms, none was more central to discussion than the word "Opinion." [15] For the Neo-Stoics, "Opinion" meant not simply what most people think but false impressions, or sense impressions that have not been corrected by reference to the "design." Stradling's translation of Lipsius defines it as an "impure commixtion," a *"vaine image and shadow of reason,"* and associated it with the contrary of fire—earth—the normal source of sense impressions.[16] In Thomas James's translation of Du Vair it is that which "taketh occasion to band her selfe against reason," "an imagination . . . that vexeth and tormenteth vs more then the things themselues." [17] Sir William Cornwallis accounted for the supremacy of counterfeit over true virtue by explaining that "the labour of most men now adayes is not to obtaine trueths, but opinions warrant." [18] And Everard Guilpin could have been echoing Marston when he wrote

> Oh that mens thoughts should so degenerate,
> Being free borne, t'admit a slauish state:
> They disclaime Natures manumission,
> Making themselues bond to opinion.[19]

[15] See Peter Ure's excellent article on the meaning and currency of this term during this period in "A Note on 'Opinion' in Daniel, Greville and Chapman," *MLR*, XLVI (1951), 331–338.

[16] *Constancie*, p. 82.   [17] *Moral Philosophie*, pp. 103, 95.

[18] *Discourses upon Seneca the Tragedian* (1601), reprinted with an Introduction by Robert Hood Bowers (Gainesville, Fla., 1952), pp. B4, B4ᵛ.

[19] *Skialetheia*, D7ᵛ. The whole of this satire, "Satyra sexta," deals with Opinion

It is not unlikely that the currency of this idea had much to do with the far-flung interest at this time in seeming and appearances, whether that interest is met in Bacon's "Idols" or Shakespeare's plays. But for the present it suffices that in Marston's satire Opinion is the prime source of human error and the principal sustainer of corruption.

In the satires Opinion appears under many guises. It is unmistakable in Marston's practice of calling his characters "shades," "shadows," "seemings," "fictions," "apparitions," "resemblances." Not only are these "Protean forms" counterfeit men, but they also advertise false values to the world. It is no less clear in a number of the theses controlling separate poems, in, for example, the stated thesis of *Certain Satires*, I, *Quaedam videntur, et non sunt* ("Certain things seem to be but are not"), or in the thesis of *The Scourge*, I, *Fronti nulla fides* ("There is no trusting to appearances"). But these outcroppings of the idea are only reflections of a more fundamental fact. More than anything else, it is Marston's view of Opinion and of its corrupting influence that controls his fictional world. Not just the satiric types, but the murky grotesqueness, the chimeric nightmarishness of his atmosphere, proceed directly from his vision of a world sick with Opinion. In the "Satira Nova," the satire dedicated to Guilpin and added to the second edition of *The Scourge,* he defines this vision fairly precisely:

> "Opinion mounts this froth unto the skies
> Whom judgment's reason justly vilifies." [ll. 43–44]

> .   .   .   .   .

> "Shame to Opinion, that perfumes his dung,
> And streweth flowers rotten bones among!
> Juggling Opinion, thou enchanting witch!
> Paint not a rotten post with colours rich."
> But now this juggler, with the world's consent,
> Hath half his soul; the other, compliment;
> Mad world the whilst. [ll. 59–65]

Whether at this time Marston felt that *The Scourge* needed such a statement or whether he was simply taking advantage of the occasion to articulate the view clearly, it is difficult to say. In any event, the passage underscores what was already clear, that in Marston's view Opinion was the major obstacle to human fulfillment. It is to this meaning of the term that we must turn, of course, to gauge the irony of Marston's allusions "To the World's Mighty Monarch, Good Opinion."

It is with Marston's full assent, then, that the hero of *Antonio's Revenge* says, "Most things that morally adhere to souls, / Wholly exist in drunk opinion" (IV, i, 29ff.). Yet it would be a mistake to conclude that Marston's view of corruption ended with this perception. Second to Opinion, though far less prominent as a villain, was Detraction, that subverter of good works and honest programs, that frustrater of positive progress toward perfection. Actually, Marston dwelt on Detraction chiefly in passages suspected of topical application, passages where he seems to have been attacking Hall and others for their efforts in criticism. But the particularity of his attacks should not obscure the seriousness of the activity in his mind. Whatever personal animosity he may have felt toward the individuals involved, and however unfair some of his charges may seem to us, it is clear that Detraction was for him, like Opinion, a perverter of the purposes of nature. Just as he had dedicated his first book to "Good Opinion," he "presented" his second "To Detraction," that "Foul canker of fair virtuous action, / Vile blaster of the freshest blooms on earth." In this dedicatory poem, indeed, he links the two, as if to accord them equal roles:

> True judgment slight regards Opinion,
> A spritely wit disdains Detraction.

The linkage is, of course, misleading. Detraction does not loom so prominent as Opinion, and it does not enter so intricately into Marston's analysis of evil. Yet it is an influential element in his thought, one that we must take into account to extend properly the dimensions of his personal attacks and to recognize the just complexity of what critics have long dismissed as Marston's competitive spleen.

Apparently Marston's concept of Detraction was original with him: he had no clear precedent for it in the thinkers on whom he drew or in the earlier satirists. Such was patently not true, however, of most of the key images and metaphors with which he filled out his paradigm of the human condition. To develop his vision of a world writhing in the grips of Opinion and Detraction, and, even more important, to represent that world so that Opinion and Detraction would seem natives in it rather than visitors artfully added to it, he borrowed certain figurative expressions from his Neo-Stoic sources and drew heavily on the metaphoric potential of such central terms in the Stoic metaphysics as fire and earth.

The Neo-Stoic view of man's relation to God, for example, was frequently explained in terms of the analogous relationship between a fountain and a plant. According to Du Vair,

the strongest and chiefest affection of man, ought to be accounted that which ioyneth vs together with the author and fountaine of all good, to wit, godlines: for by it a man is reunited and substantiallie ingrafted in his first cause, as being the roote which keepeth him . . . in his full perfection: but contrarily, being separated from it, withereth and drieth away incontinently.[20]

And Lipsius argued:

As the Marigold and other flowers are by nature alwayes enclined towards the sunne: so hath Reason a respect vnto God, and to the fountaine from whence it sprang. It is resolute and immoueable in a good purpose . . . : the fountaine & liuely spring of wholsome counsell & sound judgement.[21]

[20] *Moral Philosophie*, pp. 109, 110. See also p. 128.
[21] *Constancie*, p. 81.

Marston borrowed this analogy intact and extended it so that he could treat in detail, not just the flow of sustenance from fountain to plant, but also the stoppage of flow. In the satires this vital connection is maintained by conduits or pipes extending between the "souls of men" and "that great soul." Marston focused, of course, on the failure of this connection—the clogging, the pollution, the accumulation of slime that broke the contact and frustrated reason. Toward the end of Satire VII in *The Scourge* he developed the figure explicitly, if rather tentatively and a bit grudgingly:

> Sure I ne'er think those axioms to be true,
> That souls of men from that great soul ensue,
> And of his essence do participate
> As 'twere by pipes; when so degenerate,
> So adverse in our nature's motion
> To his immaculate condition,
> That such foul filth from such fair purity,
> Such sensual acts from such a Deity,
> Can ne'er proceed. But if that dream were so,
> Then sure the slime, that from our souls do flow,
> Have stopp'd those pipes, by which it was convey'd,
> And now no human creatures, once disray'd
> Of that fair gem.
> Beast's sense, plants' growth, like being as a stone;
> But out, alas! our cognisance is gone.

Elsewhere he treated the figure rather more tangentially, though more positively, in numerous images that assume its rationale, but do not develop it. Clearly the whole rationale is meant to operate when he calls upon "Synderesis" to "Inspire our trunks" (*SV*, VIII, 212), or when he promises to cleanse with a flood or a river (*SV*, "Proemium Tertium," 18, 19), or when he speaks of "world-arteries . . . soul-infected / With corrupt blood" (*SV*, III, 160, 161). It should also be noticed, however, that the figure is distinctly operative when he uses the term "purge." Finally, it

is the conduit-figure that gives the idea of purge so consistent
a place in Marston's thought. As a satirist, he conceived it his
function to cleanse the conduits of connection, to re-establish the
contact with divinity so necessary to a proper cultivation of the
mind.

But the conduit-figure is only one of the many images and
metaphors which Marston borrowed or for which he found suggestions in Neo-Stoic discourse. It is particularly important because of its central position in the complex system of figurative
language at work in the satires. It localizes the meaning of all
the images of pollution, just as it, in turn, is enriched in meaning by the inevitable association between most forms of pollution and the traditional fire-earth opposition in Stoic metaphysics.
This opposition, too, is important enough to linger on for a
moment. Lipsius' discussion of it gives some indication of the
secondary meanings involved when "earth" or its near equivalents
occur in Marston's representations of stoppage.

First you are not ignorant that man consisteth of two parts, Soule and
Body. That being the nobler part, resembleth the nature of a spirit
and fire: the base is compared to the earth. These two are ioyned together, but yet with a iarring concord. . . . The earth aduanceth it
selfe aboue the fire, and the dirty nature aboue that which is divine.
Herehence arise in man dissentions, stirs, & continual conflict of these
parts warring together. The captains are REASON and OPINION.[22]

Lipsius' description of the ascendancy of earth as a kind of be-
fouling was, of course, exactly how Marston saw it. All his noxious
variations on scum, filth, and slime are essentially variations on
the earth that is eternally at war with fire, the earth that stops
up the conduits to God. He speaks of "leprous filths," of "soul-
polluting beastliness," of the "scum" that "fatally / Entombs the
soul's most sacred faculty." Not often, but occasionally, he sets
these images against the "celestial fire" that Prometheus "Did

---

[22] *Constancie*, p. 80. See also Cornwallis, *Discourses*, C7ᵛ.

steal from heaven, therewith to inspire / Our earthly bodies with a senseful mind" or "that same radiant shine— / That lustre wherewith Nature's nature decked / Our intellectual part." But even when he does not, it is safe to conclude that the opposition is assumed. Apparently, we should notice, Marston was little troubled by the difficulty of having fiery and liquid purges operating on the same side in the struggle.

Far less consistent with the key figure of conduits, though derived as it is from Neo-Stoic discourse, is the fire-air opposition. Even in Lipsius this opposition was more rhetorical than metaphysical. For the most part it was not so significant as it was convenient to clarify the place of Opinion in the process of degeneration. In distinguishing between "constancie," (i.e., firmness) and "obstinacie," Lipsius says of the obstinate:

For they can hardlie be pressed downe, but are verie easily lifted vp, not unlike to a blown bladder, which you cannot without much adoe thrust vnder water, but is readie to leape vpwards of it selfe without helpe. Euen such is the lighthardiness of those men, springing of pride and too much estimation of them selues, and therefore from OPINION.[23]

Opinion, accordingly, puffs up the soul and makes it intractable. As Marston says in *The Scourge* (II, 14–18),

> Loose conscience is free
> From all conscience, what else hath liberty?
> As't please the Thracian Boreas to blow,
> So turns our airy conscience to and fro.

Marston's representation of air or wind as still another antagonist to fire, but, more specifically, as a metaphorical base for his representations of Opinion's influence is widespread in the satires. It enters elusively but distinctly into all his numerous uses of words like "airy," "windy," "puffy," "spongy," and the like. In *The*

---

[23] *Constancie*, pp. 79, 83. Cf. Guilpin, *Skialetheia*, "Satyra Quinta."

Scourge, IV (1. 4) Curio is a "windy bubble"; in Satire VII (1. 58) Silenus is "but a sponge"; in "In Lectores" the parade of satiric types is a "fantastic troop / Of puffy youths." Hence in "To Detraction" (ll. 13, 14) Marston protests, "My spirit is not puft up with fat fume / Of slimy ale," and in *The Scourge,* II (ll. 1–3) he screams,

> I cannot hold, I cannot, I, endure
> To view a big-womb'd foggy cloud immure
> The radiant tresses of the quick'ning sun.

Marston's vision of a world gone mad is in part of a world inflated by the gas of Opinion, of creatures bobbing in a wild inane. That this image is quite distinct from the conduit-idea need not, I think, trouble us. Either Marston did not demand a tight consistency of all the members of his figurative system or he was working with a more subtle view of the four elements than appears plainly in his work.

Yet the pervasiveness of these metaphors and of still others insists that nothing less than a system of figures is at work in the poems. Some metaphors can be neatly related to others; some stand by themselves. But all relate integrally to the central perception of a world corrupted by Opinion and Detraction, and all serve to clarify and particularize that perception. Although images of darkness are not so frequent as we might expect, they stand in a nice relationship to the fire everywhere so important. In *The Scourge,* II (ll. 12, 13) Marston attacks the "fusty world" because it makes "Jehova but a coverture / To shade rank filth." A bit later, the "dusky night" of sin is equivalent to a dark night of the soul. In the same way, images of corpulence relate neatly to the images of inflation. Corpulence is equated with degeneracy. With evidence of "fat-fed luxury on all sides" Marston cannot resist administering purges, surely not "When to be huge, is to be deadly sick" (*SV,* II, 118), "When inundation of luxuriousness / Fats all the world with such gross beastliness" (*SV,* II, 140, 141). Such images operate with a certain ambiguity, it is true: now they seem to refer to Opinion and its tendency to puff up, now to the cloacal breakdown in the conduits. But always they serve to fill out the picture of corruption, and they succeed because of the ultimate coherence of that picture.[24]

Of the prominent images and metaphors in the satires, only those dealing with effeminacy serve to embolden the central perception without clear reference to any of the central ideas. Effeminacy is a visible sign of the perversion of nature in the satires. It proceeds from Opinion, and in Marston's mind it could easily have been part of the opposition between masculinity and femininity that was commonplace in alchemy and astrology, where these qualities were respectively associated with fire and earth. Marston hinted at this broader context in the sonnet "To Perfection," when he associated "deformity" with "hard-favoured feminines." It would be rash, however, to push all this too far: the poems do not readily bear out such associations, and for Marston's purposes they are hardly necessary. The central subject of *The Scourge*, VIII, effeminacy is widely encountered in the amorists and gallants darting in and out of the individual poems. It deepens and enriches the commentary on corruption rather by identifying Opinion's effects than by clarifying its nature.

[24] For a different reading of the philosophy of Marston's verse satires see Kernan, *Cankered Muse*, pp. 123–126. Kernan argues that Marston's thought in the satires was, if anything, consistently Calvinistic. In drawing this conclusion, however, he seems not to have taken sufficiently into account fundamental Neo-Stoic principles and, accordingly, forces himself into a number of doubtful premises. He must assume, for example, that Marston was only temporarily a Calvinist, that he became a Neo-Stoic when he turned playwright, and that his ridicule of the Puritans in the verse satires was a form of self-ridicule. The consequences of this conclusion, moreover, are even more gravely misleading. Since Kernan finds no coherence in Marston's verse satires and since they constitute his principal example of Renaissance satire, he argues that the Elizabethan satirist "never quite manages to bind his diverse materials together," that "no author of Elizabethan formal satire had a clear idea of what was basically wrong with his society" (p. 86), and that "the full exercise of the satiric function is not . . . a logical, balanced activity" (p. 117).

Taken in the aggregate, these patterns of figurative and technical terms constitute the principal lines of Marston's discourse in
the verse satires.[25] The battery of devices considered earlier—the
use of thesis to control particular poems, of *exempla* and character sketches to illustrate thesis, of a shifting persona to adjust
tone and manner to purpose—all these are, finally, but the literary
means used to further that discourse. Of course the terms of
Marston's discourse were in large part traditional to Stoic and
Neo-Stoic discussion. But his example offers a particularly startling proof of a very different use of figurative language from that
practiced widely today and, indeed, assumed by many critics of
imagery in Renaissance works to have been practiced then. His
images are inseparable from his ideas, not arbitrarily, if judi-
ciously, chosen to embody them. His verse satires are never free
of the shadows of Epictetus, Seneca, and (unless the evidence is
grossly misleading) Lipsius and Du Vair. Yet however great
Marston's indebtedness was, it should not obscure that in some
measure the voice and vision of the verse satires are distinctly individual—derivative, to be sure, but animated by a deep-seated
integrity.

That Marston, like the other Neo-Stoics, differed from the classical Stoics on certain doctrinal points is amply evident in his attacks
on Seneca and on the Stoics as a group. He had, for example, little
use for Stoic apathy ("Preach not the Stoic's patience to me" *SV*,
II, 6). In *Antonio's Revenge* Antonio at one point reads a key
passage from Seneca arguing the value of Stoic indifference (II,
ii, 45ff.) only to dismiss it as inadequate for a person actually
steeped in grief. And in the same play Pandulpho, who up to a
point plays the ideal Stoic in adversity, finally breaks down, admits
he has been deceiving himself, and joins Antonio's plot. This play

---

[25] The evidence favors the conclusion that these terms can be met rather
widely in his contemporaries of the Neo-Stoic persuasion. We have seen
them in Guilpin and Cornwallis. Note the interesting speech by Ingenioso
at the beginning of *2 Return from Parnassus*, I, i, 84–117, ed. J. B. Leishman
(London, 1949). See also Ure, "A Note on 'Opinion.'"

unmistakably approves of action of the kind that Andrugio decides to take in *Antonio and Mellida* even though such action is inconsistent with the ideal of rational control. Apathy, apparently, was for Marston too close to the lethargy that he was at pains to attack in the satires. In the same way, Marston unequivocally denounced the early Stoics and Seneca for holding that virtue could be achieved independently of God (*SV*, IV, 145–166). On this subject, indeed, he also brushed aside the ancients and the School-men for holding that virtue is acquired by habit or only after knowing vice (*SV*, IV, 93–160). Neither willing virtue, nor practicing it, nor knowing vice was sufficient, he maintained, to motivate a genuine progress of the soul, because none of these put the individual in touch with his highest faculties—his reason and his ability to know and participate in the divine plan. Achieving virtue depended, in Marston's view, on maintaining contact with the divinity and on drawing strength from divine grace. Hence the necessity of the purge to re-establish contact.

Marston's view of virtue achieved, however, was substantially the orthodox Stoic view. His fullest representation of it in *Sophonisba* indicates quite clearly a state of being or well-being the chief trait of which was "constancie" and serenity. In that play Massinissa says several times that doubt is "the highest misery of man": doubt is akin to fear, symptomatic of degeneracy, inimical to well-being. Perfection realized, on the other hand, was by no means joy, as Sophonisba emphasizes in the line "How near was I unto the curse of man—Joy." [26] "Happiness makes us base," she goes on, implying that it begets the complacency and lethargy so fatal to the good life. Indeed, even the terms "constancie" and "serenity" do not adequately comprehend the full sense of perfection that Marston was striving for in Sophonisba and Massinissa. Perhaps Marston himself came closest to supplying an adequate term when he has Massinissa say of Sophonisba at her death, "O glory ripe for heaven." In the last scene Scipio, too, speaks of

---

[26] V, iii, 89. I have accepted Deighton's punctuation here. See K. Deighton, *Marston's Works: Conjectural Readings* (London, 1893), p. 13.

"the glory of [her] virtue," and Massinissa's final speech clearly
sets forth a kind of perfection the fiery nature of which seems
better described by "glory" than by "serenity" or "constancie":

> Thou whom, like sparkling steel, the strokes of chance
> Made hard and firm, and, like wild-fire turn'd,
> The more cold fate, the more thy virtue burn'd,
> And in whole seas of miseries didst flame;
> On thee, loved creature of a deathless fame,
> Rest all my honour! [V, iv, 49–54]

In general, Marston's vision of fulfillment through spark and fire
was far more active and turbulent than any his Stoic or Neo-
Stoic brethren expounded.

For all his dependence on others, then, Marston's version of
Neo-Stoicism was distinctly his own, and we have every reason to
believe that he took it as the foundation of his life and work.[27]
Small wonder that his thought permeates his satires: that his
language, the direction of his discourse, and even the nature of
his aims as a writer were seriously conditioned by his convictions
about the state of the world and the destiny of man. Small wonder,
too, that his conception of the total role he was playing bore
strong resemblances to that played by his preceptors. To grasp
that total role adequately, we must recognize that the combination of the orphan poet and snarling satirist was not simply sanc-
tioned by his thought but significantly extended by it. To describe

---

[27] We find additional evidence that his contemporaries were abundantly
aware of his thought in their ridicule of it. Everyone who has written on
Marston, Jonson, or the poetomachia has pointed out Jonson's ridicule of
Marston's language. It has been insufficiently recognized that Jonson and
others also ridiculed Marston's philosophical pretensions. If we can trust
the elusive evidence of the poetomachia, and surely we can trust some of
it, Jonson's thrusts at Marston's thought are illuminating. See *Every Man
Out* (H & S, III, 502, 503) and *The Poetaster* (H & S, IV, 234, 235, 312,
313); also the possible parody in Furor Poeticus' speeches in *2 Return from
Parnassus*, pp. 305, 306.

what is substantially a trifold role, we must examine these sanctions and the example of his preceptors.

Although on the face of it neither Stoicism nor Neo-Stoicism would seem to be particularly hospitable to the postures of the orphan poet or the snarling satirist, the practice of Stoics and Neo-Stoics as teachers reveals several important points of contact. The first is a distinct similarity of tone. Despite Epictetus' reputation for sweetness and kindness, he was capable of surprising vehemence when pounding home his philosophy. "Very well," he could say to the man caught in adultery, "be an adulterer and faithless and a wolf or an ape instead of a man; for what is there to prevent you?" [28] Like Seneca, in other words, he counseled against anger, yet condoned the use of harsh language and stern reproofs by moral directors. The justification for this departure from serenity is found in the Stoic view of the teacher's function; briefly, the Stoic teacher-philosopher was typically unserene in his dealings with students. To teach was to be a healer of souls, and the tactics of healing were for them, as for most, frenzied.

Perhaps nothing illuminates the kinship of the Stoic teacher-philosopher and the Renaissance satirist as well as the medical analogy used to describe both. The conception of the teacher as moral healer traces back at least to Epictetus, who said: "The lecture-room of the philosopher is a hospital; you ought not to walk out of it in pleasure, but in pain. For you are not well when you come." [29] But the idea is commonplace in Stoic and Neo-Stoic writings. Seneca used it, and later Du Vair used it. And Lipsius provided the most pertinent discussion of it of all by making explicit the connection between the teacher as moral healer and the vehemence allowed him.

The first skirmish seemed to mee verie hot, wherefore interrupting him I replyed, what libertie of speech is this that you vse? Yea what bitter taunting? Do you in this wise pinch and pricke me . . . ?

[28] *Discourses*, I, 237. See also I, 263, 379; II, 161.
[29] *Discourses*, II, 181.

Langius smiling at this, I perceive then (said he) you expect Wafer cakes or sweete wine at my handes: but ere whiles you desired either fire or razor: and therein you did well. For I am a Philosopher (*Lipsius*) not a Fidler: my purpose is to teach, not to entice thee: To profite, not to please thee: To make thee blush, rather than smile: And to make thee penitent, not insolent. *The schoole of a Philosopher is as a Phisitians shoppe* (So said *Rufus* once) whether we must repaire for health, not for pleasure. That Physitian dallyeth not, neyther flattereth: but pearceth, pricketh, razeth, and with sauorie salt of good talke sucketh out the filthie corruptions of the minde. Wherefore looke not hereafter of me for Roses, Oyles, Pepper: but for thornes, launcing tooles, wormwood, and sharp vinegar.[30]

The similarities between this view of the teacher's activity and the Renaissance satirist's view of his activity as barber-surgeon, flaying away infected flesh and administering purges, are too patent for comment.

Not so obvious is that Marston found not only sanctions for the role of satirist in his preceptors but also concrete suggestions for extending that role. Neither the Stoics nor the Neo-Stoics were content, of course, that the teacher should merely upbraid. Epictetus says that "the real guide, whenever he finds a person going astray, leads him back to the right road, instead of leaving him with a scornful laugh or an insult," [31] and all these writers of course gave their attention overwhelmingly to constructive philosophy. That Marston probably derived from them the impulse to elevate satire by overlaying it with moral philosophy is clear enough. The probability all but yields to certainty when we see that even the details of Marston's program for satire were faithful to the Stoic theory of learning. Epictetus could have been describing Marston's purpose in the satires when he talked of making a beginning in philosophy through "a recognition of the conflict between the opinion of men . . . and a condemnation of mere opinion, coupled with a skepticism regarding it." [32] Despite all the

---

[30] *Constancie*, pp. 91, 92.   [31] *Discourses*, I, 291.
[32] *Discourses*, I, 287.

contemporary and earlier satiric models from which Marston could have taken the suggestion to combine exhortation with derision, accordingly, it is probable that he was governed in the matter by his preceptors' example. Just as they furnished him with the essentials of his philosophy, they provided him in the role of the teacher-philosopher with a way to dignify and ennoble the status of the satirist. With this extension of the satirist's role in mind, Marston could say, "It is a sacred cure [office] / To salve the soul's dread wounds" (*SV*, IV, 114, 115). With a full awareness of his contribution to satiric tradition he could boast:

> O how on tip-toes proudly mounts my muse!
> Stalking a loftier gait than satires use.
> Methinks some sacred rage warms all my veins,
> Making my sprite mount up to higher strains
> Than well beseems a rough-tongu'd satire's part;
> But Art curbs Nature, Nature guideth Art. [*SV*, IX, 5–10]

It is, finally, only against the backdrop of Marston's thought and of his indebtedness to the Stoics and Neo-Stoics that the complexity of his conception in the satires can be satisfactorily gathered up. Although we need but a short step from the pride just illustrated to return to the independence, haughtiness, and exclusiveness of the orphan poet, to take the step would be pointless unless it were clear that we are not ultimately concerned with the relationship between one role and another so much as with the three roles and their interrelations. For clarity I have said that Marston's performance in the verse satires is governed by a trifold persona; but that performance is also, of course, the work of one man, the expression of one man's beliefs, aims, and desires, the representation of a highly complex attitude toward the Renaissance world. If the complexity and variety of the satires are best explained in terms of the trifold persona, their unity, too, depends on its unity. Only by apprehending the verse satires in this way can we grasp the full intention of such terms as "scourge," "villainy," "purge," and "Good Opinion." Only in this way can we see the essential consistency of much in the satires that has been scored with contradiction and insincerity:

> In serious jest, and jesting seriousness,
> I strive to scourge polluting beastliness;
> I invocate no Delian deity,
> No sacred offspring of Mnemosyne;
> I pray in aid of no Castalian muse,
> No nymph, no female angel, to infuse
> A sprightly wit to raise my flagging wings,
> And teach me tune these harsh discordant strings.
> I crave no sirens of our halcyon times,
> To grace the accents of my rough-hew'd rhymes;
> But grim Reproof, a stern hate of villainy,
> Inspire and guide a Satire's poesy.
> Fair Detestation of foul odious sin,
> In which our swinish times lie wallowing,
> Be thou my conduct and my genius,
> My wits-inciting sweet-breath'd Zephyrus.
> O that a Satire's hand had force to pluck
> Some floodgate up, to purge the world from muck!
> Would God I could turn Alpheus river in,
> To purge this Augean oxstall from foul sin.
> [SV, "Proemium Tertium," 1–20]

As Marston turned from verse satire to the drama, from a genre that required a well-defined persona to one that did not, his explicit concern with intentions naturally diminished. But he never abandoned the role of the teacher-philosopher, as we shall see: his characters speak frequently of Opinion and degeneracy, and the plays as totalities suggest that the concept of satirical comedy gradually evolved and perfected during the next six or seven years was seriously conditioned by the Neo-Stoicism so prominent in the verse satires. Moreover, he never really abandoned the characteristic attitudes of the orphan poet and snarling satirist, though he gradually suppressed these roles as tangible features in his work. Much concerning the language and structure of his plays traces unmistakably, if not to the snarling satirist, to the assumptions about Renaissance satire that made snarling and violence so unavoidable in it. In the same way much of the experimentation of the plays, of Marston's originality and ambition in dramatic conception, suggest the orphan poet become orphan playwright. The principal difference between the verse satires and the satirical comedies is the expected one: in the plays Marston worked gradually toward a completely dramatic expression of the richly complex view of his world so self-consciously communicated by his verse satires.

Chapter IV

Playwright for
the Child Actors

THE waning years of the sixteenth century were full of important decisions for Marston. Not only did he give up the law for literature, much to his father's regret, but he chose to make his reputation among the new poets and, soon afterward, among the dramatists who were then writing for the child actors at St. Paul's and Blackfriars. During these years he was in continuous residence at the Middle Temple, for the most part sharing his father's rooms until that gentleman's death in 1599. Otherwise the records are silent. All we know in addition to his movements at the Middle Temple is to be inferred from his work and those external events that clearly affected it.

The question of precisely when Marston ended his apprenticeship in verse satire and turned to the theatre is still unsettled. O. J. Campbell has argued that the Order of Conflagration of June 1, 1599, effectively put an end to activity in verse satire and forced the satirists to take up dramatic satire as a substitute.[1] But Campbell's thesis does not readily explain Marston's activity at this time, for even a rough chronology of his work during this period suggests that he had probably turned to writing plays before the Order of June 1. Certainly he had completed the bulk of his work in verse satire between March of 1598 and September of that year, when *The Scourge of Villainy* was entered in the Stationers' Register. Between September of 1598 and June of 1599 he completed only one additional satire, the "Satira Nova," published in the 1599 edition of *The Scourge*. In view of the slightness of his output in verse satire after September of 1598 and in view of the probability that his first play, *Histriomastix*, was produced in August or September of 1599 (see Appendix A), it is reasonable to conclude that he had begun to rewrite the old *Histriomastix* before the Order of June 1.[2]

Marston had good reasons for working on *Histriomastix* that were apparently unrelated to the Order of June 1. If the old plays known to have been produced early in the revival of the children's companies are a fair reflection of the managers' tactics at that time, *Histriomastix* was admirably suited to the kind of revival they planned. We have several references to these plays. In the "Induction" to *Cynthia's Revels* (1600) Jonson calls them "the *umbrae*, or ghosts of some three or foure playes, departed a dozen yeeres since" (H & S, IV, 41). In *Jack Drum's Entertainment* (1600) Marston calls them "mouldy fopperies of stale Poetry, / . . . drie mustie Fictions" (*Plays*, III, 179), and "mustie fopperies of antiquitie" (p. 234). Of extant plays these "mustie Fictions" probably included *The Wisdom of Doctor Doddipole*, *Love's Metamorphosis*, *The Maid's Metamorphosis*, and *The Contention between Liberality and Prodigality*, all of which were performed very early in the revival and all of which resemble the

---

[1] *Comicall Satyre*, p. vii.

[2] Campbell's thesis might still be sound: living in the Middle Temple, Marston could have gotten wind of the Order of June 1 early, hence shifted, knowing his literary outlet would soon be blocked.

airy mythological moralities so popular with the child actors earlier.[3] It is probable that *Histriomastix,* just such an Interlude-Morality, was one of the group and that Marston, newly risen to prominence as a writer for the intelligentsia, was commissioned to refurbish it. If he had any intention at all of turning to the drama, certainly he might well have been drawn to *Histriomastix.* As we shall see, it offered him unusual opportunities to indulge the satiric and didactic propensities so conspicuous in his work to date.

A consideration of *Histriomastix,* accordingly, offers a useful introduction to the early phase of Marston's work in satirical comedy as a kind of middle ground between the theory and practice of the verse satires and that of the satirical comedies. Although it is not a good play, it has the happy merit of structural simplicity and as a first exercise in playwriting reveals Marston almost more clearly than one dare hope in the act of translating the technique of his verse satires into dramatic terms. Perhaps the play's great value in Marston's career is that apparently it taught him that in drama these techniques would have to yield to others.

Histriomastix is a crude allegorical dramatization of two Renaissance commonplaces. The first is the idea that the fortunes of society are governed by a continuous cycle, an idea neatly summarized in the gnomic tag of the fifteenth century:

> Pees maketh plente.
> Plente maketh pryde.
> Pryde maketh plee.
> Plee maketh pouert.
> Pouert maketh pees.[4]

[3] C. C. Stopes gives us a full list of the known performances of the Children of the Chapel Royal from 1566 to 1599 in *William Hunnis and the Revels of the Chapel Royal* (Louvain, 1910), pp. 271–272; but such titles as the *Mask of Apollo and the Nine Muses, The Play of Fortune, The Lady of the Lake, The History of Loyalty and Beauty* are sufficient, perhaps, to identify the type.

[4] R. H. Robbins (ed.), *Secular Lyrics of the XIVth and XVth Centuries* (Oxford, 1952), p. 81.

The idea is everywhere to be met in the Renaissance as well as earlier, notably in Marot, Lodge, Jean de Meung, and Simon Harward.[5] It takes variant forms, some more complex than this; but it always includes these elements. The second thesis offers a way out of the cyclical trap through learning: it maintains that

[5] R. Simpson, *The School of Shakespeare* (London, 1878), has discovered these occurrences of the idea. Simpson writes (II, 87–88):

"Clement Marot, in a letter to the Duchess Marguerite in October, 1521 from the Camp in Hainault says: 'Minfaut bears witness in his comedy of *Fatal Destiny*, saying:

> Peace begets Prosperity:
> Prosperity breeds Wealth:
> Of Wealth come Pride and Luxury:
> Pride with Contention swell 'th:
> Contention looks to War for health:
> War begets Poverty:
> Poverty breeds Humility:
> Humility brings Peace again:
> So turn over deeds in endless chain.'
>   (*Clement Marot;* by Henry Morley. Vol. I, p. 31).

"So Lodge, *A Fig for Momus*, 1595, F4 verso. Satire 5.

> Briefly, the greatest gifts whereof we boast
> Are those which do attempt and tire us most.
> Peace brings in pleasure; pleasure breeds excess;
> Excess procureth want; want works distress;
> Distress contempt, etc.

"Puttenham (p. 217 Arber's reprint) quotes Ihean de Mehune, the French poet—

> Peace makes plenty, plenty makes pride;
> Pride brings quarrel, and quarrel brings war:
> War brings spoil, and spoil poverty,
> Poverty patience, and patience peace:
> So peace brings war, and war brings peace.

"Simon Harward—*Solace for the soldier and sailor*, 1592, B3 verso. Peace hath increased plenty, plenty hath wrought pride, pride hath hatched disdain, and disdain hath brought forth such strifes and debates, such suits of law, such quarrellings and contentions, as never were heard of in any age before us."

only the learned, and particularly those deeply read in what here, because it is so general, may be described as Christianized Stoicism, are well armed to stand off life's vicissitudes. All this, of course, was grist for Marston's mill.

Based on the outline furnished by the cycle, the action of the play is divided into six acts, each dealing with one phase of the cycle. In each act the appropriate allegorical figure and his or her attendants preside over the action and influence in characteristic ways the three classes of society (four, including the special class of players). Thus the play opens with the entrance of Peace and her attendants Grammar, Logic, Rhetoric, Arithmetic, Geometry, Music, and Astronomy. After they have identified themselves briefly, the action traces their effects on the three major social classes: the nobility, the merchant and professional class, and the commoners. Mavortius, Philarchus, Larius, and Hiletus, the noblemen, are moved to adopt the arts; Fourcher, Voucher, Velure, and Lion-rash, the merchants and lawyers, are likewise prompted to improve themselves through study; the commoners, represented in this act by the "harvest folk" who sing a song of plenty, simply rejoice in rosy content. In the remaining acts this pattern is repeated, except for minor variations, as Plenty, Pride, Envy, War, and Poverty successively usurp the role of presiding deity. The cycle is completed in the sixth act when Poverty flees at the return of Peace.

Within this symmetrical scheme the learned man, Chrisoganus, and the players are mobile elements. By remaining steadfast in the face of mutability, Chrisoganus illustrates the thesis about learning and Stoic fortitude. In the course of the play he confronts at different times each of the social classes, encouraging them to study, exhorting them to abandon their pride, pointing the moral like a chorus or didactic poet when they grow envious and give themselves up to war, and, finally, preaching the value of Stoicism in a world "most full of change and contrariety." The players are the buffoons, serving primarily to sweeten the pill of didacticism with horseplay and burlesque. We shall take up their role in detail when we consider their relation to the theatre war in which *Histriomastix* doubtless played a part.

But first it is important to see where in this general outline Marston's hand is most prominent. Of course it is impossible to determine precisely the extent of his revisions (see Appendix A); for all we know, Fleay's guess that he wrote all of it may be correct.[6] The evidence we have already seen concerning Marston's style and preferences in subject matter, however, favor the more conservative estimates of Small, Chambers, and Besig, who, guided almost entirely by criteria of style, ascribe to him considerable portions of Acts III, IV, and V.[7] They also attribute other lines and passages to him on the basis of what they imagine to have been his intentions regarding Jonson and the public companies; but since the bulk of the passages occur in these acts, it is to them that we shall give most attention.

Perhaps the most conspicuous fact about these acts is that they deal with those phases of the social cycle that would have had an obvious appeal to Marston—society as it degenerates first to pride, then to envy, and ultimately to war. Up to and including the first half of Act III we find that only two passages have been attributed to him, one that supposedly introduced Jonsonian traits into the character of Chrisoganus and one that burlesqued the public companies.[8] Midway in Act III, however, the verse becomes characteristically Marstonian and remains so, particularly for the satiric and didactic passages dealing with society's descent

[6] "Shakespeare and Marston," *Shakespeariana*, I (Feb. 1884), 103. Fleay's claim has recently been supported by Alvin Kernan, "John Marston's Play *Histrio-Mastix*," *MLQ*, XIX (1958), 134–140.

[7] See E. K. Chambers, *The Elizabethan Stage* (Oxford, 1923), IV, 17; Roscoe Addison Small, *The Stage-Quarrel between Ben Jonson and the So-called Poetasters* (Breslau, 1899), p. 67; and Emma M. S. Besig (ed.), "Histrio-Mastix; or The Player Whipt" (M.A. thesis, Cornell University, 1929), p. 23.

[8] These passages are in Mavortius' speech on pp. 257–258 (*Plays*) and Chrisoganus' reply and the passage on pp. 264–265 from the song to the entrance of a "roaring Divell." Small, Chambers, and Besig agree on these attributions.

to pride, envy, and war, until the end of Act V. In the latter half of Act III we find a number of scenes made to order for Marston—the short scenes illustrating the pride of the players and professional men and culminating in a scene showing the ascendancy of envy among the nobles. Act IV, on the other hand, suggests revision throughout. To begin with, it accords to envy an importance which, though unusual in conventional statements of the thesis, was utterly consistent with Marston's convictions about Opinion and Detraction and his subsequent explicit concern with envy in Feliche in *Antonio and Mellida*. Secondly, it is both shorter than the other acts and structurally different in that it departs from the pattern found at the beginning of the others and consists of a simple stringing-out of speeches in which the characters speak of their suffering under the influence of envy. The design of the act, by which each of six characters first sets forth in turn the envious state of his soul and then Chrisoganus comments sagely on the general situation, recalls immediately the structure of the satires. To be sure, the characters reveal themselves more completely here than the satiric types do in the satires, but the pattern of exposure followed by explicit criticism is substantially the same. Furthermore, Act V, though it contains a number of scenes in which Marston apparently had no part, reveals essentially the same pattern. After the speeches by War and his attendants, which are clearly in Marston's manner, and the short scene dealing with the players' induction into the army, which only Small attributes to him,[9] we find a series of short scenes that represent the effect of War on each of the social classes and that again conclude typically with the appropriate didactic summaries by Chrisoganus.

From the evidence of these revisions we can infer that in making the transition from verse satire to the drama Marston apparently chose what was for him the path of least resistance. Whatever else it might have been, the old *Histriomastix* was clearly a play rich in opportunities for a combination of satire and didac-

[9] *Stage-Quarrel*, p. 67.

ticism like that which Marston had worked out in his satires. Moreover, it was a play that permitted him both to use verse very like the verse he had been writing for his satires and— perhaps most important in our consideration of Marston's developing conception of structure—to use a design governed by a structural thesis. The story of Marston's development as a satirist is substantially the story of his progressive modification of the theory and technique of his verse satires and his adaptation of them to dramatic needs. In large part it is the story of his movement from structures of thesis such as are found in the satires and *Histriomastix* toward imitative structures.

For the moment, however, we should see clearly that in this play Marston was still very close to the verse satires. Like the satires, *Histriomastix* is largely designed to arouse feelings of moral distress, feelings that are here directed and relieved by Chrisoganus' philosophical speeches. In this respect it is a rather crude prototype of the first kind of satirical comedy that Marston was to write, that kind which balances and contains exhibitions of absurdity, grotesqueness, and depravity by concurrently communicating a distinct sense that ideal alternatives exist. But at this point he was barely discovering the type, and, apparently, he was not the only new playwright engaged in such experimentation. It was by no means accidental that Jonson followed *Histriomastix* with *Every Man Out of His Humour,* also a play in which, as Campbell has already shown, the structural principles of verse satire were imitated and in which displays of decadence were balanced by criticism.[10] We cannot be certain of the precise effect that Jonson's activity had on Marston. While we might guess that Marston was encouraged, it is clear that he was by no means convinced of the soundness of his first attempt. In his next play he continued to experiment with the type, but, unlike Jonson, he departed sharply from the structural principles of the satires and *Histriomastix* in favor of a different structural conception.

Marston's progress in the matter of dramatic structure must

[10] *Comicall Satyre,* pp. 3–81.

wait, however, until we have assembled a fuller picture of his activity at this time and of the conditions influencing it. Although it is clear that many of his artistic decisions in *Histrio-mastix* were anticipated in his earlier practice, it should also be recognized that he was influenced in this play and that he continued to be influenced by such external factors as the war of the theatres and the special talents of the child actors for whom he wrote. When he cast in his lot with the fashionable theatres that opened at the singing school at St. Paul's in 1599 and at Burbage's new theatre within the precincts of Blackfriars in 1600,[11] he automatically engaged himself in the rivalry that had developed between the private and the public houses. This rivalry has been called the "war of the theatres," a phrase that, unfortunately, occasions some confusion since at least two other rivalries have also been designated by it. The best-known, at least the most extensively documented, was the quarrel that pitted Jonson against Marston and Dekker.[12] From time to time this quarrel will be invoked to clarify passages in Marston's work; for convenience I shall call it the "poetomachia." Less well known is the rivalry that R. B. Sharpe has investigated in his book *The Real War of the Theatres,* the rivalry that apparently grew out of the competition between the Burbage and Henslowe interests. Since, as Sharpe has pointed out, the private theatres served only to intensify this competition,[13] this rivalry lies outside our immediate interests. It is primarily the third rivalry that will command most of our attention, that between the private and public theatres and the child and adult actors.[14]

Late in 1599, probably in August or September,[15] the children's

[11] The consensus of opinion favors these dates. See Chambers, *Stage,* II, 19, 20, and 41, 42.

[12] See, in addition to Small, *Stage-Quarrel,* Josiah H. Penniman, *The War of the Theatres* (Philadelphia, 1897).

[13] *Real War* (Boston, 1935), p. 131.

[14] The fullest treatment of this rivalry is to be found in Harbage's *Rival Traditions;* but see also Chambers, *Stage,* I, 378–386.

[15] Small, *Stage-Quarrel,* pp. 77–91; Fleay, "Shakespeare and Marston," p. 103; and Chambers, *Stage,* IV, 18.

companies were revived under circumstances that suggest an attempt to provide London with fashionable theatres. It is possible that this revival was conditioned by the need to circumvent the Privy Council's Order of 1597 limiting London to no more than two playing companies at one time. This order could explain the decision to base the revival on the technically private grounds of Paul's and Blackfriars, where the companies could take refuge in the Act of the Common Council of 1574, which excluded performances at "pryvate houses" from regulations governing public performances.[16] But since a third company had always managed to survive despite the law,[17] this was probably a minor consideration. What seems to have been uppermost in the minds of the entrepreneurs involved was to establish theatres that would capitalize on the discontent among sophisticates with popular poetry and drama, theatres that would give the new generation of writers an opportunity to write plays and men of mode an intimate, exclusive atmosphere for viewing them.

Alfred Harbage has already pointed out that the private houses were in physical character designed to be exclusive. Appropriately, they were small: the second Blackfriars seated about nine hundred and Paul's seated four hundred at the most, while the Swan had a capacity of more than two thousand and the Fortune of more than twenty-five hundred.[18] In addition, the private houses were completely under cover, and they used artificial light. To accommodate the gallants of the day, they were located within easy reach of the Inns of Court and the scenes of fashionable life. And to discourage attendance by playgoers of the common sort they demanded admission prices ranging from sixpence to one shilling and sixpence, prices that must have been prohibitive for the average theatregoer who paid only one, two, or three pence at the public houses.[19]

In view of Marston's avowed allegiance in "Pygmalion's Image" and the satires to the new generation of poets, it was only natural

[16] Chambers, *Stage,* IV, 273–276.   [17] Chambers, *Stage,* II, 366.
[18] *Rival Traditions,* p. 43, and *Stage,* II, 526.
[19] Harbage, *Rival Traditions,* p. 45.

he should cast in his lot with the dramatists of the intelligentsia. After taking this step in _Histriomastix_, he may have flirted briefly with the public companies (see Appendix A), but, if so, it was only to return and remain a playwright for the private theatres throughout his brief career—perhaps the most typical of the private playwrights. All his known plays belong unmistakably to the private repertories. Their use of fewer scenes and locales than we find in public plays reflects the limited physical conditions of the private houses.[20] In addition, although one can hardly find in them, as Harbage claims to, a corpus of unconventional attitudes suggestive of a clique, they are shot through with the satire and Neo-Stoicism then in vogue in educated circles. Perhaps the most striking and readily isolable of their traits in common with other private plays, however, is Marston's fulsomeness in assuring his audience of its exclusiveness and superiority. We must allow for some dimension of irony in so generous a passage as the "Prologue" to the _Parasitaster, or The Fawn:_

> For we do know that this fair-fill'd room
> Is loaden with most attic judgments, ablest spirits,
> Than whom there are none more exact, full, strong,
> Yet none more soft, benign in censuring.
> I know there is not one ass in all this presence—
>
> .   .   .   .   .
>
> O you are all the very breath of Phoebus.
> [_Works_, ll. 23–31]

But his concern with the tastes and general superiority of his audience here and elsewhere is symptomatic of the rarefied at-

---

[20] References to the smallness of the stage are quite frequent; in _Jack Drum_ Sir Edward says, "Good Boy Ifaith, I would thou hadst more roome" (_Plays_, III, 234); in _Antonio and Mellida_ Piero says, "The room's too scant; boys, stand in there, close" (V, i, 173); in the "Induction" to _What You Will_ Atticus says, "Let's place ourselves within the curtains, for good faith the stage is so very little, we shall wrong the general eye else very much" (97–99); and Chambers cites two or three others (_Stage_, II, 536)

mosphere in which this rather avant-garde movement was thought to be taking hold. Finally, even the proportion of comedies, tragedies, and histories in Marston's canon—eight comedies, three tragedies, and no histories—roughly corresponds to the proportion in the private repertories, which was 85 per cent comedies and 15 per cent tragedies against the 49 per cent comedies, 30 per cent tragedies, and 21 per cent histories typical of the public repertories during this period.[21]

Once committed to the private theatres, Marston must have found the old *Histriomastix* peculiarly suitable not only as a vehicle for his transition to the drama, but also as a contribution to the developing rivalry with the public playhouses. Chambers has argued that the old *Histriomastix* was the product of the earlier rivalry between the poets and players in which Greene took so prominent a part.[22] But even if we set aside this possibility, for the early history of the play is highly problematical, the play clearly required little doctoring to serve Marston's purpose to satirize the public companies. Throughout the play this satire centers in the burlesque behavior of Posthast's band of players organized under the aegis of Sir Oliver Owlet. These so-called actors constitute a class supplementary to the three classes representing society in the play and vulnerable, like those classes, to the social cycle. Like Shakespeare's homespuns, they are for the most part tradesmen: a beard-maker, a fiddlestring-maker, and a peddler. As homespuns with artistic pretensions, however, they embody what the intelligentsia apparently deplored most about the public companies. It is all too plain that they are ignorant. Of them, only Posthast pretends to a knowledge of the arts, and his pretensions make even Bottom look talented. When they undertake to draw up their contract and the scrivener asks their "appellations," Posthast must explain, "Your names he meanes; the man's learned." Yet ignorant though they are, they presume to to be able to teach rarer spirits:

[21] This is Harbage's count; see *Rival Traditions*, p. 85.
[22] Chambers, *Stage*, I, 376–386.

Why Lords we are heere to shew you what we are,
Lords wee are heere although our cloths be bare,
In steed of flowers, in season, yee shall gather Rime and Reason.

[p. 260]

Throughout the play their foolishness, clumsiness, and clownishness are harmless enough—suitable to be laughed at; but as artists preparing their art for the most refined sensibilities in the kingdom they are grotesque impostors.

Secondly, their taste in plays is precisely of the kind that erudite critics of the popular drama such as Joseph Hall persistently ridiculed.[23] Their bad taste is first evident in their penchant for the pathetic. While rehearsing a scene from *The Prodigal Child*, Posthast feels constrained to point out in an aside, "This is a passion, note you the passion?" (p. 259). Moreover, their repertory is especially rich in full-blown romantic and heroic plays. Their *Troilus and Cressida* is an extravagant example of heroic romances like *Sir Clyomon and Sir Clamydes* and *Mucedorus* that continued to be popular in the public theatres. Later we shall see how these romances and even their relatively subdued descendants were constantly coming under fire of the private playwrights.[24]

Finally and most damning of all, Sir Oliver Owlet's men are committed to what was for the new generation of writers the reprehensible practice of catering to the multitude. When they reject Chrisoganus' play and he insists that it is a superior piece of work, Gut answers, "Will not our owne stuffe serve the multitude?" To this Chrisoganus replies in a speech (quite clearly Marston's) that neatly summarizes the intelligentsia's view of the public companies:

[23] See his *Virgidemiarum*, in *Collected Poems*, pp. 12–17.
[24] A number of attempts have been made to identify the public plays burlesqued. See Sharpe, *Real War*, pp. 51, 133; C. W. Wallace, *The Children of the Chapel at Blackfriars* (University of Nebraska, 1908), pp. 167, 168; and Henry Wood, "Shakespeare Burlesqued by two Fellow-Dramatists," *AJP*, XVI (Oct. 1895), 273–279.

Write on, crie on, yawle to the common sort
Of thickskin'd auditours: such rotten stuffs,
More fit to fill the paunch of Esquiline,
Then feed the hearings of judiciall eares,
Yee shades tryumphe, while foggy Ignorance
Clouds bright *Apollos* beauty: Time will cleere,
The misty dullnesse of Spectators Eeys,
Then wofull hisses to your fopperies,
O age when every Scriveners boy shall dippe
Prophaning quills into Thessaliaes Spring,
When every artist prentice that hath read
The pleasant pantry of conceipts, shall dare,
To write as confident as *Hercules*.
When every Ballad-monger boldly writes:
And windy froth of bottle-ale doth fill
Their purest organ of invention:
Yet all applauded and puft up with pryde,
Swell in conceit, and load the Stage with stuffe,
Rakt from the rotten imbers of stall jests:
Which basest lines best please the vulgar sence
Make truest rapture lose preheminence. [pp. 273–274]

To be sure, this speech is the most vehement attack on the public companies to be found in the play: the burden of the attack actually resides in the lighthearted burlesque provided by the players' scenes. But the speech effectively brings to light the assumptions on which the burlesque was based, indeed the assumptions on which much of the plentiful burlesque in the plays of the private companies was based. Moreover, we must not overlook the concern here with decadence. The concealment of "*Apollos* beauty" and the perversion of the "purest organ of invention" are substantially the same concerns met in the verse satires, and the deplorable state of the public stage is represented as a triumph of "shades," "misty dullnesse," and "windy froth." Although Marston had good business reasons for attacking the public theatres, in other words, his attack seems also to have been grounded in his profoundest convictions.

It is only recently, however, that scholars and critics have begun to recognize the influence of the rivalry between the public and private companies on the plays produced during this time. For a long time the term "war of the theatres" meant the quarrel that saw Jonson pitted against Marston and Dekker for an indeterminate time and in an indeterminate number of plays. In the last eighty years much scholarly energy has been spent upon tracking down covert attacks and deceptive allusions, and the books of R. A. Small and J. H. Penniman devoted exclusively to this subject have failed to put an end to conjecture. Even the general outline of the quarrel is still highly problematical. We have only four dependable pieces of evidence: (1) *Jonson's Conversations with Drummond,* in which he mentions that Marston represented him on the stage and that he retaliated with *The Poetaster,* (2) *The Poetaster* itself, (3) Dekker's *Satiromastix,* and (4) 2 *Return from Parnassus,* in which an obscure reference to Shakespeare's part in the quarrel occurs. On the basis of this evidence Marston's plays up to *The Malcontent,* which he dedicated to Jonson, have been ransacked for clues to his part in the quarrel, as have Jonson's plays up to and including *The Poetaster.* Although no two theorists agree in every detail, taken together they exhibit considerable unanimity of opinion on important matters, and almost all ascribe to *Histriomastix* a crucial part in the growth of the poetomachia.

According to Small, whose opinion is standard in the matter, Marston attempted to compliment Jonson in the portrait of Chrisoganus, but his compliment went awry. Jonson, Small argues, construed the compliment as an insult and replied to it in *Every Man Out.*[25] This "exchange" of insults supposedly set off a series of attacks from both sides that involved, in addition to the plays already mentioned, *Jack Drum's Entertainment, Cynthia's Revels,* and *What You Will* and that ended sometime before the publication of *The Malcontent* in 1604. Actually, Small and the other

[25] *Stage-Quarrel,* pp. 89, 91.

theorists all attempt to prove considerably more than the identification of Chrisoganus with Jonson in *Histriomastix*. Small tries to identify Posthast with Anthony Munday,[26] while others try to identify Posthast with Shakespeare,[27] Posthast's plays with Shakespeare's,[28] and Sir Oliver Owlet's company with Pembroke's company.[29] All this conjecture, of course, is shot through with difficulties, and even the identification of Chrisoganus with Jonson has not gone unquestioned. Penniman, though he accepts the identification, has justly pointed out that "there is no passage in the play which has been proved to be a definite and unmistakable allusion that will apply to Jonson and to no one else." [30]

What is important in our consideration of Marston's developing concept of satiric form is that, however great or small the part played by *Histriomastix* in the poetomachia, the poetomachia need hardly be conjured up to explain the character of the play. Clearly the poetomachia was a real issue; it offers the only reasonable explanation for many details in the work of Marston and Jonson. But it has probably been overworked by scholars; and certainly it is not the indispensable factor in a consideration of these plays that Fleay claimed it was.[31] As an external factor that probably influenced Marston during the composition of these plays, it is by no means as important as the rivalry between the public and private companies; it is at most helpful in explaining passages in the relevant plays.

Far more important, though usually overlooked, is the contribution of the child actors themselves to the revision of *Histriomastix*. Was this old play particularly suitable for child actors that Marston chose it rather than another? The question seems

---

[26] *Stage-Quarrel*, pp. 86, 88, 173–175.   [27] R. Simpson, *School*, II, 11.
[28] H. Wood, "Shakespeare Burlesqued," pp. 273–279.
[29] Penniman, *War*, p. 42.   [30] *War*, p. 34.
[31] "Any criticism of any play bearing as a date of production one of the three years 1599 to 1601 which does not take account of this, for the time, stage-absorbing matter, must be imperfect and of small utility." This statement, from Fleay's *History of the Stage* (p. 119), is quoted by Small, *Stage-Quarrel*, p. 1.

fair enough; but no sooner is it asked than it inescapably raises a battery of problems concerning the child actors. What kind of actors were they, after all? How did they influence dramatic production at the private houses? And did they predispose the playwrights to write particular kinds of plays? These are matters not easily disposed of. Scholars and critics who have written about the children's companies have done a good deal toward straightening out their history,[32] but by and large the commentators have neglected to ask whether the child actors were significantly different from the adults and in what these differences consisted.[33]

The tacit assumption made in most criticism of English Renaissance drama is that Elizabethan child actors—and particularly those who played Shakespeare's women—were unbelievable prodigies. Unfortunately, this belief has rarely been examined, for if it had been it would have soon broken down under the mathematical improbability of one city's producing so many prodigies at the same time. If it had been, moreover, its failure to stand up might have forced us before this to make certain preliminary distinctions between the classes of child actors to be met in English Renaissance drama and to draw preliminary inferences about these classes from the repertories with which they were associated. Even a cursory examination tells us that the boys who acted for the public companies were a quite different group from those belonging to Blackfriars and Paul's. Their legal standing was different: the public boys were apprenticed in the normal way; the private boys were impressed into service and kept as long as they were useful. Their acting assignments were frequently different: the public boys always took women's parts (and, of course, children's) and often had to cope with complex character studies; the private boys played all parts and for much of their history spe-

[32] The best histories of the children's companies are to be found in H. N. Hillebrand, *The Child Actors* (University of Illinois Studies, 1926); Chambers, *Stage*, I, 378–386, II, 8–76, III, 130–154; and Wallace, *Children of the Chapel.*

[33] Hillebrand's last chapter in *Child Actors*, entitled "Plays and Influences," is, as far as I know, the only extended treatment of these differences.

cialized in singing and dancing. If a more intensive study of their history does not finally explain that most perplexing matter: how a boy played a satisfactory Cleopatra to Burbage's Antony, perhaps it can lead to a reasonable explanation of Marston's decision to revise *Histriomastix* as his first play for the child actors. Such a study, however sketchy, is clearly indispensable in a book on Marston since he wrote all his plays for the child actors.

We are primarily concerned, of course, with the children who did the acting for the private houses. However fascinating the youth who "boyed" Cleopatra may be, he is only incidentally relevant to the children at Paul's and Blackfriars. These are the children whose long and fairly illustrious career is so profoundly involved in theatrical history under the Tudors, and their strengths and weaknesses were those with which the private playwrights had to reckon when the private houses reopened in 1599–1600. Their activity divides itself neatly into two periods: the first running from 1515 to 1590, after which they were temporarily disbanded; the second from 1599 to 1616, the period of our immediate concern. The hiatus offers a useful way of approaching what appears to be an important distinction between their normal activity and the rather specialized form of it that developed early in the revival, and *Histriomastix* falls pat as a means of clarifying this distinction because, even if it was not a play of the earlier period, it was sufficiently like them to have been one of the "mustie fopperies of antiquitie" with which the managers of the private houses launched the revival. It is probable, therefore, that *Histriomastix* can tell us something about the tradition of the child actors before and immediately after the revival.

During the period from 1515 to 1590 the principal children's companies emerged and enjoyed their greatest popularity.[34] The children from the chapel of the reigning monarch, trained and directed by masters who themselves often wrote the plays, flourished under the title of the Children of the Chapel Royal. The children from the choir and schoolhouse at St. Paul's cathedral

[34] See Chambers, *Stage*, II, 8–60, for their history.

rose to eminence as the Children of Paul's. Before 1576, the year
in which the first public theatre was built, these players dominated
the English drama. Thereafter, they went into a steady decline
as the adult players gained popularity, until finally in the early
1590's their theatres were closed.

The history of these children is important here for what it can
tell us of their acting style and special talents before 1590. However specialized they became after the revival, they must have
done so within limits that not only nature but also tradition had
imposed on them. It is commonplace, of course, that they were
trained singers and dancers and obvious that by weight and size
they were admirably suited to the floats and sets used in spectacular displays. These qualifications fitted them for the pageantry
that was apparently their forte at court and elsewhere. Their
plays, moreover, indicate that they could handle the flat allegorical characterizations of the Interlude-Moralities.[35] What is
not quite so evident is that apparently they were also found to be
suitable for satire early in their history. Even before the history
of the children's companies is clear enough to follow, the boys'
special talents for burlesque were apparent in the tradition of the
Boy Bishop.[36] Each year on St. Nicholas' Day, December 6, boys
were elected to officiate as bishops and priests until Holy Inno-
cents' Day, December 28. During this time they counterfeited
ceremonies, including the Mass, and in general debunked the
dignity and solemnity of the religious officials and institutions.
Later, it is probable that their talents in this vein were again
drawn upon in the Marprelate Controversy, in which, according to
Chambers, they ridiculed the gravity of the Martinists in scur-
rilous plays by Lyly and Nashe.[37] Hillebrand, at least, claims that
the dissolution of their theatres in 1590 was in part caused by
their role in the Marprelate Controversy [38] and goes on to argue

[35] See Stopes, *Wm. Hunnis*, pp. 220–272.
[36] For a full discussion see Hillebrand, *Child Actors*, pp. 24–27.
[37] *Stage*, I, 294, 295.   [38] *Child Actors*, pp. 144–149.

that even the Interlude-Moralities that were their stock in trade during this early period were heavily freighted with satire. Although conjecture of this kind is always rather tenuous, the evidence of the few plays that survive, the titles of the lost plays, and the extant contemporaneous commentary seem to bear him out.[39]

If we can conclude, at any rate, that traditions in pageantry, in the Interlude-Morality, and, less emphatically, in satire are clear in the history of the child actors, perhaps we can further clarify their talents and limitations by considering briefly what they did not do as a rule, probably because they did not do it well. We can begin by observing that before 1576 they apparently did everything the adults did. The dramatic simplicity of the time imposed few, if any, limitations on their activities; and although they inclined toward the farce and allegory of the Interlude-Morality, while the adults inclined toward romantic plays of adventure, their extant repertories are very like those of the adults. After the foundation of the first public theatre, however, and after the development of actors among the adults to meet the needs of playwrights like Marlowe, Kyd, and Greene, the children's limitations became readily apparent. Soon it was obvious that however talented they might be with songs, dances, masquelike spectacle, and satire, they were not capable of serious power. Accordingly, soon the plays of the adults became distinct as a group, comprising plays of crude violence, robust adventure, and tragedies of blood, kinds of plays not to be found among the children's bright comedies and fanciful moralities. This schism culminated in the work of Lyly, a playwright whose work constitutes in Hillebrand's mind "the only body of plays of which one may say: 'these were written for children and could have been written for none but them.' " [40] Lyly's plays represent clearly the child actors' fitness for plays of light, fanciful comedy and elaborate artifice; indeed, they mark an early fruition of that kind of play. Yet fine

[39] *Child Actors*, pp. 78–86, 258.   [40] *Child Actors*, p. 262.

though Lyly's plays are of their kind, even they failed to arrest the decline that resulted in the temporary extinction of the children's companies in the early 1590's.

By 1599 times had changed: a new literary generation had arisen, and in its wake followed the Henry Evanses, Nathaniel Gyleses, and Robert Keysars, who revived the children's companies on an altogether different basis from any ever known. The first significant fact about the revivals of 1599 and 1600 is that the companies were organized for the first time as businesses. Actual control passed from the Master who had previously trained and directed the children to a financial syndicate, "associated," as Chambers points out, "much on the principle adopted by the ordinary playing companies." [41] This syndicate was hardly concerned about restoring a dormant theatrical tradition: its chief interest in the child actors was unmistakably the money it could make with them. Accordingly, when the old plays with which they had reasonably enough initiated the revival failed, they quickly abandoned them for the plays that enabled them temporarily to carry the day in the rivalry that soon developed with the public companies.[42]

The extant lists of plays produced during the first few years of the revival [43] reveal a decisive movement toward instrumental music, song, dance, and satire, all of which, apparently, were very popular with the fashionable clientele at Paul's and Blackfriars.

[41] *Stage*, I, 379.

[42] Chambers quotes the crucial pieces of evidence documenting their ascendancy (*Stage*, I, 380, 381): from *The Poetaster* (H & S, IV, 255, 256) this speech by Histrio, who is the spokesman for the company being satirized: "this winter ha's made vs all poorer, than so many staru'd snakes: No bodie comes at vs; not a gentleman, nor a—"; and from *Hamlet* (II, ii, 45ff.) the famous passage ending:

Ham. Do the boys carry it away?
Ros. Ay, that they do, my lord, Hercules and his load too.

[43] See Hillebrand, *Child Actors*, pp. 279–323, and Harbage, *Rival Traditions*, pp. 343–350.

None of this was new to the child actors (though, of course, it was all new to this group of them); but for the first time in their history these special talents were emphasized to the near exclusion of all others. Unfortunately, we do not know what went on during, say, the rehearsals of *Antonio and Mellida*. From the rash of satirical comedies generously padded with music, song, and dance, however, we might reasonably conclude a concentration on and a rapid improvement in these specialties, particularly the children's satiric talents. As we shall see, the plays actually suggest not just improvement, but a wholesale exploitation of their capacity for satire. They imply, in fact, an acting style that is sufficiently different from the normal style to be inferred from the earlier repertory to justify separate attention, a style some understanding of which is indispensable to a study of the children's drama after 1599.

The problem of defining this style is beset by numerous difficulties. Contemporary remarks about it are neither so numerous nor so unequivocal as to be conclusive. Moreover, the plays in which the style was probably practiced provide at best a rather slippery footing, since to use them as a basis for clarifying a style that we wish ultimately to argue is essential to them inescapably entails some circularity. Furthermore, since the style we are concerned with was substantially what I shall call a burlesque style, defining it necessarily requires establishing with some precision what it was a burlesque of and inevitably involves us in the whole thorny question of Elizabethan acting. Finally, none of the available evidence is reliable by itself; only in the aggregate is it persuasive, and then only after it has been very carefully pieced together.

At the very heart of this matter is the obvious but usually neglected fact of the children's natural aptitude for satire. Although all the critics who have written on the children's companies have noticed that their repertories after 1599 reveal a decided preference for satirical comedy, few of them have explored this preference. Ignoring that the children were apparently active in satire before 1599, most have been content to explain the satire at the turn of the century by the fact that the private companies were engaged in a rivalry with the public theatres, hence, fond of satirizing them. Even Hillebrand does not penetrate very deeply into the matter: he explains the preference in terms of the private companies' aim "to gain the public ear by shocking" and the children's peculiar immunity as minors to legal reprisal.[44] A more satisfactory account of the children's concentration on satire probably ought to begin with the recognition that children from ten to fifteen years of age were and are naturally fitted by size, voice, and general immaturity to burlesque the adult world. In summing up the effects that these actors probably had on their audience, Hillebrand observes, as Creizenach had before him,[45] that however satisfied the audiences were of the fitness of the boys to play women,

surely they found no illusions when boys impersonated men, they who knew Burbage and Alleyn. Boys on the stage must have seemed to them largely what boys on the stage now seem to us—masqueraders. They had charm, of course, the charm of piquant strangeness and the genuine charm of delightful music and nimble dancing, the vivacity of rattling comedy, often precocious skill, as in Salathiel [Salmon] Pavy's old men; but granting all that and making allowances for the perpetuating instincts of an old tradition, I cannot help feeling that the fundamental attraction of the boy actors for the Jacobean audience was the whimsical charm of a masquerade. "The apes in time will do it finely," said Brabant Senior of the boys of Paul's, most happy in his descriptive noun. Hamlet's little eyases that "cry out on the top of the question" is a commentary from an unfriendly source, bearing witness to a popularity which throve in spite of limitations as clearly perceived as they would be today.[46]

[44] *Child Actors*, pp. 269, 270.

[45] *The English Drama in the Age of Elizabeth* (Philadelphia, 1916), p. 414.

[46] *The Child Actors* (University of Illinois Studies; Urbana: University of Illinois Press, 1926), p. 271.

Certainly this represents a reasonable assumption. Even if we grant that the children were probably not out of key in such plays of elaborate artifice as *The Maid's Metamorphosis* and *The Wisdom of Dr. Doddipole*, they must have seemed something more than strange taking adult parts in the bustling domestic worlds of *The Family of Love* and *Jack Drum's Entertainment*. Indeed, the epithet "apes" so frequently applied to them suggests fairly precisely the effect they must have had. In *Volpone*, Act III, scene iii, Nano, the dwarf, explains the term as follows:

> Else, why doe men say to a creature of my shape,
> So soone as they see him, it's a pritty little ape?
> And why a pritty ape? but for pleasing imitation
> Of greater mens action, in a ridiculous fashion.
> [H & S, V, 70]

Of all the epithets applied to the child actors, this is easily the most frequent.

Unfortunately, Hillebrand does not account for the children's satire in this way; nor, in my opinion, does he take the implication of his observation far enough. If we grant that the sophisticated turn-of-the-century audience probably felt a disparity between what the children pretended to be and what they obviously were, surely it is not rash to assume that not only the audience, but the producers, the playwrights, and the actors as well were aware of this disparity. From this it is but a short step to conclude that they exploited this disparity not only for the "charm of a masquerade," but also for its inherent comic and satiric effects. We have seen that apparently from the first the child actors showed a talent for satire. In the annual burlesque on religious officialdom enacted in the Boy Bishop ceremonies they had not been chosen because of their immunity to legal reprisal, but because their size and immaturity poked fun at the gravity they mimicked. Likewise, their part in the Marprelate Controversy was probably delegated to them chiefly because they had an aptitude for the ridicule appropriate to the anti-Martinists' purposes. In 1599, accordingly, when it was perfectly apparent that the child actors did not have the range and depth demanded by the drama then on the public boards and when it was discovered that the airy mythological romances and Moralities for which they were suitable could not be revived with success, the managers of their companies quite understandably turned to the one kind of play that fitted the children's talents, that was in vogue with the connoisseurs frequenting the private houses, and that provided gratuitous opportunities to ridicule the public companies—satirical comedy. This decision could not have been taken if the child actors did not have a natural aptitude for the burlesque acting style that we must now define as precisely as the evidence permits.

Our chief source of evidence concerning the details of the children's acting styles is, of course, the plays produced by the private houses shortly after 1599. This evidence is of two kinds: (1) those direct comments on or descriptions of the actors performing, and (2) those passages the bold satiric nature of which imply the outline of a burlesque acting style. All of this is tricky, but it is sufficiently clear to suggest a number of ways in which the managers and playwrights exploited the children's aptitude for satire and tried to convert their limitations as actors to positive advantage.

The direct comments indicate unmistakably that the child actors did not try to duplicate the effects within the grasp of their adult rivals, but were, as they were so often called, chiefly, "apes" —mimics or impersonators—relying heavily on inherent incongruity and exuberant gesticulation and movement for comic and satiric effects. In the "Induction" to *Cynthia's Revels* Child 3 refers to them as "rascally tits, . . . wrens or pismires" and in his two extraneous impersonations exemplifies their talent for virtuoso mimicry (H & S, IV, 39–42). In *The Gentleman Usher*, Bassiolo's advice to the boys whom he is readying for the entertainment in Act III goes far in illuminating such impersonations:

Bas. What stir is with these boys here! God forgive me.
   If 't were not for the credit on't, I'd see
   Your apish trash afire, ere I'd endure this.

.   .   .   .   .

            Hence, ye brats!
   You stand upon your tire; but for your action
   Which you must use in singing of your songs
   Exceeding dextrously and full of life,
   I hope [i.e. expect] you'll then stand like a sort of blocks,
   Without due motion of your hands and heads,
   And wresting your whole bodies to your words;
   Look to 't.[47]

But it is Marston who provides us with the most telling comments in the "Induction" to *Antonio and Mellida*. In Alberto's advice to the actor playing Piero, the tyrant, Marston unequivocally outlines an acting style weighted heavily with burlesque intention:

Alb. O! ho! then thus frame your exterior shape
      To haughty form of elate majesty,
      As if you held the palsy-shaking head
      Of reeking chance under your fortune's belt
      In strictest vassalage: grow big in thought,
      As swoln with glory of successful arms.
Piero. If that be all, fear not; I'll suit it right.
      Who cannot be proud, stroke up the hair, and strut? [ll. 7–14]

If we assume that the advice of Bassiolo and Alberto refers to the normal manner of the children while acting satirical comedy, we are in a good position to understand why caricature rather than characterization was the rule of their plays.

   This much seems secure enough; it is only when we try to

[47] *The Plays and Poems of George Chapman*, ed. Thomas Marc Parrott (London, 1914), II, i, 166–176.

move beyond these generalizations that the picture becomes intricate. The details of this acting style are easiest to follow, perhaps, in those passages in various plays that imply burlesque. But the passages are troublesome. To begin with, their satire is sometimes problematical because much of it is aimed at the public companies, and to identify its intention precisely, one must recognize what in the public companies was being satirized. Obviously such recognition is not always easy for usually it consists in seeing what in the adult style of acting was being satirized and, hence, involves the whole problem of Elizabethan acting.

This is, of course, no place to try to settle definitively the problem of Elizabethan acting. In my opinion the evidence favors the arguments of Alfred Harbage and B. L. Joseph that it was, fundamentally, what they call a formal or conventionalized style, a style depending on relatively standard decorums in speech, movement, and gesticulation.[48] Certainly the contemporary references to actors' heightened gestures and exaggerated walk, as well as those few to actors performing, support the claim for such a style; [49] and only such a style renders certain facts intelligible: that Elizabethan actors could tour frequently and successfully in foreign

[48] Alfred Harbage, "Elizabethan Actors," *PMLA*, LIV (1939), 685–708, and B. L. Joseph, *Elizabethan Acting* (London, 1951).

[49] See especially the passage cited by Harbage, "Actors," p. 698, from the MS play "The Cyprian Conqueror": "The other parts of action is in ye gesture, wch must be various, as required; as in a sorrowfull parte, ye head must hang downe; in a proud, ye head must bee lofty; in amorous, closed eies, hanging downe lookes, & crossed armes, in a hastie, fumeing, & scratching ye head & . . ."; Robert Greene's statement that acting is "a kind of mechanical labour" (*Francesco's Fortunes*, 1590, in *The Life and Works of Robert Greene*, ed. A. B. Grosart, London, 1881–1886, VIII, 132); the passage quoted by Joseph, *Acting*, p. 153, from T. Gainsford's *The Rich Cabinet* (London, 1616): "[a] Player is like a garment which the Tailor maketh at the direction of the owner: so they frame their action, at the disposing of the Poet"; and the reference quoted by A. G. H. Bachrach in "The Great Chain of Acting," *Neophilologus*, XXXIII (1949), 167, from John Gaule's *Mag-Astro-Mancer* (London, 1652) to the "subtlety and industry" of actor's hands.

countries;[50] that they could maintain such staggering repertories;[51] and that acting itself was so often linked with oratory
and the teaching of oratory.[52] But even what we might imagine in
the light of our knowledge of the Elizabethan theatre about the
actor's problem on a bare stage in broad daylight, with little more
to bring his audience to focus on him than his handsome costume
and whatever he could do with voice and gesture seems to insist
on a stylized, distinctly larger-than-life mode of acting. And to
discover this basis in Elizabethan acting is not to deny that variety
and a considerable range in quality were both possible and probable.

At the end of the sixteenth century there is every likelihood that
acting underwent a development in some ways comparable to the
development in drama itself. Bottom's illustration of "Ercles' vein"
and Falstaff's of "King Cambyses' vein" apparently refer to acting
not much earlier, but distinctly cruder than the best to be met in
Shakespeare's day.[53] Yet to claim that Elizabethan acting developed is not to read Hamlet's famous speech on the subject as a
plea for a fundamentally different kind of acting from that of thirty
years before. As Harbage has argued, why assume a complete
change?

Why not simply an improvement in formal acting—an increase in grace,
in restraint, in mastery of the stylized gesture, and, above all, in the
clear, musical, and expressive reading of lines?[54]

[50] This fact is well known; but see Chambers, *Stage,* I, 342–346, especially
the quoted passage by Fynes Moryson (343).

[51] Chambers, *Stage,* II, 94, 122, 143.

[52] See, for example, Sir Thomas Overbury's "An Excellent Actor" in *The
Miscellaneous Works in Prose and Verse of Sir Thomas Overbury, Bart.,* ed.
Edward F. Rimbault (London, 1890), p. 147; Chambers, *Stage,* II, 86; and,
again, Joseph, *Acting, passim.*

[53] See also John Stow, *Annals,* or *A General Chronicle of England* (London, 1631), p. 698 (a passage added in 1615); and Richard Brome, *The
Antipodes* in *The Dramatic Works of Richard Brome* (London, 1873), III,
260 (Letoy's speech).

[54] "Actors," p. 705.

And if we can assume such improvement, we can still conclude that the turn of the century saw a considerable range in the quality of acting: at one extreme were actors of the cruder, earlier type who were ridiculed in Bottom's and Falstaff's imitations; at the other were the Burbages and Armins who exemplified the style at its best.

Some of our confusion on this subject no doubt results from the terms we have come to argue with, particularly the terms "formal" and "conventional." Although Harbage's and Joseph's arguments for stylized, exaggerated acting seem valid, nothing is really gained by calling it formal or conventional acting. We are not sure of the norms implied by these terms; and even if we infer rudimentary decorums from handbooks on oratory, as Joseph has done, by the time of Burbage the technique of the best actors was almost certainly as far from them as a good actor always is from the simple lessons of a how-to-act manual.

From the evidence all we can be certain of is that the Elizabethan acting style was a heightened style of the sort suggested in Richard III's exchange with Buckingham:

> *Rich.* Come cousin, canst thou quake, and change thy colour,
>   Murder thy breath in middle of a word,
>   And then again begin, and stop again,
>   As if thou were distraught and mad with terror?
> *Buck.* Tut, I can counterfeit the deep tragedian,
>   Speak, and look back, and pry on every side.
>   Tremble and start at wagging of a straw,
>   Intending deep suspicion: ghastly looks
>   Are at my service, like enforced smiles. [III, v, 1–9]

An even more vivid and detailed discussion of it occurs in Letoy's advice to his actors in Richard Brome's *The Antipodes* (1638). Though this play is rather late, the passage has a general relevance to our period; and neither its distinction between the style of *Hercules Furens* and the comic style nor its disapproval of

mannered gesticulation carried to extremes obscures that Letoy
is implying as standard a stylized, heightened style.

> *Letoy.* . . . Let me not see you act now,
>   In your Scholasticke way, you brought to towne wi'yee,
>   With see saw sacke a downe, like a Sawyer;
>   Nor in a Comicke Scene, play *Hercules Furens*,
>   Tearing your throat to split the Audients eares.
>   And you Sir, you had got a tricke of late,
>   Of holding out your bum in a set speech;
>   Your fingers fibulating on your breast,
>   As if your Buttons, or your Band-strings were
>   Helpes to your memory. Let me see you in it
>   No more I charge you. No, nor you sir, in
>   That over-action of the legges I told you of,
>   Your singles, and your doubles, Looke you—thus—
>   Like one o' th' dancing Masters o' the Beare-garden;
>   And when you have spoke, at the end of every speech,
>   Not minding the reply, you turne you round
>   As Tumblers doe; when betwixt every feat
>   They gather wind, by firking up their breeches.
>   Ile none of these, absurdities in my house.
>   But words and action married so together,
>   That shall strike harmony in the eares and eyes
>   Of the severest, if judicious Criticks.[55]

Of course it might be argued that all stage acting, as distinct from
movie or television acting, is heightened, and few would debate
the point. The further point is that Elizabethan acting seems to
have been more emphatically heightened than, say, the relatively
naturalistic style of our time. To call it a heightened style does not
mean that the actors were marionettes; it means simply that they
relied on a distinctly larger-than-life, stylized use of the voice,
gesture, and movements. The term "heightened style," moreover,
has the further advantage of embracing more than "formal" or

---

[55] *Works of Brome*, III, 259.

"conventional" can. It suggests how an actor might have moved from such magnified periods as Lear's "Blow, winds, and crack your cheeks" to the quiet intensity of "Pray you undo this button" while keeping to the same style—that is, without mixing styles, as S. L. Bethell claims they must have done.[56] What, after all, was to prevent an amazing range in a style that was fundamentally heightened, but not tied to rigid decorums?

In concluding this digression, then, we can confidently assume that the acting style fundamental to the adult actors was a heightened style. Further, we can assume that it was practiced with different degrees of success. Alberto's advice in the "Induction" to *Antonio and Mellida* to the boy playing the tyrant Piero suggests a burlesque on the style as it was still to be seen at its worst. Shakespeare's phrases "tearing a passion to tatters," "strutting and bellowing," and "imitating humanity abominably" come to mind. It was this version of adult acting that was especially vulnerable to impersonation by Marston's ten-to-fifteen-year-old virtuosos and that was, accordingly, most frequently ridiculed.

Most of the extant plays produced at Paul's and Blackfriars during the first five years of the revival bear unmistakable traces of this kind of burlesque. Sometimes the burlesque seems to have been woven through a whole play, particularly when the matter is of that conspicuously passionate or heroic stripe that normally the child actors never attempted. The production of the "Jeronimo" play mentioned in the "Induction" to *The Malcontent* (1604) is a case in point. Here we learn from Condell that the King's Men produced *The Malcontent* in part because the children at Blackfriars had performed their "Jeronimo" (ll. 53, 54). Although we do not know which of the "Jeronimo" plays this statement refers to, it probably refers to *I Jeronimo* (*ca.* 1600), since, as far as we know, Shakespeare's company never played the old *Spanish Tragedy*.[57] But it hardly matters; either play would have seemed outrageously old fashioned to the sophisticated Blackfriars audience,

---

[56] "Shakespeare's Actors," *RES*, N.S. I (July, 1950), 193–205.
[57] Chambers, *Stage*, III, 396.

and both required for a serious production acting talents far beyond anything that the child actors could manage. Difficult though it is to imagine, the alternative seems more reasonable: that the production referred to was not a serious production, that the Blackfriars boys sustained a burlesque through the whole of their "Jeronimo in decimosexto."

The style is even clearer, however, in plays or parts of them that deal with stock features of the adult repertories in a patently burlesque fashion. Sometimes the burlesque centers in character types from the public stage, sometimes in overworked situations or stock scenes. For most of the plays, of course, we do not have passages conveniently describing how the parts were played, though from time to time we do find jokes about the actors' size that sharpen the sense of incongruity.[58] But usually the plays are pitched in a sufficiently extravagant key to make the playwright's intention clear. If we only remember the actors' age and size, the large number of braggarts and aging lechers in these plays become distinctly grotesque. Imagine, for example, a little "Eyase" crying out on top of the following question:

Hippolite: . . . Wenches, by Mars his sweaty buff-jerkin (for now all my oaths must smell o' the soldado), I have seen more men's heads spurned up and down like foot-balls at a breakfast, after the hungry

---

[58] See, for example, *The Family of Love, The Works of Thomas Middleton*, ed. A. H. Bullen (London, 1885), III, 26. Gerardine announces that he has just come from a play:

Ger. . . . where we saw most excellent Sampson excel the whole world in gate-carrying.
Dryfat. Was it performed by the youths?
Ger. By youths? Why, I tell thee we saw Sampson, and I hope 'tis not for youths to play Sampson.

In *Blurt, Master Constable* (Middleton's *Works*, I, 38) Imperia, a courtezan, answers Doyt's remark, "At your service," with the *double entendre:* "Alas, thou canst do me small service!" And in the "Induction" to *Cynthia's Revels* (H & S, IV, 38) when Child 3 is attacked by Child 1 and Child 2, he cries, "I'lde crie, a rape, but that you are children."

cannons had picked them, than are maidenheads in Venice, and more legs of men served in at a dinner than ever I shall see legs of capons in one platter whilst I live.[59]

This passage is typical of the rant spoken by such characters as Lazarillo de Tormes, the "Son of Mars" in *Blurt, Master Constable,* Medice in *The Gentleman Usher,* and Captain Quintiliano in *May Day.* And just as absurd as the braggarts are the aging lechers and young lovers luxuriating in the febrile love poetry that the verse satirists had ridiculed so relentlessly. In fact, the burlesque centering in young lovers—since they are usually important characters —often includes a burlesque of one or several stock situations as well as a burlesque of character. The balcony scene, for example, seems to have been a particularly popular object of ridicule. Many of these plays have one;[60] and in them the young lovers invariably strike all the conventional poses and speak all the conventional speeches. In Chapman's *May Day* a third character, Angelo, is present to point the satire through his exasperated comments ("You'll be whipped anon for your amorosity"), as he ostensibly assists Aurelia in his wooing of Aemelia.[61]

The precise nature and extent of the satire leveled at the public companies by the children's companies is, of course, a subject too vast and complex to be here given a full treatment. It is sufficient for our purposes to recognize a burlesque acting style in these few examples so that we can identify it in plays providing fewer clues to the way they were acted. But recognizing a burlesque acting style in these plays is of the utmost importance. As Marston pointed out in his "Preface" to *The Fawn:* "Comedies are writ to be spoken, not read; remember the life of these things consists in action." Although we have no conclusive evidence that he was thinking here of the losses involved in reading a play that was

[59] *Blurt, Master Constable* (Middleton's *Works,* I, 6).

[60] See, for example, *The Poetaster* (H & S, IV, 286–289); Chapman's *May Day* (*Plays,* III, iii); and *Jack Drum,* pp. 196ff.

[61] *Plays,* IV, ii, 79, 80.

originally intended to be acted in a broad vein of burlesque, the quotation applies. Moreover, it is only by assuming such a style that many of the children's satirical comedies produced early in the revival can be visualized as not only intelligent but intelligible productions.

Before we leave the subject of the burlesque acting style, however, it should be pointed out that not all of the burlesque was specifically directed at the public companies. Frequently, as we shall see, it was much more general in character. When it was, the children became the agents of a pervasive burlesque on the adult world, apes mimicking adult foibles and vices, impersonators bringing contempt down upon foolishness of which they, as children, were palpably innocent. Put to this use, the child actors constituted a major satiric premise: that adults are often children. And, capitalizing on the possibilities offered by burlesque, they affirmed the logic of the premise by showing that, the more peculiarly adult the follies and vices of their characters became, the more like children their characters seemed.

This account of the child actors' burlesque style, of course, suggests but faintly their normal style in performing tragedies. Although Marston's tragedies, notably *Antonio's Revenge,* contain moments for which the burlesque style was appropriate, they are for the most part utterly unsuited to a burlesque treatment. Whatever else they may be, the tragedies produced at the private houses—Marston's and Chapman's tragedies, Daniel's *Philotas,* and Mason's *The Turk*—are unmistakably serious plays, and they call for a style of acting that, however different it may have been from the style practiced at the Globe, must have been sober and dignified. We have only the evidence of some nine or ten plays to suggest what it was like, yet even this small body of evidence indicates that, like the comedies, the tragedies did not demand complex characterizations or realistic action. On the contrary, they avoided realism and emphasized stylization and artificiality. These qualities are especially evident in the tragedies produced during the first five or six years of the revival, plays that abound in long set speeches, tableaux effects, and other devices intended to formalize the action. As plays, they are distinctly abstract and intellectual when compared with most plays like them being done at the public houses. Although it is difficult to generalize further about the mode of representation used for them, we can conclude from this that they too seem to have been adapted to the children's limitations. That the children had little in the way of special talents to bring to them may help to explain why so few tragedies were written for the private companies.

It was, at any rate, for actors thus gifted and thus limited that Marston undertook a career as playwright in 1599. I have discussed them at length because they account for so much in his first few plays and in all the plays produced at Paul's and Blackfriars during the first half-dozen years of the revival. They, more than anything else, encouraged in the private theatres the development of satirical comedy and the refinement of the critical perspective crucial to Marston's and Jonson's best work. They, better than anything else, explain the peculiarities of the tragedy produced at the private theatres.

It would be too simple and rather misleading, however, to imply that the child actors continued to exert this kind of influence on their playwrights through the whole period of the revival. To imply this is to assume that the personnel of the children's companies was much the same at all times, and this we have reason to disbelieve. In the first years of the revival most, if not all, of the child actors were, it is true, from ten to fifteen years of age. Nathan Field was thirteen in 1600; Clifton states that his son was thirteen when he was abducted in 1600; and Salmon (Salathiel) Pavy must have been ten in 1600, since Jonson says he was "scarce thirteen" at his death in 1603.[62] But we should not overlook that many of the boys in the extant actors' lists for 1600–1603 continued with these companies for some time.[63] Nathan

----

[62] See Chambers, *Stage*, II, 44 and 295ff. under "Actors."

[63] These lists are easiest to compile from Sir Henry Clifton's Complaint (see Hillebrand, *Child Actors*, pp. 160–164) and Jonson's lists of actors for *Cynthia's Revels* and *The Poetaster*.

Field appears to have remained with the Blackfriars children until 1613; and even in 1609, when he acted in *Epicoene,* he was twenty-two years old. Likewise, William Ostler and John Underwood, though they appear in the lists by 1601, evidently did not leave for the King's Men until about 1608. On the other hand, the Commissions granted Nathaniel Gyles in 1604 and 1606 indicate that he was continuously recruiting. The Commission of September 13, 1604, could be interpreted as a routine confirmation resulting from the accession of James of Gyles's right to impress children, except that the Commission of November 7, 1606, which was expressly designed to restrain him from recruiting for the stage, bears out that he actually was still impressing them.[64]

It follows from all this that the personnel of the children's companies changed in the course of the revival. At first the "boys" were literally boys, ranging in age from ten to fifteen and possessing the talents and limitations discussed above. But by about 1605 and thereafter the membership had become mixed and included youths as well as boys, with the result that the actors doubtless exerted a rather different influence on the playwrights from that exerted earlier. The effect of this change on Marston's work will be considered later; for the present suffice it to say that it accounts in part, at least, for the differences between *The Poetaster* (1601) and *Epicoene* (1609).

Of course, such changes came considerably later than *Histriomastix*. As one of the earliest, indeed one of the first plays of the revival, *Histriomastix* was acted by what seems to have been a homogeneous group of youngsters, boys peculiarly suited to broad satire and burlesque. If these capabilities are only partially in evidence in the play, it is because the play is substantially one of the prerevival type, an Interlude-Morality, on which is grafted the satire on the adult actors. It is this combination of elements that makes *Histriomastix* so useful as a transitional piece. In its over-all didactic structure, in the figure of the critic Chrisoganus, and in the denunciation backed by general Stoic ideals, we can

[64] *Malone Society Collections,* I, pts. 4 and 5, ed. E. K. Chambers (London, 1911), 353–359.

easily discover Marston the snarling satirist and Neo-Stoic. In
the *buffo* burlesque on the public companies, however, we find
him in a new role: devising satire that is neither snarling nor
particularly elevated, but unmistakably intended to be funny.
Against a conception of what the child actors were capable of
and predisposed to, it is now possible to see that in the process
of revising this play Marston worked for the first time with elements calculated to elicit laughter. In view of his decisive movement in his next few plays toward gaiety and hilarity, this facet
of *Histriomastix* is important. It was Marston's attention to the
uses of laughter in satire that subsequently made possible fresh
combinations of the elements seen first in the verse satires and
then seen reappearing in *Histriomastix*, and it was from these
fresh combinations that he hammered out his conception of satirical comedy.

Chapter V

Lovers-in-Distress
Burlesques and
Antonio's Revenge

THE next phase of Marston's work reflects his vigorous efforts to master the role of private playwright while retaining as much as possible of the theory and practice of the verse satires. His experience with *Histriomastix* had persuaded him that the didactic, thesis-dominated structure was inadequate for dramatic purposes. In the "Introduction" to *Jack Drum's Entertainment* he apologized, accordingly, for his false start by vowing "not to torment your listning eares / With mouldy fopperies of stale Poetry, / Unpossible drie mustie Fictions" (p. 179), and in his next two plays he worked for the first time with imitative structures, that is, dramatic structures the controlling purpose of which is the development of an action of a certain kind rather than the illustration of a thesis. This decision focused his attention for the first time on the technical problems of designing an action capable of moving an audience in a relatively controlled way. It required him to look carefully at such matters as the system of probabilities at the core of his action, governing the reasonableness of the play's events. It forced him as a playwright with something to say to subordinate explicit argument to the larger considerations of plot and to center his persuasion not in theoretical statement but in the plot's power to evoke a fairly specific set of attitudes and emotions.

His first effort along these lines in *Jack Drum* (see Appendix A) traces so intimate a concern with his new task that in it the snarling satirist and Neo-Stoic only fitfully intrude on the new-fledged playwright. The play contains characteristic satiric passages and occasional flights into Neo-Stoic theory, it is true; but more striking by far is Marston's attention in it to the immediate, practical problems of devising a dramatic action both suited for child actors and productive of comic pleasure. *Jack Drum* represents a neat, if not very impressive, solution to the problem. It involves a skillful exploitation of the children's talents for burlesque, songs, and dances, and it substitutes for character-interest the utterly flat characters who readily become targets of satire and criticism. Moreover, it embraces these elements in an action the over-all shape of which is governed by its own inner principles rather than by a thesis.

Jack Drum's Entertainment, or The Comedy of Pasquill and Katherine revolves round the three women in Sir Edward Fortune's household and their suitors. In the first scene we are prepared for a keen bout at courtship when Sir Edward, a roistering gentleman of High-gate, determines to permit his daughters, Katherine and Camelia, complete freedom in their choice of husbands. Katherine's rejection of Mamon, the aging usurer from London, quickly identifies her as a conventional romantic heroine. Camelia, who dotes on Brabant Jr. at the beginning of her first scene, is a capricious young woman whose maid Winifride much too easily persuades her to shift from Brabant Jr. to John Ellis. Winifride, whose guile and ambition are particularly clear in the soliloquy in which she gloats over the ease with which she handles Camelia, is an enterprising wench interested only in the profit her mistress' marriage may bring her. By the final scene in Act I, in which all the suitors come on stage and indulge their foibles or vices, the main lines of the multiple courtships to ensue are clear. The remainder of the action consists in large part in the working out of the farcical and satiric possibilities of this situation.

In the next two acts the courtships get under way. In three successive balcony scenes Katherine rejects a pipe-smoking gallant name Puffe, rejects Mamon a second time, and then surrenders passionately to Pasquill. But a complication develops when Mamon hires John fo' de King, a lecherous Frenchman whose ardors fix on Winifride in the subsequent action, to murder Pasquill. Although John fo' de King, whom we know from a thumbnail sketch to be a "faithfull pure Rogue," quickly reveals Mamon's plot to Pasquill, and although Pasquill feigns death and then beats the gloating Mamon, Brabant Jr. and Planet hear only the false report of his death. In the next scene, accordingly, still another balcony scene in which this time Camelia rejects Brabant Jr. and then in his presence encourages the melancholy simile-hunter John Ellis, Planet mentions Pasquill's death while he and Sir Edward try to calm the furious Brabant Jr. This disclosure sends Katherine off tearing her hair and Sir Edward to security in a "Butt of Canary Sacke." Pasquill enters, just too late for the first of several times in the play, only to learn that Katherine has disappeared.

Act III opens with a scene of courtship on a lower social level when Jack Drum, Sir Edward's devil-may-care steward, and John fo' de King vie for the favors of Winifride. Unlike her superiors, Winifride ostensibly yields to both, though she has no intention of yielding to either. On the one hand she tells Jack Drum to hide in a sack in her chamber, while on the other she tells John fo' de King that she will be in the sack and that he is to carry it away.

After this piece of comic business has been primed, Planet and Brabant Jr. catch Camelia and John Ellis at amorous dalliance. When Brabant Jr. makes still another plea to Camelia, Planet criticizes him and then criticizes Camelia for her stupidity. But when Planet sees that Brabant Jr. will persist in his foolishness, he draws Winifride aside to bribe her to woo Camelia in his behalf. Meanwhile, Pasquill and Katherine are reunited in a chance meeting that culminates in hyperbolical ardors, only to be separated again when, in Pasquill's absence, Mamon throws a poison in Katherine's face. With Katherine fled, Pasquill becomes distracted; but he delays his pursuit long enough to punish Mamon by tearing up his indentures, and Flawne completes this punishment by reporting Mamon's financial disaster.

Act IV begins with the working out of the sack trick. Embarrassed at being detected by Planet, Brabant Sr., and Brabant Jr., Jack Drum saves face, and John fo' de King accepts the compensation offered by Brabant Sr., who as would-be intriguer plans to embarrass him again by taking him to still another wench— this time to Mistress Brabant. Unknown to Brabant Sr., after he leaves John fo' de King and his wife alone, she kindly agrees to show John her chamber. Meanwhile, Winifride, acting on Planet's promises, persuades Camelia to give up John Ellis in favor of Planet, and Camelia rejects the confident Ellis as he makes nuptial arrangements. Once Camelia is confronted with Planet, however, Planet reviles her to avenge his friend Brabant Jr., but initiates still another complication when Brabant Jr. misconstrues Planet's conversation, becomes jealous, and resolves to murder his friend.

Act V brings each of the lines of action to an orthodox resolution. After Brabant Jr. has arranged to have Planet killed off stage, he disguises himself as his victim and learns from the capricious Camelia that he has grossly wronged Planet. While Sir Edward and the others are trying to prevent him from suicide, Planet enters, and the Page hired to do the murder explains why he had not done it. Amid the subsequent rejoicing, Katherine and Pasquill enter. Katherine has been cured by a "skilfull Beldame," and

Pasquill, though mad when he appears, is soon miraculously restored by music and the sight of Katherine. These joyful reunions rapidly give place, however, to a series of punishments. First, we learn that Mamon has been committed to Bedlam; next we see the inconstant Camelia rejected by all her suitors. Finally, the high-spirited Brabant Sr. is shattered by the backfire of his own joke when John fo' de King enters to thank him for the wench. With the achievement of this plateau the play closes as Sir Edward calls for feasting and revelry.

Even this summary suggests that *Jack Drum* is not intended as a conventional treatment of its plot materials. By type these materials resemble strongly those of the lovers-in-distress plays popular in the previous two decades, those plays the primary interest of which centers in what is called at the end of *Antonio and Mellida* "The comic crosses of true love." Such Elizabethan pot-boilers as *Common Conditions* (*ca.* 1576), *Mucedorus* (*ca.* 1590), *Sir Clyomon and Sir Clamydes* (*ca.* 1591), and Robert Greene's *Orlando Furioso* (*ca.* 1591) readily define the category, to which the prose romances were a nondramatic cousin. By way of departing from this type in *Jack Drum* Marston has emphasized the conventionality of its nakedly conventional action with the clear purpose of magnifying and thus rendering more ludicrous its naïve romanticism. Moreover, he has taken every advantage of the occasions provided by the action to graft on it the method of his verse satires. The result is a burlesque of the traditional lovers-in-distress plays filled out with satiric passages and songs and dances.

Symptomatic of Marston's intentions is his all but complete indifference to the long-range sentimental interests ordinarily met in such plays, the interests that usually center in the lovers and their struggle against obstacles. He has ignored even the most obvious means to make the lovers interesting or the action suspenseful. The line of action concerning Katherine is very mechanically drawn out by repetitious complications; and if the action concerning Camelia is more economically handled, its focal point,

Camelia, is hardly complex enough to sustain interest for long. The action concerning Winifride, on the other hand, is telescoped into one piece of farce-business, and Winifride herself is so shuttled to the background that at the end her final punishment is only implied. Even the rift between Planet and Brabant Jr., though intrinsically interesting since they are easily the most attractive characters in the play, comes too late to be central, while such conventional interest as the other characters provide is evident only in the scenes in which they are exposed and ridiculed. Whether as a result of deliberate choice or inexperience, therefore, Marston has here committed himself to a structure comprised of multiple short-range interests focused in scenes or small groups of scenes. It is on these units that he has spent his ingenuity, and it is primarily from them that the play derives its unusual combination of criticism and gaiety. Although it is probably fair to say that the lovers-in-distress materials predicated this structure to some extent, that Marston knew what he was doing is quite clear in almost every aspect of the action he has designed.

Conventional interest is chiefly reduced, perhaps, through his widespread use of the extremely flat, burlesque characters then popular with the private playwrights. Where we most expect pathos and most expect the characters to move us to unalloyed sympathy, in the vicissitudes of Katherine and Pasquill, Marston has reversed the technique of a public playwright by ridiculing the conventionality of the characters and underscoring their absurd extravagance. In their first meeting in the burlesque balcony scene in Act II, they strike the stock postures and gush the appropriate hyperboles; yet even here a burlesque intention is clear in Pasquill's obtrusive fulsomeness and his incongruous tendency to slip from the poetry of superlatives to images of a "snoring world" and of a content "Bung[ed] up . . . within the whoopes / Of a stuft dry Fatt"—and all this as Mamon lurks to the side, grunting "Ha, ha, yong Pasquill, have I found you out?" (pp. 198, 199). In their second meeting the intention to play for moment-to-moment burlesque rather than for long-range interest is even more conspicuous. As Pasquill laments the loss of "that rich *Idea* of perfection," Katherine, in a petticoat, approaches the place where Pasquill was supposed to have been murdered and, as she observes that even nature reflects the loss, prepares to join her lover in the grand manner. Of course Pasquill stops her, and as usual they are reunited in hyperboles:

> *Pas.* Hold, hold thou miracle of constancie,
>   First let heaven perish, and the crazde world runne
>   Into first *Chaos* of confusion. . . .
>   Amazement of thy Sex. . . .
>   Divinitee of sweetnesse. . . .
> *Kath.* Heaven of Content, Paphos of my delight.
> *Pas.* Mirrour of Constancie, life-bloud of love.
> *Kath.* Centre to whom all my affections move. [p. 215]

No actors, I submit, could have delivered these lines convincingly at this time in English dramatic history, and least of all the child actors. Indeed, in view of the sophistication that we must assume in Marston's audience, the lines are clear evidence that Marston was not interested in Pasquill and Katherine as frustrated lovers, but as the agents of a burlesque on amorists both in and outside the drama. The lovers' transparent simplicity, their magnified conventionality, their absurd artificiality, and their trite extravagance, all qualities which were doubtless heightened by the child actors, deprive them of even routine interest.

Much the same tendency to reduce and distort for the purposes of caricature is also met in the other important characters. Sir Edward Fortune, though important chiefly as an instrumental character whose liberality makes the multiple courtships of the play probable and whose hedonism provides occasions for much of the singing, dancing, and revelry, is also something of a caricature of the frolicking knight of the Sir Richard Mounchensey (*The Merry Devil of Edmonton*) type. The stupidity of his laissez-faire attitude toward Camelia and his gross attempts to be philosophical in a butt of Canary sack effectively undercut the sentimentality of his heartiness, but are not meant to complicate the characterization appreciably. Camelia, on the other hand, is a simple embodiment of contemptible caprice, who, since her capriciousness has no serious consequences, arouses little more than the mild punitive desires that are gratified when all her suitors reject her. Winifride, moreover, is much the same kind of character. The remaining characters, with the exception of Planet, are for the most part satiric types who plainly owe much to their predecessors in the verse satires and whose foolishness is exposed and derided in much the manner of the satires. John Ellis, the melancholy amorist (as opposed to Pasquill and Brabant Jr., who are dedicated amorists), recalls the melancholy "inamorato Lucian" in Satire III of *Certain Satires* and Briscus in Satire I, who also entertains his mistress with music. The satiric crux of John Ellis' characterization is that his melancholy is distinctly a symptom of his stupidity. The grandiloquent Puffe savors of the fashionable Curio of *The Scourge*, Satire VI, the image of courtesy of *Certain Satires*, Satire II, and the clotheshorse, complete with Ganymede, in Satire III of *Certain Satires*. John fo' de King is a French Luxurio, without Luxurio's perversions. And Brabant Sr., the self-appointed critic and would-be intriguer, most resembles the "judicial Torquatus" of Marston's prefatory letter in *The Scourge*. On the other hand, Mamon, the old Jewish usurer, is not derived from a character in the satires, but from the *commedia dell' arte* Pantalone of the famous fiery nose, black suit, and ineffectual villainy.

Of all the important characters in the play, only Planet wholly escapes ridicule, and even he is notably flat. His character most nearly approximates the persona of the Neo-Stoic satirist; as Campbell has pointed out, his name probably owes something to the popular notion that corruption and change visited only those regions of the universe on which the moon cast its shadow and that the planets, accordingly, were pure.[1] At any rate, he is free

---

[1] *Comicall Satyre*, p. 163. Marston's use of names appropriate to his characters persisted from the verse satires. The "Chrisoganus" of *Histriomastix*

of the blemishes marking all the other characters (for even Brabant Jr. is a fool in loving Camelia), and, like the satirist-philosopher, he spends most of his time criticizing and attacking them from the fringe of the action. Yet for all his moral superiority Planet evokes very little sympathy and anxiety, if only because he does not become engaged in the action in any way endangering his good fortune until late in the play. Before he is exposed to the threats of Brabant Jr.'s plan to murder him, he fills the single function of directing opinion through his criticism.

Planet's function as satirist-philosopher, however, brings us to the second important means by which Marston has tailored his lovers-in-distress materials to a rather episodic burlesque. In addition to throwing away the conventional effects of such an action by ignoring the standard means for securing long-range interest, he has exploited most opportunities for satire. Planet is the chief of several agents calling our attention to foibles and vices in characters who are, whatever they may lack in human interest, boldly etched, very lively caricatures. Much as the satirist had discussed the satiric types with Lynceus in the poems, here Planet discusses them with Brabant Jr., drawing them out, as he draws out Puffe in Act I, and denouncing them, as he denounces Brabant Sr. in Act V:

> I do hate these bumbaste wits,
> That are puft up with arrogant conceit
> Of their owne worth, as if *Omnipotence*
> Had hoysed them to such unequaled height,
> That they survaide our spirits with an eye
> Only create to censure from above,
> When good soules they do nothing but reprove. [p. 229]

---

raises problems of derivation and meaning (see William Smith, *Dictionary of Greek and Roman Biography and Mythology*, London, 1844, and Guilpin's *Skialetheia*, London, 1931, Epigram 30), and he could not have intended the conventional associations for "Pasquill" (see A. Davenport's note on the name in Hall's *Collected Poems*, p. 231). But otherwise his usages seem to have been quite regular.

Yet Planet is not the only such commentator in *Jack Drum*. In his absence others readily assume the critic's function; in fact, in the early comedies it was Marston's practice to disperse the criticism in this way. In Act II Jack Drum takes it upon himself to denounce Mamon, Jews, and usurers, and earlier Sir Edward speaks authoritatively against the corruption at court. In the last scene of Act I Brabant Jr. temporarily shares Planet's role when he introduces a number of the satiric types in thumbnail sketches reminiscent of the verse satires. Taken in the aggregate, this commentary undercuts the values normal to an action of this kind by forcing it into a critical perspective.

Some elements of the satire, of course, are not so clearly labeled as others. The dimension of burlesque, for example, is not always easy to identify because some of the scenes in which a burlesque intention seems clear have no critic to direct opinion. But Puffe's balcony scene with Katherine at the beginning of Act II is a good example of how the satire can proceed from outrageous exaggeration alone, and surely there can be no mistake about Pasquill's use of Seneca in his posturing lamentation at the end of Act III.[2] Unless an intention to burlesque is assumed, at any rate, unless a purpose to see and to have us see this action from an unusual point of view is granted, much of the play is unintelligible. More than any other elements, the lighthearted burlesque and playful exposures of grotesquery define the highly conscious attempt here to achieve exuberance and gaiety in a context distinctly, but by no means savagely, satiric.

Granting this general purpose, then, it will be useful to consider more briefly the other means by which Marston fashioned this otherwise melodramatic action to make the most of its farcical and satiric possibilities. To begin with, he has handled the

---

[2] After Katherine has been poisoned and has run off, Pasquill uses a familiar passage from the *Hercules Furens* (ll. 1138–1139) as part of his lamentation:

> *Quis his locus? quae Regio? quae Mundi plaga?*
> *Ubi sum?* Katherine, Katherine, *Eheu* Katherine.

threats to the relatively sympathetic characters so that they cannot be taken seriously. The threats to the lovers stem chiefly from Mamon, and his villainy is too conventional to evoke much anxiety. Like Pantalone, ridiculed by all, beaten physically and disgraced at every turn, he is a clown—so blatantly the Elizabethan Jew-usurer *commedia dell' arte* butt as to be incapable of inspiring fear. Accordingly, we anticipate the failure of his plot to kill Pasquill, and, in fact, Marston has John fo' de King betray it twenty lines after he has agreed to do it. In like manner the other threats, the poison thrown in Katherine's face, Pasquill's madness, and Brabant Jr.'s plan to have Planet killed, are all rendered innocuous by their stark conventionality, by their vagueness, or by the manner of their execution. In each case Marston has left a wide margin of probability for the comic resolutions appropriate in the conspicuously unterrifying world he has created.

Marston's treatment of the world of the play, moreover, forces still further qualifications because, of all the play's structural features, it most clearly reflects his intention to fashion not just a "Jacke Drums entertainment" in the proverbial sense of "brusque reception," but an entertainment in the more general sense as well. To embrace both comic and satiric variety, he needed a fictional world in which the improbable was distinctly probable. In the first few scenes, accordingly, he defines an atmosphere in which the satiric grotesques are at home, in which songs and dances are the rule rather than the exception, in which vague disappearances and chance meetings are perfectly normal, and in which dangers and misfortunes of a serious order would be completely out of place. The open, rural world of the first scene is noisy, carefree, plentiful, and healthful, a world in which Sir Edward presides and in which only Mamon, the city man, seems grotesque enough to be strange. Here the many songs and dances seem perfectly natural. Some of them are simply entertainments, extraneous songs and dances designed to give the child actors opportunities to exercise their specialties. Indeed, some of them seem to have been elaborate, if the stage directions for the morris dance and song in Act I and the length of Ellis' song in Act V are any indication. The others, however, clearly relate, if somewhat loosely, to the satiric line of the play. Mamon's love song in Act II, "Chunck, chunck, chunck, chunck, his bagges do ring," and John fo' de King's song in Act IV, "By gor den me must needs now sing," are extravagant expressions of character that emerge quite naturally from the action and the particular fictional world defined.

In general, then, Marston's treatment of the lovers-in-distress action in this play has made the most of its comic and satiric values and stamped it with ebullience. It would be a mistake to deny the ethical interest of the satire and criticism and a mistake to overlook the familiar Neo-Stoic strain in Planet and even in Sir Edward's abhorrence of the Opinion of the "drunke reeling Commons" (pp. 184–185). But one is not so aware of these elements as of sheer variety in the play—of satire and serious commentary, it is true, but also of songs, dances, roguish burlesque, and farce gags. Even Marston's language reflects this variety. I have already discussed his practice of modulating his verbal style in the satires to accord with the different facets of his satiric persona. Such modulation is no less in evidence in the plays, though in the plays it is more extensive in scope because it is dependent on the range of characters involved. In *Jack Drum* there is the plain conversational prose spoken by Jack Drum, Timothy Twedle, and others; there is the rather plain verse like that spoken by Planet when he bribes Winifride in Act III; there is the extravagant verse of the amorists' speeches; and, finally, there is the familiar harsh verse of the critical speeches. Frequently, these speeches turn on the terms integral to Marston's thought in the satires when, for example, Brabant Jr. describes himself as "a man / . . . not so clogd with durt as others are" or speaks of "the bright models of eternitie" (p. 212). But such emergences of Marston's intellectual commitment are fugitive and decidedly subordinate to the primary task of executing what was for him the new literary task of designing a particular kind of dramatic action.

To summarize we must return to this crucial shift in Marston's interests. Marston's attention in *Jack Drum* was consumed by the structural, largely technical problem involved in executing this kind of dramatic design. As his first full-scale effort in the drama, the play obviously has many flaws. The dispersion of its criticism tends to deprive it of a moral center. Many of the punishments are unsatisfactory, either because they are altogether arbitrary, like Mamon's financial failure, or because they are crudely farcical. Moreover, the play involves an unfortunate tension between its gamboling farcicality and its satire. The satire tends to undercut the hilarity, and the gaiety of Sir Edward's world tends to undercut the satire. Marston only later solved the problem of reconciling such disparate qualities, of uniting and harmonizing them in a dramatic action. For all its shortcomings, however, *Jack Drum* constitutes a reasonable and mildly successful attempt to design a play suitable for the child actors, relevant to the needs of the private theatre, and, at the same time, productive of a distinctly satiricomic pleasure.[3] In the story of Marston's development it establishes the first of the several distinctly different dramatic actions that he was to experiment with in carrying out this artistic aim. If it emphasizes lighthearted, trivial fun at the expense of the higher seriousness met in the satires, it does so because Marston apparently found it necessary to work through this kind of action before he was able to realize more fully the peculiar comic seriousness he felt appropriate to satirical comedy. Undoubtedly, it reveals the seriocomic attitude at the core of all Marston's satirical comedies in its most ribald aspect.

In what appears to have been his next play, *Antonio and Mellida* (see Appendix A), he has left us a brief statement of

[3] It has been argued, of course, that it was also designed for the poetomachia. See Penniman, *War*, pp. 71–73, and Small, *Stage-Quarrel*, pp. 95–100.

intentions that neatly sums up his ambition to combine the methods of laughter with those of satire. The mock dedication to "*The
most honourably renowned* NOBODY" conveniently brings into the
open the jaunty superiority of the orphan poet, the lightness and
ebullience of *Jack Drum*, and Marston's elusive seriousness, all
epitomized in his description of his attitude as "seriously fantastical." I had better quote the "Dedication" in full:

> Since it hath flowed with the current of my humorous blood to affect
> (a little too much) to be seriously fantastical, here take (most respected
> Patron) the worthless present of my slighter idleness. If you vouchsafe
> not his protection, then, O thou sweetest perfection (Female Beauty),
> shield me from the stopping of vinegar bottles. Which most wished
> favour if it fail me, then *Si nequeo flectere superos, Acheronta movebo*.
> But yet, honour's redeemer, virtue's advancer, religion's shelter, and
> piety's fosterer, yet, yet, I faint not in despair of thy gracious affection
> and protection; to which I only shall ever rest most servingman-like,
> obsequiously making legs and standing (after our free-born English
> garb) bareheaded. Thy only affied slave and admirer,
>
> J.M.

The chief trouble with this statement is that it does not clarify
precisely how serious being "seriously fantastical" is. As Marston
ridicules in his own person the conventionality and extravagance
so pervasively ridiculed in the plays, his language is essentially
that of Pasquill. The irony, accordingly, is difficult to gauge. Yet
the blend of playfulness and of a slightly concealed, but firmly
derisive attitude toward romantic conventions is unmistakable.
As we shall see, this blend is a permanent and a progressively
more impressive feature of his satirical comedy.

Actually, the burlesque intention of *Antonio and Mellida* does
not differ significantly from that in *Jack Drum*. Again, Marston
was concerned with writing to the child actors' special talents;
accordingly the play is abundant in songs, dances, and comic
grotesques. At the same time he was concerned with fashioning
a dramatic action that would effectively deliver both gaiety and

criticism, and again his efforts produced a plot emphasizing scenes or small structural units. The important difference between *Antonio and Mellida* and *Jack Drum* is that in *Antonio and Mellida* the burlesque is linked with more devices to render the laughter serious, to temper the dominant quality of gaiety with didactic or philosophical substance.

Unlike *Jack Drum*, for example, *Antonio and Mellida* has an "Induction" the chief function of which is to prepare quite deliberately for the rather off-key frolic to follow. As we have seen from Alberto's advice to the actor playing Piero, the "Induction" consists of a discussion of the various players' parts. All the actors taking male parts come on stage *"with parts in their hands; having cloaks cast over their apparel";* and each in turn is introduced. In this way the satiric types are sketched briefly much after the fashion of the thumbnail sketches of the satires, and the character of Feliche, the critic-spectator deriving from the satirist himself through Planet, is quickly defined. In addition, the pervasive burlesque on the public companies is explicitly set up in Alberto's comments on Piero's role as a stock tyrant:

> such rank custom is grown popular;
> And now the vulgar fashion strides as wide,
> And stalks as proud upon the weakest stilts
> Of the slight'st fortunes, as if Hercules
> Or burly Atlas shoulder'd up their state. [ll. 15–19]

Having thus economically disposed of these preliminaries, Marston realized at least two important advantages. First he was enabled, after the initial exposition of Antonio's opening soliloquy, to collapse the action and to achieve the rapid pace necessary to farcical effects. Secondly and more important, he made it possible to develop, not more strands of action than we discovered in *Jack Drum*, but contrasting strands of action that qualify and extend each other and that require for the effectiveness of the contrast a fuller development than strands of action set up in parallel would require.

The plot of *Antonio and Mellida* is contrived in large part to realize the effect of the contrast between the satiric scenes at Piero's court and the scenes in which Andrugio philosophizes at the seashore. To the extent that Andrugio's Neo-Stoicism is relevant to the degenerate folly at court, the hand of Marston the satirist-philosopher is easy to recognize. But it would be misleading to push the importance of the contrast too far. Even though Andrugio has counterparts at court in Feliche and Rossaline, the respective lines of action are constructed not according to the predications of a thesis, but according to the inner requirements of the action. In other words, though Marston's penchant for didacticism is again prominent in this structure, the structure itself is not ordered by didactic principles.

The satiric line of action centering in the scenes at Piero's court is not unlike the plot of *Jack Drum*, built as it is around the relations between Mellida and Rossaline, Piero's daughter and niece respectively, and their suitors. The main action concerns Mellida and her Romeolike suitor, Antonio, who has been denied Mellida's hand by Piero because of a long-standing family enmity and who, before the represented action of the play begins, has been defeated along with his father Andrugio. In Act I Antonio comes to Piero's court disguised (grotesquely enough for a child actor) as an Amazon, desolate at his defeat and the loss of his father, but determined to take Mellida at all costs.[4] Here he is immediately befriended by Mellida and Rossaline, to whom he recounts the pathetic and purely fictitious tale of Antonio's death at sea. In Act II, after becoming so wrought up at seeing Mellida on the arm of the Florentine, Galeatzo, that he falls into one of his frequent swoons, he manages to reveal himself to Mellida and to give her a note containing his plan for their flight. Of course Mellida loses the note, and in Act III Piero finds it to initiate a complication. But before Piero's lieutenants can apprehend the lovers, Antonio

---

[4] The actors seem to have been abundantly aware of the absurdity of the role of Amazon; see "Induction," ll. 69–88.

is warned of the discovery by Feliche. Then, in the very presence of the overconfident Piero, Antonio makes his escape disguised as a sailor, shouting "He went that way," and Mellida, disguised as a page, literally dances past untouched. In Act IV the lovers are reunited in eighteen lines of saccharine Italian dialogue, only to be separated again when Balurdo recognizes Mellida and Piero captures her and condemns her to marry Galeatzo immediately. But this final complication is overcome in Act V: Andrugio moves Piero to repentance by volunteering his head for the reward Piero has offered, and Antonio tricks Piero into yielding Mellida by pretending to have died of grief.

Parallel to this line of action, though sufficiently different from it to set off Antonio and Mellida as a relatively attractive couple, the action concerning Rossaline and her suitors is rigorously satirical. It consists almost wholly of a parade of the satiric types vying for Rossaline's hand, and its probability derives almost wholly from the character of Rossaline. Rossaline has frequently been compared to the characters of Shakespeare's romantic comedies, and, indeed, her name, her wit, and certain verbal echoes make it probable that she derives from them.[5] But if Marston copied these heroines in drawing Rossaline's character, he put her character to a use quite as different as that made of his romantic materials. Rossaline's wit and vivacity serve chiefly to qualify her as a witty intriguer capable of attracting the thirty-nine suitors of whom she boasts for the sheer pleasure of observing them indulge their follies. When Piero asks her which one she will marry, she answers,

---

[5] Cf. Castilio's description of Rossaline's wit (II, i, 64, 65) with the description of Beatrice's wit in II, i, 231–234 of *Much Ado;* cf. Alberto's lines, "For woods, trees, sea, or rocky Apenine, / Is not so ruthless as my Rossaline" (V, i, 66, 67), with the "false gallop of verses" in *As You Like It* (III, ii, 87, 88); and cf. Rossaline's line, "O, to have a husband with a mouth / continually smoking, with a bush of furze on the ridge of his chin . . ." (V, i, 144–146) with Beatrice's remark (II, i, 29), "I could not endure a husband with a beard on his face."

Nobody, good sweet uncle. I tell you, sir, I have thirty-nine servants,
and my monkey that makes the fortieth. Now I love all of them lightly
for something, but affect none of them seriously for anything. . . .

[V, i, 153–156]

Instead of taking them seriously, she delights in drawing them
out to scathe them with a wit that Castilio says "stings, blisters,
galls off the skin with the tart acrimony of her sharp quickness"
(II, i, 64, 65). Consequently, she is, like Feliche, a critic in the
line of action at the center of which she stands, a critic, moreover,
who is particularly interesting because her humor sometimes runs
to mimicking the folly that she ridicules. In Act III, scene ii,
where, like Balurdo, she sets her face before a mirror, she would
be indistinguishable from the fashionable Martia of *The Scourge*,
Satire VII, if her character had not already prepared the audience
for the extra dimension of self-conscious mockery.

Taken as a whole, this line of action involves very little, if any,
development. The satiric types vying for Rossaline's hand simply
reveal themselves in conversations with her, Feliche, or each
other, and at the end of the play they find themselves in the same
situation that prevailed at the beginning, except that Rossaline
has at last promised Piero that she will make a choice, when she
has heard how Mellida likes wedlock and when she has taken a
survey of her servants. Despite the slightness of development in
these scenes, however, they are extremely prominent. The comic
grotesques do much to establish the dominant quality of the play,
and their shortcomings force the audience to judge Antonio and
Mellida with some sympathy, as well as Andrugio and the Neo-
Stoicism of which he is the preacher with some awareness of its
validity.

Only the line of action concerning Andrugio represents a
marked departure from the structure of *Jack Drum*. Wholly serious, unlike anything in that play except for one or two of Planet's
speeches, it provides a careful, if very general, exposition of Marston's Neo-Stoicism that bears significantly on the satiric burden

of the play, and particularly on Piero's corrupt, effeminate court. Andrugio emerges at the beginning of Act III, heartsick because of his defeat at the hands of Piero and his loss of Antonio. Carefully and eloquently, he articulates the wisdom of freedom from externals to his old friend Lucio, and thereafter he struggles to maintain this freedom against the pressure of Opinion and habit. In the first scene of this act he fights a losing battle with the press of passion. After taking the orthodox Neo-Stoic stand that

> There's nothing left
> Unto Andrugio, but Andrugio:
> And that nor mischief, force, distress, nor hell can take.
> Fortune my fortunes, not my mind, shall shake [III, i, 59–62]

he vacillates between this attempt at rational control and an attitude of militant defiance. After he has applauded the man "unmov'd / Despite the justling of opinion" (IV, i, 57–57), he backslides and orders Lucio to spit on him: "for I am turnèd slave: Observe how passion domineers o'er me" (83–84). Later in the act, after he has been reunited with Antonio, he again turns Neo-Stoic and, Learlike, beseeches his son to "remember to forget [himself]" and to retire with him to a house "which fortune will not envy" (120, 125). But when Antonio loses Mellida later in the act, Andrugio once more reverts to his intention to die in combat, "like old Andrugio, / Worthy [his] birth" (306, 307). In other words, Andrugio never completely wins the palm of Neo-Stoic content. He comes closest to it in the last act when with the kind of un-Stoic aggression of which Marston approved he offers his head to Piero, indifferent to all but his fixed resolve. But even here Marston has not emphasized a triumph. Throughout, he has used the character rather to clarify the Neo-Stoic position than to represent its final victory. Andrugio's scenes add very little to the play in terms of action, for his bout with the angel of Neo-Stoicism is wholly inward—Senecan, like the many quotations in his speeches. But they constitute a serious commentary different from that in *Jack Drum, Histriomastix*, and the verse satires in that it reflects Marston's increased attention to the art of securing persuasion through indirection.

In general, the plot of *Antonio and Mellida* reveals, then, a partial return to the conspicuous high-mindedness of Marston's earlier work even as it retains much of the lightness and gaiety of *Jack Drum*. Its kinship to *Jack Drum* is quite clear. Many of its controlling devices have exact counterparts in the devices already considered in *Jack Drum*, and even distinctive structural details are common to both plays. Despite such similarities, however, it is the differences between *Jack Drum* and *Antonio and Mellida* that are most important in the development of Marston's satiricomical style; and these, too, have structural causes.

Like his use of contrasting lines of action, for example, Marston's elaborate use of explicitly critical and didactic speeches is crucial to the over-all dramatic image provided by *Antonio and Mellida*. In the bizarre world of Piero's court Feliche and, to a lesser extent, Rossaline draw the satiric types out, attack their folly, and generalize on their degeneracy. But it is symptomatic of Marston's particular emphasis here that Feliche, though clearly related in spirit and function to Planet, is much more serious and more philosophical than he—and much more widely used. Feliche's speeches of self-characterization identify him unmistakably as a Neo-Stoic of Marstonian stripe. Although some have said that his disclaimers of envy reflect Marston's attempt to differentiate him from Jonson's Macilente, these protests hark back even more clearly to Marston's elaborate concern with envy in *Histriomastix*.[6] His simultaneous cultivation of "calm hush'd rich Content" (III, ii, 1–24)—his name means "The contented man"—and the aggressive contempt of the satirist, on the other

---

[6] Passages dealing with envy in *Antonio and Mellida* are found in the "Induction," ll. 112–124, and III, ii, 7, 9, 41, 43, 47, 64. Campbell, *Comicall Satyre*, pp. 140–141, sees a connection with *Every Man Out*, which had been acted in 1599.

hand, is utterly consistent with Marston's blend of the roles of snarling satirist and Neo-Stoic. There is no contradiction, as some have claimed, between his speaking at one moment of his serenity and his attacking at the next the depravity of Piero, Forobosco, and Castilio. If we recall Epictetus on teaching and Marston's own dismissal of classical Stoic apathy, a speech like the following is a completely probable utterance for Marston's version of a philosopher mired in his society:

> O that the stomach of this queasy age
> Digests, or brooks such raw unseasoned gobs,
> And vomits not them forth! O! slavish sots!
> Servant, quoth you? faugh! if a dog should crave
> And beg her service, he should have it straight:
> She'd give him favours too, to lick her feet,
> Or fetch her fan, or some such drudgery:
> A good dog's office, which these amorists
> Triumph of: 'tis rare, well give her more ass,
> More sot, as long as dropping of her nose
> Is sworn rich pearl by such low slaves as those.
> [II, i, 94–104]

Like the composite of the orphan poet, the snarling satirist, and the Neo-Stoic of the satires, Feliche is fundamentally a philosopher; like the trifold persona, too, he is continuously on the offensive. Andrugio's outcast state, on the other hand, gives him every opportunity to speak clearly, feelingly, and rather more generally of the values of this philosophical position. If his speeches tend to be abstract, they are never so abstract that they lose the quality of obvious relevance both to his own situation and to the conditions of Piero's court.

> Why man, I never was a prince till now.
> 'Tis not the barèd pate, the bended knees,
> Gilt tipstaves, Tyrrian purple, chairs of state,
> Troops of pied butterflies that flutter still

In greatness' summer, that confirm a prince:
'Tis not the unsavoury breath of multitudes,
Shouting and clapping, with confusèd din,
That makes a prince. No, Lucio, he's a king,
A true right king, that dares do aught save wrong;
Fears nothing mortal but to be unjust. . . .   [IV, i, 46–55]

Only Andrugio's personal struggle to practice what he preaches saves him from a purely choral function in the play.

Taken together, these satiric and didactic speeches stand in counterpoint to the local exhibitions of moral disorder in the play. They direct the feelings of distress aroused, and by their prominence they affirm a viable alternative to the ubiquitous degeneracy. Far more impressive and persuasive than any comparable feature in *Jack Drum,* they account in large part for the comic power of *Antonio and Mellida* to control and contain its extremes of hilarity and unpleasantness.

The greater harmoniousness of *Antonio and Mellida,* however, is also the result of Marston's having turned to a setting more capable than the English locale of *Jack Drum* of encompassing his disparate materials. In this play there is little, if any, of the tension detected in *Jack Drum* between didacticism and levity. On the contrary, Andrugio's solemnity seems strangely appropriate alongside the wildest of episodes. This compatibility proceeds in large part from Marston's use of an Italian locale and of the wider range of probabilities that this superlatively sophisticated, notoriously wicked, and yet conveniently remote setting provided. However knowledgeable the contemporary Englishman was about Italy, it is reasonable to assume that he would accept distortions in an Italian context—as long as the distortions were in scale—where he could not in an English one. Marston's decision to relinquish the English scene for Italy, accordingly, was important to his more effective control in this play of the grotesqueness and incongruity inherent in the unity he desired. Andrugio's surrender and Antonio's feigned death do not seem so gross in the Venice of Piero as they would in Highgate, and characters differing as widely as Andrugio and Castilio seem perfectly normal together. The explanation for this lies in the innately more melodramatic, more distinctly fictional atmosphere of Piero's Venice. Italy and things Italianate provided, apparently, just the quality of chiaroscuro for the kind of play Marston was trying to write.

Against this backdrop, Marston's array of comic grotesques, burlesque figures, philosophers, and critics mingle with ease. Antonio is a repetition of Pasquill with several minor differences, an amorist to the manner born. Throughout the play the pathos of his situation and the passion of his effusions are steadily undercut by such devices as his Amazon disguise, his tendency to swoon in a crisis, his habit of foreswearing metaphor and then going ahead to develop one, and his complete failure to remain intelligible at one point. But as an amorist he is chiefly rendered ridiculous, as Pasquill had been, through his extravagant protestations, a good example of which occurs in his speech to the disguised Mellida.

> Then hast thou seen the glory of her sex,
> The music of Nature, the unequall'd lustre
> Of unmatch'd excellence, the united sweet
> Of heaven's graces, the most adorèd beauty,
> That ever strook amazement in the world!
> [IV, i, 163–167]

Mellida, on the other hand (her name derives from *mellitus* or *melito*, meaning "honied"), perhaps nowhere reveals her comic dimensions more clearly than in the ridiculous understatement of her reply to this adventure in superlatives, when she says, "You seem to love her." Taken together, Antonio and Mellida constitute the principal long-range interest in the play, such as it is. We rejoice mildly at their success, it is true; but our primary interest centers in the moment-to-moment burlesque for which their characters are carefully tailored.

More obviously relevant to the structural emphasis on scenes
and short-range interests are the young blades at Piero's court, the
satiric types who seem to have stepped from the pages of an
Italian dictionary and Marston's verse satires. Forobosco, meaning a "sneaking, prying, busie fellowe," [7] is a parasite plainly
modeled on the toady in Satire II of *Certain Satires* and Ruscus
and Gnato of *The Scourge*.[8] Matzagente, meaning a "killer or
queller of people," is a "modern braggadoch" and combines Tubrio
and Martius, the swaggering braggart and the martialist.[9] Alberto
and Galeatzo, meanwhile, are amorists of the type pervading both
the satires and the early plays, while Balurdo, meaning "a foole
. . . or giddie-head," derives through Puffe of *Jack Drum* from
Curio (*CS*, II) and the clotheshorses (*CS*, IV). Castilio, of course,
whose name derives from "Castiglione," duplicates the Castilio
of the satires, though his boast about Rossaline's letter in Act
III, scene i, also recalls the spruce Duceus of *Certain Satires*, Satire III.

Of the important comic characters in the play, only Piero apparently owes nothing to the portraits of the verse satires. Instead,
he is a thoroughgoing burlesque of the stock tyrant of contemporary melodrama, a King Cambyses in miniature. In keeping with
his resolve in the "Induction" to "be proud, stroke up the hair, and
strut" (l. 14), throughout he commands, condemns, grows sinister,
congratulates himself on his good fortune, and fumes when he
is thwarted. Yet, though his will runs contrary to our desire for
the more attractive characters, he elicits no painful expectations,
none of the anxiety that such genuine villains in lovers-in-distress
plays as Segasto, Bremo, and Bryan Sans Foy are designed to call
forth. He is a hollow tyrant, emptied of all seriousness, disqualified

[7] When I quote dictionary definitions for these names, I shall be quoting
from John Florio's *New World of Words* (London, 1611). This is the augmented edition of his *A Worlde of Words* (London, 1598), the dictionary
that Marston doubtless used, if he used one.

[8] Satire III, 53–68; "In Lectores," 52–56.

[9] Satire I (*CS*), 89–125, and II (*CS*), 118, 119. Satire I (*SV*), 1–8, IV
(*SV*), 2–8, VIII (*SV*), 72–83, and X (*SV*), 52–73.

as a source of serious threats. Despite his blustering and his quotations from Seneca, when he is confronted with a problem such as the flight of Antonio and Mellida, he quickly descends to stuttering impotence:

Forobosco, Alberto, Feliche, Castilio, Balurdo! run, keep the palace, post to the ports, go to my daughter's chamber! whither now? scud to the Jew's! stay, run to the gates, stop the gundolets, let none pass the marsh! do all at once! Antonio! his head, his head! Keep you the court, and rest stand still, or run, or go, or shout, or search, or scud, or call, or hang, or do-do-do su-su-su something! I know not who-who-who what I do-do-do, nor who-who-who, where I am. [III, ii, 177–185]

A little later in the scene Marston completes the image of absurdity by having both Antonio and Mellida escape from under his nose. Actually, the plot of this play turns in large part on the probabilities offered by Piero's peculiar combination of wickedness and incompetence. Surely the absence of genuine seriousness in his threats to Antonio, Mellida, and Andrugio is indicative of Marston's dominant comic emphasis.

In other ways, too, the seriousness implicit in these plot materials is steadily undercut. It would be risky to try to say more about the mode of production practiced than I have already tried to say under the general heading of the burlesque acting style. But at least it should be clear that Marston's stage directions both bear out my contention and supply details of a bustling burlesque rendition of the text. The comic entrances are, perhaps, most suggestive. In Act II, scene i, the stage direction reads: "*Enter* Forobosco, *with two torches:* Castilio *singing fantastically;* Rossaline *running a coranto pace, and* Balurdo; Feliche *following, wondering at them all.*" In Act III, scene ii, Castilio enters sprinkling himself with sweet waters. Later in the same scene Balurdo enters backwards, admiring himself in a mirror, and Flavia enters backwards, holding a mirror for Rossaline. And near the end of Act III, Antonio runs on stage, disguised as a sailor, and Mellida, disguised as a page, enters dancing. Such clues to a light ebullient production are perfectly consistent with details like Rossaline's innocent proposal to Antonio as Amazon that they be bedfellows —a proposal that forces a dangerously tender moment back into perspective at the end of Act I—and perfectly in key with the numerous songs and dances. Although it is difficult to say much about the songs, since none of them has been printed, we can infer from the context that at least one of them—the one in which Flavia "descants" on the obscene names of Catzo and Dildo—is light, while all of them are extraneous to the action, apparently having been included simply to give the children opportunities to sing. The dances, on the other hand, distinctly serve to heighten the comic value of the scenes in which they are used. The dance in Act II, where three sets of characters dance in such a way that their conversations are successively overheard, imposes a delightfully incongruous order on the movements of characters then in the process of revealing their enormity.

The effect of all these elements in dramatic synthesis is, of course, the combination of seriousness and playfulness, thoughtfulness and gaiety, met initially in the phrase "seriously fantastical." There is unpleasantness, to be sure, and sober highmindedness. Moreover, the exposure of the satiric types and the unfavorable turns in the fortunes of Antonio, Mellida, and Andrugio evoke a mild sense of distress and anxiety. But in any total view of the comic power of the play these feelings are balanced and controlled by the burlesque just as the levity is balanced and, when it is satiric, directed by the didacticism.

In *Antonio and Mellida* Marston attempted a fresh combination of the leading qualities of the satires and the leading qualities of *Jack Drum*, a combination that realizes its effects, moreover, through an integrated dramatic action. Within its limitations the play is doubtless a success. But the limitations of the form are perhaps more grave than has thus far appeared. If, as I have argued, Marston has made the combination work, has harmonized, that is to say, burlesque, satire, and philosophy in a single dramatic image, we must not overlook that he has done so here at the expense of anything like genuine intensity at any point. It has always been characteristic of burlesque that its source of fun is usually too local to elicit intense comic responses. But the fault here seems to proceed not from the burlesque alone so much as from the combination. Although Marston has succeeded in unifying trivial fun, social criticism, and philosophy in *Antonio and Mellida,* the total harmony lacks the potential intensity of its parts. As a dramatic structure the play works efficiently, but it proves incapable of an impressive comic power.

Marston's decision to write burlesques at this stage of his career is easy to understand. We have seen how the predilections of his literary group favored mocking the popular forms of the immediate past, as well as how the rivalry with the public companies and the special talents and limitations of the child actors could have encouraged this kind of play. In addition, we should not forget that his first effort, "Pygmalion's Image," was a parody and burlesque and, in fact, that young writers in all ages have a penchant for this kind of imitation. But these explanations—however valid and useful—do not tell the whole story. If they account for what Marston was trying to do and why he was trying to do it, they tell us very little about how he was trying to do it and nothing at all about what he learned from effort to effort.

Most elusive of the features of Marston's work in the lovers-in-distress burlesques are the discoveries he made about his craft during this period. These discoveries depend utterly on particular circumstances—that one John Marston was trying to achieve particular effects by means of a particular treatment of particular materials. To clarify their value, we must keep in mind the one technical decision that, more than any other, conditioned what he learned as well as what he accomplished: that in these plays he abandoned the structures of thesis used in the verse satires and *Histriomastix* for structures of plot, relinquished structures designed to illustrate a key idea for structures designed to set a certain kind of dramatic action or dramatic image before an audi-

ence. I emphasize this point because this decision was by no
means inevitable. Indeed, Ben Jonson, who began writing satirical comedy at the same time and under much the same conditions,[10] decided quite differently.

Actually, Jonson's early comedies provide an illuminating contrast to Marston's, not just because they are different but because
they are so very similar and yet different. O. J. Campbell has
argued that Jonson and Marston established the dramatic type
that he calls—following Jonson's lead—"comicall satyre." But in
concentrating on the common features of these plays Campbell
tends to lose sight of the differences between them and to assume too easily that there was only one kind, the best example of
which is to be found in Jonson's work. Arguing from the undeniable similarities between Marston's early comedies and Jonson's, he concludes that Marston was trying to emulate Jonson's
performance or to approximate the ideal form of "comicall satyre"
implied by it, but that Marston unhappily failed in the attempt.

This argument is manifestly unfair to Marston. Despite the
many similarities between Marston's early comedies and Jonson's,
they embody important differences, and perhaps none is more
important than that, unlike Marston's early comedies except *Histriomastix*, Jonson's "comicall satyres" are all structures of thesis.
Jonson, too, was very self-conscious of his first steps as an orphan
playwright. In his first "comicall satyre," *Every Man Out of His
Humour* (1600), he elaborately defined the peculiar nature of the
play in the lengthy "Induction" and used the choral characters

---

[10] The one important exception to this statement is *Every Man Out*,
which was produced by a public company, the Lord Chamberlain's Men. It
is safe to assume, however, that it was primarily written for the enlightened
classes that Jonson had already won with *Every Man In*. Herford and Simpson argue convincingly that "the second Humour play was addressed even
more directly to the intellectual part of his audience, and it put their intel-
lectuality to severe tests. . . . For such 'gentle' academic hearers and
readers *Every Man Out of His Humour* . . . was obviously calculated."
Indeed, in 1616, he dedicated the work to "those noblest nurseries of humanity and liberty in the Kingdom, the Inns of Court" (H & S, I, 22, 23).

of Mitis and Cordatus throughout to direct opinion to a proper appreciation of it. The play itself is constructed, as Campbell has shown, according to principles that Jonson deduced from verse satire (particularly Marston's verse satires).[11] As a structure it is best understood as a calculated dramatization of the satiric pattern—character exposure, followed by commentary. The individual scenes stand in no necessary relationship to each other; the satiric types simply come on stage and indulge their humours while Macilente criticizes them. Even in the second half of the play, where there is some causal connection between the scenes for the purposes of bringing the characters out of their humours, the plot devices used are very arbitrary. Taken as a whole, accordingly, the structure of *Every Man Out* is largely controlled by a predetermined pattern.

Jonson's next two comicall satyres trace his efforts to perfect the use of this pattern in drama. Unlike Marston, who as early as *Jack Drum* went beyond the structural principles of his verse satires, Jonson was apparently determined to convert them into a dramatic structure of a rather unique kind. To improve on his performance in *Every Man Out,* he apparently tried to lend focus and depth to the satire in *Cynthia's Revels* and *The Poetaster* by constructing these plays to support didactic theses that would permit a richer, more tightly integrated dramatization of the satiric procedure. Both *Cynthia's Revels* and *The Poetaster,* consequently, are best explained as structures of thesis: in *Cynthia's Revels* the satiric careers of the sham courtiers and the three-point program calculated to bring them out of their humours to true courtliness are ordered by the proposition that "A vertuous *Court* a world to vertue drawes" (H & S, IV, 181); in *The Poetaster* the careers of the degenerate poets are seen in the context of the idea that false standards and moral degeneracy in the arts are the prelude for the collapse of the arts and the state.[12] The

[11] *Comicall Satyre,* pp. 2–81.

[12] This thesis is most clearly set forth in passages on pp. 276, 277, and 282 (H & S, IV).

concern in both plays with not just the satiric types but with satiric types as they relate to the court and the world or to the arts and the state gives these plays a depth and interest lacking in *Every Man Out*. Like *Every Man Out,* however, their structure is determined by didactic principles rather than imitative principles.

After *Histriomastix,* on the other hand, Marston's dominant artistic interest centered in how to put together a dramatic action that by its own nature was endowed with the power to move an audience to a relatively controlled state of thoughts and feelings. How to make such action work with an air of reasonableness and inevitability! How to make it express what he wanted it to communicate by virtue of its own thrust! As we have seen, his dedication to this task soon forced him to subordinate the orphan poet, the snarling satirist, and the Neo-Stoic to his new role as private playwright. The composite that emerged is nowhere perfectly clear, partly because the author's voice is rarely clear in this kind of play and partly because the composite itself seems to have varied from play to play as first this role and then that was more fully indulged. But to the extent that Marston is discernible behind the multitude of artistic decisions embodied in the plays, he seems always to have been primarily concerned with the task of forging a dramatic action adequate to his needs. It was his dedication to this task that prompts me to trace his development in satirical comedy in terms of the three types of dramatic action that he worked with. It is my firm belief that the quality of his achievement in satirical comedy is directly related to his mastery of these types of dramatic action as well as to their suitability for his mixture of the comic and serious.

But even in *Antonio and Mellida* certain advances are evident. In writing it he had begun to eliminate the faults of arbitrariness and had come to understand the possibilities of contrasting lines of action. More important, he had apparently discovered that the lovers-in-distress action, however ironically handled, would not yield the impressive union of the comic and the serious that he desired. How conscious this discovery was with him and how deliberately he moved from it to the work of the next few years are questions, of course, impossible to determine. We have only the *fait accompli* that with his next efforts in satirical comedy he turned to another kind of dramatic action and that with it he achieved a full expression of his seriocomic view of the late-Renaissance world.

Before Marston entered the next phase of his work in satiricomic forms, however, he made good the promise of the "Induction" to *Antonio and Mellida* by writing a "second part," *Antonio's Revenge*, the first of his three tragedies (see Appendix A). Although *Antonio's Revenge* is not indispensable to the story of Marston's development as a satirist, it would probably be a mistake to regard it as a mere digression. Certainly he undertook this first flight into the realms of tragedy with typical seriousness, and certainly the play, however imperfectly it embodies the attitude that is our central concern, contains much that he devoutly believed. More precisely, *Antonio's Revenge* is important in our inquiry as a representation of Marston's beliefs when they are uncomplicated by irony and comic perspective. It will be useful to see to what extent Marston's serious fantasticalness could be accommodated to what he considered a tragic view of the human condition and in what, essentially, his tragic view consisted.

Like the lovers-in-distress burlesques, *Antonio's Revenge* is an innovative adaptation of a conventional and popular dramatic action. Its kinship to revenge plays of the type established by *The Spanish Tragedy* and fully realized in *Hamlet* has long been recognized; [13] with them it shares the common elements of revenge, a distracted revenger, complex intrigue, and abundant slaughter. In fact, even its concluding act of vengeance is accomplished by the strategy of a masque like that used earlier in *The Spanish*

[13] See, for example, A. H. Thorndike, "The Relations of *Hamlet* to Contemporary Revenge Plays," *PMLA*, XVII (1902), 156–159, and C. V. Boyer, *The Villain as Hero in Elizabethan Tragedy* (London, 1914), pp. 133–139.

Tragedy. But, as usual, Marston's governing intention was not imitation; true to the pattern of his behavior elsewhere, he has re-shaped his conventional materials along highly individualistic lines, and, as usual, he has not hesitated to say so:

> O that our power
> Could lackey or keep wing with our desires,
> That with unusèd paize [heaviness] of style and sense,
> We might weigh massy in judicious scale.
> ["Prologue," ll. 27–30]

We might approach a formulation of his intention in this play, then, by first trying to see what he meant by the "unusèd paize of style and sense," in what his departures from the conventional revenge type consisted.

Burlesque, of course, played no prominent part in his adapta-tion. Although the play contains burlesque elements as well as other comic elements, they are far less important than his depar-tures from the conventional revenge action. Considered as a group, these departures suggest that he wished to design a revenge action expressive of his personal version of Neo-Stoicism. The dramatic situation and the characters, for example, were furnished by *Antonio and Mellida* and duly adjusted to the requirements of a normal revenge action. Instead of the stuttering, burlesque tyrant of the first play, Piero is an incarnation of Machiavellian villainy, a creature capable of every crime, a monster who demands that someone take a righteous vengeance. But in addition to being the villain, he is also a particularly vivid example of the deformity that, according to Marston's thought, comes from a total dedication to the false values of the world and an indispensable foil to the Stoics and Neo-Stoics in the play. In the play's opening scene he and his assistant Strotzo (from *strozzare*, meaning "to strangle" or "kill") introduce us to a world strangling in evil as he rejoices— his arms still smeared with blood—in his murder of Andrugio and Feliche and luxuriates in his plan to defeat Antonio and then marry Andrugio's widow, Maria. In the subsequent action he is the cause of all the trials in adversity that the men of philosophy undergo, the force of evil that they oppose.

Piero's chief antagonists—Antonio, Pandulpho, and Alberto—are, by contrast, Stoics and Neo-Stoics whose responses to the condition of life in Piero's Venice serve to delineate Marston's philosophy. With his assurance to the imprisoned Mellida that he "will not swell, like a tragedian, / In forced passion of affected strains" (II, ii, 109–110), Antonio clearly disassociates himself from the burlesque character of *Antonio and Mellida*. Here he is a wholly serious youth, who, when he finds himself caught in a maze of crime, seeks what is initially a conventional justice through revenge. But his approach to the act of vengeance and his deliberations on its justice are by no means conventional, though they owe something to the Senecan revenger. Unlike Pandulpho and Alberto, orthodox Stoics for whom patience and indifference are the highest responses to misfortune, Antonio argues the necessity for action and finally persuades them to act. His reflections on evil and the world and his formulation and execution of a plan by which to correct the condition that has been thrust upon him, accordingly, are prolonged in the interests of a careful exposition of the active hostility that we have already seen in the verse satires. In all this he is distinctly a Marstonian Neo-Stoic, a man sickened by the spectacle of wrong and committed to combating it. Indeed, Campbell has argued that he is really only a variation on the satirist and the critic of the earlier plays, an argument that has for support the ghost's choral speech at the beginning of Act V in which Antonio is called "The scourge of murder and impiety" (1. 25).[14] But Antonio is also different from the critic. When Alberto suggests to him at the beginning of Act IV, scene i, that he abandon his disguise as a fool for "Some habit of a spitting critic" (1. 4), he rejects the counsel and continues in his fool's disguise. As a revenger, he is much more intricately engaged in his world

[14] *Comicall Satyre*, pp. 153, 154.

than the critic or satirist is. Like the satirist, he is corrective; but unlike the satirist, he is affected by something more personal than crimes and vices at large and, consequently, is incapable of the detachment required of satire.

A more precise view of what Marston wished to embody in Antonio can best be obtained by comparing him with Pandulpho and Alberto, characters whose main function is to provide commentary on the progress of attitudes in the play. Act I, scene ii, and most of Act II are designed to represent fully a set of different responses to the deaths of Andrugio and Feliche and Piero's charge that Mellida has been caught in adultery with Feliche on the eve of her wedding. In the first of these scenes Alberto gives Antonio conventional advice and initiates a running discussion that continues into the next scene:

> Sweet prince, be patient. [I, ii, 270]
>
> 'Tis reason's glory to command affects. [I, ii, 275]
>
> Nay, sweet, be comforted, take counsel. [II, ii, 1]
>
> Will you endeavor to forget your grief? [II, ii, 39]

But Antonio rejects the advice and in a series of speeches dismisses patience as a "slave to fools" (I, ii, 273), "a parasite, a flattering jack" (I, ii, 287), a refuge for small men. His fullest statement on the subject comes in Act II, scene ii, when, having been left alone to seek solace in a volume of Seneca, he reads and dismisses a key passage from *De Providentia*—*Ferte fortiter: hoc est quo deum antecedatis* . . . ("Bear yourself with fortitude: it is in this you can surpass the gods . . .") (chapter vi, 4). A few moments later he tells Mellida that he is ready to right her wrongs (l. 112), and in the next scene he clearly indicates to his mother that, unlike the Stoics, he believes that not taking revenge would constitute yielding to chance, that this is a wrong he can and must do something about:

May I be fetter'd slave to coward Chance,
If blood, heart, brain, plot ought save vengeance.

[III, i, 90–91]

The most important foil to Antonio, however, is Pandulpho, the murdered Feliche's father. Still another conventional Stoic, he is elaborate in his attempts to win inward serenity through an indifference to external things. He concludes Act I with a long speech that is both orthodox and sound, as far as it goes:

> 'Tis not true valour's pride
> To swagger, quarrel, swear, stamp, rave, and chide,
> To stab in fume of blood, to keep loud coils
> To bandy factions in domestic broils,
> To dare the act of sins, whose filth excels
> The blackest customs of blind infidels.
> No, my lov'd youth: he may of valour vaunt
> Whom fortune's loudest thunder cannot daunt;
> Whom fretful gales of chance, stern fortune's siege,
> Makes not his reason slink, the soul's fair liege;
> Whose well-pais'd action ever rests upon
> Not giddy humours but discretion.
> This heart in valour even Jove out-goes. [ll. 325–337]

Pandulpho's position is clarified still further in the next scene both by what he says in his interview with Piero and by Piero's asides as Piero tries to enlist him in his conspiracy against Antonio. But although Pandulpho wins a victory by resisting Piero's invitation to passion and by penetrating the slander on Antonio, his triumph is but a part of an *a fortiori* design to compound the evidence of Antonio's superiority. Ultimately, after Antonio has been accused of the double murder and has gone into disguise, Pandulpho acknowledges the supremacy of his active hostility by renouncing his passivity and indifference. At the end of Act IV, both Pandulpho and Alberto form a league with Antonio against Piero, and in Act V they are joined by still another man of good will, the foolish courtier Balurdo, who has been imprisoned for speaking against Piero. Together they execute the intricate and notably bloody vengeance. The play ends, significantly, not with their deaths, but with thanks from the court for ridding Venice of a monster and their announcement that they intend to withdraw from the world.

In general, then, *Antonio's Revenge* is an adaptation of a revenge action along lines that permitted Marston a Neo-Stoic interpretation of revenge materials. All the typical features of the revenge play are here: the grotesque and exceedingly cunning villain, the ghost crying for vengeance, the revenger, hesitant, distracted, groping toward justice, and the crimes executed in conspicuously gruesome detail. An appreciable portion of the represented action, indeed, consists in the violence of Antonio's preliminary vengeance in the murder of Julio, Piero's son, Strotzo's murder at Piero's hands, and the long debacle of the last scene, in which Antonio and his allies first cut out Piero's tongue, then serve him a dish of Julio's flesh, and only then stab him to death. And an equally substantial portion of the action concerns the lamentations of Maria, Mellida, Pandulpho, and Antonio. But where these elements usually serve to heighten terror and pathos to a largely sensational end in most melodramatic revenge actions, here they are integral to the total design in that they intensify a sense of the need for the Neo-Stoic attitude finally articulated. Actually, it is difficult to say with confidence that this purpose entirely explains the extravagant gruesomeness of the final scene; it is probable that we cannot wholly understand so much apparently gratuitous horror until we more fully understand why Marston's age found high seriousness in the same kind of thing in Seneca. But to the extent that such "black-visaged shows" do not blur the design by calling attention to themselves alone, they support the Neo-Stoicism that elsewhere governs and that pervasively erupts in choral speeches like Maria's in Act I, scene ii, on outward glitter and inward grace.

In most respects the remaining features of the play are relevant either to this design or to such problems as accommodating the play to the child actors. Much of the verse is conventionally figurative and distinctly lyrical; passages like Antonio's speech on dawn—

> Darkness is fled: look, infant morn hath drawn
> Bright silver curtains 'bout the couch of night;
> And now Aurora's horse trots azure rings,
> Breathing fair light about the firmament [I, ii, 66–69]

reflect a sober intensity appropriately different from the jarring tonalities of the satirical comedies. The play's six songs, on the other hand, suggest the usual exploitation of the children's special talents, while Marston's emphasis on type characterization, long speeches, and a fictional world far more phantasmagoric than realistic reveals his deliberate attempts to keep to a mode of representation within his actors' limitations. The play's three dumb shows, the use of off-stage voices in clear defiance of realistic probabilities in Act II, scene ii, and Act III, scene i, and the ritual character of the last act, with its masque and the Ghost of Andrugio *"betwixt the music houses,"* confer on the action—an action already slow, even static—an air of stylization and abstractness reminiscent of the Interlude-Moralities with which the child actors had so long been associated. In the total design, of course, these qualities are perfectly consonant with the intellectual emphasis on the inward drama.

Of the prominent elements in the play, only the comic elements are ambiguously adjusted to the main design. It is easy to see in Balurdo's entrance, *"with a beard, half off, half on,"* in his comic variation on Antonio's prophetic dream, and in his tendency throughout—even in the scene of vengeance—to undercut the serious interest with outrageous comments a kind of fitful burlesque like that so prominent in the satirical comedies. But neither his foolishness, nor Nutriche's comic earthiness, nor the hazy assemblage of grotesques hovering in the background bring more than a certain ill-digested variety and murky density to the total picture. Certainly they do not prompt the critical attitude toward the action that their counterparts in the satirical comedies encourage; and that Marston did not intend them to is most evident in the negligible place in the play of the satiric types carried over intact from *Antonio and Mellida*. To the extent that such comic elements interrupt from time to time the otherwise pervasive solemnity, they serve to broaden the base of the tragedy. But the laughter they elicit has no place in Antonio's attitude and no place of consequence in the response the play as a whole seems fashioned to call forth.

Perhaps the chief problem in *Antonio's Revenge* is that Marston's attempt to represent a Neo-Stoic attitude capable of mastering the condition of life in Piero's Venice depends so much on the characterization of Antonio. We have already seen that as a spokesman for Marston he is quite different from the satirist or the critic of the earlier plays because the revenge action compels him to engage himself in his world so personally that detachment toward it is impossible to him. Deprived of this detachment, he expresses a notably uncomplicated point of view. By comparison with the trifold persona of the satirist, he has none of the satirist's capacity for ironic and comic insight and, accordingly, no capacity for his kind of mastery. Yet even as a Neo-Stoic, fashioned here for the purposes of carrying Marston's didactic burden, he is only partially successful. Although he claims rational control, the revenge action forces upon him acts of violence that make inescapable the inference that he suffers brutalization in the process of exercising it. The murder of Julio and the orgy of vengeance in the last scene are proofs too strong to be set aside by the logic of Marston's theoretical position, and the unconventional conclusion permitting Antonio and his allies to live seems, however intended, inevitably arbitrary.

The unsuitability of a revenge action for Marston's purpose is even clearer, perhaps, when it is held up against the Stoic view of tragedy. After all, Stoics of all denominations hold that the truly virtuous man, the man who has achieved rational control, cannot finally suffer failure. If a man fails, he has lost control through his foolishness and weakness, and such a loss is not tragic, but merely unfortunate. For the Stoics, as well as for Marston in this play, the tragic flaw is met, not in men, who are potentially perfect and whose imperfection is a matter of faulty training, but in the world and in the insidious way in which it operates on men. The tragic vision of *Antonio's Revenge* centers on the fact that Antonio must work out his fulfillment in a world, as Mellida says, "too cunning for honest natures to converse withal"; the tragedy consists in the tension between the virtuous man and the corrupt world. As long as Marston is able to sustain that tension, to keep Antonio undefiled in the face of all threats, Antonio's superiority is intact; but when he is compelled by the revenge materials to illustrate what he considered a just hostility in acts of gruesome violence, the tragic opposition yields to something else and the image of Neo-Stoic mastery blurs. The attempt to sustain in Antonio a consistent embodiment of rational mastery, accordingly, is in some measure frustrated by the very nature of the task Marston has set for himself.

For our purposes, however, *Antonio's Revenge* is chiefly important for its relevance to Marston's seriocomic attitude and to his progress in technical skills. Of course, for all the play's echoes of the serious fantasticalness met earlier, it by no means achieves an ample representation of it, and it would be unfair to argue that Marston intended one. Although it is altogether possible that he wished to complicate the dominant Neo-Stoic stance with such fugitive intrusions of the satirical spirit as we meet in Balurdo, Nutriche, and Matzagente, if he did, we must conclude that these elements are finally swallowed up by a pervasive solemnity utterly foreign to his satirical comedies.

In general, the differences between the state of thoughts and feelings elicited by *Antonio's Revenge* and that elicited by the satirical comedies are best explained by the key difference of distance. As a revenge tragedy *Antonio's Revenge* is relatively philosophical and abstract, but it unavoidably involves as well a closer, more moving study of the consequences of evil than the satires or the satirical comedies provide. Like Antonio, the audience, too, is unable to sustain a detached view of the play's representation of suffering and crime, unable to hold at mind's length in the manner of the satirist so crushing a burden of sorrow. Perhaps we can conclude from this that critical distance is indispensable to the amalgam of profound concern and amused detachment at the core of Marston's seriocomic attitude. Without sufficient distance Marston's response to the world centers, as it does here, in the monochromatic sobriety of Antonio's Neo-Stoicism; with sufficient distance the highly complex, richly ironic view of the satirical comedies becomes possible.

In the satirical comedies that followed *Antonio's Revenge* the seriocomic attitude emerged in all its amplitude. As we shall see, moreover, at least some of the technical skill responsible for his success in these plays was learned in *Antonio's Revenge,* for it seems highly probable that the characters of Antonio and Piero were early studies for the critics and comic villains immediately to follow, that the device of Antonio's disguise provided the impulse for the disguise plots used in his next three plays, and that the pattern achieved in the action of this play was imitated in *The Malcontent.* Aside from its interest as the first of Marston's three efforts in tragedy, then, *Antonio's Revenge* marks a necessary stage in the story of Marston's experimentation with satiricomic forms. It throws light on Marston the artist and the thinker without which we might easily distort the image of Marston the satirist.

Chapter VI

The Disguise-Plot Plays

THE "Induction" to *What You Will* is an eminently useful preface to Marston's work in the disguise-plot plays.[1] Quite obviously an outgrowth of the poetomachia, it has the happy merit of revealing him in the act of defending not only himself (presumably from Jonson's censure) but also his dramatic theories against rival theories. Marston's argument here suggests that he was plentifully aware of the differences between his and Jonson's structural means to the end of satirical comedy. He treats his own practice—we may assume that he particularly has in mind the practice of *Jack Drum, Antonio and Mellida,* and *What You Will* —as a reversion to conventional, well-established methods of dramatic composition. At first glance his contempt for innovators might even suggest that he had deserted the aim of novelty, though, of course, he had not. In the "Induction" he is still the innovator, enough so, at least, to be reluctant to describe his play as either "comedy, tragedy, pastoral, moral, nocturnal, or history" (ll. 89, 90), lest its uniqueness go unappreciated. What is rather

---

[1] The question of the date of *What You Will* is taken up in Appendix A.

startling is that he claims to have conducted his experiments within what he calls the "rules of art," by which he seems to have meant the principles of construction met in conventional dramatic plots.

The "Induction" consists chiefly of a dialogue between Doricus and Philomuse. A third character, Atticus, is present, but he does little more than hurry the others along by warning them that they are trying the audience's patience. The main discussion develops when Doricus expresses his fear that Sir Signior Snuff, Monsieur Mew, and Cavaliero Blirt will spoil the play with their usual shows of vulgar contempt. Philomuse hastens to assure him that the author is "higher blooded than to quake and pant / At the report of Scoff's artillery" (ll. 26, 27). In a long speech that suggests unmistakably a retaliation on Marston's part to attacks suffered, Philomuse then develops at some length the idea that the artist must be emancipated from the pressures of Opinion:

> Shall he be crest-fall'n, if some looser brain,
> In flux of wit uncivilly befilth
> His slight composures? Shall his bosom faint,
> If drunken Censure, belch out sour breath
> From Hatred's surfeit on his labour's front?
>
> .   .   .   .   .
>
> Why, gentle spirits, what loose-waving vane,
> What anything, would thus be screw'd about
> With each slight touch of odd phantasmatas?
> No, let the feeble palsey'd lamer joints
> Lean on opinion's crutches; let the—[ll. 28–48]

But before Philomuse can denounce the "feeble palsey'd lamer joints" to his heart's content, Doricus interrupts and attempts to qualify this view of artistic freedom in the speech that is the core of this "Induction" and that contains, perhaps, Marston's most revelatory comments on his art.

In essence, Doricus says that dramatic invention must be grounded in the expectations of the ordinary theatregoer, however inferior he may be as a critic. Artistic freedom, he contends, can go too far; and in illustration he cites, surely with the Jonson of *Every Man Out* and *Cynthia's Revels* in mind, the "tight brain" that has flouted the "better audience," indeed insulted it, by prescribing methods of censure. "Music and poetry," he argues,

> were first approved
> By common sense; and that which pleasèd most,
> Held most allowèd pass: know, rules of art
> Were shaped to pleasure, not pleasure to your rules;
> Think you, if that his scenes took stamp in mint
> Of three or four deem'd most judicious,
> It must enforce the world to current them . . . ? [ll. 61–67]

Doricus caps this apology for dramatic invention based on the audience's normal expectations with the threat that if Philomuse's friend, the author, once talks of "squinting critics, drunken censure, splay-footed opinion, juiceless husks," he has done with him (ll. 77–82). Philomuse is able to reassure him only by insisting that the play is, indeed, *What You Will*.

The importance of this "Induction" in the history of Marston's work in satirical comedy cannot be overstressed. Taken by itself, it might be construed as a commitment to plays of a conventional kind, plays always well within the bounds of what was known and liked by theatregoers. Taken in the context of his work in verse satire, his early work in the drama, and his continued association with the private theatres, however, it records both Marston's personal recognition of his debt to tradition and his claim to uniqueness. If the pattern thus far traced in Marston's works can be trusted at all, we may conclude that he was defending here the decision first met in *Jack Drum* to treat conventional dramatic actions innovatively, to recast traditional actions in the image of the world as he saw it. And well he might acknowledge a heavy debt to the "rules of art," for, unlike Jonson in the "comicall satyres," he was in the older, imitative tradition. But just as he had wrenched the lovers-in-distress plots in *Jack Drum* and *An-*

tonio and Mellida to satiric ends and had re-shaped the revenge action of *Antonio's Revenge* in a highly individualistic way, so also he exploited the disguise plot to achieve the peculiar power characteristic of his best satirical comedies.

Many years ago P. A. Daniel pointed out in a note published by Bullen that Marston had borrowed the plot materials for *What You Will* from Sforza d'Oddi's *I Morti Vivi*, which was first published in 1576.[2] Picking up Daniel's suggestion, Paul Becker examined his claim and proved it beyond a doubt in his *Das Verhältnis von John Marston's "What You Will" zu Plautus' "Amphitruo" und Sforza d'Oddi's "I Morti Vivi."*[3] Becker's work is primarily a source study: he has pointed out plot similarities and differences and has collected a convincing number of parallel passages. But since he has done very little to explain why Marston chose to use certain parts of D'Oddi's play, while ignoring others, the task remains of relating Marston's use of D'Oddi to the play he was trying to write. This attention to Marston's use of his source should deepen our understanding of his theoretical claims in the "Induction" to this play.

I Morti Vivi is a romantic comedy of the sort that had a considerable vogue in Italy in the sixteenth century and in England in the last two decades of that century.[4] Its plot, as its title suggests, effects the happy return of two characters to scenes rendered chaotic by their supposed loss. The first is Alessandra, a young Moslem from Alexandria, who before the represented action of the play had met Ottavio, a young gentleman from Ancona, and had fallen in love. Although he returned her love, her father had prevented a match for religious reasons, and then a war had broken out that had sent Ottavio back to Italy and that, apparently, had put a marriage out of the question. But Ottavio was

---

[2] This note is to be found in *Works,* I, lxviii.   [3] Halle, 1904.

[4] According to Becker, Sforza d'Oddi (1540–1610) was an important follower of Raffaelle Borghini in the sixteenth century. His known plays are *L'Erophilomachia, La Prigione d'Amore,* and *I Morti Vivi.* Although *I Morti Vivi* was published in 1576, I have had to use the edition (Florence) of 1608.

so enamored of Alessandra that he had sent a friend, Moretto, to Alexandria to fetch her for him. Only when Moretto had returned with the tale that she had been taken from him by robbers did Ottavio sink into the melancholy in which he is discovered at the beginning of the play and consent, because he was now penniless, to marry the rich widow Oranta. This is their situation at the beginning of the play. The audience quickly learns, of course, that Alessandra is not dead, but is a new member of Oranta's household using the name Rossana. As Rossana, she is befriended by Oranta and soon learns of the impending marriage between Oranta and Ottavio. Subsequently, she even meets Ottavio, who fails to recognize her, and learns from him that he still cherishes some faint hope for his Alessandra. In a series of such meetings, this line of action is tied into delicate knots by scruples of various kinds: Alessandra loves Ottavio, but cannot declare herself because of her debt to Oranta; Ottavio is fond of Oranta and needs her financial support, but cannot desert the memory of his Alessandra; and Oranta, though troubled less by scruples than the lovers, does not wish to give pain and, besides, has her pride to think of.

The second of the characters thought to be dead is Tersandro, Oranta's husband, and of his death no one has any doubts. So certain is everyone of this that Luigi, whose suit to Oranta has been rejected, plots with Fabrizio, his servant, and Marcone, Oranta's factotum, to disguise one Jancola from Capua as Tersandro, spread rumors that Tersandro lives, and in this way ruin the impending marriage between Oranta and Ottavio with "Tersandro's" reappearance. Before they can bring the plot off, however, their secret gets out. Thus, when Tersandro himself suddenly appears, he is met with scoffs and jeers. Jancola beats a hasty retreat to Capua, without ever having faced the principal characters in his disguise, and Tersandro is left with the difficult task of convincing friends and neighbors that he is, in fact, Tersandro.

D'Oddi's purpose in creating these complications is artfully carried out in his resolution of them. Throughout, he treats the line of action involving Alessandra, Ottavio, and Oranta so as to make the most of the delicate sentiment of their misgivings, doubts, desires, and fears. Alessandra as Rossana makes the supreme sacrifice by telling Ottavio, after she has convinced him that she knew Alessandra, that Alessandra would want him to marry Oranta. Then, having made her position in Oranta's house impossible, she silently takes her leave, only at the last minute— as she is leaving the city—confiding her secret to Ottavio's servant and, by note, to Oranta. On the other hand, D'Oddi treats the line of action involving Luigi's plot and Tersandro's unexpected return for its potentialities in lively farce and sudden comic reversals. After suffering the ignominy of being jeered at by his friends and servants, Tersandro finally convinces Marcone of his identity. But at this point he, too, contrives a scheme and in his subsequent scene with Oranta tries to persuade her that he is the false Tersandro so that he might learn how intimate she has been with Ottavio. Even here he fails, however: Oranta has already learned the truth; and her defense against his charges is so good that he is forced to back down and blame Luigi for slandering her. Finally, of course, everything turns out well. Alessandra is returned to Ottavio, and explanations and forgiveness are offered all round. To gild the lily, moreover, Tersandro has brought information that Alessandra's father has given both his consent and his money to support his daughter's choice.

Even a rudimentary survey of the selection that Marston exercised in using *I Morti Vivi* clarifies considerably his intentions in *What You Will*. Certainly the cardinal fact is that, despite his use of lovers-in-distress actions in *Jack Drum* and *Antonio and Mellida,* he decided against using any part of the Ottavio-Alessandra action. Instead, he took as his essential action, the action providing the framework of probabilities supporting all the other elements, the Tersandro-Oranta story, including the scheme of Luigi. In other words, he borrowed something less than half of the represented action of *I Morti Vivi,* though by far the livelier part of that play. This action he stretched over five acts, reshaping and changing it, renaming the characters, and adding considerable new matter. In the final structure of *What You Will* the outline of the material from D'Oddi is to be found in Act I, where we meet Jacomo, who, like D'Oddi's Luigi, laments his rejection and evolves the crucial scheme, and where we learn first of the rich widow who is about to remarry; in Act III, scene ii, where Albano, like D'Oddi's Tersandro, returns unexpectedly and confronts the would-be bridegroom only to be laughed at by all present; in Act IV where Jacomo's plot fails and Albano again suffers ridicule; and in the second half of Act V, where Albano finally succeeds in establishing his identity. These scenes furnish the skeletal structure for the action.

Marston's choice of the relatively spare Tersandro action over the intricacy of the whole plot of *I Morti Vivi* gave him abundant opportunity for amplification and addition. A great many of his additions and all of his changes reveal his general purpose to enlarge the satiric and farcical content of the play; some few capitalize on the child actor's special talents; some bring to the play the Marstonian seriousness utterly absent in D'Oddi's treatment of the Tersandro action. Perhaps the main direction of his adaptation is best epitomized in his crucial changes in the character of Celia, who corresponds to D'Oddi's rich widow Oranta. Whereas Oranta is a high-minded woman whose unrequited passion for Ottavio arouses considerable sympathy, Celia is closely modeled on the stock character of the gay widow. The fact that she does not appear until Act IV indicates how little Marston wanted to interest the audience in the delicacies of her situation. On the contrary, he has made of her the kind of widow who might give hospitality to a large, assorted following of gallants and admirers. With the latitude in probability offered by this change, he was able to fill out the skeletal framework from D'Oddi with much the kind of substance he had worked with before.

In Act I Jacomo and Albano's brothers concoct the scheme to disguise Francisco, a perfumer, as Albano, to spread rumors that Albano lives, and at the eleventh hour to break up Celia's mar-

riage to Laverdure. The remainder of Act I and all of Act II deal
with Marston's new satiric characters and their buffoonery. In the
morning of the single day covered by the play, Quadratus, an
Epicurean gallant and critic, first meets Jacomo, whom he draws
out and denounces as an effeminate amorist. Later in the morning,
in Act II, he goes to the lodgings of Laverdure, Celia's fiancé, in
the company of Lampatho Doria and Simplicius Faber to tease
and fulminate while each of them—Laverdure, the absolute Castilio, Lampatho, the scholar who is renouncing scholarship to
cultivate the felicities of fashionable life, and Simplicius, the effeminate gallant and toady—parades his folly at length. Moving,
then, in the general direction of Celia's house, this group stops at
the school, where Laverdure speaks to Pedante about his nuptial
arrangements and Simplicius acquires a servant, Holofernes Pippo.

In Act III these broadly satiric lines of action develop complications. The act begins with a scene not represented in D'Oddi,
though implied, in which the plotters disguise the perfumer as
Albano and rehearse him in his role, while Bidet, Laverdure's
page, eavesdrops and gloats to think how pleased his master will
be to hear of the scheme. Taking full advantage of this opportunity for surprise, Marston then introduces Albano unexpectedly
in the next scene. At first Albano bemoans Celia's disloyalty, but
at the approach of Laverdure and his company he withdraws and
after a few moments comes forward to revenge himself on the
interloper. Since Laverdure and his friends have already learned
of Jacomo's plot from Bidet, of course, Albano gets only ridicule
from them. And to make matters worse, he succeeds no better
with Jacomo and his brothers, who come in toward the end of the
scene to compliment him on his good performance and to twit
him for having appeared too early. In the last scene of this act,
these comic cross-purposes recede briefly while Bidet, presiding
over the Court of Pages, delineates a plot to disgrace Simplicius
and to trick him into parting with some of his money. The pages
conspire to disguise Holofernes Pippo as a merchant's wife who
is to persuade Simplicius that she is enamoured of him. Bidet
plans to play the go-between himself.

Celia appears in Act IV and in the first scene listens for the most part while her sister Meletza takes stock of their suitors. Then, after Laverdure and his friends have come in, she learns from him of Jacomo's plot and of their rout of the person whom they assumed to be the false Albano. Unlike the characters in *I Morti Vivi*, at this point no one, except Albano and his page Slip, knows that Albano has actually returned. To accommodate this difference and, at the same time, to add another strand of complication, Marston has Laverdure propose in jest at this juncture that they ought to disguise a fiddler as Albano to confound the false Albano when he appears. Accordingly, when Albano and Francisco do turn up a moment later, shouting simultaneously for entrance, Celia and the company assume that Laverdure has already done what he suggested; and before Laverdure has an opportunity to explain, both Albanos are admitted. Joined by Jacomo and Albano's brothers, who, meanwhile, have rushed in and tried to upset the marriage by proclaiming Albano's return only to learn that their plot is by this time old hat, the whole company ridicules Albano. Outraged and confused, even he wonders about his identity as he goes off in search of the duke and justice. Immensely pleased with themselves, the gallants disport in a dance and then join Celia for dinner.

Act V, of course, unravels all these complications. In the first scene the plot against Simplicius is carried out, and he is disgraced when his friends, who discover the pages playing dice for their loot, learn how the pages have tricked him. Then, in the presence of the Duke, Albano is finally permitted a hearing of a kind. In the face of his continued protestations, Laverdure belatedly comes forward to recognize him and to beg his pardon. Moments later, when Albano shows Celia a telltale mark and threatens to reveal details of their intimate conversation, even she is convinced. Albano, true to the spirit of these events, however, holds no grudges. "I'll know all, I'll pardon all—and I'll laugh at all," he says. Appropriately, the play closes on his invitation to celebrate this evening in rejoicing at his house.

From this outline alone it is possible to see that this kind of action is admirably suited to Marston's peculiar blend of light and shadow. It consists of an essentially serious human situation that with strategic distortions and emphases can be treated humorously. It abounds, unlike the earlier burlesques, in built-in elements for a picture of characters skittering into absurdity. And even its relative spareness has the special advantage of opportunities for easily internalized and integrated additions. Marston's principal task in reshaping it was to adjust and tailor it in keeping with his more ambitious design. His treatment of the disguise and of the disclosures concerning it, for example, was plainly calculated to increase the comic value of the sudden reversals and the confusion produced. By withholding from all except the audience that Albano has actually returned, by accounting for the second "false" Albano through Laverdure's suggestion, and then in the final scene by surprising the know-it-alls, who are deliriously pleased with themselves for having surprised the plotters, he manages a highly effective double turn instead of the single reversal in D'Oddi. In much the same way, by representing the scene in which Francisco is disguised immediately before the sudden appearance of Albano and by contriving the actual confrontation of Albano and Francisco, he realizes the maximal possibilities of the situation for satire and farce.

His treatment of character is perfectly consistent with these changes. With the possible exception of Albano, he has for the most part reduced the fairly complex characters borrowed from D'Oddi to the extremely flat, though highly animated, burlesque figures met in his earlier plays. Neither Celia, as we have seen, nor Albano can be entirely explained by this tendency to reduction; but they are unquestionably far funnier than Oranta and Tersandro, and Celia wins not a fraction of the interest Oranta does. Jacomo and Laverdure, on the other hand, are relatively simple transformations. Like Luigi, Jacomo is an intriguer capable of creating the plot that is the spring behind most of the play's complications, but he is also an amorist of the wailing, hair-tearing kind seen earlier in Pasquill and Antonio. In the first part of Act I he laments his wretchedness in terms that prompt Quadratus to say, "He speaks like a player: ha! poetical" (l. 32). Then, after Quadratus has departed, he woos Celia with music (in still another burlesque of the balcony scene) and receives for his pains a willow branch. Laverdure, moreover, is nothing like D'Oddi's Ottavio. Considerably simpler, he resembles by turns the clothes-horse (*CS*, III) as he orders Bidet to display his wardrobe and Curio (*SV*, VII, VIII, X) as he dances the "French passage"; but he is best summed up in the absolute Castilio (*CS*, I; *SV*, III), the professional gallant, perfect in address, appearance, and bearing, if somewhat at odds to support himself.

Like Jacomo and Laverdure, furthermore, the characters invented by Marston are for the most part agents of the satire and farce, incapable of arousing long-range concerns, but highly engaging while they dominate the stage. Simplicius Faber is a typical effeminate gallant who closely resembles the fawning Sporo in Satire I of *Certain Satires* and the toady in Satire III. The pages who disgrace him bear a clear likeness to the saucy servants in D'Oddi's play; but the Court of Pages scene and the scene in which their plot against Simplicius is carried out are entirely Marston's. Indeed, the device of the mock court at which each of the pages cites his master's shortcomings is, essentially, a simple variation on the procedure of the satires, except that, instead of the satirist, Bidet and the respective pages heap criticism on their masters. Meletza, on the other hand, unmistakably derives from the Rossaline of *Antonio and Mellida*. A critic in a minor way, Meletza, too, is a witty young woman with a large number of suitors, but no great desire to marry. In Act IV, scene i, the scene that could have been suggested by Act I, scene ii, of *Two Gentlemen of Verona*,[5] her sole function is to take the roll of her suitors

---

[5] Becker suggested that two scenes were borrowed from Shakespeare: IV, i, from I, ii, of *Two Gentlemen;* and II, ii, the schoolroom scene, from IV, i, of *The Merry Wives* (see Becker, pp. 28, 37). The scene involving Celia, Meletza, Lyzabetta, and so on, could easily have been suggested by *Two Gentlemen,* though the idea is commonplace enough that Marston could

and Celia's, much as the satirist takes the roll of the satiric types, while later, she fills the strategic function of drawing the gallants out and crossing their excessive behavior with appropriate comments.

Among the characters added by Marston, only Quadratus and Lampatho Doria obviously do more than carry out Marston's intention to enlarge the satirical and farcical content of the play. Quadratus, whose name derives from *quadrato,* meaning "squared," or "fowre-square," is the inevitable critic, hovering over the action to direct opinion to a proper appreciation of, and contempt for, the ridiculous goings on.[6] But he is a quite different critic from any Marston had used to this point and any, indeed, that he was to use in later comedies. On the other hand, Lampatho Doria, whose name is derived from *lampazo,* meaning "bur," and perhaps *dorio,* meaning a "musician who plays grave music," is primarily a satiric character, now playing the toady for Laverdure in an effort to make the transition from scholarship to courtliness, now playing the amorist for Meletza, but doing both with a distinct awareness of himself that is entirely new for a satiric type. On one occasion he is even permitted to talk seriously and at length about his wasted life.

Like the simpler satiric characters, the Duke has been cut from a pattern met earlier, in his case that of the degenerate Luxurio (SV, III), and more than any other character, with the exception

---

also have hit upon it on his own; IV, i, in *Merry Wives,* on the other hand, is substantially different from Marston's schoolroom scene. To begin with, Shakespeare's scene does not take place in a schoolroom, but on the street, where Sir Hugh Evans examines William Page in grammar. His interrogation resembles Pedante's quiz, of course, but it is only narrowly possible that it suggested the idea of the scene to Marston.

[6] This meaning of the name is played on several times: viz. II, i, 152, 168; IV, i, 119. In addition, there was a considerable number of reasonably well-known men from classical times by this name. Smith lists more than a dozen (see Smith, *Dictionary of Mythology*); but no one of them seems more appropriate as Marston's model than any other. Perhaps Marston had in mind the Quadratus mentioned by Epictetus (II, 177); he was a wealthy citizen at whose house philosophers sometimes gathered.

of Quadratus, he has been fashioned to lend atmosphere to the world of the play. He appears only twice, in the first act (where he does not speak) and in the last; but both appearances are handled so that his enormity as the political and social leader epitomizes the grotesque distortions everywhere and fixes a background of Italianate depravity. In Act I Jacomo describes him as "the loose Venice Duke," who carouses all night and sleeps all day and who "scorns all plaints; makes jest of serious suit" (i, 230). Then, in Act V, he himself emphasizes the moral dislocation in his realm when he complains that libertine excesses are no longer satisfying because now everyone enjoys them.

But doubtless the character most adequately reflective of the play's complexity—of its elusive blend of qualities—is Quadratus, the Epicurean critic. Quadratus is in the foreground more than any other character, almost simultaneously exploding in denunciations, calling for songs, dances, and wine, and imposing his own good humor, his "fantasticalness" as he calls it, on the proceedings. His mock defense of "fantasticalness" is a kind of index to both his mixture of levity and seriousness and his self-consciousness as a participant in the life of this rather anomalous Venice. In Act II, scene i, outraged at Lampatho for suggesting that he might criticize him, he undertakes to justify the fantastical man, by which he apparently means the wildly unconventional man. To do so, he argues for what he calls *phantasia incomplexa*, meaning uncircumscribed or unfettered imagination. This mental faculty he defends by marshaling the functions ordinarily associated with the fantasy or imagination and by then proceeding to show that without the fantasy man is on a level with the beasts.[7] His argu-

---

[7] The terms "fantasy" and "imagination" were frequently synonymous (see Pierre de la Primaudaye, *The French Academie* [London, 1618], p. 410); but sometimes they were used to complement each other. In this passage Quadratus expounds ideas that go back to Aristotle (see Harry Austryn Wolfson, "The Internal Senses in Latin, Arabic, and Hebrew Philosophic Texts," *Harvard Theological Review*, XXVIII [1935], 69–133). For contemporary expositions see de la Primaudaye, pp. 410, 414, and Puttenham, *Arte*, pp. 18, 19. Quadratus' term, *phantasia incomplexa*, however, seems

ment, as such, involves a fatal equivocation since he identifies unconventionality or fantasticalness with fantasy on the basis of the similarity of terms.[8] But the passage is not so important for its logic as it is for the rhetoric that enables Quadratus for the remainder of the act to refer the other characters to "fantasticalness" as if to a highly admirable standard in behavior. "He can scarce be saved," he says a few lines later, "that's not fantastical: I stand firm to it" (ll. 210, 211). And his behavior throughout the play proves that he has every desire to be saved.

In general, Quadratus combines the Epicurean *bon vivant* and the critic. In the former role he often resembles Falstaff. Like him, he is fat, carefree, devoted to food and drink, and, if Meletza's comment that "he lives by begging" can be credited, to some extent even parasitic.[9] Like Falstaff in *I Henry IV*, he undertakes a play extempore (Act V) that is interrupted; and like Falstaff his philosophy, insofar as either can be said to have one, is rooted in a pessimistic view of civilization. To this extent, perhaps, a case can even be made for his having been a burlesque version of Shakespeare's comic titan; actually, of course, we shall probably never know to what extent a similarity was intended or to what extent it was pure chance or a matter of borrowings. But, if Quadratus was patterned on Falstaff, clearly Marston had no intention whatever of trying to approach Shakespeare's conception in depth and complexity. For all his multiple facets, Quadratus is a relatively flat character, a rowdy burlesque figure who carries his seriousness lightly. Surely the child actor who packed his girth and strutted and fumed, calling for wine and denouncing his

---

to be Marston's coinage. Although dozens of distinctions were made with reference to the *phantasia* (see Sextus Empiricus, *Adversus Mathematicos*, Paris, 1569), none of the authorities on the subject mentions *phantasia incomplexa*.

[8] Lampatho, the former scholar, apparently notices the fallacy; at least he says, "Most fantastical protection of fantasticness" (l. 203).

[9] IV, i, 36, 37. Yet at several points Quadratus suggests that it is Lampatho who borrows from him; see IV, i, 119ff.

brother-gallants, was humorous to behold; but it is doubtful that
he troubled himself about an intricate characterization.

Yet a certain seriousness Quadratus does have. A great number
of his speeches are in the vein of Planet, Feliche, and, before
them, the snarling satirist. He attacks and reviles; and his criticism,
like that of the critics in the earlier comedies, constitutes one of
the chief ways in which Marston controls the peculiar seriousness
of *What You Will.* After the gallants have assembled, for example,
he turns aside to say:

> Is not this rare, now? Now, by Gorgon's head,
> I gape, and am struck stiff in wonderment
> At sight of these strange beasts. Yon chamlet youth,
> Simplicius Faber, that hermaphrodite,
> *Party per pale,* that bastard mongrel soul,
> Is nought but admiration and applause
> Of yon Lampatho Doria, a fusty cask,
> Devote to mouldy customs of hoary eld;
> Doth he but speak, "O tones of heaven itself!"
> Doth he once write, "O Jesu admirable!"
> Cries out Simplicius. Then Lampatho spits,
> And says, "faith 'tis good." But, O, to mark yon thing
> Sweat to unite acquaintance to his friend,
> Labour his praises, and endear his worth
> With titles all as formally trick'd forth
> As the cap of a dedicatory epistle.
> Then, sir, to view Lampatho: he protests,
> Protests and vows such sudden heat of love,
> That O 'twere warmth enough of mirth to dry
> The stintless tears of old Heraclitus,—
> Make Niobe to laugh! [II, i, 44–64]

Characterized wholly on the basis of such speeches, he might
almost be indistinguishable from Planet and Feliche. Actually, he
is far from being a simple spokesman of Marston's views. He is
not a Marstonian Neo-Stoic, as Planet and Feliche had been, but

an Epicurean devoted to pleasure and laughter. Perhaps Marston sought to unify the *bon vivant* and the critic in the character of Quadratus because he felt, what any reader of *Jack Drum* and *Antonio and Mellida* must feel, that Planet and Feliche would be more effective if they were more integrally engaged in the action, as, say, Antonio is in *Antonio's Revenge*. As it is, Planet and Feliche stand on the verges of the intrigue, commenting and philosophizing, but seldom merging with the action in any but a very mechanical way. To remedy this fault, Marston could well have set for himself in *What You Will* the task of creating a critic who could with probability be on stage frequently, who could participate in the lighthearted proceedings, and who could at the same time turn at any moment into the familiar scourge. Quadratus obviously fills these needs. A gallant himself, indeed, a half-hearted suitor to Meletza, he is, nonetheless, a stern censor and a rather jaundiced philosopher whose hedonism proceeds from his widely expressed conviction that life offers little else.

As a critic, accordingly, Quadratus is involved both in the play's merriment and its seriousness. His pessimistic moments are part of the fabric of serious matter that stands in counterpoint to the lightness and gaiety of the play. To a large extent, this serious matter consists of speeches by him, Lampatho, and Albano, speeches declaring the transience of human joy, the obscurity of human destiny, and the decay of all things. More particularly, Quadratus is both the rather buoyant spokesman of a *carpe diem* resignation:

> Gulp Rhenish wine, my liege; let our paunch rent;
> Suck merry jellies; preview, but not prevent,
> No mortal can, the miseries of life [V, i, 363–365]

and an embittered observer of the human scene:

> Hang love.
> It is the abject outcast of the world. [I, i, 59–60]
>
> Why, turn a temporist, row with the Tide. [II, ii, 195]

But none of these speeches embodies the philosophy of the play. Taken together, they crystallize only one response to its world, though a response that is the more sobering because we see in his speech on Cato (V, i, 240–262) that Quadratus is aware of an ideal alternative to Venetian depravity.

Like Quadratus, Lampatho Doria, the character that best qualifies as a satiric portrait of Jonson, also contributes to the triviality of this Venice and at the same time under-cuts it. In large part he contributes to the general image of deformity as a contemptible sycophant; but he has more than routine interest because he does so with considerable perspective on himself. At one point, after the others have left the schoolroom, he remains with Quadratus to reflect on his wasted life as a scholar; and briefly he erupts into a rich portrait of degeneracy. The whole scene is very skillfully contrived. As Lampatho reflects amid the scenes of his former labors, Simplicius calls from without, as if calling him to his new life and its emptiness. In quick strides Lampatho rises to accents of eloquence unmatched elsewhere in the play:

> I was a scholar: seven useful springs
> Did I deflower in quotations
> Of cross'd opinions 'bout the soul of man.
> The more I learnt the more I learnt to doubt:
> Knowledge and wit, faith's foes, turn faith about.
>
> .   .   .   .   .
>
>   Delight,
> Delight, my spaniel slept, whilst I baus'd leaves,
> Toss'd o'er the dunces, pored on the old print
> Of titled words, and still my spaniel slept.
> Whilst I wasted lamp-oil, bated my flesh,
> Shrunk up my veins; and still my spaniel slept.
> And still I held converse with Zabarell,
> Aquinas, Scotus, and the musty saw
> Of antic Donate; still my spaniel slept.
> Still went on went I; first *an sit anima*,
> Then, and it were mortal. O hold, hold! at that

> They're at brain-buffets, fell by the ears amain
> Pell-mell together; still my spaniel slept.
> Then whether 'twere corporeal, local, fix'd,
> Extraduce; but whether't had free will
> Or no, ho philosophers
> Stood banding factions all so strongly propp'd,
> I stagger'd, knew not which was firmer part;
> But thought, quoted, read, observ'd, and pried,
> Stuff'd noting-books; and still my spaniel slept.
> At length he waked and yawn'd and by yon sky,
> For aught I know he knew as much as I. [II, ii, 151–180]

This is doubtless impressive. But it is also important to notice that almost as quickly as this moment of self-revelation develops, it ends, and Lampatho resumes the antics of the toady. Essentially, Lampatho is a satiric type, a toady boldly drawn in grotesque outline; but, like Quadratus, he is a relatively more complex character than any we have met thus far. His self-awareness and the speeches it gives rise to actuate undercurrents of criticism that complicate and darken the dramatic image as a whole.

Albano, too, is delicately adjusted to the play's "serious fantasticalness." In addition to his speeches of sobering commentary,[10] he is the only character borrowed from D'Oddi who has been in some ways rendered more serious. Marston decided against engaging him in a scheme like that by which Tersandro attempts to trick Oranta into revealing her infidelity, and this change alone makes him a more sympathetic victim than Tersandro had been. Moreover, Marston has supported this claim for sympathy by enhancing the poignancy of his failures to be recognized. He has replaced Marcone, Oranta's factotum, with Randolpho and Andrea so that it is Albano's own brothers who do not know him, and he has contrived the actual confrontation of Albano and Celia, at which time she does not know him. Most important of all, he has endowed the whole circumstance of mistaken identity with meaning that it did not have in its farce context in *I Morti Vivi*.

---

[10] See especially III, ii, 41–67.

The various failures to recognize Albano can hardly be restricted to a discussion of him because they are so intimately tied up with the whole question of identity in the play. In general, Marston has taken the relatively simple plot device of mistaken identity and treated it as a problem common to the world of the play. It appears most conspicuously, of course, in Albano's inability to establish his identity. But it suggests itself also in the widespread interest among the satiric characters in clothes and appearances: in Laverdure's passion for his pawned finery in II, i, and in the concern of Lampatho and Simplicius to appear to be gallants at all costs. It is, perhaps, even apparent in Simplicius' failure to recognize Pippo in the disguise of a merchant's wife. Jacomo first touches squarely on the problem when in the process of disguising Francisco he says,

> Apparel's grown a god, and goes more neat;
> Makes men of rags, which straight he bears aloft,
> Like patch'd-up scarecrows to affright the rout
> Of the idolatrous vulgar that worship images,
> Stand awed and bare-scalp'd at the gloss of silks,
> Which, like the glorious A-jax of Lincoln's-Inn
> (Survey'd with wonder by me when I lay
> Factor in London), laps up naught but filth
> And excrements, that bear the shape of men,
> Whose inside every daw would peck and tear,
> But that vain scarecrow clothes entreats forbear.
> [III, i, 13–23]

Jacomo's assertions receive plenty of support from Albano, who after his tribulations is so confused that he, too, wonders about his identity.

> My brothers know not right Albano yet?
> Away! 'tis faithless! If Albano's name
> Were liable to sense, that I could taste, or touch,
> Or see, or feel it, it might 'tice belief;

But since 'tis voice, and air—Come to the Muskcat, boy;
Francisco, that's my name. . . . [III, ii, 293–298]

Albano's confusion as well as the general tendency to value false
impressions to a point where individual identity is lost recalls, of
course, Marston's familiar convictions about Opinion and its power
to corrupt. The Venice of *What You Will* wriggles in the grips of
this perverter of thought and feeling; in the play Opinion tinges
even the zaniest of episodes with hints of mutability and futility.

Taken together, these features of Marston's treatment of the
action of *What You Will* complicate and qualify the exuberant
frivolity of the play. Yet lest by discussing them in isolation they
assume an importance that they do not deserve, it bears repeating
that *What You Will* is dominantly lighthearted, a comedy that
rises on the outrageous behavior of its characters and that fre-
qently lilts with lyrical moments of song and dance. The text
contains stage directions for seven songs and two dances. We have
no notion of the length of the songs or of the elaborateness of the
dances, since the songs have not been printed and the directions
for the dances are very brief; but Marston's practice in his earlier
comedies suggests that some of them, at least, could have been
fairly substantial. Even the play's most serious moments, moreover, are carefully controlled. To prevent Albano's failure to establish his identity from becoming too pathetic and his character
from becoming too sympathetic, Marston resolves speeches that
could well rise to heartbroken eloquence in incoherent stuttering.[11] In Act III, scene ii, for example, Albano begins well, but
finally collapses in comic confusion:

[11] Although Marston had used stuttering to something like this end in
the character of Piero in *Antonio and Mellida*, it is just possible that he
derived the idea of using it in this play from D'Oddi, whose Beccafico
stutters: "Orsù in buon' hora, parla di me costui. Vo far mi inanzi, e con
buona creanza dirgli se vuol' altro. Tiriri, ri, ri, Tiriri, Tirira, Tirisandro, che
commanda altro la Reverentia vostra?" (*I Morti Vivi*, p. 145). Marston was
hardly the only playwright to use stuttering for comic effect; cf. Red Cap's
stuttering in *Look about You* (Malone Society Reprints, Oxford, 1913).

> Babes and fools I'll trust;
> But servants' faith, wives' love, or female's lust,—
> A usurer and a devil sooner. Now, were I dead,
> Methinks I see a huff-cap swaggering sir
> Pawning my plate, my jewels mortgage; nay,
> Selling outright the purchase of my brows,
> Whilst my poor fatherless, lean, totter'd son—
> My gentry's relics, my house's only prop—
> Is saw'd asunder, lies forlorn, all bleak
> Unto the griefs of sharp necessities,
> Whilst his father-in-law, his father-in-devil, or d-d-d-d-devil-f-f-f-
> father,
> Or who, who, who, who,—What You Will!—
> When is the marriage morn? [ll. 69–81]

At such moments the audience forgets, briefly, the pathos of Albano's situation and sees only a frenzied man of passion.

As a whole, therefore, *What You Will* combines much the same elements found in *Jack Drum* and *Antonio and Mellida.* Its diversity, like the diversity of those plays, is conspicuous in its styles: in the supercharged effusions of Jacomo's speeches of lamentation, in the straightforward blank verse in which he lays his plot, in the euphuistic extravagance of Lampatho at his most obsequious, and in the battering cadences of Quadratus' denunciations, but most often in the racy conversational prose that is the standard speech of the play. Using the structural scheme derived from D'Oddi, Marston has assembled a world that reels, totters, and staggers in an almost frantic effort to enjoy itself. Lampatho bitterly renounces the search for truth and raises the cup. Quadratus praises the way of Cato, but follows the way of Falstaff. Albano loses all sense of identity and submits to the spirit of bedlam, and the Duke in his whimsical, jaded licentiousness sums up the whole tipsy carnival. But it is not a world that totters inevitably to fall. Quadratus does acknowledge the superiority of Cato and in other ways praises the value of high-minded pride in self, and Albano does recover his identity to the rejoicing of all. In other words, the dramatic action of *What You Will* affirms Marston's usual alternative to a life in the swamp of Opinion even as it vividly and compellingly represents the nature of life in the swamp.

Technically, *What You Will* reflects clear advances over the earlier satirical comedies in unifying all the elements that Marston felt intrinsic to this dramatic type in a more concrete and better-integrated dramatic image. It would be too simple to attribute its more effective accommodation of parts to the whole, its greater variety and subtlety of satiric method, and its greater liveliness of comic invention to the disguise plot alone. Indeed, strictly speaking, the plot of *What You Will* is as dependent on mistaken identity as it is on disguise. But the distinction is not especially important here since, however the plot is described, it opened up to Marston exactly the structural possibilities exploited in *The Malcontent* and *The Fawn*. It is probably more to the point to say that the plot of *What You Will*—a disguise plot in part at least—enabled Marston to abandon or refurbish much of the explicit direction of his first efforts in favor of inference and indirect controls, to internalize such devices as the disengaged critic, the parade of satiric types, and the set speeches of Neo-Stoic preachment. With this kind of action he was able to turn even so elementary a matter as the order of disclosures to comical satiric effect. The fact in *What You Will* that the audience is possessed as early as Act III, scene ii, of all the information necessary to unravel the situation provides a point of vantage from which the characters, now luxuriating in their pretensions, now engaging in plots the audience knows cannot succeed, and now acting on opinions the audience knows to be false, heightens their comic and satiric value beyond anything that explicit comment can do. If *What You Will* represents the crudest treatment of this kind of plot that we shall meet, it is nonetheless a vastly superior play to Marston's previous efforts in satirical comedy.

The advantages of Marston's discovery of the disguise plot are nowhere more clear or impressive than in his next and, I think, his best play, *The Malcontent*. Unfortunately the evolution of this play and of *The Fawn* is rather difficult to explain. We have neither Marston's immediate sources for them nor any conclusive evidence that he knew plays or stories that might have furnished him with hints for the disguise plots used. He had used disguise in his own plays, notably in *Antonio and Mellida* and *Antonio's Revenge;* and, indeed, Antonio's assumption of a fool's disguise to enable him to prowl around Piero's court and carry out his revenge could easily have led to Malevole and *The Malcontent*. But it is also possible that Marston did not make the leap from disguise as a device within a plot to disguise as an axis on which to build a plot until he reworked D'Oddi's play. And it is always possible that he was stimulated by a contemporary play, perhaps Middleton's *The Phoenix*, or even *Measure for Measure*, though the dates of these plays create problems.[12]

While the question of his source or sources remains open, it is perfectly clear that Marston exploited the idea of using disguise as the foundation for a plot in *The Malcontent* and *The Fawn*. It is important to see, moreover, that out of the wide variety of disguise plots at his disposal he chose a rather specialized type for his own purpose. V. O. Freeburg has made a study of the disguise plot as it was used by the Elizabethans in his *Disguise Plots in Elizabethan Drama*.[13] After tracing the history of the plot from the Greek and Roman plays through the medieval romances, the Italian *novelle,* and the Italian, French, and Spanish plays, he classifies the various types of disguise plots that are to be found in Elizabethan plays.[14] Within the framework of these classifica-

---

[12] Nothing is known about *Measure for Measure* before Dec. 26, 1604, when it was performed at Court, but J. Dover Wilson thinks that it existed considerably earlier; see his edition of the play (Cambridge, 1950), pp. 103–105. The only positive piece of evidence that we have concerning *The Phoenix* is that it was published in 1609, though Chambers thinks that a performance of it may have been seen by the King on Feb. 20, 1604 (*Stage*, IV, 118), and R. C. Bald puts it in 1602 ("The Chronology of Middleton's Plays," *MLR*, XXXII [1937], 35, 36). *The Malcontent*, on the other hand, almost certainly existed before 1604 (see Appendix A).

[13] New York, 1915.   [14] Pages 31–60.

tions we find that Marston, having exercised a high degree of selectivity, fixed upon the duke-in-disguise plot, a rather unusual and infrequent type. The reasons for his choice are not difficult to discover.

Like all disguise plots, the duke-in-disguise plot enabled Marston to regulate seriousness and levity by controlling the nature of the character in disguise. It is probably fair to say that with plays of this kind our expectations for a happy or unhappy outcome depend to a large extent on the nature of the character disguised. If the disguised character is admirable, the fact that his disguise is successful disposes us to feel hopeful of a happy issue. If, on the other hand, the disguised character is a villain, our expectations become fearful for the same reason. Without attempting to formulate a dramaturgic law, we might say that, in general, our feelings about a character, whether good or bad, are generalized to the world of the play when that character successfully goes into disguise. For Marston, who was always hard pressed to control his unusual fictional worlds, such a character was invaluable to undercut plot materials too melodramatic for his purposes and to render plot materials intrinsically too trivial more serious.

More particularly, the duke-in-disguise plot provided Marston with a disguised character that easily assumes the multiple functions of protagonist, intriguer, critic, and judge. The very fact that this character is a duke gives him an important stake in all that happens, particularly in all the vice and folly to which he is exposed; and, at the same time, his rank makes him capable of punishing all offenses. Hence, by simply making it probable that this character be in the midst of the action at all times, Marston was able to qualify whatever happens in the play with the knowledge that it is being observed and will be punished or put to rights. Again, as in *What You Will*, the quality of the action is in large part defined by the order of disclosures: the audience's reception of the action depends on what it knows against what the characters in the play know. Armed with the knowledge that the duke is deceiving the other characters until a moment propitious for his undisguising, the audience anticipates the punishment of the immoral characters even as they parade their folly and wickedness with complete confidence in their security. In other words, the audience sees the characters in a perspective that renders their activities ironic; indeed, it sees the whole spectacle of manners represented in the play in this perspective.

The Malcontent, probably Marston's first play for the company at Blackfriars, the company with which he was associated for the remainder of his career, was the first of the two plays in which he used the duke-in-disguise plot.[15] Traditionally it is thought to be a very serious play, either a very bitter comedy or a tragicomedy, and as a matter of record it was called a *tragiecomedia* when it was entered in the Stationers' Register.[16] Other comments by Marston, however, suggest that he did not think the play different in intention from his previous satirical comedies. In his preface "To the Reader" he hopes that his "supposed tartness . . . may modestly pass with the freedom of a satire" and himself calls the play a comedy. Moreover, he has taken as a motto for the play part of Laronia's speech in Juvenal's second satire: *Dat veniam corvis, vexat censura columbas* ("Our censor absolves the ravens and passes judgment on the pigeons"),[17] a statement that accords perfectly with Webster's assertion in the "Induction" that the play deals with "such vices as stand not accountable to law" (ll. 73, 74). The implication that the play was constructed, despite its plethora of usurpations, attempted murders, and disloyalties of all

---

[15] The question of the date of *The Malcontent* is taken up in Appendix A.

[16] *SR*, III, 268:

Quinto die Julii

William Aspley   Entred for their Copie under the hands of
Thomas Thorpe   Master Pasfield and Master Norton Warden
                     an Enterlude called *The Malcontent*
                     tragiecomedia.

[17] This line is printed in the margin of the first page of text in the old editions.

kinds, to mend not major but minor vices is, perhaps, best verified by giving sufficient attention to Marston's treatment of the disguise plot. Only by tracing the long-range effects of the duke in disguise are the, admittedly, highly melodramatic parts of the play seen in the proper comic perspective, and only when the seriousness of the parts has been related to the comic orientation of the whole does Langbaine's description of the play as an "honest general Satyr" seem accurate.[18]

The plot of *The Malcontent* is based on easily the most melodramatic materials to be found in Marston's satirical comedies. Consisting largely of an intricate pattern of revenges and betrayals, it resembles a revenge plot and harks back to *Antonio's Revenge*. But it is marked by the important difference that none of its revenges is carried out successfully, save the protagonist's, and his is notably tame alongside those found in regular revenge plays. In brief, the plot is a representation of the process by which the banished Altofronto regains the dukedom of Genoa. Yet a simple straightforward description of this process would serve only to distort the plot's character, for the peculiar character of the plot results from the unusual adaptation that Marston has made of essentially very serious plot materials in the interests of comic seriousness.

At the center of a Genoa stronger in the will to sin than in sin itself stands Duke Altofronto, who a year previous to the two days covered by the play had been banished by the usurper Pietro. When the play opens, Altofronto's fortunes are low, but giving conspicuous promise of improvement. To begin with, he has established himself in the court of the usurper, where, with all the privileges of a court jester, he plays the part of the malcontent Malevole. In the course of the first scene the world of Pietro's

---

[18] It should be pointed out that Langbaine used the phrase to distinguish the play from satires on particular persons: "I take [it] to be an honest general Satyr, and not (as some malicious Enemies endeavour'd to persuade the world) design'd to strike at particular persons" (*An Account of the English Dramatick Poets*, Oxford, 1691, p. 350).

court passes in parade, and, as Malevole teases and reviles its chief members, it becomes clear that it is not a discouragingly formidable world. Duke Pietro, for example, learns from Malevole that he has been made a cuckold by Mendoza, and he rushes off to avenge himself. And Mendoza, who soon reveals himself to be the villain of the piece, is not unlike an amorist in his first appearance, when he goes off to write a sonnet on Pietro's wife, Aurelia. Besides these reassuring signs, Altofronto has at least one loyal friend among Pietro's followers in Celso, with whom he plots in secret. Together, they await the moment when Altofronto can take full advantage of the disguise that hope has bade him assume.

In Act I, scene ii, the initial impression of confusion among the villains offers still another reason to hope for the best. Ferneze, one of Pietro's courtiers, and Maquerelle, a bawd, deceive Aurelia into believing that Mendoza has been disloyal to her, whereupon she makes a rendezvous with Ferneze for that night and denounces Mendoza to his face. Bewildered, Mendoza is in the next instant confronted by Pietro, who is bent on killing him. With all the boldness of a consummate Machiavellian, however, he brazens out Pietro's charge, saves himself, and initiates his vengeance on Ferneze and Aurelia by simply offering to prove that Ferneze is the guilty party. With this one stroke he apparently foils Altofronto's first plot, though subsequent events prove that the reversal actually works to Altofronto's advantage.

As Mendoza's fortunes rise in Act II, Pietro's sag perceptibly, and Altofronto's continue promising through the maze of intrigue that turns gradually in his favor. Typically, their scenes are interspersed with light satiric moments involving Malevole, Maquerelle, the ladies of the court, or Bilioso. Pietro completes his plot to ambush Ferneze in Aurelia's chamber and dismisses Malevole for having wrongfully accused Mendoza. At the same time, he is so heartbroken about Aurelia's disloyalty that even after Ferneze has been waylaid and supposedly killed by Mendoza, he derives no satisfaction from the revenge. Having blundered by naming Mendoza as his heir, moreover, he next makes the error of leaving

Mendoza with the irate Aurelia, and together they hatch still another plot, this time with Pietro as victim. But the probable efficacy of all this dire design is undermined when the act concludes with the surprising development that Ferneze has not been successfully dispatched. Though wounded, he is helped off by Malevole, a fact that prepares for his subsequent conversion.

In Act III Altofronto's conviction that "the wind begins to come about" (l. 228) reinforces our expectation for a happy outcome even as Mendoza's villainy multiplies in schemes and counter-schemes. For one thing, Celso brings news that the people now regret having turned against Altofronto. For another, Altofronto is confident that the Duke of Florence, who had supported Pietro's usurpation, will desert him once he learns that his daughter, Aurelia, is an adulteress. But perhaps most important of all is the fact that Mendoza makes the fatal error of enlisting Malevole to assist him in his schemes. It is Malevole whom he sends to assassinate Pietro and to whom he confides his intention to banish Aurelia and marry Maria, Altofronto's wife, at present Pietro's prisoner. Pietro, meanwhile, diminishes considerably as a possible threat to Altofronto's restoration. At this point he is not only much conspired against, but incapable of more than a paralytic melancholy. When Malevole, armed to the teeth and supposedly determined to carry out Mendoza's plan to murder him, comes upon him in the final scene and reveals to him the extent of Mendoza's treachery, he easily bends to Malevole's will and, unwittingly, joins the ranks of the man whose place he had usurped.

So strong is Altofronto's position by Act IV that even Mendoza's superb villainy arouses little anxiety about the ultimate outcome. Of course, Marston was not interested in melodramatic suspense: he could easily have manipulated these materials for thrills, but he did not. Instead, he put Mendoza, who would otherwise be the architect of all terror, in the absurd position of thinking that he is being wonderfully diabolical, while actually he is building only the flimsiest of Gothic sand castles for himself. Once Mendoza engages Malevole as his hatchet man, Altofronto as Malevole quite clearly controls events. He returns to the court with Pietro, who is disguised as a hermit, to report that Pietro has committed suicide, whereupon Mendoza, as Pietro's heir, is proclaimed duke. Now supremely confident of himself, Mendoza immediately banishes the stunned Aurelia and then, in separate interviews, orders both Malevole and Pietro-as-hermit to kill the other. Almost as quickly, of course, Malevole and Pietro tell each other of the double treachery, and the counterplot against Mendoza nears fruition. Pietro, now thoroughly humbled by the spectacle of what men can be, thoroughly chastened by the knowledge that even Aurelia is repentant, and thoroughly convinced of the futility of his own situation by Bilioso's news that the Duke of Florence has ordered Altofronto's restoration, wishes aloud that he might make amends to Altofronto. With magnificent timing, Malevole undisguises himself, and the reformed sinners, Pietro and Ferneze, join the men of good will, Altofronto and Celso, in a league to unseat Mendoza.

But Mendoza is not actually unseated until the very last moment. Through most of the final act he continues to receive assurances that his dark plots are succeeding and that his position is more secure than ever, even as Altofronto's restoration becomes inevitable. When Altofronto, still disguised, goes to Maria to sue in Mendoza's behalf, he not only finds her faithful, but also picks up another ally in the loyal captain who guards her. And when he returns to Mendoza with her reply and the false report that the hermit is dead, he anticipates Mendoza's attempt to poison him by tricking Mendoza into using an empty poison box. By the end of Act V, scene ii, Mendoza exults in the knowledge that Ferneze, Pietro the hermit, and Malevole are dead, that Aurelia is banished, and that Maria is completely in his power. In this state of mind he orders the masque that sets the stage for the denouement.

In the last scene Mendoza's sand castle is dashed by a single wave. As he tries first to persuade and then to coerce Maria into yielding just one more victory to him, Altofronto and his allies enter disguised as masquers and take their ladies to dance. With the conclusion of the dance they unmask, and Mendoza and his court see the whole truth in an instant. Altofronto, now restored, is contemptuous but clement in his punishments. Appropriately enough, in view of Mendoza's actual achievement as a villain, he simply kicks the Machiavellian into banishment. Then, after sending Maquerelle to the suburbs and cursing Bilioso as a perfect knave, he takes Maria and his loyal friends to his bosom, and the play concludes.

The dominant qualities of the plot of *The Malcontent* are quite clearly established in Marston's treatment of Mendoza and Altofronto. The former is a villain who, in any other play, could well be a Machiavellian monster like Piero in *Antonio's Revenge,* from whom he probably derives. He has no conscience, and his fertility in wicked schemes is matched in the play only by the fertility of the court of Genoa in occasions for them. Yet everything he does and everything he plans to do is either noted or suggested by Altofronto disguised as Malevole. Throughout the play his villainy is undermined by the audience's certain knowledge that he cannot succeed. By subverting Mendoza's villainy in this way Marston has minimized the suspense that a contest of mighty opposites could have furnished and put the emphasis on the comic possibilities of Mendoza's role. Mendoza remains the most wicked figure in a world that abundantly justifies Pietro's and Altofronto's disgust, but his villainy is deprived of its edge. As Waith has remarked, evil in *The Malcontent* is largely an atmosphere,[19] an atmosphere appropriate to the didactic and satiric burdens of the play and at the same time appropriate to the comic resolution.

This general view of Marston's purpose is confirmed by the details of his treatment of Mendoza. Our first impression of Mendoza is comic. In Act I, scene i, after he has dismissed the favor-seekers and Malevole, he has a long soliloquy in praise of princely favor and "sweet women! most sweet ladies! nay, angels! by heaven . . ." (ll. 324–357). But a few moments later, in Act I, scene ii, when he enters reading his sonnet to Aurelia, he is met

[19] *Pattern*, p. 70.

by her scorn; and in his second soliloquy, exactly parallel to the first, he denounces "women! nay Furies; nay, worse . . ." (ll. 85–102). Only after he has been scaled down in this fashion does he emerge, in the subsequent scene with Pietro, as a villain of considerable cunning. Thereafter, though he commands interest as a stock Machiavellian, his enormity is undercut by what the audience knows and he does not know about his situation. When in Act III, scene i, he seizes upon Malevole's plan to murder Pietro, chuckling with glee: "O unpeerable invention! rare! / Thou god of policy! it honeys me" (ll. 329, 330), he does not know that he is playing into his enemy's hands. And, in Act IV, scene i, when he has arranged, as he thinks, the murders of Malevole and the hermit he cannot know how hollow he sounds as he gloats satanically,

> We that are great, our sole self-good still moves us.
>
> . . . . .
>
> One stick burns t'other, steel cuts steel alone:
> 'Tis good trust few; but, O, 'tis best trust none! [ll. 234–241]

The child actors, of course, were perfectly suited to exploit the comic possibilities of this top-heavy villainy. But by whoever acted, Mendoza is clearly only a caricature of the stock Machiavellian type so frequently seen on the public stages.

Altofronto, on the other hand, cannot be summed up so easily. Although we are continually reminded that he is a banished duke who hopes to be restored and who, to effect that end, pretends to be a malcontent in the court of his enemy, much that he says and does as the malcontent is just as important to the structure of the play as what he says and does as Altofronto. A great deal has already been written about the origins of Malevole's character and his probable relations to Kyd's Hamlet, to Jaques, Macilente, and a dozen or more other characters.[20] It is doubtful, however, that

[20] See, especially, E. E. Stoll, "Shakespeare, Marston and the Malcontent Type," *MP*, III (Jan. 1906), 281–303; R. S. Forsythe, *The Relations of*

any of this work offers more likely precedents for the character than those that Marston had ready at hand in Antonio, Feliche, Planet, and the commentator in the satires; and it is extremely doubtful that this attention to sources throws any light at all on Malevole's specific function in *The Malcontent*. For our purpose it suffices to recognize that the malcontent enabled Marston to unify in a single character the functions filled by several characters in the early satirical comedies. Altofronto as Malevole is at once the critic, poised to denounce vice and folly, the protagonist, arousing some concern about his prospects for good fortune, the intriguer, foiling the villain and shaping the action to his own advantage, and the judge, providing the standards that in the final analysis order the world of the play.

As Malevole, the critic and intriguer, "a man, or rather a monster, more discontent than Lucifer when he was thrust out of the presence" (I, i, 27–29), he harks back to the screech owl with his "vilest out-of-tune music," while at the same time he keeps events in alignment with the audience's hopeful expectations. Like the earlier critics, he pounces on the other characters one by one, summing them up, just as the satirist had, as toadies, lechers, or panderesses. When he is not drawing out Bilioso, Maquerelle, or Mendoza, he is punctuating their excesses with wry comments. He is the jaundiced yet amused observer of a world in the coils of Opinion, a world in which no one is what he seems, in which characters shift from one role to another with shocking facility, in which some characters do not even know themselves. Of all Marston's fictional worlds, the Genoa of *The Malcontent* best achieves the sense of chimerical, nightmarish instability striven for in the verse satires. As the critic and intriguer, Malevole directs opinion to a proper assessment of it.

As Altofronto, on the other hand, the protagonist and ultimately

---

Shirley's Plays to the Elizabethan Drama (New York, 1914), pp. 288, 289; H. W. Wells, *Elizabethan and Jacobean Playwrights* (New York, 1939), p. 29; and Theodore Spencer, "The Elizabethan Malcontent," *J. Q. Adams Memorial Studies* (Washington, 1948), pp. 523–535.

the judge, he is the sympathetic, but not too sympathetic, leader of the party of reform in the world of Genoa. Some time ago J. Le Gay Brereton claimed that the audience is indifferent to Altofronto's success.[21] This assertion is obviously a bit extreme, but it verges on a very shrewd and important insight into the nature of Altofronto's role in the play. Actually, we are not very anxious about Altofronto's welfare, not because, as Brereton has claimed, he rails and is a "burrowing vermin," but because of the conspicuous security of his position, indeed, because he himself is not overly anxious about it. His security proceeds, of course, from his disguise, but it is reflected in his attitude toward the other characters. Though a banished duke who has to deal with adversaries who seem prepared to stop at nothing, he is, as Waith has pointed out, notably unbloodthirsty:[22] he does not feel it necessary to kill Pietro; he is quite content with simply disturbing Pietro's peace of mind; moreover, he does not rejoice when Ferneze, one of Pietro's courtiers, is removed from his path; instead, he deplores the moral turpitude that led to Ferneze's being wounded:

> Thy shame more than thy wounds do grieve me far:
> Thy wounds but leave upon thy flesh some scar;
> But fame ne'er heals, still rankles worse and worse;
> Such is of uncontrollèd lust the curse. . . . [II, iii, 214–217]

Altofronto is as much interested in the morality of his fellowmen as he is in their immediate relations to him. In his reflective moments he broods over the corruption of mankind:

> O heaven, didst hear
> Such devilish mischief? suffer'st thou the world
> Carouse damnation even with greedy swallow,
> And still dost wink, still dost thy vengeance slumber?
> If now thy brows are clear, when will they thunder?
> [III, i, 342–346]

[21] *Writings on Elizabethan Drama* (Melbourne, 1948), p. 53.
[22] *Pattern*, pp. 67–68.

This preoccupation with morality and the general conditions of life puts his moral superiority in the play beyond question; but it does little to suggest that he is in any danger.

To put the matter another way, Malevole as critic and Altofronto as judge are primarily choral in the structure of the play. In these roles he calls attention to vice and folly and meditates on human degeneration, underscoring the moral character of the action. Not all of his criticism is, of course, as solemn as the passages just quoted; indeed, the greater part of it consists of sardonic remarks—light satiric thrusts from Malevole, perfectly true in substance, but appropriately humorous. Malevole as intriguer and Altofronto as protagonist, on the other hand, constitute the built-in guarantee in the play of a favorable outcome. In these roles he is the major agency through which Marston subordinates the play's potential melodramatic concerns to immediate satiric effects and focuses the spectacle of manners as a whole as an instructive dramatic image.

Marston's treatment of the other characters in the play serves to embolden the outline clearly established by Mendoza and Altofronto. Like the earlier satirical comedies, this play, too, has its full complement of simple satiric characters. If, for some reason, they do not resemble characters from the satires as closely as do those in the other plays, they are drawn, nonetheless, on the same lines and tagged, as so many of the earlier characters are, with names from an Italian dictionary. Actually, it is one of the minor problems of *The Malcontent* that for once the correspondence between the Italian names and the characters themselves is not uniformly tight. Mendoza, meaning "corrupted" or "full of errors that may be mended," Altofronto, meaning "high forehead," Malevole, meaning "malevolent" or "spiteful," and Celso, meaning "high," "noble," or "bright," are all names appropriate enough. But among the simple satiric characters only Maquerelle and Passarello, the clown added in the augmented version of the play, have names that characterize them. Bearing a name that was rather widely used by English writers, Maquerelle, meaning "panderess," is precisely that, the "old coal" in the court, who though she cannot flame herself is "yet able . . . to set a thousand virgins' tapers afire." And Passarello is substantially the clown that his name designates. Bilioso, meaning "full of anger," on the other hand, is not nearly so much the "old choleric marshal" described in the *Dramatis Personae* as the toady (CS, II). Particularly in the augmented version of the play, it is his willingness to flatter and shift loyalties as convenience demands that is exploited at considerable length. Guerrino, meaning "little war," moreover, is nothing like the martialist that the name suggests; he is called a flatterer by Malevole; and, when he gives his elaborate instructions for the dance, he is most like the Curio of the satires (SV, VI, VIII, X). Ferrardo, Prepasso, and Equato, furthermore, have names the exact forms of which are not to be found in a contemporary Italian dictionary. That the first might mean "locksmith" or "blacksmith," the second "the preferred one," and the third "equal one" or "one made equal" is almost irrelevant, especially since in his thumbnail sketches in Act I, scene i, Malevole identifies Ferrardo as an effeminate amorist, Prepasso as a gamester and dancer, and Equato as a scholar who has deserted his ideals. At any rate the failure to find a neat correspondence between these last satiric characters and their names is not a matter of great importance. At most they parade their follies for only a few moments in the represented action of the play; and even in the scenes devoted to burlesque and mockery they are decidedly minor.

The prominent characters in the satiric scenes are Bilioso, Maquerelle, Bianca, Passarello, and, of course, Malevole. At one point Malevole draws out Maquerelle, Bianca, and Emelia; at another Maquerelle schools her protégées in the virtues of a posset and the uses of youth and beauty; at another Bilioso descants on his turncoat tactics, a subject that is considerably amplified in the augmented version; and at still another Malevole cautions him about leaving his wife unguarded in an Italian palace. Frequently, Marston uses these characters to prevent moments that might otherwise be too serious from getting out of hand. In Act I, scene ii, Ferneze's seduction of Aurelia and her fury at what she understands to be Mendoza's betrayal of her is accompanied by Maquerelle's transparent speeches in support of Ferneze, support given as Ferneze surreptitiously stuffs her hands with money and jewels. In Act III, scene i, Pietro's suffering might easily be too serious for Marston's purposes if Bilioso were not standing at his shoulder, suggesting such ridiculous cures for melancholy as *Physic for Fortune* and *Lozenges of Sanctified Sincerity*. And the whole of the first part of Act V, scene ii, when Altofronto in disguise tries to seduce his own wife in Mendoza's behalf, is buoyed up by the presence of Maquerelle, whose amoral chatter diverts attention from the latent enormity of the situation. In every act except Act IV these characters appear regularly and frequently to exemplify the ludicrously grotesque side of vice and folly that Mendoza, Pietro, Aurelia, and Ferneze often neglect. Taken together, their activities constitute a considerable portion of the represented action of the play. Through their vicious absurdity they serve to reinforce the play's comic orientation by balancing the elements that evoke serious disapproval and a sense of moral distress.

Of the less important devices by which Marston has controlled the proportions of seriousness and levity in the play, perhaps two are important enough to deserve mention. The first is the pattern discernible in the way in which Marston has arranged scenes in sequence. Except in Act IV, which poses special problems, practically every incident of serious matter is accompanied by or followed immediately by a brief explosion of light immoral grotesquery. Most often these moments proceed from Maquerelle or characters like her. But sometimes it is impossible not to discover traces of this lightness even in characters drawn on more serious lines. This patterned arrangement produces a spectacle of evil that is usually ludicrous almost as soon as it is serious. The second of these devices, which is intimately related to the first, consists simply in the way in which Marston has tailored the behavior of

the more serious characters to erupt in moments of broad burlesque. Certainly in the version of the play performed by the
child actors many of the details and speeches were calculated to
make the most of the children's talents for burlesque. It is difficult to imagine how the child playing the role of Malevole could
have made his entrance in Act III, scene ii, weighted down with
a crossbow, sword, and pistol, and avoided being funny or to
imagine how Pietro and Malevole could have mouthed the series
of exclamations beginning, "Death and damnation" in Act I,
scene i, without sounding a bit ridiculous. Perhaps even more
conspicuous, however, are Mendoza's periodic descents into the
hell of his Machiavellian imagination:

> Nothing so holy,
> No band of nature so strong,
> No law of friendship so sacred,
> But I'll profane, burst, violate. . . . [II, i, 14–17]

Such moments arrest the mind as it moves along the paths of
serious reflection; and, when it again moves on, it does so in a
quite different spirit. It is in part through Marston's controlled
use of such moments, regardless of whence they proceed, that
The Malcontent achieves its unusual fusion of laughter and seriousness.

The peculiar power of *The Malcontent* is perhaps Marston's
most important contribution to the English drama. He had succeeded in provoking laughter before, and he had succeeded to
some extent in uniting it with seriousness. But he had not covered
the emotional range covered in this play before, and he had not
handled a diversity of materials as well. *The Malcontent* is doubtless Marston's most effective dramatic equivalent for his "seriously fantastical" Neo-Stoic view of the world. At one moment it
arouses teeth-grating contempt, at the next exhilarating levity.
Almost simultaneously it touches on extremes of moral distress
and moral reassurance. One of the play's problems is that it moves

so rapidly between extremes, while one of its great merits is that it does so persuasively—without sentimentality. To explore further the unusual integrity of the whole, however, we must first isolate and examine those parts of the plot that produce its seriousness.

It is clear that the melodramatic machinery of threats and dark plots has only an indirect effect on the seriousness of the play, undercut as this machinery is by the device of Altofronto's disguise. The melodramatic materials serve chiefly to create a world in which horrid forms of latent evil are forever promising to become active but never quite do, a semibarbarous world abounding in distortions and dislocations and accommodating as grotesque a crew of characters as appear in any of Marston's plays. It is a world that completely justifies Altofronto's melancholy and distress, even though he is in a position to control it. But instead of emphasizing these materials, Marston has chosen to develop only those strands that could be made to stand in a significant relationship to the satiric burden of the play. Rightly considered, this was a rather unusual choice for a dramatist writing at that time. Mendoza and the threats he poses offered an obvious and, for most, a perfectly respectable source of seriousness. But Marston was apparently not interested in that kind of seriousness: it could at most be a melodramatic seriousness, arising mechanically as the villain generated more and more danger and disappearing magically when the villain was caught. On the contrary, Marston was interested in the kind of seriousness that could be produced through a representation of moral suffering and reformation. And, obviously, moral suffering and reformation could be related significantly to the satiric interest in folly and degradation.

Accordingly, Marston has represented the characters of Pietro, Aurelia, and Ferneze in the process of undergoing a moral awakening, suffering remorse, and choosing repentance. Of these three portraits Pietro's is by far the most elaborate. In *What You Will* Marston had brought some depth and complexity to the image of deformity by having Lampatho, an otherwise simple satiric character, talk about the past and present in such a way as to reveal the nature of his degeneration. In Pietro Marston takes this technique a few steps farther. From the start Pietro is a character irretrievably committed to the role of victim. Although he has usurped Altofronto's dukedom, in the represented action of the play he is battered in every act but the last by a series of blows that he is incapable of defending himself against. Plainly, he is the "too soft duke" in Celso's phrase, the "weak lord duke" in Altofronto's phrase, and the "weak-brained duke" in Mendoza's phrase—too sluggish a specimen to survive in the world of *The Malcontent.* He is not a complex character and hardly a very engaging one. But he does command some interest as a victim. After he has learned from Malevole that he has been cuckolded and has been deceived by Mendoza into thinking that Ferneze is the guilty party, he avenges himself on Ferneze only to receive his wife's unbridled hatred for his pains and later to escape being murdered only by the fact that Malevole is hired to do it. Through all this, his suffering increases perceptibly. As he instructs the men engaged to carry out his vengeance on Ferneze, he says,

> I strike, but yet, like him that 'gainst stone walls
> Directs, his shafts rebound in his own face;
> My lady's shame is mine, O God, 'tis mine! [II, ii, 91–93]

As he waits for his courtiers to prepare for the hunt, he tries in vain to rid himself of his grief:

> O vain relief!
> Sad souls may well change place, but not change grief.
> [III, i, 6–7]

By the time he has seen the full extent of Mendoza's villainy and has also seen the faithless Aurelia broken on the wheel of treachery, he is ready for the remorse that pours from him toward the end of Act IV.

The changes in Aurelia and Ferneze are not nearly so fully

developed. After Ferneze is helped off, wounded, by Malevole at
the end of Act II, he does not reappear until the end of Act IV,
by which time he has recovered from his wounds, reformed, and
joined forces with Altofronto. Aurelia, on the other hand, is consistently despicable until Mendoza banishes her. She is faithless
to Pietro with both Mendoza and Ferneze; when Ferneze is
thought to have been killed, she plots Pietro's murder with Mendoza; and, when news is brought of her husband's death in the
midst of her preparations to dance, she flippantly ignores it.
Moreover, the process of her reformation, like Ferneze's, is not
represented; but, when she appears under guard and pours out
her remorse to the hermit who is her husband in disguise, she has
undergone a profound change:

> I can desire nothing but death,
> Nor deserve anything but hell.
> If heaven should give sufficiency of grace
> To clear my soul, it would make heaven graceless. . . .
> [IV, ii, 32–35]

Marston has treated these characters so that their careers converge on a point at the end of Act IV where the action takes a
decisive turn. Act IV is unquestionably the most serious act in
the play. In it Mendoza's villainy reaches its acme, while Pietro's
despair and ultimately Aurelia's find the depths. Moreover, Marston has carefully intensified this seriousness by diminishing considerably in this act the number of light satiric moments so conspicuously interspersed throughout the other acts. As a whole
Act IV prepares elaborately for the profound sense of moral distress which descends on Pietro and Malevole and which Malevole,
ever the chorus, provides the clearest expression of:

Think this:—this earth is the only grave and Golgotha wherein all
things that live must rot; 'tis but the draught wherein the heavenly
bodies discharge their corruption; the very muck-hill on which the sub-
lunary orbs cast their excrements: man is the slime of this dung-pit,

and princes are the governors of these men; for, for our souls, they are as free as emperors, all of one piece; there goes but a pair of shears betwixt an emperor and the son of a bagpiper; only the dying, dressing, pressing, glossing, makes the difference. . . . [IV, ii, 141–151]

The moment this low point is reached, however, prompting Pietro to renounce his regency and repent his wrongs to Altofronto, it provides the basis for a reorganization of energies that offer fresh hope. Such is the nature of repentance and reformation; and Marston has exploited it by resolving the moment in which Pietro cries out for forgiveness in the establishment of a league between the men of good will, Altofronto and Celso, and the reformed sinners, Pietro and Ferneze.

Marston could easily have derived the idea of such an alliance from the alliance sealed by Antonio, Pandulpho, and Alberto at the end of Act IV in *Antonio's Revenge*. Whether he did or not, the establishment of a league between the men of good will and reformed sinners at the end of Act IV in *The Malcontent* amounts to an affirmation of the possibility of good that has been implicit all along in Malevole's disguise and the existence of such characters as Celso. It is an affirmation made trebly impressive by the fact that Altofronto interrupts Pietro's darkest moment with his forgiveness: "Thy vows are heard, and we accept thy faith" (IV, ii, 164), and then, to Pietro's amazement, undisguises himself. Immediately, Ferneze and Celso enter, and Altofronto seals the union:

> Banish amazement: come, we four must stand
> Full shock of fortune: be not so wonder-stricken.
> [ll. 165–166]

Almost before the echoes of Malevole's Golgotha speech have died away, as Altofronto he enunciates a counterstatement that has the benefit of his approval when undisguised and has the position of emphasis at the end of the act:

Who doubts of providence,
That sees this change? a hearty faith to all!
He needs must rise who can no lower fall:
For still impetuous vicissitude
Touseth the world. . . . [ll. 172–176]

Although it is doubtful that the audience develops an intense interest in the characters of *The Malcontent*, it does develop an interest in the human relations represented. After the lying, snarling, cuckolding, and treachery of the first three acts, the chastened air that settles over the relations between characters at the end of Act IV is like the dawning of a new day. Clearly, Marston could easily have had Pietro, Ferneze, and Aurelia killed off; indeed, in an ordinary revenge play he probably would have. Instead, he has saved them for the uses just described, neglecting the seriousness that would proceed from their deaths in favor of the act of faith that he has achieved.

Of course the careers of these characters do not alone account for the distinct sense of moral distress evoked by *The Malcontent*. The enormity of Bilioso, Maquerelle, Bianca, and the other satiric types, if carefully controlled for humorous effect, is also sufficiently heightened to contribute to the sense of distress. Moreover, a dukedom is at stake in the play, not, as in *What You Will*, a wife; and although Altofronto is in a position to control the intrigue and arouse active expectations that justice will prevail, he has the problem in the play of restoring himself to the role of justice's instrument. Until he does, his indictments of his world seem perfectly justified. The necessity at the end of *The Malcontent* for the punishments, however mild, of Mendoza, Bilioso, and Maquerelle marks out clearly the qualitative difference between this and the satirical comedies Marston had written to this point.

The Malcontent, then, represents Marston's first completely successful fusion of the solemn and the grotesque in a dramatic action, his first altogether adequate embodiment of the unusual power which his verse satires and early satirical comedies indicate he was striving for. It is the most effective specimen he was ever to produce of that kind of satirical comedy the peculiar harmony of which depends on a balance of represented depravity and viable alternatives to it. Moreover, much of the play's impressiveness depends on the integrity of that balance. Comedy is so easily and so frequently vitiated by invoking too facilely ideal alternatives to flawed behavior. This is the besetting weakness of sentimental comedy, in which good-natured, virtuous behavior is always just an easy stride from moral laxity. But to Marston's credit it must be said that his alternative to the Court of Genoa, the way of Altofronto, is not easy. In all his plays—but especially in *The Malcontent*—Marston's presentation of superior behavior is always accompanied by a full sense of its difficulties, of the intractability of the human material that must be reformed. In *The Malcontent* the ascendancy of Altofronto is persuasive chiefly because the play and Altofronto as Malevole within the play are so relentless in their exposure of that intractability.

One final matter remains to consider: the additions included in the augmented version of *The Malcontent*. This is the only play in Marston's canon for which we have two distinct versions: one that was acted by the child actors at Blackfriars and an augmented version that was acted by the adult actors at the Globe.[23] Since it is now fairly certain that Marston made the additions himself, the play offers a unique opportunity to sift more finely the differences between private and public productions and to check the hypothesis set forth above as to its design and effect.

In Webster's "Induction" to the augmented version Burbage explains to Sly that the additions are "not greatly needful; only as your salad to your great feast, to entertain a little more time,

[23] W. W. Greg has established that there are three distinct editions of the play: two editions of the short version and one of the augmented version. See his "Notes on Old Books," *Library*, II (1922), 49–57, or his *A Bibliography of the English Printed Drama to the Restoration* (London, 1939), I, 323, 324.

and to abridge the not-received custom of music in our theatre (ll. 87–91). There seems to be no reason to question the first part of this statement; Burbage's assertion that the additions are "not greatly needful" is perfectly true. His reasons for them, however, deserve closer examination. To begin with, what he meant by the "not-received custom of music in our theatre" is not immediately clear. Apparently, he was not referring to the songs and incidental music within the play because a comparison of the stage directions of both versions reveals that the directions for song and music are exactly the same in both. Surprisingly enough, *The Malcontent* contains only four songs and one elaborate dance. It is just possible that the songs were more elaborate in the private production than in the public, but we have no evidence to suggest that they were. In any case, Burbage was probably referring to the entr'acte music that at the children's theatres usually amounted to brief concerts. Both versions contain directions for music to be played before the acts and often as accompaniment to the first few minutes of them, but these directions could well have called for brief musical introductions at the Globe, while at Blackfriars the same directions indicated fairly substantial preludes.

Granting Burbage's assertion, then, that the additions served to "abridge the not-received custom of music," it is nonetheless important to see how Marston chose to "entertain a little more time" and why he chose to make these additions rather than others. The signal fact about Marston's additions is that of the approximately 460 lines that were added practically all are satiric and relatively light in character. Some 112 additional lines were given to Malevole, most of them lines of satiric commentary. Of the rest, most of it was given to Bilioso and Passarello, the clown created in the augmented version, in new scenes or in scenes in which Bilioso's part is considerably amplified. It is possible that the character of Passarello was created to engage the talents of Robert Armin, who had succeeded Will Kempe in 1599 and who specialized in fool's parts at the Globe until his withdrawal in

1609. It is also possible that Bilioso's role was increased from 42 to 195 lines in the augmented version to accommodate another actor. Bilioso's resemblance to Polonius suggests that the part may have been enlarged for the actor who played Polonius. At any rate, Marston chose to amplify the light and humorous facets of the satire for the adult production rather than the serious parts. In view of the conclusions already reached about the differences between the child and adult actors, it is tempting to infer that through his additions he was compensating for the measure of satire and burlesque that proceeded normally from the children's acting style, but that the adults could not easily duplicate.

Certainly it is useful to recall that in writing Marston seems always to have taken into his calculations something more than ever appears in print. His concern over the dramatic values supplied by performance is, perhaps, nowhere more clearly seen than in his concern with their loss in the printed texts of his plays. In the preface to this play, he says,

Only one thing afflicts me, to think that scenes, invented merely to be spoken, should be enforcively published to be read. . . . I shall entreat . . . that the unhandsome shape which this trifle in reading presents, may be pardoned for the pleasure it once afforded you when it was presented with the soul of lively action.

If his additions to the adult version of *The Malcontent* were made to preserve the quality of the children's version, it is hardly surprising that neither he nor Webster offered to explain the problem to the audience, for it is doubtful that anyone would have understood. But the problem was probably very real for Marston and very important in *The Malcontent,* where the adjustment between seriousness and lightness is so crucial to the structure.

In his brief preface to *The Parasitaster or The Fawn* Marston quite unambiguously confirms the picture of himself as private playwright that has been presented thus far.[24] His opening sen-

[24] See Appendix A for a discussion of the date of this play.

tences hark back to the fashionable poet rather self-consciously protesting that he should be engaged in more serious pursuits than writing. Although it is still difficult to know how much of this is ironic pose and how much a sincere expression of regret, we cannot ignore his concern that he has neglected self-knowledge for knowledge about his craft—not in view of the philosophical bent so obtrusive in his past and of the renunciation of public fame soon to come. Actually, this rivalry between self and art was intrinsic, even necessary, to the role he was playing. On the one hand, he was the craftsman, admitting that he had been seduced by "the delights of poetry," worrying about the problem of printing plays, "whose life rests much in the actor's voice," and theorizing about his work:

If any desire to understand the scope of my comedy, know it hath the same limits which Juvenal gives to his *Satires*:—

> Quicquid agunt homines, votum, timor, ira, voluptas,
> Gaudia, discursus, nostri farrago libelli est.

("Whatever men do—desire, fear, anger, pleasure, joy, discourse—is the medley-subject of my little book").

On the other hand, he was still speaking of his "bosom friend, good Epictetus" and still measuring his activity in terms of its relevance to personal perfection. These interests are not contradictory; they are important facets of the private playwright as he developed, in this case, from the orphan poet, the sharp-fanged satirist, and the Neo-Stoic. Still another facet reflects the sophisticated, playful man about town. Marston had not yet relinquished the modishness of these qualities, and, in an image from Persius that very effectively unites his seriousness with his fantasticalness, he admits himself half a clown, though one who hopes to bring his verse to the consecrated repositories of poets:

> Ipse semipaganus
> Ad sacra vatum carmen affero nostrum.

The Fawn is a reasonable expression of this many-sided purpose and, technically at least, no mean successor to *The Malcontent*. In fashioning this particular "farrago" Marston has put to good use the lessons of his experience. Yet in the "Epilogue" even he acknowledges that the play is distinctly lighter than previous efforts, and no one would claim for it a comic power so complex or so impressive as that of *The Malcontent*. The cardinal fact is that in *The Fawn* Marston has turned his skills to an action essentially simpler and more limited than that of *The Malcontent*. In important respects *The Fawn* turns on the familiar formula consisting of the satirist and the parade of satiric types. Marston has added to the formula the duke in disguise and has amplified it with skill and ingenuity such as he commanded only at the height of his powers. But the whole makes a relatively simple appeal and offers very few of *The Malcontent's* possibilities for meaningful discovery and reversal and none of its opportunities to explore extremes of distress and reassurance. Ultimately, it is the action chosen for *The Fawn,* not Marston's use of it, that explains the relative mildness of the play.

The plot of *The Fawn* is built squarely on the Duke of Ferrara's plan to trick his son Tiberio into marrying Dulcimel, the daughter of the Duke of Urbin. To effect this marriage, Ferrara sends his son to Urbin to woo the girl for him, hoping that Tiberio's exposure to her will prompt him to take her for himself, and accompanies him disguised as Faunus to do what he can to encourage this betrayal. In Urbin Ferrara fortunately finds an indispensable ally in Dulcimel, who falls in love with Tiberio and determines to have him. Although she is not aware until the end that she is playing a part of which the Duke of Ferrara wholly approves, her plan to win Tiberio by deceiving her meddlesome father is chiefly responsible for the fulfillment of Ferrara's hopes. Ferrara is in a position, of course, to assist her without her knowing it, and he does assist her by prompting Tiberio at crucial moments. But in this matter, at least, Dulcimel is more than director of incident than he.

Langbaine was the first to point out that Marston may have derived the idea of Dulcimel's scheme from Boccaccio's *Decameron* (Story 3 of the third day).[25] Although this seems a highly probable source, the debt, if there was one, was very general. While in the *novella* the lady-intriguer is triumphant without qualification, in *The Fawn* Dulcimel's victory and the intrigue that produces it are constantly under scrutiny by the Duke of Ferrara. There is no doubt that, like Boccaccio's heroine, Dulcimel is wondrous clever. but she is different in that Marston has represented her cleverness so that the audience knows that she is contriving to do only what her supposed enemy in this affair, the Duke of Ferrara, wants her to do and is doing it, moreover, as the Duke looks on and assists. As we shall see, this is one of the ways in which Marston managed a perspective that is rather new in his work, a perspective by which no character is beyond embarrassment.

This situation, at any rate, furnishes the platform of probabilities on which the rest of the play is erected. Having provided himself, characteristically, with the convenient locale of a court, Marston was able to people the play with whatever characters he liked, and it is symptomatic of the general quality of *The Fawn* that he fixed almost exclusively on the familiar simple satiric characters. From Gonzago, the Duke of Urbin, down to his most abject courtier, the inhabitants of the Court of Urbin are, with very few exceptions, fools and would-be knaves, zanies and buf-

[25] *Dramatick Poets*, p. 351. Becker also cites Terence's *The Adelphi* as a possible source for the play (see *Das Verhältnis*, p. 11). No doubt there are resemblances between the plays. In both a father manipulates the marriage of his son, though in *The Adelphi* Micio, the stepfather, does not have to trick his son Aeschinus: Aeschinus wants to marry the girl all along. In both plays, moreover, there are two fathers, one of whom is tricked by his child. But all resemblance is rather vague.

More likely than *The Adelphi* as an immediate source for *The Fawn* is Chapman's *All Fools*, which was itself based on *The Adelphi*. In Chapman's play there is, in addition to the duped father, a subplot dealing with a jealous husband that is rather like, though with differences, the Zuccone-Zoya action.

foons, who are easily summed up in a phrase and appropriately tagged with Italian names. It is important to observe that their activities account for more of the represented action than the execution of Ferrara's plan to effect the marriage of Dulcimel and Tiberio.

The first act provides the situation subsequently exploited for the gay sense of absurdity dominant in the play. In the first scene, Hercules, the Duke of Ferrara, arrives at the outskirts of Urbin and outlines for his friend Renaldo his plan to trick Tiberio into marrying Dulcimel. Inside the palace a page announces to Herod and Nymphadoro that "the city's a-fire" with festivities to celebrate the Princess Dulcimel's birthday. Presently, Gonzago, Dulcimel, and their attendants enter, and when they are joined by Tiberio, the disguised Hercules, and Tiberio's train, Dulcimel makes it clear that she is much more interested in Tiberio than in his father. But Tiberio is apparently as impervious to female charms as his father had feared. Accordingly, when these characters leave the stage to Hercules, Herod, and Nymphadoro, Hercules goes ahead with his plan to establish himself in the court and, by criticizing the presumption of the Duke of Ferrara for wishing to marry one so young as Dulcimel, quickly wins the confidence of the courtiers and the rare opportunity of hearing them damn him. Indeed, so enchanted are they with Faunus that they promise to secure him a place in Gonzago's retinue. Left alone, finally, Hercules ponders these events and, realizing what an unusual opportunity his disguise affords him to look behind the scenes for a change, dedicates himself to the further purpose of undoing the deceivers and especially the flatterers that cross his path. Appropriately he vows to revenge himself on them while playing the role of the consummate flatterer himself:

> I vow to waste this most prodigious heat,
> That falls into my age like scorching flames
> In depth of numb'd December, in flattering all
> In all of their extremest viciousness,

Till in their own lov'd race they fall most lame,
And meet full butt the close of Vice's shame.
[I, ii, 352–357]

In Act II Hercules' resolve to revenge himself and all honest
men on counterfeits takes concrete form, while his plan to trick
Tiberio takes a favorable turn that he could hardly have anticipated. In the series of scenes that constitute the first two-thirds of
the act his newly won acceptance at court and his limitless supply
of flattery prove more than sufficient to gain for him the confidence of his victims-to-be. Amid the holiday atmosphere of the
banquet in progress he first exchanges witticisms with Herod and
Nymphadoro and then meets Herod's brother, Sir Amoroso Debile-Dosso, a decaying debauchee who is now finding it difficult to
sire an heir. When Sir Amoroso goes off, Hercules flatters Herod
into admitting that Garbetza, Sir Amoroso's wife, is in fact with
child by him. Next he loosens the tongue of Zuccone, who boasts
that he has not shared his wife Zoya's bed in four years, but who
agonizes at the thought that someone else has. When Dondolo
brings the news that Zoya is with child and then Zoya enters
during Zuccone's absence to reveal that she has lied about the
child to revenge herself for his jealousy, Hercules quickly takes up
the scheme and convinces Zuccone on his return that he should
be divorced. Thus with flattery and disguised kindness he un-
covers each of the petty intrigues currently in progress in Urbin
and even manages with the unwitting help of the foolish Gonzago
to adjust without Dulcimel's knowing it to her scheme to marry
Tiberio. At the end of the act Hercules' position is secure, but his
imagination has been staggered by what he has observed:

                            I am left
                As on a rock, from whence I may discern
                The giddy sea of humour flow beneath,
                Upon whose back the vainer bubbles float,
                And forthwith break. O mighty flattery! [II, i, 588–592]

In Act III, Hercules discovers still more bubbles. The first part of the act finds Nymphadoro exhibiting himself at length, confiding to Hercules that he can always find something to love in a woman and attempting to prove his sincerity by wooing both Donnetta and Garbetza. Nor do his hollow declarations cease with the entrance of Dulcimel and Philocalia, though they are interrupted when Philocalia asks the gentlemen to leave. Alone with Philocalia, Dulcimel tries to justify her unmaidenly plan to win Tiberio and reveals how she is using her father as intermediary. When Gonzago, Hercules, and Granuffo enter, she again pretends to submit to Gonzago's wisdom, renewing her claim that Tiberio has been wooing her and this time producing letters and an embroidered scarf to prove it. Gonzago, of course, promptly confronts the nonplussed Tiberio with this evidence and demands that he mend his ways. With the crafty Hercules at his ear to prompt him, however, Tiberio finally realizes that he would like very much to be guilty of the disloyalty of which he is accused and leaves convinced that he has a right to be disloyal. Hercules is pleased at his progress, but still bewildered at the deviousness of life at court.

The strands of intrigue that curl about the figure of Hercules in the first three acts move decisively in Act IV toward the general exposure of all the fools and knaves and toward the wedding of Tiberio and Dulcimel. Herod has a preliminary comeuppance in the early part of the act, when Hercules and Garbetza, Herod's mistress and his brother's wife, overhear Puttotta, a virtuous laundress, denounce him for writing her a love letter. This infidelity prompts Garbetza to revenge herself on him by using his own bastard child to deprive him of the inheritance he hopes to achieve, and then Hercules disintegrates him by reading his letter to Puttotta aloud. Zuccone, meanwhile, has obtained his divorce, and, steeled by self-righteousness, he scorns Zoya as she follows him on her knees begging for mercy. But his bubble also bursts when a moment later he sees her sought after and entertained and learns that she has deceived him only to be rid of him. Half-crazed by self-inflicted torment, he submits almost willingly to the taunts of Hercules, Herod, and Nymphadoro and almost acquiesces in Hercules' argument that he has done Zoya a service by setting her free. Dulcimel, on the other hand, has every reason to rejoice. With one last lie she conveys to Tiberio by means of her preposterous father the arrangements that she has made for their secret wedding, even as Gonzago continues to pride himself on his daughter's devoted submission and his own efficiency in meeting the crisis of Tiberio's passion. Once Tiberio has been pushed to the brink of the ceremony, Hercules cannot resist asking him about his father; and even Hercules feels a bit ridiculous when he learns that Tiberio does not greatly care. But the feeling lasts only a moment; before Hercules lie the marriage and the Parliament of Cupid, where he will have a final opportunity to settle all accounts with the deceivers in Urbin.

Act V brings Hercules a full measure of success. After assisting Tiberio in his ascent to Dulcimel's chamber and watching a repetition of the mercy-begging scene, this time with Zuccone begging on his knees, he serves as prosecuting attorney in the Parliament of Cupid. In theory the Parliament has been called as part of the round of festivities in Urbin for the purpose of surveying Cupid's laws and punishing transgressors. Actually, it gives Hercules an opportunity to mete out the disgrace and embarrassment that the inhabitants of the court so justly deserve. One by one he summons them to the bar: Nymphadoro for having more mistresses than he can effectively handle, Sir Amoroso for being a counterfeit lover, Herod for boasting about conquests he never made, Zuccone for slandering Cupid's liege ladies, and Granuffo for abusing women by feigning wisdom through silence. This parade of folly and vice culminates in the arraignment of Gonzago for having tried to cross true lovers while he unwittingly brought about their union; and this fool even Gonzago damns mirthfully until he learns that it is himself he has damned. Once the secret is out, however, and the newlyweds appear, Hercules has only to undisguise himself to stamp the union with his approval. On this note of discovery and rejoicing the play ends.

Despite its apparent complexity, the plot of *The Fawn* is not just simpler than that of *The Malcontent*, but distinctly lighter and gayer. On the single foundation of Hercules' intrusion into the life of Urbin, Marston has constructed a series of petty intrigues that he has worked out largely with the single trump card of Hercules' disguise. The sum total of these parts has little qualitative diversity, and its strands never converge to produce a discovery like that at the end of Act IV in *The Malcontent*. In fact, the separate intrigues have very little to do with each other: at the end they are very mechanically assimilated in the Parliament of Cupid. At no point, moreover, does this action contain a serious threat to anyone or even a serious alternative to the outcome anticipated. Unlike Altofronto, Hercules is never involved in anything so important or so complicated as a restoration, and his ambitions to see Tiberio married and the fools and knaves of Urbin embarrassed pose no alternatives of great consequence. These features of the action alone explain in part why the mood of *The Fawn* is almost sportive by comparison with that of *The Malcontent*.

But the differences between these plays go far beyond differences in mood. Unlike *The Malcontent*, the chief merits of *The Fawn* consist rather in the effectiveness of its parts than in the impressivness of their amalgamation in a dramatic action. However episodic its structure, *The Fawn* abounds in delightful comic moments that, cumulatively, endow its dramatic image with great vitality. This vitality derives largely from the familiar material of short episodes that expose and ridicule simple satiric characters. To a man the characters are the conspicuous successors to the cast of satiric types met in the satires, and each is animated by a dominant folly or vice and tagged with an Italian name. Granuffo, whose name derives from *gramuffa*, meaning a "kinde of staring, stately, staulking, puffing looke," is Gonzago's silent lieutenant, who accompanies him constantly and says nothing, tacitly accepting his assurances that silence signifies wisdom and passively absorbing his interminable, fatuous pronouncements on policy. When in the last act, he is finally made to speak, like Pope's Sir Plume, he speaks nonsense:

> *Herc.* . . . Speak, speak; is not this law just?
> *Gran.* Just, sure; for in good truth or in good sooth,
>   When wise men speak, they still must open
>   their mouth.
> *Herc.* The brazen head has spoken. [V, i, 384–387]

Don Zuccone, on the other hand, speaks too much. Consistent with his name, which means "shaven pate . . . a gull, a ninnie, a ioulthead," he is a typical jealous husband, whose raving desire to find his wife unfaithful results in his divorcing and almost losing her. Sir Amoroso Debile-Dosso, the amorist of the weak back, is essentially a broken-down Luxurio, a sex debauchee whose youthful excesses have cursed his middle years with disease and a dependence on aphrodisiacs. Dondolo, "a gull, a fool, a thinge to make sport of," is the bustling Nuntius in Urbin, a court fool always bursting with news and nonsense. Nymphadoro, "an effeminate, wanton milk-sop, perfumed ladies courting-courtier," descends from the large crew of amorists in the satires. And Herod Frappatore, "a bragger, a boaster, a craker . . . , a cony catcher," is the lineal descendant of the spruce Duceus of *Certain Satires* (III), perhaps slightly more contemptible than the others for his base disloyalty to his brother, but also too grotesque to be a source of serious concern or distress. Even the women are conveniently summed up in their names: Garbetza, meaning "sourness" or "tartness," Poveia, meaning a "butterfly or ladybird," Donnetta, meaning a "goodie flurt or goodie driggle-draggle," and Puttotta, meaning "a good handsome, plum-cheekt wench." In this class of characters only Gonzago has a conventional name. But his absurd preoccupation with the ripeness of his wisdom and the freshness of his eloquence clearly demonstrates that he is drawn on the same simple lines:

Daughter, for that our last speech leaves the firmest print, be thus advised. When young Tiberio negociates his father's love, hold heedy guard over thy passions, and still keep this full thought firm in thy reason: 'tis his old father's love the young man moves (is't not well thought, my lord, we must bear brain), and when thou shalt behold Tiberio's lifeful eyes and well-fill'd veins, complexion firm, and hairs that curls with strength of lusty moisture (I think we yet can speak, we ha' been eloquent), thou must shape thy thoughts to apprehend his father well in years. . . .

> . . . and do not give thy thoughts
> Least liberty to shape a diverse scope
> (My Lord Granuffo, pray ye note my phrase)
> So shalt thou not abuse thy younger hope. . . .
> [I, ii, 82–97]

Marston had never presented simple comic enormity with more wit or economy.

Hercules' description of these characters as "bubbles" is entirely accurate: they have all been inflated with the gas of a single folly or vice, and they can be deflated just as easily. Yet taken together, they furnish much of the play's ribald buoyancy and vitality. Moreover, it is worth observing that Marston has taken more pains than usual to tailor them for his child actors. By this time it is possible that because the child actors were on the average older than earlier, greater pains were necessary to secure comparable burlesque effects. Some of the actors were, we know, young men by 1604; besides, the fact that Marston has used but one song and two brief dances might suggest some changes in his acting personnel. In any event, Marston has provided strikingly clear opportunities for the buffo antics so characteristic of the children's satiric style. The absurdity inherent in Amoroso's background in debauchery, in Herod's boasts of sexual capacity, and in Nymphadoro's prodigious ambition along these lines hardly needs comment. And the four old men in the play fairly cry out for burlesque treatment in the hands of child actors, or even of youths. Gonzago, with his insistence on the conjunction of wisdom and age, is doubtless the most obvious, but even Hercules is not beyond embarrassment on this score.

Having shaped the action of *The Fawn* chiefly from these rather loosely joined materials, then, Marston placed relatively few controls on their capacity to generate a sense of Daumierlike frolic. For the first time he has not qualified the levity with the sober denunciation of a critic. Although Hercules is a critic in his fashion, he observes, judges, and ultimately brings the satiric types to justice without resorting to the excoriation so characteristic of his predecessors. The result is that the sequence of comic moments is largely uninterrupted and the level of holiday liveliness achieved early is uniformly maintained. Yet a few devices for control Marston has used. The satiric commentary so prominent earlier is present here, if only by implication, and the satiric characters, no less than the spectacle as a whole, are constantly subject to the tempering influence of Hercules, who from the fortress of his disguise not only directs the various intrigues, but also extends the comic dimensions of all he surveys by serving as a persistent reminder that the fools and knaves are destined for embarrassment and disgrace. As a duke in disguise, he—or rather his presence on the scene—serves to place this "mere spectacle of life and public manners" so that its absurdity and the futility of its folly are heightened.

The exact nature of Hercules' function, however, is best defined by reference to his own declaration of purposes. Fortunately, he is explicit on this point. After confiding to Renaldo at the beginning of Act I that he is going into Urbin in disguise to promote a marriage between Dulcimel and Tiberio, he admits a moment later, when left alone, that he is also indulging his inclination for a lark. Too long, he feels, he has deprived himself

> of exorbitant affects,
> Wild longings, or the least of disrank'd shapes.
> But we must once be wild. [I, i, 48–50]

Then at the end of Act I, scene ii, after he has sampled the conduct of courtiers as their equal, he resolves to use his disguise to achieve one further end—revenge on counterfeits for himself and all honest men. Prompted by these motives, he assumes the disguise of Faunus, wins a position of prominence in Gonzago's retinue, and manipulates affairs to the end he desires. In doing so his combined attitude of frivolous fun-seeking and serious social criticism qualify the action with a much lighter, less acid irony than that operative in *The Malcontent*. Apparently Marston had no wish here to use the duke in disguise for the darker effects of *The Malcontent*. Not only is Hercules less crucially involved and more secure than Altofronto had been, but his roguishness in Urbin is calculated to define a gayer, more briskly ridiculous, distinctly less distressing dramatic world than that of Altofronto's Genoa. It is, indeed, in a spirit of Puckish playfulness that Hercules dominates the play.

Yet it would be a mistake to ignore that Hercules has a serious side and that the life of Urbin has been controlled in more than one way for serious implication. In general, these serious elements consist of the speeches, the twists of characterization, and the turns of incident fashioned with special attention to the problem of deformity. In the aggregate these elements constitute the principal unifying theme of the spectacle. Renaldo first calls our attention to it when he worries that Hercules has determined to "break forth / Those stricter limits of regardful state" (I, i, 10, 11); and when he has gone, Hercules gives us a full exposition of the problem:

> And now, thou ceremonious sovereignty—
> Ye proud, severer, stateful compliments,
> The secret arts of rule—I put you off;
> Nor ever shall those manacles of form
> Once more lock up the appetite of blood.
> 'Tis now an age of man whilst we, all strict,
> Have lived in awe of carriage regular. . . .

But we must once be wild. . . .
Shall I, because some few may cry, "Light! vain!"
Beat down affection from desirèd rule?
He that doth strive to please the world's a fool.
. . . No, thou world, know thus,
There's nothing free but it is generous. [ll. 40–65]

Of course this concern with the consequences of perverting nature has its counterpart in the action, where they are represented in some detail. They are seen quite clearly in Granuffo, who guards an unnatural silence, in Tiberio, who refuses to become interested in women, and in Gonzago, who insists on turning the course of true love; but nowhere are they more conspicuous than in Zuccone, who out of unfounded jealousy has refused to share his wife's bed for four years. In every case the represented portions of the play touching on the problem are undeniably comic in quality, yet the problem, enunciated and illustrated as it is through the length and breadth of the play, nonetheless emboldens the familiar outline of Marston's thought. However gay and free-wheeling the total image, the zanies of Urbin are "bubbles" and Urbin itself is a "giddy sea of humour" in every sense implied by Marston's Neo-Stoic convictions. Even this ostensibly trivial action represents an attempt to find a dramatic equivalent for the ideas and interests explicitly presented earlier, although it is an attempt to find a different equivalent from that found in *The Malcontent*.

In summary, Marston's achievement in the disguise-plot plays consists of a series of attempts to produce completely dramatic equivalents for the thought and interests that control the verse satires and the early plays. If we can conclude that the direction of that achievement was clearly laid down in the "Induction" to *What You Will* in his stated preference there for conventional dramatic actions over the innovative forms of "tight brains," the forms of the achievement were largely determined by the structural tactic central to them—that of constructing actions on the

axis of disguise. In this we must not overlook Marston's originality. Disguise had long been a popular device with comic
dramatists; but Marston was the first to use it as the key control
in a comic action.

It would be far too simple, of course, to explain Marston's
accomplishment in these plays solely in terms of his mastery of
this structural tactic. Even in our age of precision in criticism, we
must allow that Marston was improving as a playwright partly as
a result of experience, experience in the sheer mechanics of
writing plays and dramatic verse, as well as experience in adapt-
ing plays to the peculiar conditions of the private theatre. Unquestionably these plays reflect a sophistication greater than any
that can be found in his first satirical comedies. It is perfectly
evident, for example, in the verse of these plays, verse so much
less spectacular than that met earlier, but so much better controlled.

Yet much that is characteristic of and crucial to this achievement rests unmistakably on Marston's success in devising disguise plots. Once in control of that structural tactic, he succeeded
in either internalizing or discarding most of the devices derived
from the verse satires. In *What You Will* and *The Malcontent* we
see the familiar critic transforming gradually from the trifold
persona of the satires to a character rooted in the action. In *The
Fawn* he practically disappears altogether. In the course of these
three plays, moreover, we meet the harsh satiric style less and
less frequently until, in *The Fawn*, it also disappears. It is true
that in these plays Marston began to use heroes and heroines
sufficiently admirable to supply by inference the contrasts and
judgments handled explicitly earlier. Women like Maria and Dulcimel are especially useful in this way. But we must not overlook that such elements were also predicated in part by the
exercise of devising this kind of plot. Even the satiric types, characters who, though more skillfully drawn in these plays, remain
substantially unchanged, were as Marston's skill increased dis-

entangled from the pattern of exposure and derision, fixed securely in a system of probabilities, and far more subtly integrated than they previously had been.

In short, by concentrating his energies on the fullest exploitation of the disguise plot Marston succeeded in objectifying dramatically his serious-fantastical view of a world drunk with Opinion; he succeeded in realizing the comic power striven for, but only crudely achieved, in the lovers-in-distress plays. At this point it seems a long way from the satiric types dancing like puppets on the satirist's strings, but the distance covered has been largely technical. Marston's beliefs in *The Fawn* seem to be what they were in *Certain Satires*. The big difference is that by *The Fawn* Marston had learned to make the puppets dance on their own— had learned to animate the total dramatic image with a power of its own.

Chapter VII

Final Experiments

DURING the years that saw the appearance of *What You Will*, *The Malcontent*, and *The Fawn* John Marston became a successful and controversial figure. It was during this period—roughly from the beginning of 1601 to the end of 1604—that he engaged in his famous quarrel with Jonson. In 1601, moreover, he had been a central figure in the brief battle of verse satires involving W. I.'s *The Whipping of the Satyre*, Nicholas Breton's *No Whipping, Nor Tripping*, and the anonymous *The Whipper of the Satyre*. Despite all his enemies might do or say, however, he apparently prospered. Sometime after 1602, probably in 1603, he bought from Henry Evans a one-sixth share in the Blackfriars organization.[1] And in all probability the next year saw his endorsement by an adult company, when Shakespeare's company produced the augmented version of *The Malcontent*. In the latter part of 1601 he had lost his rooms at the Middle Temple for failure to pay his fees while absent from London.[2] But he was restored to "Fellowship" there; and, since he apparently lived in London

[1] Chambers, *Stage*, II, 50–55.   [2] "Life," p. 163.

during these years, he doubtless continued to move in this society. Only after 1605 and the temporary exile that followed *Eastward Ho* does the evidence suggest that he began to sever his ties with London and the Inns by living, part of the time at least, in or near Coventry.

By all odds the most important biographical event bearing upon his work in satirical comedy yet to be done was his reconciliation with Jonson at some time prior to the publication of *The Malcontent* in 1604. Their reconciliation made possible their collaboration with Chapman early in 1605 on that happiest product of Renaissance collaboration, *Eastward Ho*. Although the collaboration alone does Marston considerable credit, in my view it also marked a final turning point in his work in satirical comedy. Of course the relations between *Eastward Ho* and *The Dutch Courtezan* are profoundly entangled in questions of authorship and chronology, but it can be demonstrated, I think, that for all its problems the collaboration offers a highly reasonable explanation for his striking departure in structural methods in *The Dutch Courtezan*.

This approach to *The Dutch Courtezan* by way of *Eastward Ho* has been overlooked largely because most students of the Marston-Jonson-Chapman collaboration have assumed that *The Dutch Courtezan* preceded *Eastward Ho*.[3] Guided by this assumption, they have approached the question of authorship in *Eastward Ho* with the conviction that Marston had written a play similar in structure to it not long before he joined Chapman and Jonson. It is not surprising that they have interpreted the structural analogues between these plays to mean that Marston was probably responsible for the structural outline of *Eastward Ho*.[4]

On one point in this argument there is little room for disagreement: despite all the differences between *The Dutch Courtezan*

[3] The most important scholars on this subject are Parrott, in his edition of Chapman, and Herford and Simpson in their edition of Jonson. See *Plays and Poems*, pp. 841–848, and H & S, II, 40.

[4] *Plays and Poems*, p. 841; H & S, II, 40.

and *Eastward Ho,* they are undeniably similar in structural outline. Both plays are organized in terms of sets of character contrasts. In *The Dutch Courtezan* Freevill, a carefree, but principled
man about town, is contrasted with his friend Malheureux, a
moralist with rules but little understanding, and Beatrice, Freevill's lawful love, is contrasted with Franceschina, a courtezan. In
Eastward Ho Touchstone's virtuous apprentice, Golding, is contrasted with his debauched apprentice, Quicksilver; and his duti-
ful daughter, Mildred, is contrasted with his social-climbing
daughter, Gertrude. In addition, both plots have subsidiary
actions involving bourgeois grotesques, Mulligrub in *The Dutch
Courtezan* and Security in *Eastward Ho;* and in both plays these
subsidiary actions function primarily to focus the principal action
by serving as farcical obbligatos. Though such similarities in an
age when multilinear plots were commonplace and broad contrasts inevitable do not necessarily imply a connection between
the plays, in this case the prejudice in favor of a connection has
still more to recommend it.

But the argument concerning indebtedness must begin with
the question of chronology. There are good reasons to doubt that
The Dutch Courtezan preceded *Eastward Ho,* and certainly the
external evidence concerning the dates of these plays does not
confirm that order. That *The Dutch Courtezan* was entered in the
Stationers' Register on June 26, 1605, and *Eastward Ho* on September 4 of the same year need hardly lead to the conclusion that
The Dutch Courtezan was the earlier play. Of course the probable
date of *Eastward Ho* is a cardinal consideration. Its limits are
conveniently set by an unmistakable allusion in the "Prologue" to
Westward Ho, which was very probably produced at the end of
1604,[5] and the entry in the Stationers' Register for September 4,

[5] On the basis of the Stationers' entry for March 2, 1605, and the internal
references to the length of the siege of Ostend (ended in September, 1604)
and to cold weather, scholarly opinion has unanimously favored the late fall
or early winter of 1604 for the rough date of its first production. See Stoll,
Webster, p. 14, and Mary Leland Hunt, *Thomas Dekker* (New York, 1911),
pp. 101, 102.

1605. Within the period from the end of 1604 to September of 1605 one striking piece of evidence suggests a production very early in 1605: that three men were engaged to write a play that was in part at least an answer to *Westward Ho* implies that the play was to be written quickly so that it might follow the first play closely. All the available evidence concerning *The Dutch Courtezan*, in addition, suggests that it was not written before the early part of 1605. First, the entry for June 26, 1605 itself treats the play as if it were a recent production: "A booke called the Dutche Curtizan, as yt was latelie presented at the Blackeffryers. . . ." Secondly, the title page omits the usual formula—added in Sheares' edition of 1633—"as it hath been sundry times playd" in favor of "as it was played." And thirdly, in the "Prologue" Marston refers to his "Slight hasty labours" in writing the play. If we can infer from this evidence that the play was written hastily and produced shortly before June, 1605, we can conclude it improbable that *The Dutch Courtezan* was written before *Eastward Ho*, though at the same time this argument does not decisively place the play after the composition of *Eastward Ho*. In view of the extremely brief period of time during which both plays were apparently written, it is distinctly probable that they were written concurrently, or very nearly concurrently, though this, too, is a matter that cannot be conclusively settled on the basis of the available external evidence alone.

A case for placing *Eastward Ho* earlier, if only by a few weeks, than *The Dutch Courtezan* is suggested more strongly by the character of *Eastward Ho* and the probable role that Marston played in its composition. There has never been any doubt that Marston was responsible for a part of the play; we have the evidence of the title page:

Eastward / Hoe / As / It was playd in the / Black-friers. / By / The Children of her Maiesties Reuels / Made by / Geo: Chapman. Ben: Ionson. Ioh Marston / At London / Printed for William Aspley. / 1605.

and we have Drummond's report to attest conclusively to Marston's participation: "He [Jonson] was delated by Sr James Murray to the King for writting something against the Scots in a play Eastward hoe & voluntarily Imprissonned himself w^t Chapman and Marston, who had written it amongst y^m." [6] The problem, therefore, has always been to determine the exact limits of his contribution and those of his collaborators. This problem readily resolves itself into two questions: (1) to what extent was Marston responsible for the structural outline of the play and (2) what parts of the whole did he himself write? Only the first question is immediately relevant to our concern. [7]

In generously giving to Marston full credit for the structural outline in *Eastward Ho,* scholars have overlooked two facts about Marston's practice as a comic dramatist. To begin with, though the technique of constructing plots based on broad contrasts in character was fairly commonplace in Marston's time, it is significant that Marston did not use it—except in *The Dutch Courtezan.* On the contrary, in his earlier satirical comedies he had divided his interest between lovers-in-distress plots and disguise plots. Contrasts in character can be found in these plays, as indeed they can be found in any narrative involving more than one character; but Marston was singularly not interested in constructing his plots to pursue these contrasts closely. Secondly, scholars have overlooked a basic structural feature in *Eastward Ho* that distinctly sets it off from Marston's typical work in satirical comedy. In all Marston's plays the plots are grounded in a characteristic value system. If we understand "value system" to mean the specific platform of assumptions concerning character and society on which a particular play is erected, we can easily see—though we

---

[6] H & S, I, 140. Drummond was mistaken about Marston's imprisonment. It is clear from the letters of Chapman and Jonson, the title page of the second edition of *The Fawn,* and A. Nixon's reference to the matter in *The Black Year* (quoted by Chambers, *Stage,* III, 255) that he escaped.

[7] For a brief attempt to answer the second question see Appendix A.

have not considered the fact before—that in Marston these assumptions are by no means narrowly limited: in all his satirical comedies the follies and vices treated range widely over the spectrum of faults possible in a world governed by Opinion. Indeed, although he frequently features the Italianate deformities of amorists and Castilios, even these deformities run the gamut from John Ellis' affected melancholy to Mendoza's political villainy. In *Eastward Ho,* on the other hand, the value system is, as in so many Jonsonian comedies, distinctly economic: the characters are distinguished from each other largely on the basis of economic virtues and vices. In fact, even Gertrude's social ambition, which is not economic, was not a fault that Marston had shown a previous interest in, as, say, Jonson had in Chloe in *The Poetaster.* At any rate, the importance of this distinction is obvious. Although an author's choice of value system probably has little to do with the structure of the play he ultimately writes, this choice is usually characteristic of the particular way in which he transforms the matter of life into the matter of art. It is significant that *Eastward Ho* is not only different in this respect, but that Marston did not vary the value system characteristic of his other satirical comedies until *The Dutch Courtezan,* and then only in the subsidiary action.

In the light of these considerations, therefore, it is distinctly improbable that Marston devised the structural outline of *Eastward Ho.* On the contrary, the evidence supports the hypothesis that *The Dutch Courtezan* was written either concurrently with or after *Eastward Ho* and that Marston derived much of his technique in it from the collaboration. If I had to point to one source for the structural outline of *Eastward Ho,* I would look with the author of the article that appeared in *Blackwood's* over a century ago,[8] to Jonson. Not only the play's value system but also the subtlety and sophistication of its plot and particularly the unusual way in which it brings the guns of ridicule to bear on virtuous

---

[8] "Notices on Old English Comedies: Eastward Hoe," *Blackwood's Edinburgh Magazine,* X (Sept. 1821), 136. The article is signed "J.C."

and vicious characters alike savor of Jonson far more than of Chapman or Marston.

If we can conclude that Marston's collaboration with Jonson and Chapman resulted in his acquiring ideas and methods that he put to immediate use in *The Dutch Courtezan*, then, it only remains to see what kind of play *Eastward Ho* is and what, precisely, Marston might have learned about comic structure from it. We need not be troubled by the fact that Marston did not write all of *Eastward Ho* or by the fact that we do not know exactly what parts he did write. It is enough to know that he had a hand in the play and that he was forced to deal with its structural problems at extremely close range.

The plot of *Eastward Ho* is markedly different from any that Marston had thus far used in that its structure is based squarely on a scheme of related character contrasts. In Act I Touchstone's apprentices, Quicksilver and Golding, "the one of a boundless prodigality, the other of a most hopeful industry," are contrasted; Touchstone's daughters, Gertrude and Mildred, "the [first], of a proud ambition and nice wantonness; the other of a modest humility and comely soberness," are contrasted; and the couples, Sir Petronel Flash and Gertrude, Golding and Mildred, and Touchstone and his wife, are contrasted. Early in the play these contrasts are developed explicitly through Touchstone's denunciations and praise and implicitly through juxtaposition; and in Act II the contrasts are elaborated as the characters engage in actions exhibiting them more fully. Gradually the distance between contrasted individuals increases. Quicksilver, expelled from Touchstone's employ, takes refuge with the usurer Security, with whom he completes the details of Sir Petronel's plan to exchange Gertrude's lands for the money needed for the Virginia expedition they are planning. Later Sir Petronel himself confirms the details of the arrangement and dupes Security into assisting him in his plan to elope with Security's wife. Gertrude, meanwhile, prepares to go off with her mother and Sindefy, her new maid, formerly Quicksilver's mistress, to find Sir Petronel's castle in the country, while Golding and Mildred muddle on, aglow with virtue and hard work. Once the maximum distance between the contrasted characters is achieved in Act III, scene ii, when Gertrude, having signed her lands over to Security, rejects Touchstone, Golding, and Mildred and rushes off to establish herself in Sir Petronel's fictitious castle, each line of action takes a decisive turn. Gertrude, of course, finds no castle and returns to London to be rejected by Touchstone; the Virginia venture, oiled by the money obtained from the sale of Gertrude's lands, is launched and wrecked off the shores of Cuckold's Haven. Only Golding and Mildred prosper, and they succeed beyond even Touchstone's fondest expectation when Golding is named Alderman's Deputy by his Guild.

All the lines of action converge in Act V. Gertrude is reduced to poverty, and Quicksilver and Sir Petronel are charged by Touchstone and committed to prison by Golding, where they are soon joined by Security. Only when Gertrude is reconciled to Mildred, and when Golding tricks Touchstone into witnessing the repentance of the wayward Quicksilver and Sir Petronel in the prison scene, is forgiveness finally exchanged all around. Then, with the reunions of husbands and wives and apprentice and master, the state of normalcy with which the play opened is restored. But it should be noticed that it is an unusually comic state of normalcy that this fictional world is returned to. The characters have been brought out of their humours, it is true, but only so far as it has been convenient for them to be brought out; the thesis of Quicksilver's "Repentance Ballad"—"Seek not to go beyond your tether"—has been illustrated, but with no very serious view toward its inculcation. The final chord in this composition, like those in so many of Jonson's plays, is triumphantly comic.

The crowning merit of *Eastward Ho* is that all of its parts are contrived so that each contributes maximally to the comic and satiric effect of the whole. This merit is, perhaps, most clearly seen in the major controls placed on the action. What might pass for relatively serious villainy in many another comedy, for example, is here rendered nonserious by the treatment of the villains. Security, Sir Petronel Flash, and Quicksilver are all highly comic; Security is even grotesquely comic. The objects of their villainy, moreover, are not virtuous characters, but each other; and their aspirations never result in more than financial threats to any character, except in Sir Petronel's threat to Security's marriage. At the same time, the virtuous characters in the play are so excessively virtuous as to be comic themselves. When Touchstone promises to make Mildred's wedding feast the equal of Gertrude's, Golding replies in a spirit of frugality that is more absurd than laudatory:

Let me beseech you, no, sir; the superfluity and cold meat left at their nuptials will with bounty furnish ours. The grossest prodigality is superfluous cost of the belly; nor would I wish any invitement of states or friends, only your reverent presence and witness shall sufficiently grace and confirm us. [II, i, 164–169]

Throughout *Eastward Ho,* accordingly, the satire is double-edged, cutting finely but surely into the complacency of Touchstone and his group just as it cuts into the humorous extravagance of Sir Petronel and his associates. Touchstone is an honest tradesman as the fashionable audience at Blackfriars conceived of such honest tradesmen. With his tag line, "Work upon that now," his "good wholesome thrifty sentences," his terror at learning what his daughter's wedding is costing him, his self-righteousness and vindictiveness when he learns that he has the prodigals in his power, and his childish gullibility and sentimentality when exposed to proofs of Quicksilver's reform, he does not deserve Mistress Touchstone's denunciation of him as an ass, but he does carry economic values too far, if Quicksilver does not carry them far enough. Likewise, Golding and Mildred are so excessively thrifty and modest in all things that ambition in them seems de-

prived of desire. The explicit norms of behavior established by
Touchstone, Golding, and Mildred, consequently, are as comic
as the deviations from them. The over-all effect of this instability
is that the world of *Eastward Ho* shimmers with a comic unity
exhilarating to behold.

The playwrights have maximized this exhilaration in certain
clearly definable ways. The large number of represented scenes
of revelry and high-spirited horseplay re-enforce the satiric content with explosions of ebullience. The scene after Gertrude's
wedding, when Quicksilver is drunk, the scene of carousing fare-
wells at the Blue Anchor, the scene in which Poldavy schools
Gertrude in the tripping walk of a lady, and the scene of Gertrude's departure, with its complaining ostlers and curious citizens' wives, all serve to intensify the sense of comic liberation. In
addition, the playwrights have provided abundant opportunities
for the child actors to perform in a broad vein of burlesque. The
usurer Security, wringing his hands at the prospect of dishonest
gain, the self-important Touchstone, the swaggering Seagull, the
fashionable Sir Petronel, and the mincing, affected Gertrude were
all conceived, to some extent at least, with the child actors' special
talents in mind. Consider with what effect a child actor (a trained
dancer) could mimic the affected movements of a fashionable
lady:

Gertrude. . . . How must I bear my hands? Light? light?
Poldavy. O ay, now you are in the lady-fashion, you must do all things
  light. Tread light, light. Ay, and fall so: that's the Court-amble. (*She
  trips about the stage.*)
Ge. Has the Court ne'er a trot?
Po. No, but a false gallop, lady. [I, i, 218–224]

Or consider the entrance of Sir Petronel Flash "*in boots, with a
riding wand*":

Pe. I'll out of this wicked town as fast as my horse can trot! Here's
  now no good action for a man to spend his time in. Taverns grow

dead; ordinaries are blown up; plays are at a stand; houses of hospitality at a fall; not a feather waving, nor a spur jingling anywhere. I'll away instantly. [II, iii, 211–215]

The subsidiary action concerning Security and his wife and Sir Petronel's plan to carry her off to Virginia with him, furthermore, has been designed to focus the comic value of the principal action. Security is fundamentally an instrumental character who enables Sir Petronel to deprive Gertrude of her lands and finance his Virginia expedition. At the same time, however, the line of action in which he assists Sir Petronel in what he understands to be the knight's plan to elope with Bramble's wife by providing both the idea for a disguise and the gown in which his own wife subsequently deceives him is a farcical accompaniment to the main action that adjusts our attitude toward it. Taken all in all, the plot of this play embodies a superb example of the world seen from afar. Of the playwrights involved, only Jonson has managed in other plays the almost Olympian outlook that here simultaneously ridicules, enjoys, and affirms what is seen.

Eastward Ho is undoubtedly a minor masterpiece in the annals of English Renaissance drama, and certainly it is a credit to Marston that he had any part in it at all. But given the probabilities afforded by his experience up to this time and the markedly different structure found in the play, it is extremely improbable that he can be credited with anything so substantial as the plot. Indeed, the singular fact that *Eastward Ho* is practically devoid of literal seriousness is sufficient cause to suspect that Marston had little to do with its general outline. His conception of satirical comedy did not run to the kind of sunlit image of comic confusion so masterfully handled here as much as to a chiaroscuro of forms quite distinctly evaluated. Yet Marston was throughout his brief literary career an innovator of sorts, one who might have raised his glass at the Blue Anchor and taken "Eastward Ho" as his motto in his struggle to go beyond stale convention. Having once worked on *Eastward Ho* and having seen how effective a dramatic structure ordered by contrast could be, it is altogether probable that he would experiment with one like it in his next play in this mode.

The Dutch Courtezan represents Marston's last attempt to generate by dramatic means the blend of moral distress and moral reassurance, ironical levity and ironical earnestness so peculiar to his satirical comedies. Its plot, like that of *Eastward Ho,* is based on a simple scheme of character contrasts that are carefully set up in the early acts. Unlike the contrasts in *Eastward Ho,* however, those in *The Dutch Courtezan* are developed, not through separate strains of action, but within a single line of action in which Marston plays off three key characters against the central figure of the courtezan, Franceschina, either by juxtaposing them to her or by illuminating them through their responses to her. In Act I, scene i, for example, Freevill and Malheureux, who are fast friends, have an intellectual and moral falling out when Malheureux learns that Freevill has enjoyed and continues to enjoy an association with Franceschina. Their discussion establishes Freevill as an intelligent, carefree man about town who is aware that he has debased himself, but who has too much respect for the vagaries of natural impulse to be excessively severe either with himself or with the institution of courtezans. At the same time, it establishes Malheureux as an austere young man of unbending and untested moral convictions. Later, in Act II, scene i, Beatrice, an attractive young woman who hopes to marry Freevill, is introduced as an antitype to Franceschina. With these—the most important figures in the play—as with other figures in the play, Franceschina serves as a touchstone to moral character, and the line of action concerning her is developed to amplify and clarify the contrasts she occasions.

In general, *The Dutch Courtezan* is constructed to exploit these contrasts for satiric and didactic interest. When Freevill and Malheureux visit Franceschina in Act I, scene ii, Malheureux unexpectedly succumbs to her charms, to his bewilderment and Freevill's amusement. This representation of misdirected passion is then followed by a balcony scene in which Freevill and Beatrice declare their love, after which Beatrice gives Freevill a ring and Freevill decides to break with Francheschina. When Malheureux confesses his infatuation for the courtezan to Freevill, accordingly, Freevill only too willingly seizes upon the simple expedient of vacating his place in Franceschina's favors for him, and together they go to her. But Franceschina is not so willing to be exchanged. Suspicious that Freevill plans to marry Beatrice, she tests his fidelity by asking for Beatrice's ring and, when Freevill refuses to part with it and leaves her, flies into a rage. Bent on revenge, she chooses Malheureux as her instrument and in return for Freevill's death and Beatrice's ring promises to surrender to him. Although Malheureux at first agrees to kill Freevill, when he is alone, he fortunately decides to tell his friend everything.

In Acts III and IV further complications develop out of the counterplot of Freevill and Malheureux against Franceschina and Freevill's private plan to teach his friend a lesson. When Malheureux lays before his friend the dark design of the courtezan, Freevill devises a scheme by which at a celebration in honor of Freevill's engagement to Beatrice he and Malheureux will seem to quarrel and then leave as if to prepare for a duel. While he is in hiding at Master Shatewe's, Malheureux is to claim that he has killed his friend, show Franceschina Beatrice's ring, and demand his reward. In keeping with this plan the friends stage a dispute at Sir Hubert Subboy's party and subsequently go their separate ways, Malheureux to Franceschina's and Freevill, supposedly, to Master Shatewe's. But at this point Freevill determines to go still farther with his deception. By not informing Master Shatewe or anyone that he is unharmed, he leaves his friend to the treachery of the courtezan in the hope that this experience will cure him of his dangerous excess. As insurance, moreover, he disguises himself as a bravo and enrolls in Franceschina's employ, where he is able to survey this labyrinth at close range.

Everything happens as Freevill predicts. True to her plan,

Franceschina has Malheureux arrested and uses every device within her reach to torment Beatrice with Freevill's infidelity; and when Malheureux cannot prove his claim that Freevill is alive, he is tried and condemned to be hanged. Of course Freevill has only to undisguise himself to save Malheureux and put an end to Beatrice's distress; but he delays and only in the shadow of the gallows, when the picture of villainy is complete, reveals the whole story. The play ends according to Freevill's design: Franceschina is packed off to prison in a fury; Malheureux indicates that he has been chastened by his narrow escape; and the lovers reunite amid general rejoicing.

Thus briefly set forth, this action faithfully follows Marston's source, the story of Dellio and Cinthye in Nicholas de Montreux's *Le premier livre des bergeries de Juliette*.[9] But De Montreux's tale is by no means conspicuously comic and satiric, and, characteristically, Marston de-emphasized its melodramatic and sentimental values in favor of latent comic and satiric ones. To begin with, he has minimized the courtezan's ominousness by making her a comic villain, a woman scorned, whose wounded pride and explosive temper propel her to the extravagant revenge she formulates, but whose frustration results most frequently in outbursts of comic fury.[10] After she reminds herself of Beatrice, she

[9] John J. O'Connor, "Chief Source of Marston's *Dutch Courtezan*," SP, LIV (Oct. 1957), 509–515.

[10] This point is illuminated by comparing Marston's play with a Restoration adaptation of it, Christopher Bullock's *A Woman's Revenge or A Match in Newgate* (1758). (For Bullock's play see *A Complete Collection of the Best Modern Plays*, London, 1759, XII.) In *A Woman's Revenge* Corinna (Bullock's Franceschina) is not Dutch and has no comic accent. Moreover, because her motivation is clearer—Freeman (Bullock's Freevill) was her first lover—and because her rage does not run to excessive displays, she poses more serious threats to the lovers than Franceschina's. These changes in her character are consistent with Bullock's general aim in his revision, which removes satiric elements in favor of the intrigue of romantic comedy. Bevil (Bullock's Malheureux) does not have moral pretensions that he fails to live up to; he is committed from the start to the course of seducing Corinna. Miranda (Bullock's Crispinella), on the other hand, does not love

raves, "God's sacrament, ick could scratch out her eyes, and suck
the holes" (II, ii, 86, 87); and just as she is about to betray
Malheureux, she insists, "If dat me knew a dog dat Freevill love,
/ Me would puisson him" (V, i, 14, 15). This comic excess is
heightened, of course, by her thick Dutch accent (apparently all
accents were funny to the Jacobeans). Further, Marston has effectively undercut and controlled the seriousness of this action
through his familiar use of a character in disguise. The tactic of
having Freevill disguise himself as a bravo (IV, ii) and secure a
place in Franceschina's service (IV, iv) so that he can oversee
everything and forestall moments of genuine distress is entirely
Marston's invention. Again the device depends on disclosures, on
what the audience knows against what the majority of the characters in the play know at a given time. When Freevill goes into
disguise and successfully establishes himself in a position that will
enable him to control his plan, we see that there is every probability that he will succeed and that Franceschina will fail.
Franceschina's apparent success—it is apparent only to her and
other characters in the play—becomes for us a subject for ironic
contemplation and her fury only the more ridiculous because it
will obviously go unrequited.

The plot as a whole, indeed, provides plentiful assurances of a
happy issue. The character of Malheureux's friendship with Freevill as it is established in Act I, scene i, for example, when Malheureux pleads with Freevill to desist from his waywardness, and
in Act II, scene i, when Freevill is jubilant that Malheureux has
found himself human after all ("now I could swallow thee, thou
has wont to be so harsh and cold") makes it distinctly improbable
that Malheureux will kill him, despite his desire for Franceschina
and his moment of vacillation. By the end of the second of these
scenes he has decided to tell his friend, and two scenes later he
does tell him. Moreover, no part of the friends' scheme against

-----

a witty Tysefew, but Bevil, whom she marries at the end. Furthermore, a
number of Marston's satiric characters—Caqueteur, Putifer, and Burnish—
are eliminated outright.

Franceschina or of Freevill's plan to teach Malheureux a lesson is withheld. Everything is revealed to the audience so that the emphasis falls not on melodramatic suspense, but on the action's comic and satiric dimensions. Even the rather remote possibility that Freevill's marriage to Beatrice will run afoul of complications when she learns about his past is rendered highly improbable by Beatrice's character. So generous and so deeply in love is she when she thinks Freevill dead and she receives from Franceschina the venomed proofs of his waywardness that their reunion, when it does occur, resolves easily into rejoicing.

In addition to these controls, the play has two subsidiary actions that strengthen and accentuate its comic focus. The first, the rather spare line of action concerning Tysefew's courtship of Crispinella, involves very little development beyond a brief quarrel and the subsequent agreement to marry; but it serves to introduce two extremely lively characters who invite comparison with, and strengthen our perception of, the superiority of the principal couple, and a comic grotesque in the person of Caqueteur. The second of the subsidiary actions, moreover, the action concerning Cockledemoy and Mulligrub, represents a substantial part of the play that consists wholly of scenes of ribald farce and satire.[11]

Like the action in *Eastward Ho* concerning Sir Petronel's plan to elope with Security's wife, the action here concerning Cockledemoy's systematic destruction of the sharking vintner Mulligrub qualifies the main action by punctuating it with loud outbursts of exuberant comic activity. Through five acts Cockledemoy gradually drives the bourgeois villain Mulligrub to the brink of insanity by a series of skillfully executed deceptions. In Act I we learn from Mulligrub that Cockledemoy has just cheated him of a supper and made off with some goblets. In Act II Cockledemoy disguises himself as a barber, trims Mulligrub, places a coxcomb on Mulligrub's head, and then steals the money with which Mulli-

---

[11] On the sources of this subplot see James L. Jackson, "Sources of the Sub-plot of Marston's *Dutch Courtezan*," *PQ*, XXXI (1952), 223–224.

grub had planned to replace the goblets. In Act III, disguised as a French peddler, Cockledemoy eavesdrops as Mulligrub buys a "standing cup" from Master Burnish and then, posing as Burnish's servant, steals the cup by convincing Mistress Mulligrub that Mulligrub had wanted it engraved. To heap insult on injury, he then returns to Mistress Mulligrub and carries away the jowl of salmon with which he had gilded his first lie with credibility. In Act IV, with Mulligrub desperate for vengeance by this time, Cockledemoy has only to call the constables to have him arrested and placed in the stocks when Mulligrub seizes his cloak while pursuing him. Disguised as a bellman, Cockledemoy then visits Mulligrub, accepts money from him on the promise that he will talk to the constables for him, and tells the constables a tale that prompts them to put Mulligrub in prison. Only at the last moment is Mulligrub released from torment. Even at the gallows Cockledemoy, disguised as a sergeant, makes an assignation with Mistress Mulligrub for after the hanging and reminds Mulligrub of his dishonest past. When Mulligrub confesses and forgives his tormentor, Cockledemoy at last drops the disguise and in turn forgives him.

The conspicuous farcicality of the Cockledemoy action need not be dwelt on; but in the sequence of represented scenes its prominence can hardly be ignored. As a substantial part of the plot the Cockledemoy action serves to complement the subtler, more incisive humor of the principal action with raucous laughter and to qualify it by tracing through five acts a tenuous parallel to it. On the surface the parallel is not readily apparent, though when considered together, Freevill's and Cockledemoy's apologies for prostitution, Freevill's and Cockledemoy's disguises, and the respective arrests toward the end of both actions offer some evidence of the linkage. But these details are probably not as important as the fact that Cockledemoy's corrective gulling of Mulligrub is a counterpart to Freevill's plan to teach Malheureux a lesson, just as Mulligrub's comic fury is a counterpart to Franceschina's rage. One of the less conspicuous factors that characterizes

Franceschina as a comic villain is that she is in many ways like Mulligrub. And in much the same way the whole Cockledemoy action serves to adjust the perspective on the Franceschina action by infusing the play with the exuberance of a fabliau. Cockledemoy, it is important to recall, has the play's final speech:

Why, then, my worshipful good friends, I bid myself most heartily welcome to your merry nuptials and wanton jigga-joggies.—And now, my very fine Heliconian gallants, and you, my worshipful friends in the middle region,

> If with content our hurtless mirth hath been,
> Let your pleased minds at our much care be seen;
> For he shall find, that slights such trivial wit,
> 'Tis easier to reprove than better it. . . . [V, iii, 159–168]

Even after an allowance has been made for the conventionality of the speech, it is as *envoi* for this play decidedly in key.

In summary, then, *The Dutch Courtezan* represents an attempt to achieve with a dramatic structure that was fairly new to Marston a working power like that of his other satirical comedies. It elicits much the same seriocomic attitude toward moral deformity and moral improvement and delivers much the same mixed affirmation of a world drunk with self-deception. It is properly considered a final experiment in Marston's work on satirical comedy chiefly because it differs from *What You Will*, *The Malcontent*, and the others in the dramatic means used.

Much of the technique of *The Dutch Courtezan*, however, points to continuities in workmanship that must not be overlooked. Already familiar as a device for directing opinion is the use Marston makes of Freevill as a choral character. By this time Marston had replaced the earlier critic-spectator by a character firmly rooted in the action who could from time to time fill the choral function explicitly filled by Planet and Feliche in earlier plays. Altofronto as Malevole is such a character in *The Malcontent*, and Hercules is such a character in *The Fawn*. In *The Dutch Courtezan* Freevill fills this function in part, at least, by the very nature of his position in the latter part of the play, where he is a disguised character possessed of the power of putting matters to right whenever he pleases. Yet even before he becomes an intriguer bent on teaching his friend a lesson, he takes a prominent part in directing opinion. Throughout Act I, for example, when Malheureux's turnabout could easily resemble Angelo's in *Measure for Measure*, Freevill sustains a spirit of levity by mocking his friend relentlessly, even to throwing his moral saws back in his face after he has succumbed to Franceschina. At the crucial moment of Malheureux's fall, for example, he unmistakably pinpoints the response aimed at; "By the Lord! he's caught! Laughter eternal" (I, ii, 247). In his relations with Beatrice, moreover, his lightheartedness serves as a curb to the danger of their being taken too seriously. As young lovers go in Marston's satirical comedies, Freevill and Beatrice are easily the most attractive, if only because the plot turns on more scenes than usual in which their affection for each other is prominent. To prevent its becoming too important, however, Marston has resorted to two or three familiar devices, not the least of which is a balcony scene in which Freevill's lighthearted good sense serves to undercut their passion. In the balcony scene which, though not so replete with elements of parody and burlesque as those we have already examined, is at least tinctured by these elements, Freevill, like all good Romeos, is carried away by verbal extravagance. But, significantly, he perceives his fault and breaks off in the middle of a word:

> My vow is up above me, and like time,
> Irrevocable: I am sworn all yours.
> No beauty shall untwine our arms, no face
> In my eyes can or shall seem fair;
> And would to God only to me you might
> Seem only fair! Let others disesteem
> Your matchless graces, so might I safer seem;
> Envy I covet not. Far, far be all ostent—
> Vain boasts of beauties, soft joys, and the rest:
> He that is wise pants on a private breast. [II, i, 28–37]

When he continues, he does so in a less exalted vein, having deftly
distanced the moment with his self-awareness.

But the problem of the lovers cannot be dismissed so easily.
Having admitted that they are easily the most attractive couple
in Marston's comedies and having said, still earlier, that the character of the denouement is to a large extent determined by emotions aroused by their reunion, we have touched on a romantic
strain that is by no means entirely undercut by comic controls. Its
prominence in the play is in some measure explained by the
source, where it is much more tender and pathetic. But the question of how much interest and sympathy the lovers arouse and
how prominent their vicissitudes are in the play can only be answered by looking more closely at Marston's treatment of them, a
subject that brings us to another continuous feature of his technique, his treatment of character.

For the most part the characters in *The Dutch Courtezan* are
the extremely flat characters tending to caricature so numerous
earlier. Only Freevill and Beatrice are notably different, and even
they do not greatly depart from the general rule. By way of a
change, it is true that Marston represents here love scenes or exhibitions of the lovers' affection that are not severely undercut as
are those of Pasquill and Katherine and of Antonio and Mellida.
But recognizing that Freevill and Beatrice are relatively free of
the gross exaggeration that so quickly identifies Pasquill and
Katherine as burlesque characters is really no more important
than recognizing that they do not approach in interest a Rosalind
and an Orlando. All in all they are a fairly attractive couple who
encounter what seems to Beatrice to be an impediment to their
marriage; yet, despite Beatrice's genuinely serious laments and
Freevill's remorse in Act V, scene ii, when he goes too far with his
deception and causes Beatrice to faint, they remain flat as characters whose good fortunes are never endangered so as to arouse
anxiety, as, for example, the fortunes of Dellio are endangered in
the source when his beloved almost dies. What Beatrice takes to
be an impediment to their marriage, the audience knows all along

to be a skillful deception that can only end happily for her; and the anxiety expressed by this threat is a fair index to the anxiety aroused for them throughout. In other words, the lovers elicit interest and sympathy, but only enough so that they contrast effectively with Malheureux and Franceschina. Even their success at the end is in large part the rather abstract success of virtuous young love over the machinations of a harlot, just as the high spirits at the end are rather the result of critical distance achieved than of sentimental desires fulfilled.

Certainly Marston's treatment of the other characters is in most respects the standard treatment accorded to satiric characters. In keeping with the cosmopolitan London that he has substituted (again, perhaps, at the suggestion of *Eastward Ho*) for the familiar Italian locale, he has drawn names from English as well as from French and Italian. But whatever the national source, the characters are the lineal descendants of Puffe, Castilio, and Maquerelle. Mary Faugh, whose name derives from an English expression of disgust, is a bawd who prides herself on the assistance she has given Franceschina. Putifer, from the Italian *putiferio*, meaning "stench," is a nurse, young in desire but old in body. Caqueteur, a French word meaning "idle prater," is precisely that and cowardly as well. And Mulligrub is a grubbing vintner whose only joy in life is material gain, however dishonestly acquired, and whose wife is devoted to him only so long as he shall live. Crispinella, whose name betrays her crispness, and Tysefew, whose name derives from the French combination *tiser* and *feu*, meaning "to feed a fire," serve in their modest ways to draw out the satiric types and furnish the play with what little explicit criticism it has. Crispinella savors strongly of such earlier critics as Maletza in *What You Will* and Rossaline in *Antonio and Mellida*, and her barbed remarks on love, marriage, and suitors serve, as her predecessors' had, to embolden the satiric quality of the action. Cockledemoy, the meaning of whose name is obscure, is, for all his witty fantasticalness, chiefly an instrumental character whose knavery produces the series of comic disasters that befall Mulligrub. Although his exuberance and buoyancy are extremely prominent and important, he, too, is drawn from a very simple pattern.

Of the remaining characters, only Franceschina and Malheureux are more than simple satiric types, and even they are flat. Franceschina (her name doubtless derives from the *commedia dell' arte* doxy) is a comic villain whose fulminations heighten the exhilaration of her complete frustration. Malheureux, "the unhappy one," is a dour young idealist whose moral pretensions are rendered humorous by the series of shocks that teach him what he is and what the world is. He is, it is worthy of note, the only satiric butt of his kind in the plays, the only one, that is to say, who errs, initially at least, on the side of strictness. But he has clear forebears in the puritans of *Certain Satires*, Satire II, and *The Scourge*, Satire IX, and his fault, strictly considered, constitutes a departure from the reason of nature as serious as any other surrender to Opinion. In the represented action of the play, of course, Franceschina and Malheureux fill the crucial function of contrasting with Freevill and Beatrice. Yet like the others, they have no more complexity than is necessary to propel the action in the direction of the serious fantasticalness aimed at.

To gauge more finely the effect of such characters, we must again recall that they were played by child actors, or by this time, perhaps, by youths. The whole subject of prostitution must have seemed more than usually grotesque in a dramatic world peopled by children. Surely speeches like those in which Freevill and Cockledemoy undertake libertine defenses of whores must have sounded strangely ironic. Consider the comic enormity of Mary Faugh's self-defense:

I ha' made as much o' your maidenhead—and you had been mine own daughter, I could not ha' sold your maidenhead oft'ner than I ha' done. I ha' sworn for you, God forgive me! I have made you acquainted with the Spaniard, Don Skirtoll,—with the Italian, Messer Beieroane. . . . Is this my reward? Am I called bawd? [II, ii, 12–23]

If anything, the grating incongruity of hearing such vulgarity from youngsters is more frequent here than in previous plays; this is, in fact, the most censorable play in Marston's canon—though not for its alleged obscenity so much as for its coarse scatalogical references. But the grotesqueness that results is perfectly consistent with the world as Marston has represented it, and indeed with the human condition as he saw it. As a satirist he was always given to exaggeration; and here, as elsewhere, his exaggeration is never merely rhetorical.

In general, *The Dutch Courtezan* recalls the structural strategy of many of Marston's satirical comedies, that of recasting essentially melodramatic materials for the peculiar union of levity and seriousness that seen from a certain point of view they are capable of yielding. All things considered, and despite my emphasis to this point on Marston's attention to satire and satiric devices, the play provides a relatively somber version of the serious fantasticalness typically achieved. Although it is generously interlarded with light, comic scenes and although it contains five songs and a dance clearly calculated to brighten the whole, its total effect is much more like that of *The Malcontent* than that of *The Fawn*. Franceschina's viciousness is grounded in an impressive integrity; however comic, she more than once suggests the disturbing paradox of the white devil. Moreover, the poignancy of Beatrice's grief is genuine and profound, even though it lasts but a short time. Actually both her pain and her earlier tenderness are necessary to give meaning to one of the two contrasts on which the plot is founded—that, as Marston puts it in his *Fabulae Argumentum*, "betwixt the love of a courtezan and a wife." Finally, the over-all sense of a world snatching at phantoms is sometimes especially heavy in *The Dutch Courtezan*, at times even oppressive. Perhaps the endeavors of Malheureux best epitomize the confusion of values on the personal level. In some respects he recalls the figure of Ixion so frequently used by Marston, the Ixion who embraces clouds and begets centaurs in the belief that he is embracing the queen of the gods. He is clearly central to Marston's familiar concern with nature perverted. A man of propriety guided by inherited moral principle, he comes to realize that the highest morality cannot be divorced from an awareness of what man is and of the difficulties involved in making him better; Freevill, meanwhile, comes while trying to be a man of nature guided by reason to understand as he had not understood before the implications of the depravity he had cavalierly flirted with.

The total dramatic image, at any rate, generates much the same combination of amusement and zeal met in the earlier satirical comedies, much the same sense of sovereign detachment admixed with outraged concern, but with the accent on distress to a degree met earlier only in *The Malcontent.* If *Jack Drum* and *The Dutch Courtezan* can be said to identify the extreme variations in the seriocomic attitude communicated by Marston's satirical comedies, *The Dutch Courtezan* reveals the attitude in its most saturnine aspect.

After *The Dutch Courtezan* Marston apparently began to disengage himself by stages from the society and career that had been so important to him since 1595. In the latter half of 1605 he was forced to flee London because of the trouble occasioned by *Eastward Ho.* Although we do not know how long he was away, we know that he was also out of the city in 1606 when the first edition of *The Fawn* appeared. When he returned to oversee the second edition, we know from his note "To the Reader" that he had finished *Sophonisba,* a tragedy (see Appendix A), and by July 31, 1606, when his *City Pageant* (see Appendix B) was presented as one of the entertainments in honor of the King of Denmark, he had apparently restored himself in King James's favor. That he was asked to write the *Ashby Entertainment* (see Appendix B) for a presentation at Ashby-de-la-Zouch in Leicester in 1607, however, strongly suggests that in that year he spent some time at least in the neighborhood of Coventry; actually, he could well have spent much of his time among the scenes of his boyhood after 1605. Aside from his part in *The Insatiate Countess,* he worked on no further plays that we know of. And even his last complete play, *Sophonisba,* bears signs of a break with the purposes that had governed his work to this point.

The Tragedy of Sophonisba constitutes a curious penultimate effort in a career almost all of which had been dedicated to satiri-comic expression. On the one hand, it is in some sense anticipated in Marston's earlier attempt to write a Neo-Stoic tragedy in *Antonio's Revenge* and in his continuous commitment to the Neo-Stoic position discussed earlier; on the other, it reflects a complete, if temporary, abandonment of the satiric attitude that it had so long been his labor to represent and a neglect, at least, of those refinements on classical Stoicism characteristic of his personal version of Neo-Stoicism. It is possible that we have already seen evidence of a shift in focus in Marston's expressed concern in the "Preface" to *The Fawn* about his neglect of serious interests. Doubtless he wrote this "Preface" in 1606 for the first edition of that play at the same time that he was engaged in writing *Sophonisba*, which he mentions later in that year in a note to the second edition. Such hints of personal dissatisfaction, at any rate, taken in conjunction with the fact that in *Sophonisba* he has re-stricted himself to the austerities of the Stoic persuasion suggest a disenchantment with the satiric attitude, perhaps even the initial signs of the re-evaluation that led him ultimately to renounce the theatre for the church.

Certainly of all Marston's plays, *Sophonisba* has the least rele-vance to the satiric attitude. T. S. Eliot has called attention to its "exceptional consistency of texture . . . and its difference of tone, not only from that of Marston's other plays, but from that of any other Elizabethan dramatist." [12] These qualities proceed from the all but total exclusion of comic and satiric elements from the play and the scrupulous avoidance of mixed tonalities. Despite Marston's central position in the satiric movement at the turn of the century, in other words, he has here deliberately eschewed the satiric elements that were then making such inroads into the tragedy being written in favor of a singleness of effect that even his most Senecan contemporaries would have thought chaste. Perhaps he had been persuaded by his experience in *Antonio's*

[12] *Elizabethan Essays*, p. 194.

Revenge that the complexity produced by satiric intrusions was not germane to the kind of tragedy he wished to write. Perhaps, on the other hand, he was genuinely, if temporarily, dissatisfied with the satiric attitude and freshly stimulated by classical Stoic ideas. In any event, *Sophonisba* is designed to affirm Stoic values in by all odds the simplest, most homogeneous dramatic action that Marston was ever to construct.

Drawn chiefly from the histories of Appian and Livy, the action of the play is designed to define and heighten progressively the impressiveness of Sophonisba's and Massinissa's Stoic virtue. The key structural strategy is the device of the test or trial. In Act I Sophonisba and Massinissa are interrupted as they prepare to consummate their marriage by the news that Scipio is leading a Roman army on Carthage and that Syphax, whom Sophonisba had rejected in favor of Massinissa, has taken his forces over to the Roman side. As Massinissa takes his leave and Sophonisba approves his resolve to do so, the ample representation of their self-denial mounts steadily to Massinissa's declaration

> Wondrous creature! even fit for gods not men:
> Nature made all the rest of thy fair sex
> As weak essays, to make thee a pattern
> Of what can be in woman! [I, ii, 226–229]

In Act II several such tests are represented. The first confronts Gelosso, an older Carthaginian of firm virtue, and then Sophonisba with the plan of the Machiavellian leaders in Carthage to betray Massinissa by giving Sophonisba to Syphax; Gelosso's and Sophonisba's rejection of the plan ends in Gelosso's praise of her:

> A prodigy! let Nature run cross-legg'd,
> Ops go upon his head, let Neptune burn,
> Cold Saturn crack with heat, for now the world
> Hath seen a woman! [II, i, 156–159]

The second test confronts Massinissa with Gisco, the assassin sent by the Carthaginian leaders to poison him, and it ends with

Gisco's astonished recognition of Massinissa's magnanimity in deciding not to execute him. The third confronts Gelosso with Asdrubal, Sophonisba's father and one of the leaders of the Machiavellian faction, and ends with Gelosso's heroic departure for execution and a vivid representation of dissension and discord in Asdrubal's group.

In the remaining acts the pattern by which the Stoic heroes are exposed to threats so that they can meet them magnificently is not repeated so simply as it is in Acts I and II, but it continues to govern the action. In Acts III and IV Sophonisba meets three assaults on her virginity by Syphax and finally eludes him only after he has recognized her a "Creature of most astonishing virtue" and has sought the help of Erictho, a witch, who in turn tricks him into making love to her by masquerading as Sophonisba. Massinissa's fortitude, meanwhile, is tested largely by Scipio, whom he has joined and who, reminding him of his losses, gives him every inducement to lapse into passion only to find him still undaunted. Finally, Massinissa meets and kills Syphax in personal combat, and he and his Roman allies win the war. But the Stoic heroes undergo one ultimate trial in meeting Scipio's resolve to take Sophonisba back to Rome a prisoner. To eulogies from all sides, Massinissa and Sophonisba also rise above this obstacle by jointly contriving her suicide. The play ends with a death march and appropriate encomiums on the "loved creature of a deathless fame."

Marston's intention to achieve simple massiveness here through a straightforward illustration of Stoic virtue is unmistakable. The play's subtitle, *The Wonder of Women,* is an accurate guide to one of the main responses aimed at, admiration, and H. Harvey Wood's remarks about the play as a harbinger of Restoration Heroic Tragedy are not idle.[13] Yet despite the play's simplicity by Renaissance standards and despite its frequently facile technique, it has an authoritative power that is honestly won, however unusual it may be. Certainly the apparently naïve division of characters into heroes or villains, the obvious simplicity of characteri-

[13] *Plays,* III, xiv.

zation, and the pervasive stateliness of presentation are not faults, but matters to be explained by the peculiar nature of tragedy at the private theatres. Moreover, even these apparent limitations did not keep Marston from a searching analysis of the condition he has represented. Although his villains are rather flat and melodramatic, they are handled so that what they represent is by no means simple. Asdrubal articulates clearly the need for Machiavellian tactics in a world where power dictates (II, iii), but also his regret that he must be a "statist" rather than a man (II, ii, 41). His fellow-conspirators' insecurity throughout and their vicious recriminations in Act II, scene iii, when they meet unexpected obstacles, stand in effective contrast to the Stoic serenity embodied in Massinissa and Sophonisba. And, in perhaps the most striking scene in the play, Erictho deepens the meaning of Syphax's evil by associating him with the unnaturalness and disorder crystallized by her witchcraft. By such devices a considerable density is achieved through an action that is notably simple, even deliberately abstract.

The general tendency in the play toward formality and abstractness, of course, was probably required by the peculiar conditions of the private theatres, particularly the peculiar talents and limitations of the child actors. Marston's awareness of such conditions is obliquely attested to in a note appended to the first edition:

After all, let me intreat my Reader not to taxe me for the fashion of the Entrances and Musique of this tragedy, for know it is printed only as it was presented by youths, and after the fashion of the private stage. . . .

But even without this acknowledgment, it is again perfectly clear that he has tailored his characterizations to his actors' capacity, that he has made the most of the opportunities for music, dance, and masquelike ceremony, that, in general, he has paced and pointed his action to give it the abstract emphasis of the Interlude-Morality. Eliot's comments on its tone, Peter Ure's on its "deliberate slowing-down of pace," [14] and the general observations already made about its simplicity all point to this emphasis. The explicit quality of the character oppositions, the tendency of the characters to discuss philosophical theory, and the sobriety of most of the play's verse, moreover, support this emphasis. Yet perhaps no single feature of the play is more germane to this emphasis than the elaborate use made of masque elements. The bridal ceremony in Act I, scene ii, is typical. The "Stage Direction" reads,

Enter four Boys, anticly attired, with bows and quivers, dancing to the cornets a fantastic measure; Massinissa *in his night-gown, led by* Asdrubal *and* Hanno, *followed by* Bytheas *and* Jugurth. *The boys draw the curtains* [to the bed] *discovering* Sophonisba, *to whom* Massinissa *speaks.*

After a highly formal greeting, "Massinissa *draws a white ribbon forth of the bed, as from the waist of* Sophonisba" and sings "Io to Hymen," to be followed by the "*Chorus, with cornets, organ and voices* [singing] *Io to Hymen!*" Sophonisba's and Asdrubal's rimed speeches then follow, and they, too, are punctuated by the "*Chorus* [singing] *Io to Hymen!*" The whole ceremony is aimed at a static, tableaulike effect, rich in atmospheric and symbolic values; and comparable effects are aimed at in Sophonisba's solemn "sacrifice" in Act III, scene i, in Erictho's elaborate spell-binding ceremony in Act IV, scene i, and in Sophonisba's death march in Act V, scene iv. These masque elements crystallize the stylized formality less obviously secured by the action of the play as a whole and identify the abstract quality of a paradigm at the heart of *Sophonisba's* uniqueness.

In the context of Marston's career to this point, of course, nothing he has done in *Sophonisba* is highly surprising. What is mildly bewildering is that he should have determined at this juncture to carry the peculiarly classical version of Stoicism reflected

[14] "John Marston's *Sophonisba:* A Reconsideration," *Durham University Journal,* N.S. X, no. 3 (1949), 88.

here to such lengths with scarcely a look back to the qualifications in theory and temper that he had cherished through his entire literary life. Some critics have applauded the change by arguing that *Sophonisba* is his best play.[15] If the play marks a change, however, it was probably only a temporary one. His last effort in drama strongly suggests a return to the more difficult, more complex, but in most respects more authoritative way of dealing with his world embodied in the satiric attitude.

Unfortunately, *The Insatiate Countess* is hardly a reliable guide to Marston's activities and interests because of its manifold authorial and textual problems. The most one can say with confidence is that the available evidence indicates Marston's return to the satiricomic plot, since, of the two actions making up the play, his hand is most evident in the comic one (see Appendix A). If this conclusion is sound, we can credit him in this play with an action not unlike in design his earlier satirical comedies. The comic rage of Claridiana and Rogero is ingeniously exploited in a series of scenes in which they successively fume at learning that they are neighbors, scheme to cuckold each other, fulminate when each thinks the other has cuckolded him, and all but dissolve in fury as the Duke delays the execution they demand for a crime they did not commit. The technique of this action strongly resembles Marston's dramatic method. The characters are boldly and simply drawn—caricatures shading into burlesque figures in the mock heroes, Claridiana and Rogero. The episodes are firmly plotted and rich in the outrageousness characteristic of Marston's comic action. And even the complications are handled so that key characters are at all points in possession of the truth and the emphasis falls squarely on comic exhibitions of deformity. Finally, the whole design is laced with such characteristic features of Marston's dramaturgy as a burlesque wooing in Mendoza's scene with Lady Lentulus, an elaborate masque in Act II, and passages of exceedingly vigorous dialogue. Taken as a dramatic unit, the comic action of *The Insatiate Countess* reveals nothing new in

[15] Giuliano Pellegrini, *Il Teatro di John Marston* (Pisa, 1952), p. 165.

Marston's career in satiricomic forms; indeed, it reflects a far simpler exercise in satirical comedy than any of his full-scale plays. If we can accept that Marston wrote it, however, it has interest as his last attempt at satiricomic expression.

Actually, the play would be far more interesting if we could conclude that Marston wrote, or at least designed, all of it. It would then reveal him experimenting with still another union of comic and serious materials, still another fusion of disparate tonalities and heterogeneous elements. But the speculation is pointless. There is no evidence to suggest that Marston had a hand in the tragic action, and no further work to confirm that he was ever interested in a dramatic design like this one. At best the play offers tantalizing evidence for speculation about the last, mysterious years of Marston's association with the theatre.

On June 8, 1608, Marston was imprisoned for unknown reasons. Chambers has argued that he gave offense to the King in a play mentioned in March of 1608 by the French ambassador, M. de la Broderie, and Sir Thomas Lake; [16] but since the play is lost and since Marston is not linked with it by name, the theory must remain highly problematical. What is certain is that soon after his imprisonment, in July or August of 1608, he sold his share in the Blackfriars organization to Robert Keysar.[17] This is the last piece of evidence connecting him with the theatre. On September 24, 1609, he entered St. Mary's Hall, Oxford, to study for the Anglican priesthood, and on December 24 of that year he was ordained. He lived the last twenty-five years of his life as a priest, first at Barford St. Martin in Wiltshire, then, after 1616, at Christ Church in Hampshire. While he was at Barford St. Martin, he married Mary Wilkes, the daughter of John Wilkes, his rector and a favorite chaplain to King James. She bore him one son, who died in 1624. On September 13, 1631, Marston resigned his living at Christ Church; he died in London "in Aldermanbury his house there" on June 24, 1634, and was buried beside his father in the

[16] Chambers, *Stage*, II, 53, 54.   [17] Chambers, *Stage*, II, 54, 55.

Middle Temple Church. The curious wish expressed in his epitaph *"Oblivioni Sacrum"* was partially fulfilled when the church and its graves were destroyed during the raids in World War II.

The motives that prompted Marston to renounce the theatre for the church will perhaps never be known precisely. After *The Dutch Courtezan* it is clear that misfortune befell him in the form of the *Eastward Ho* scandal and the imprisonment in 1608, just as it is clear in his final plays that his interests shifted. Whether there was a connection between the two is entirely a matter of conjecture. Certainly he had no apparent reason to feel that he had failed as a dramatist. By 1606, the year that saw the last of the continuous stream of plays that he had begun producing in 1599, he was an important shareholder in his own company and a dramatist admired by his friends and reckoned a person of consequence even by his enemies. He had clearly achieved the outward signs of the success that had tempted him to renounce the law for literature. He was sufficiently admired to have been imitated by dramatists like Edward Sharpham [18] and to have a collection of his plays published before his death.[19] But all of this was not enough.

Perhaps we have an additional clue to his activities during the rather mysterious years between 1606 and 1609 in something mentioned in the course of his routine application for library privileges at St. Mary's. In the "Supplicat" made on December 7, 1609, he says that he has spent three years and more in the study of philosophy.[20] Of course this could easily be a meaningless state-

---

[18] See especially Sharpham's *The Fleire* (pub. 1607). Not only did Sharpham borrow materials for this play from *The Malcontent* and *The Fawn*, but he also imitated Marston's methods of presenting action and of presenting satire in dramatic form.

[19] In 1633 William Sheares published *The Workes of John Marston, being Tragedies and Comedies collected into one volume. . . .* The collection included *Antonio and Mellida, Antonio's Revenge, Sophonisba, What You Will, The Fawn,* and *The Dutch Courtezan.*

[20] The complete "Supplicat" is reprinted by R. E. Brettle, "John Marston, Dramatist, at Oxford," *RES,* III (1927), 404, 405: "Supplicat etc. (i.e.

ment made for form's sake alone. In the light of what we know of Marston's proclivities, of his relative inactivity in things literary during this period, and of the future he was soon to take up, however, it could also be a reflection of his disenchantment with the theatre, perhaps even of his dissatisfaction with himself. Certainly it is not improbable that his renunciation of London and the theatre was prompted by the very conviction about self-realization that had molded so much of his literary work. In some respects, indeed, this decision amounts to the same rather characteristic withdrawal met in the lives of so many men of the Neo-Stoic persuasion, notably the lives of Muret and Montaigne.

It is a symptom of Marston's integrity, at any rate, that most problems concerning him trace back, almost inevitably, to his beliefs, and it bears repeating that his work derives its unity from these beliefs. In this study I have examined this work so as to emphasize, not this unity, but Marston's artistic development and the continuities and discontinuities all along the line. I have focused intently on the literary persona that he cultivated and on the historical environment that conditioned that persona because Marston the dramatist was in some profound way a Marston who had assimilated the orphan poet, the sharp-fanged satirist, the Neo-Stoic, and the private playwright. I have analyzed carefully, furthermore, the different types of dramatic action used because his work in drama is in still another profound way a series of attempts to design dramatic actions of a certain kind. His achievement in drama can be usefully, if not completely, explained in terms of his handling of the lovers-in-distress plots, the disguise plots, and the other experiments in plotting that he undertook. But all this would be misleading, however useful, and relatively insignificant, however full of detail, if not seen as part of a larger effort to fashion dramatic equivalents for his seriocomical view

venerabili Congregationi) Johannes Marston bacchalaureus facultatis artium ex aula Sanctae Mariae, ut quatenus tres annos et ultra a suscepto bacchalaureatus gradus in studio philosophiae posuerit liceat ei bona vestra eum venia publicae. . . ."

of the world and, in the tragedies, of an important part of that view. Ultimately, it is this seriocomical view that traces the most profound continuities from play to play; it better than anything explains the particular power aimed at in these plays and the particular attitude of detached engagement, of constructive disapproval and amusement communicated. Finally, this is what all the roles cultivated, ideas articulated, problems faced, and fashions attacked add up to: a particular way of confronting the world of the late Renaissance in England, a particular way of charting its directions, of measuring its failures, of responding to its immediate surfaces. It is, finally, the expression of this attitude toward his world that best explains Marston's long-range aims as a writer and that best accounts for his success with his educated audience.

Yet not the least interesting aspect of Marston's work is that his satire evolves so clearly from the explicit tracing out of this view in the verse satires to the expression of it in wholly dramatic terms in the last satirical comedies. Had he not abandoned literature for the church, like his contemporaries he too might have embraced more diversity in time, just as he might have written a play of more importance than *The Malcontent*. But he did not. Our compensation is found in the remarkably unified canon he has left and the light it sheds on him and his time.

Problems of Date and
Authorship in the Plays

Histriomastix

Authorship: Although there is no clear evidence that *Histriomastix* ever existed in an earlier form, it could easily be one of the old plays acted by the child actors during the early days of their revival.[1] In the "Induction" to *Cynthia's Revels* Jonson associates these plays with the Chapel Children:

> 3 *Child.* . . . they say, the *umbrae,* or ghosts of some three or foure playes, departed a dozen yeeres since, have bin seene walking on your stage heere: take heed, boy, if your house bee haunted with such *hobgoblins,* 'twill fright away all your spectators quickly; [H & S, IV, 41]

and in *Jack Drum* (1600) Marston associates them with the Children of Paul's:

[1] Cf. pp. 100–101.

Brabant Sig. . . . they [the Children of Paul's] produce
    Such mustie fopperies of antiquitie,
    And do not sute the humorous ages backs
    With cloathes in fashion. [*Plays*, III, 234]

In style, structure, number of parts, and number of songs *Histriomastix* suggests either the fanciful moralities that had been the standard fare with the child actors in the previous decades [2] or, perhaps, an Inns of Court play; and in its original form it may well have been a product of the rivalry of that era between the poets and players.[3]

But we are concerned with what appears to be a revised version of the original play, a text that was not published until 1610, though it was probably acted as early as 1599 (see below). That Marston was responsible for this revision emerges in evidence of various kinds. To begin with, Marston seems to have been occupied with no other major literary work between September of 1598, when *The Scourge of Villainy* was entered in the Stationers' Register, and 1600, when presumably he wrote *Jack Drum.* That he was busy with something, however, is clearly established by the entry in *Henslowe's Diary* for September 28, 1599, in which Henslowe refers to Mr. Maxton, the "new poet." It is unlikely that Henslowe would have referred in this way to Marston's appearance as a verse satirist in 1598: far more likely is that he was referring to a recent effort by Marston, perhaps a dramatic work. In any event, the probability that Marston brought out a play before *Jack Drum* is increased by the "Introduction" to *Jack Drum,* in which he seems to apologize for a false start that he had made with an old play:

    [the playwright] vowes not to torment your listning eares
    With mouldy fopperies of stale Poetry,
    Unpossible drie mustie Fictions. [p. 179]

When this apparent apology is laid alongside the passage in Jonson's *Every Man Out* (1599) that seems to parody Marston and to link him with a *Histriomastix,* the probability that Marston had revised this play in 1599 becomes reasonably strong. The full passage from *Every Man Out* reads:

[2] See Chapter IV, n. 3.   [3] On this subject see Chambers, *Stage,* I, 376 ff.

Clove. . . . Now, sir, whereas the Ingenuitie of the time, and the soules *Synderesis* are but *Embrions* in nature, added to the panch of *Esquiline,* and the *Inter-vallum* of the *Zodiack,* besides the *Eclipticke line* being *opticke,* and not *mentall,* but by the *contemplatiue* & *theoricke* part thereof, doth demonstrate to vs the *vegetable circumference,* and the *ventositie* of the Tropicks, and whereas our *intellectual,* or *mincing capreall* (according to the *Metaphisicks*) as you may reade in PLATO'S *Histriomastix* - - - You conceiue me, sir? [H & S, III, 502, 503]

As parody this points quite clearly to Marston (see pp. 59–60, Chapter III, on "synderesis"), and the occurrence of the phrase "panch of Esquiline" in both the satires and *Histriomastix* is almost too striking to be accidental.

Perhaps the most persuasive evidence for linking the play with Marston, however, is the usually undependable evidence of style. Owing to the highly individualistic style that Marston evolved in his verse satires, this kind of evidence must be more seriously considered where he is concerned than elsewhere. That *Histriomastix* is, like the satires, a structure of thesis would be negligible if at the same time there did not appear in the play phrases and passages that seem excerpted from *The Scourge.* It is rather difficult to imagine that anyone except Marston at the beginning of his career could have written the following from *Histriomastix:*

> How you translating-scholler? you can make
> A stabbing *Satir,* or an *Epigram,*
> And think you carry just Ramnusia's whippe
> To lash the patient: goe, get you clothes,
> Our free-borne blood such apprehension lothes. [pp. 257, 258]

> Write on, crie on, yawle to the common sort
> Of thickskin'd auditours: such rotten stuffs,
> More fit to fill the paunch of Esquiline,
> Then feed the hearings of judiciall eares,
> Yee shades tryumphe, while foggy Ignorance
> Clouds bright *Apollos* beauty. . . . [pp. 273, 274]

> Now shall proud Noblesse, Law, and Merchandize,
> Each swell at other, as their veins would breake,
> Fat Ignorance, and rammish Barbarisme,

Shall spit and drivell in sweete Learnings face,
Whilst he half starv'd in Envie of their power,
Shall eate his marrow, and him-selfe devoure. . . . [p. 277]

Add to these passages such striking reminders of the figurative language of *The Scourge* as "To puffe up *Prides* swolne bulke with plumy
showes" (p. 280) or to "purge the aire of these grosse foggy clouds, /
That doe obscure our births bright radiance" / (p. 281) and the case is
all but complete. What seems to clinch the matter is that even the
thought of *Histriomastix* is remarkably close to that of Marston's satires.
The Stoicism of the last two acts alone is, perhaps, too general to be
very convincing,[4] but articulated as it is in the following passage it
seems irresistible as proof:

When I behold these huge fat lumpes of flesh,
These big-bulkt painted postes, that sencelesse stand,
To have their backes pasted with dignity,
Quite choaking up all passage to respect:
These huge *Colossi* that rowle up and down,
And fill up all the seate of man with froth
Of outward semblance, whilst pale *Artizans*
Pine in the shades of gloomy *Academes,*
Faint in pursuite of vertue, and quite tierd
For want of liberall food: for liberall Art
Give up the goale to sluggish *Ignorance.*
O whether doth my passion carry mee? [p. 282]

The question of the precise extent to which Marston rewrote the old
play, on the other hand, cannot be answered with nearly so much confidence. Basing my conclusions on stylistic evidence alone, I find his
hand in the following passages: II, 63–69, 261–269, 322–344; III, 78–83,
179–217, 265–316; IV (all); and V, 1–60, 103–146, 181–191, 234, 244–
267.[5] At the same time, it is only fair to say that I have found words
and phrases scattered throughout the text, suggesting that his revision
may have been very general. Such lines as the following are hardly
conclusive, but they savor strongly of Marston:

---

[4] See pp. 287, 291, 295, and 296.
[5] Here I have used R. Simpson's lineated edition of the play in *School,* II.
Cf. these attributions with the argument on pp. 85–86.

II, 20   What dullards thus would dote in rusty Arte?

II, 128   Heres no new luxury or blandishment.

III, 62, 63 . . . unbowelling the bagges
of their rich burthens in your wide-mouth'd deskes.

VI, 26, 27 And savage-like yoakes up humanity,
To bind in chaines true-born civility.

VI, 50, 51 My full-mouthd bags may now be fild with ayre.
The Divell and Ambition taught it me.

Fleay's guess that Marston should be credited with the whole play may be correct after all! [6]

Date of Composition: If *Histriomastix* was one of the "mustie fopperies of antiquitie" with which the child actors reopened Paul's, then it was probably rewritten in 1599 for a production late in that year. This hypothesis is supported by several pieces of evidence. To begin with, if the reference in *Every Man Out* to "Plato's Histriomastix" can be credited, *Histriomastix* must have been acted by the autumn of 1599, since we can say with great confidence that *Every Man Out* was acted late in that year.[7] If, on the other hand, it was a children's play, as it seems to have been from the evidence of its clear and prejudiced distinction between polite and vulgar audiences and sophisticated and popular playwrights, its abundant use of music and song, and its disproportionate use of female figures, it could not have been acted before the late summer of 1599, when, according to the best estimates,[8] Paul's was reopened. Actually, one piece of internal evidence argues for August of 1599. The line "the Spanish are come!" (p. 291) could easily have been a reference to the crisis that occurred in August of 1599, when the sudden preparations for war were begun that were discontinued in September. All this evidence, moreover, accords well with what is known about Marston's activities at the time. The entry in *Henslowe's Diary* for September 28, 1599, suggests that he had recently brought out a play; and the title pages of his other early plays confirm that he was a playwright for Paul's boys early in his dramatic career. Finally, he seems to apologize for just such a play in his "Introduction" to *Jack Drum,* which was entered in the Stationers' Register in 1600.

---

[6] See Chapter IV, n. 6.   [7] H & S, I, 373; IX, 186.
[8] Hillebrand, *Child Actors,* pp. 207–210, and Chambers, *Stage,* II, 19, 20.

A *Play for Henslowe?*

The only evidence we have that Marston ever wrote for a public theatre is the entry in *Henslowe's Diary* for September 28, 1599, in which Henslowe mentions paying a "mr maxton" forty shillings for an unnamed play. The entry reads:

> Lent vnto wm Borne the 28 of september ⎫
> 1599 to Lend vnto mr maxton the new |
>   mr mastone   ⎬ XXXXs
> poete ∧ in earneste of a Boocke called |
>   the some of. . . .[9]   ⎭

The entry is not without difficulties. Not only does the name "maxton" not exactly correspond with Marston's, but the insertion "mr mastone" is universally accepted as a forgery.[10] Moreover, if my conclusions about *Histriomastix* are correct—that Marston revised it for production in August of 1599—we must conclude that he was working for both Paul's and Henslowe at roughly the same time, a circumstance that is curious, but hardly self-contradictory, since Jonson clearly worked for the King's Men and Henslowe at the same time. Despite these problems, however, it is distinctly probable that the words "mr maxton the new poete" point to Marston; at least we know of no other with a name like "maxton" who would have qualified so well in 1599. If we can accept the identification tentatively, we can turn to the even more intricate question of the play referred to. Thus far no one has identified it conclusively.

According to one theory, Marston was the "other Jentellman" mentioned in the entry for September 3, 1599, in which Henslowe recorded payment for the lost play *Robert II, King of Scots*. That entry reads:

> Lent vnto Thomas downton the 3 of Septmber   ⎫
> 1599 to lend vnto Thomas deckers Bengemen |
> Johnson hary chettel & other Jentellman in earneste ⎬ XXXXs
> of a playe calle Robart the second kinge of scottes |
> tragedie the some of. . . .[11]   ⎭

The argument goes that this entry records the first of several payments made on this play. The next records a second payment of twenty

[9] Ed. W. W. Greg (London, 1904–1908), I, 112.
[10] Greg, *Diary*, I, xxxviii.   [11] I, 111.

shillings to "Thomas dickers & harey chettell" for "The scottes tragedi" on September 15, the third a payment of ten shillings to "hary chettell" for "the scottes tragedie" on September 16, and the fourth a payment of twenty shillings to "Bengeman Johnsone" for that play on September 27.[12] Immediately following these entries is that concerning the payment of twenty shillings to "m^r maxton" on September 28. Presumably, this entry refers to the "other Jentellman" in the first entry and completes Henslowe's payments on the play, bringing the total sum put out to six pounds, ten shillings.

The theory clearly has certain facts to recommend it.[13] The entries are so neatly consecutive as to appear to tell the financial story of *Robert II,* and the sums involved do add up conveniently to the sum that Henslowe normally spent for such work. But all this is hardly conclusive. It must not be overlooked that the "maxton" entry, even if we identify Marston in it, does not name *Robert II* as the others do. Moreover, we do not have *Robert II* and, accordingly, do not have anything against which to check this conjecture. Although it is tempting to speculate that Marston was associated with Jonson so early in his career, the evidence for believing so is very slender.

More recently and perhaps more convincingly, K. Gustave Cross has argued that the "maxton" entry refers to Marston's part in *Lust's Dominion.*[14] The chain of argument connecting the two is long and intricate, but impressive despite the problems that remain. *Lust's Dominion* was first published in 1657 by Francis Kirkman, who then ascribed it to Christopher Marlowe. This attribution stood for many years until J. P. Collier demonstrated that the play was, if not written, at least substantially revised in or after 1599 (too late for Marlowe) and that it is probably to be identified with the "spaneshe mores tragedie" mentioned in the *Diary* entry for February 13, 1599/1600:

> Layd owt for the company the 13 of febrearye
>
>   tragedie
> 1599 for a boocke called the spaneshe mores ∧ vnto   ⎱ III^{li}
> thomas deckers w^m harton John daye in
> pte of payment the some of . . . .[15]

[12] I, 111–112.

[13] Small, *Stage-Quarrel,* pp. 90, 91, and Chambers, *Stage,* III, 428, are its chief spokesmen.

[14] "The Authorship of *Lust's Dominion,*" SP, LV (1958), 39–61.

[15] *Diary,* I, 118. See J. Le Gay Brereton's edition of *Lust's Dominion* (Louvain,

In his edition of *Lust's Dominion* J. Le Gay Brereton argued at length to support the theory that the play—originally either by Marlowe or a Marlowe imitator—was substantially revised in 1599 by Dekker with the assistance of Haughton and Day.[16] Although we shall not concern ourselves with the details of his case, the identification of *Lust's Dominion* with a "spaneshe mores tragedie" written in 1599/1600 for Henslowe seems reasonable enough.

While accepting this crucial identification, Cross goes farther than Brereton by arguing that before Dekker, *et al.*, got at the play in February 1599/1600, Marston had revised it and received payment for his work on September 28, 1599. Cross's argument rests on various kinds of evidence, some of it rather doubtful, but some of it almost too striking to be set aside. He completely overlooks the unlikelihood of one man's revision's being revised later by three, and his citations of general similarities of subject matter and character types are far too tenuous to be meaningful. His remark that the use of music in the play recalls Marston's fondness for music in his plays ignores that the private theatres were the primary cause of the music in Marston's and his colleagues' plays. Moreover, his discussion of "striking parallels with Marston's work" omits all mention of striking differences, particularly in the pervasive matter of verbal style, which is in this play typically full and expansive rather than tight and elliptical in the manner of Marston's most characteristic verse. Finally, despite his claim that the "outlook, interests, and temperament" met in the play are "akin to Marston's," what is most striking is that we find in it nothing or very little of the rather clearly characterized mind of the satires or of *Histriomastix* (also a revision).

Yet despite these objections, Cross's accumulation of evidence adds up to an impressive total. Most persuasive is his list of unusual words and phrases found both in *Lust's Dominion* and Marston's work. Although one can hardly feel certain that these are Marston "coinages," as Cross claims they are, many of them are striking terms, and undeniably they occur in striking numbers. Taken with the other evidence

---

1931) for the history of scholarship on this play, pp. 246–261. See especially pp. xv–xviii on Collier's work.

[16] Pages xviii–xxxiii.

advanced, they lend considerable weight to Cross's explanation of the "maxton" entry.

In conclusion, then, it is probable, but by no means certain, that Marston, like Jonson, was briefly employed by Henslowe in September of 1599. Of the two plays that might have constituted the occasion of that employment, a stronger case can probably be made out for *Lust's Dominion* than for *Robert II, King of Scots*, though both candidates raise serious problems. In any event, since "maxton['s]" pay came to only forty shillings, his part in the project could not have been very extensive. If "maxton" was Marston, his brief experience with the public theatres was little more than a flirtation.

Jack Drum's Entertainment

Authorship: The question of the authorship of *Jack Drum* is conclusively answered by Edward Pudsey's manuscript commonplace book (*ca.* 1600–1616) in the Bodleian Library. On folio 40^v of the book Pudsey has written Marston's name after the title *Jack Drum* just as he has written Shakespeare's name after *The Merchant of Venice* and Jonson's after *Every Man Out*. The internal evidence of the title page, which shows that it was a Paul's play, the "Introduction," which suggests that it was the author's first full-scale dramatic effort, and the structure and style, which are as crude as we might expect in a first effort and which bear marked resemblances to the verse satires, simply confirm the play's position very early in Marston's canon.

Date of Composition: A forward limit for *Jack Drum* is established by its entry in the Stationers' Register on September 8, 1600. If we assume the date argued for *Histriomastix*, August of 1599, we find that Marston had approximately a year, or something less, in which to complete this play. The evidence of internal references both confirms these limits and narrows them sufficiently so that we might deduce a production of the play in the late spring or early summer of 1600. The references to the "peace with Spaine" (p. 182), to the Irish troubles: "I'le to *Ireland*" (p. 207) and "hee will waste more substance than *Ireland* souldiers" (p. 186), and to leap year: "womens yeere," i.e., 1600 (p. 186), all point to late 1599 and 1600. But the reference to "Kemps Morice" (p. 182) could not have been made before March 11, 1599/

1600, since the famous dance from London to Norwich took place between February 11 and March 11 of that year. Moreover, Sir Edward's line, "Tis Whitsontyde, and we must frolick it" (p. 182) might well have referred to a holiday outside the play as well as to one within it. The probable reference to *Histriomastix* in Marston's vow

> . . . not to Torment your listning eares
> With mouldy fopperies of stale poetry
> Unpossible drie mustie Fictions [p. 179]

suggests that that play was still fresh in the memory of his audience and that Marston had produced no other between it and *Jack Drum*.

Antonio and Mellida

Date of Composition: Although *Antonio and Mellida* was not entered in the Stationers' Register until October 24, 1601, the consensus of opinion has placed it in 1599—before *Jack Drum*. This view is supported, however, by two pieces of rather doubtful evidence. First, Brabant Jr.'s reference in Act IV of *Jack Drum* to the "new poet Mellidus" (p. 221) has been interpreted as a sly allusion by Marston to himself that proves that *Antonio and Mellida* existed before *Jack Drum* was written.[17] But it is seldom pointed out that in the subsequent dialogue a "Musus" and a "Decius" are also alluded to and that clearly these names were not derived from the titles of works. "Musus" seems to be Hall in SV, I, 5 and X, 105, though elsewhere in the satires Hall is also called "Pallas" (CS, II, 39) and "Grillus" ("Reactio," 31). We can, in other words, expect no consistency in Marston's use of Latin names. It is striking that Marston should use this name, but hardly conclusive. The second piece of evidence used to prove 1599 is the passage beginning at V, i, 11, in *Antonio and Mellida* in which Balurdo reads from a painting the year 1599 and the phrase "*Aetatis suae 24.*" Small and others have interpreted the phrase to mean "aged 24" and have concluded that it is another autobiographical reference, this time to Marston's age in 1599. Since they believed, as was long believed, that Marston was born in 1575, the phrase thus interpreted accords with the year 1599. It is now known, however, that Marston was born

---

[17] Penniman, *War*, p. 74; Small, *Stage-Quarrel*, p. 96.

late in 1576: [18] accordingly, if the reference is translated to mean "aged 24," it would necessitate a date not earlier than late 1600. But the trouble with the phrase *"Aetatis suae 24"* is that we can never be certain that it meant "aged 24" and not "in the 24th year of his age." At any rate, the argument for 1599 runs counter to every other piece of evidence bearing on the question. It is particularly unlikely that Marston would have apologized for the "mustie Fictions" mentioned in *Jack Drum* after he had produced *Antonio and Mellida*.

In the light of other evidence it seems reasonable to conclude that *Antonio and Mellida* was written in the second half of 1600. To begin with, from the evidence of the "Induction," where Marston promises a second part (l. 150), it was clearly written before *Antonio's Revenge,* the promised second part, and *Antonio's Revenge* seems to have been written for a production in the winter of 1600/1. It, too, was entered in the Stationers' Register on October 24, 1601, and its "Prologue" clearly refers to winter. If we take the winter of 1600/1—the only winter between the composition of *Jack Drum* and the entry in the Stationers' Register—as a rough forward limit for *Antonio and Mellida,* that play falls neatly into the period of the second half of 1600. Structurally and stylistically *Antonio and Mellida* is so much more sophisticated a work than *Jack Drum* that it is difficult to imagine that it was Marston's first full-scale effort.

Antonio's Revenge

Date of Composition: Entered in the Stationers' Register with *Antonio and Mellida* on October 24, 1601, *Antonio's Revenge* seems to have been written for a production during the winter of 1600/1. The "Prologue" alludes elaborately to winter. Since we know that this play was written after *Antonio and Mellida,* probably directly after, and since *Antonio and Mellida* was probably not written earlier than the second half of 1600, it is likely that this play did not come earlier than the winter of 1600/1. The Stationers' entry establishes that it did not come later. An internal reference to monopoly (IV, i, 124) points to 1601, moreover, when feeling ran very high against monopolies and

---

[18] The notice of Marston's christening was entered on October 7, 1576. See "Life," p. 22.

when the agitation against them finally culminated in Elizabeth's proclamation abolishing them on November 25.[19]

What You Will

Authorship: Small, among others, has claimed that our text of *What You Will*, which was not published until 1607, represents a revised version of the play.[20] His argument rests on three points. First, he finds cause for "strong suspicion" in the fact that the formula "as it hath been sundry times acted" is absent from the title page. A close examination of the title pages of Marston's plays reveals that they do reflect a high degree of consistency in their references to stage history and suggests that they ought to be taken seriously. But in the case of *What You Will* it is not a statement, but the lack of one that we are asked to consider. If the publisher had wished to indicate that the published text was a revision of the original, why did he not resort to the formula "with new additions," as the publisher of *The Malcontent* had? Clearly, the absence of a formula cannot be interpreted to mean anything. Secondly, it is argued that the confusion within the play of the names Celia and Lucea and Andrea and Adrian suggest a revision.[21] But this, too, is highly suspicious since it is very unlikely that the author of the play would have made such a mistake, even if he were revising it. Finally, the absence in *What You Will* of the kind of diction that Jonson had attacked in *The Poetaster* has prompted Small and others to infer that Marston revised it as a consequence of *The Poetaster*, purifying it of the diction so characteristic of his satires and early plays in the process. It is true that *What You Will* is relatively free of the diction ridiculed in *The Poetaster*, though it is probably not necessary to assume a revision to account for the fact. If we assume that Marston was so affected by *The Poetaster* that he revised *What You Will*, how can we account for the fact that he did not revise either *Antonio and Mellida* or *Antonio's Revenge*, both of which abound in this diction and both of which were probably published, though not written, after *The Poetaster* had been played? In view of the slightness of the argument for a revision, accordingly, it is preferable to assume that *What*

[19] See the entries for November 20, 21, 23, 25, 28, and 30, 1601, in G. B. Harrison's *Elizabethan Journals, 1591–1603* (London, 1938), III, 221–231.
[20] *Stage-Quarrel*, pp. 108, 109.
[21] See I, i, 29; II, ii, 200; III, ii, 83, 190, 245, 258; IV, i, 290, 295; V, i, 194.

You Will simply reflects a development in Marston's artistic powers. Unlike *Histriomastix, Jack Drum,* and the Antonio plays, it is relatively free of the diction ridiculed by Jonson; but so are all his subsequent plays. Unlike the early plays, too, it clearly represents the sophistication in structural matters that remains constant in the subsequent plays.

Date of Composition: What You Will is the only play by Marston that obviously took a part in the poetomachia (see especially "Induction" and III, iii, 165–173), which culminated in *The Poetaster* and *Satiromastix* and which had concluded by 1604, when Marston dedicated *The Malcontent* to Jonson. Those who have tried to unravel the tangle of the poetomachia have, to a man, assumed that *What You Will* was a reply to *Cynthia's Revels,* which was produced in December 1600,[22] and that it prompted Jonson to undertake *The Poetaster,* which was produced in the summer of 1601.[23] But aside from the tenuous internal relationships that might be worked out between the plays, there is no proof that *What You Will* filled exactly that role. Although it is possible that it did and that Marston wrote it in the few short months between the completion of *Antonio's Revenge* in the winter of 1600/1 and the late spring, by which time Jonson must have started on *The Poetaster,* it is also possible that he wrote it at the same time or after *The Poetaster.* All that can be concluded with confidence is that he wrote it after the completion of *Antonio's Revenge* and before *The Malcontent.* In view of the fact that Jonson's *Cynthia Revels* and *The Poetaster* were, during the poetomachia, Blackfriars' plays, and in view of Marston's allusion in the "Induction" to a very small stage (l. 98), *What You Will* would appear to have been a Paul's play.[24] If so, it was the last play Marston wrote for Paul's boys before leaving them to write *The Malcontent,* a Blackfriars' play (see below).

[22] H & S, I, 393, 394.   [23] H & S, IV, 325.

[24] Our precise knowledge about the physical conditions of the private houses is, of course, very limited. But consider Marston's other references to the small stage at Paul's.

> *Sir Edward Fortune.* Good Boy I faith, I would thou hast more roome. [*Jack Drum,* p. 234]

> *Piero.* The room's too scant: boys, stand in there, close. [*Antonio and Mellida,* V, i, 173]

I have noticed no such comments in his Blackfriars' plays.

Everything considered, *What You Will* was probably produced in 1601 or 1602. This rough location in Marston's canon is to some extent supported by the internal evidence of structure and style. Although *What You Will* still bears traces of the satires and early plays, it also reflects structural advances that become important in subsequent plays; it was, for example, the first play in which Marston used the disguise plot that he continued to use in *The Malcontent* and *The Fawn*. Stylistically, moreover, it is almost entirely free of the heavy, ponderous lines and wild diction of the satires and early plays; its general style is the racy, conversational prose and verse prominent in the later plays.

The Malcontent

Authorship: From the evidence of the title pages of the first two editions of the play, *The Malcontent* is clearly Marston's play. There is some question, however, about his responsibility for the additions inserted in the third edition. At the heart of this matter are the ambiguous title page of the third edition: "The / Malcontent. / Augmented by Marston. / With the Additions played by the Kings / Maiesties servants. / Written by John Webster." and the special head title above the "Induction": "The Induction to / the Malecontent, And / the additions acted by the kings Ma- / iesties servants. Written by John Webster." On the strength of this evidence one might conclude that Webster was responsible for both the "Induction" and the additions to the text proper. But Stoll has argued convincingly that these statements should be interpreted to mean that Marston augmented the text, while Webster added only the "Induction." [25] Certainly this is the division of labor one would expect between the author of a work and a second writer, and this is what is suggested by the additions in the text itself. As F. L. Lucas has pointed out in his edition of Webster, the additions and changes made in the text proper suggest the activity of an author carefully revising his own work.[26] A close comparison of the early editions with the third edition reveals changes, additions, and omissions so trifling that only the author himself could have been concerned enough to make them. In I, i, 35, 36, for example, the line "the elements struggle within him; his soul is at variance" becomes in

---

[25] *John Webster* (Boston, 1905), pp. 55–60.
[26] *The Complete Works of John Webster* (London, 1927), III, 297

the third edition ". . . at variance with herself." In I, i, 215–218, we find the addition of parentheses around the passage in the third edition. And in I, i, 248, the line "O, climb not a falling tower" becomes "O, no, climb not. . . ." Moreover, we find such insignificant stray additions as the line at II, ii, 34: "Fried frogs are very good, and French-like too," and such slight omissions as the omission of "new" from the line at I, i, 54: "Some arch-devil can shape her a new petticoat." But the substantial additions also support the case for Marston's authorship of the inserted passages. Satiric almost to the line, they represent subtle extensions of the satiric possibilities latent in the shorter version, extensions that Marston could well have felt necessary in order to maintain, in the adult production of the play, the balance between levity and seriousness he had achieved in the children's production.

Date of Composition: Although *The Malcontent* was not entered in the Stationers' Register until July 5, 1604, Stoll has argued that it was produced in 1600.[27] His evidence for this contention is the allusion in I, iii, 20, 21, to a horn growing in a woman's forehead twelve years before, a reference that is thought to hark back to a pamphlet of 1588 describing this phenomenon. But 1600 is clearly too early for this play. To begin with, that year would place the play in the middle of the poetomachia, with which its only tangible connection is the dedication to Jonson. Secondly, since the allusion occurs in an added passage, it would force the conclusion that the additions were inserted in 1600. Since *The Malcontent* was a Blackfriars' play and since Blackfriars was not leased by Evans until September 2, 1600, there could hardly have been time for all that would have had to happen: a production at Blackfriars, a company that Marston was not associated with at that time; an extensive revision; and a second production at the Globe. Chambers' conclusion that twelve was probably a round rather than a precise figure is probably correct.[28]

By far the more persuasive body of evidence points to 1603 for the composition of the short version. Quite clearly *The Malcontent* followed *What You Will.* Although it is in its use of the disguise plot the structural kin of that play, it appears on the strength of an allusion in the "Induction" (ll. 45, 46) to have been a Blackfriars' play—the first in the series that Marston wrote for that playhouse, while *What You Will* was apparently the last in the series that he wrote for Paul's.

[27] *Webster,* p. 60.   [28] *Stage,* IV, 432.

Moreover, the dedication to Jonson and the absence in the text of anything suggestive of the poetomachia clearly put it after that trouble and, automatically, after *What You Will*.

Taking the rough date determined for *What You Will*, 1601–1602, then, and 1604, the year of all three editions of the play, as limits, we have only to consider when within the period 1602–1604 the respective productions of the play were probable. Since all three editions of the play were issued in 1604, it is distinctly possible that both versions of it were produced for the first time in that year. If that were true, however, both versions would have had to be produced between April of 1604, when the theatres (which had been closed because of the plague since May of 1603) reopened, and November, to allow a month for the printing of the long version. This order of events may be accurate, but it is rather improbable. To begin with, it is rather improbable that the managers at Blackfriars would have permitted Marston to transfer a play to the Globe that they had produced only recently, perhaps were still producing, and also improbable that the managers of the Globe would have wanted it. It is more likely that the managers at the Globe would negotiate for a play that had been a success before the theatres had been closed in May of 1603 and would use such a play for the reopening in April of 1604. Moreover, there is one piece of internal evidence that clearly suggests that the short version was not followed closely by the long version. Sly's remark in the "Induction" that he had seen this play often (ll. 16, 17) indicates that it was not new when the long version was presented. If it had been produced after April of 1604, it most certainly would have been new. If, on the other hand, we assume that it was first produced in 1603 before the theatres were closed in May, Sly's remark makes sense and the business strategy seems reasonable.

The Fawn

Date of Composition: Although *The Fawn* was not entered in the Stationers' Register until March 12, 1606, what we can infer about Marston's activity in 1605 and the early months of 1606 suggests that the play was written before 1605. During 1605 he was apparently preoccupied with *Eastward Ho* and *The Dutch Courtezan*. We know from the allusion in the "Prologue" to *Eastward Ho*, as well as from other evidence, that it was a relatively new play when it was entered in September of 1605. We know, too, from the evidence of the entry for *The Dutch Courtezan* on July 26, 1605, where it is referred to as "latelie presented," the evidence of the title page, and the evidence of the "Prologue" (see Chapter VII, pp. 219–222) that it was a new play when it was entered. Accordingly, Marston had plenty to occupy himself with until July of 1605, without assuming that he had another play in hand. Yet it was either after the production of *Eastward Ho* in the late spring or early summer or after its publication in the early fall that Chapman and Jonson were arrested and Marston was forced to flee from London.[29] We cannot be sure how long he remained in this self-imposed exile, but it is probable that he remained away until after the first edition of *The Fawn* had been released in the spring of 1606 because the title page of the second edition mentions that he had been absent when the first edition was prepared. At any rate, in the second edition he mentioned in a note "To the Reader" that he was about to bring out *Sophonisba,* with which, we may reasonably assume, he had been busy since the production of *The Dutch Courtezan*—perhaps during his absence. In view of all this activity it is hardly probable that he wrote his longest play in 1605 or 1606.

A comparison of the title pages of both editions, furthermore, suggests that *The Fawn* was far from being a new play when it was published in 1606. Where the title page of the first edition mentions that it had "Bene Divers times presented at the blacke Friars," the title page of the second edition mentions both the production at Blackfriars and another "since at Powles." Since it is unlikely that the company at Paul's would have produced the play soon after the company at Blackfriars had introduced it or that the company at Blackfriars would have permitted them to, we must assume that the play had been introduced at Blackfriars, but had not been played there for some time when the company at Paul's acquired permission to perform it. This sequence of events would put the first production of the play at a considerable distance from the date of its first publication.

On the strength of internal evidence we may infer that *The Fawn* was probably written in 1604. To begin with, that it was written after *The Malcontent* is manifest from *The Fawn's* copious quotations from

[29] Chambers, *Stage,* III, 255.

and paraphrases of Florio's Montaigne, which was published in 1603 and which, once Marston had read it, so impressed him that his next three plays are saturated with extracts from it. Secondly, its title page mentions that it was acted by "the Children of the Queenes Maiesties Reuels," a designation that the child actors at Blackfriars bore for only a limited time. They assumed it when they received the Queen's patronage on February 4, 1604, and discontinued using it after they lost her patronage early in 1606. All three of Marston's plays that were acted during this period use the designation on their title pages, but *Sophonisba*, which was acted in 1606, does not. Moreover, this distinction is maintained consistently even in Sheares's edition of 1633, and we have no reason to think that Sheares was simply copying earlier title pages: at any rate he had not copied the title page of *The Dutch Courtezan;* he had brought it up to date by changing "as it was played" to "as it hath been sundry times played." The reliability of the title page is important; by limiting the play, as it does, to 1604–1606, it insists on the year 1604 since 1605 and 1606 can be ruled out on other grounds. The only additional evidence that we have supporting 1604 is the play's obvious kinship to *The Malcontent. The Fawn* is not only a disguise-plot play, like *The Malcontent,* but it also uses the same motto used for *The Malcontent.*

In conclusion, I should mention that E. Herz has argued that *The Fawn* influenced the plot of a German play, *Tiberius von Ferrara und Annabella von Mompelgart* (1604).[30] I have purposely ignored his claim because I find it so difficult to prove which play influenced which in such cases. Moreover, Stoll's claim that the quartering alluded to in IV, i, 310, refers to the execution of Sir Everard Digby on January 30, 1606, is even less impressive.[31] This date is too close to that of the Stationers' entry, and, besides, the allusion refers to a commonplace matter much too generally to make the Digby quartering any more eligible than, say, the Valentine Thomas quartering of June 6, 1603.

Eastward Ho

Authorship: The question of Marston's contribution to the structural outline of the play is taken up in the early pages of Chapter VII. The

----

[30] *Englische Schauspieler und englisches Schauspiel zur Zeit Shakespeares in Deutschland* (Hamburg, 1903), p. 99.

[31] *Webster,* p. 17.

question concerning the precise parts he wrote leads abruptly to conjecture.

Unfortunately, we have nothing to guide us in this matter except the play itself and the respective styles of the collaborators, insofar as they can be precisely determined. By this time Marston had given up the harsh satiric style that so indelibly stamps his early plays. On the basis of those remaining stylistic traits that might still be considered characteristic, however, one can take a calculated leap into the unknown. Basing my conclusions entirely on such stylistic evidence as unusually full stage directions, unusual verbs derived from nouns, unusual words that occur elsewhere in Marston's work, sentence structure, and the even less reliable index of pace or movement, I would say that Marston's hand is clearest in I; II, iii, up to about l. 209; III, ii, up to about l. 82; and IV, iv.

Date of Composition: This question is discussed in the early pages of Chapter VII.

The Dutch Courtezan

Date of Composition: This question is discussed in the early pages of Chapter VII.

Sophonisba

Date of Composition: Sophonisba was entered in the Stationers' Register on March 17, 1606, five days after *The Fawn* had been entered. Since *The Fawn* was probably written in 1604 and since Marston had been busy with *Eastward Ho* and *The Dutch Courtezan* during the first half of 1605, it is reasonable to assume that he wrote this second tragedy in the second half of 1605 and early in 1606, perhaps during his enforced exile after the *Eastward Ho* scandal. Actually, we have no clear proof about the duration of his exile. We know that he was out of London when the first edition of *The Fawn* appeared, sometime after March 12, 1606, the date of the Stationers' entry, and for all we know he may have been in continuous exile until he returned sometime before July 31, 1606, for the *City Pageant,* an event that indicates that King James had forgiven him. In any case, we can be reasonably certain that, despite the Stationers' entry, *Sophonisba* was neither produced nor published until the spring or summer. Apparently it was acted by the children after they had ceased to enjoy the Queen's patronage early in 1606,[32] and Marston mentioned it to his London audience apparently for the first time in a prefatory note to the second edition of *The Fawn*,[33] which surely appeared several weeks, at least, after the entry of March 12. Moreover, the statement on the title page that it had "beene sundry times / Acted at the Blacke Friers" before it was printed suggests that it was published considerably after it had been entered. In view of this evidence, we can conclude, perhaps, that *Sophonisba* was first acted in the late spring of 1606 and published in the summer.

The Insatiate Countess

Authorship: There has never been any doubt that Marston had some part in the composition of this play. Two of the four known title pages bear his name: the edition of 1613 (in two of five copies of which his name has been cut out and supplied in a Renaissance hand) and the second issue of the edition of 1631. Yet there is also external evidence to suggest that he was not its sole author. The edition of 1616 bears no author's name, and the first issue of the edition of 1631 supplies the name "William Barksteed." Moreover, William Sheares did not include the play in his collection of 1633, just as he did not include *The Malcontent*, the only other play credited as a whole to Marston by some title pages, but about which there are also authorial problems.[34]

Beginning with these facts, scholars have looked to internal evidence to determine how much of the play is Marston's and have evolved a variety of theories of authorship. At the one extreme are Aronstein, Koeppel, Ernst, and Wood, who give most of the play to Marston.[35]

[32] *Sophonisba* was the first in the series of four plays published after the Queen's patronage had been bestowed on February 4, 1604, not to bear a note describing the actors as "the Children of the Queenes Maiesties Reuels."

[33] The pertinent part of the note reads: "for such courteous survey of my pen, I will present a tragedy to you, which shall boldly abide the most curious perusal." A marginal note in the second quarto prints the title *Sophonisba*.

[34] A. B. Grosart points out in his edition of Barksted's poems (*Unique or Very Rare Books*, Manchester, 1876, III, xxii) that other reasons can be found to account for Sheare's failure to include *The Malcontent* and *The Insatiate Countess* in his collection. Most notable is that both plays were in the hands of another bookseller.

[35] Philip Aronstein, "John Marston als Dramatiker," *ES*, XX (1895), 386; Emil Koeppel, *Quellen-Studien zu den Dramen Ben Jonson's, John Marston's, und Beaumont's und Fletcher's* (Erlangen and Leipzig, 1895), pp. 30, 31; Friedrich

Less generous are the editor of the edition of 1820, who gives him only the tragic plot, and Fleay, who gives him only the comic plot.[36] At the other extreme are Bullen, Small, Curtis, and Chambers, who give most of the play to Barksted.[37] Even with this last group, indeed, there is a considerable range of opinion. Bullen and Chambers argue that Marston drafted the whole plot and that Barksted finished it, while the others conclude that Marston drafted only parts of the plot, the rest of which Barksted drafted and the whole of which he finished. Actually, no solution to the problem of authorship can be advanced with confidence until a thorough study has been made of the play's manifold textual problems, and even then the play could well remain a tantalizing conundrum. For the present we can only review the available evidence with a view toward re-evaluating it in the light of the probabilities about Marston established in this study.

The case against Marston's exclusive authorship seems solid. To begin with, several pieces of evidence link William Barksted with the play. In addition to the appearance of his name as author in the first issue of 1631, the play in all editions is identified with Whitefriars, a playhouse with which Marston had no known association, but where Barksted was an actor. Moreover, Small has isolated "no less than fourteen passages" in the play that in his view strongly resemble passages in Barksted's poems, *Mirrha The Mother of Adonis* (1607) and *Hiren, or The Fair Greek* (1611).[38] Although some of these resemblances seem a bit farfetched, three of them are verbatim repetitions. If, at any rate, this evidence can be said to connect Barksted with the play, the other arguments to support his part authorship take on importance in that they supply further guides for identifying his hand. Ordinarily, the argument first offered by Bullen that traces Barksted's hand in the unusual number of Shakespearean imitations would be negligible;[39] but since Barksted can be linked with the play on other grounds, it takes on added weight in view of his acknowledged debt to

Ernst, *John Marstons Tragödie, The Insatiate Countess* (Königsberg, 1913), pp. 65–66; Wood, *Plays*, III, xxviii.

[36] *The Insatiate Countess, A Tragi-Comedy* (London, 1820), p. xiii; F. G. Fleay, *Shakespeariana*, I (March, 1884), 137.

[37] Bullen, *Works*, I, li; R. A. Small, "The Authorship and Date of *The Insatiate Countess*," *Harvard Studies and Notes in Philology and Literature*, V (1896) 277–282; Curtis, "Life," pp. 290–295; Chambers, *Stage*, III, 434.

[38] "Authorship," pp. 279–281.

[39] *Works*, I, 1. See also Small, "Authorship," pp. 278–279.

Shakespeare in the last stanza of *Mirrha*. In the same way, the arguments used to rule out Marston on stylistic grounds are still highly problematical, but doubtless more impressive, since the full, richly allusive style that all scholars have declared un-Marstonian is strikingly suggestive of Barksted's poems.[40] Altogether, this evidence confirms Barksted's part in the play and provides guides (though admittedly unreliable ones) by which to identify that part.

Before proceeding to the task of differentiating Marston's from Barksted's part, however, we should recognize that other evidence, too, indicates that Marston was not the sole author. It is surely significant that there is no reminder in the play of the Neo-Stoicism that had so long dominated Marston's thought, nor even of the classical Stoicism so solemnly bodied forth in his most recent dramatic effort, *Sophonisba*. Indeed, no part of the play's general conception—of the ideas encountered in the action or of the intellectual terms of the choral commentary—is suggestive of Marston. On the contrary, at two points a doctrinal point is explicitly made that is not simply uncharacteristic, but conspicuously at variance with, Marston's thought, as far as we know it. In III, iv, Isabella says, "We know not virtue till we taste of vice" (l. 140), and in IV, ii, Massino repeats the point, "Till man knows hell he never has firm faith" (l. 114). This idea is central to the moral position established by the play. Yet Marston had unequivocally attacked it in *SV*, IV, 93–167, and had throughout his public life held a philosophy inconsistent with it. If this philosophical disparity can be trusted, it suggests not only that Marston was not the sole author but also that he was probably not the author chiefly responsible for the play.

What, then, was his part in *The Insatiate Countess?* Much of the evidence by which his part might be isolated proceeds from the rather negative tests discussed above, evidence that suggests another hand, presumably Barksted's. By themselves, of course, the echoes of Barksted's poems, the verse style, and the Shakespearean imitations are not very significant; but they become significant when they can be seen to cluster to an extent sufficient to delineate a pattern. Such a pattern is not difficult to discover in the play. Most of the evidence of this negative sort appears in the tragic line of action concerning Isabella,

---

[40] Small, "Authorship," p. 279, cites seventy-two such passages.

that part of the play that least resembles Marston's work in thought, manner, and tone. Of the two actions comprising the play, accordingly, apparently Marston had little, if anything, to do with the tragic action.

The comic action concerning Claridiana, Rogero, and Mendoza, on the other hand, is one that Marston might well have designed and might even have worked up to a considerable extent. Its exploitation of the hatred of Claridiana and Rogero for exhibitions of comic rage is reminiscent of Marston's earlier treatment of Franceschina and Mulligrub. Its technique of revealing the whole situation to the audience and to certain characters in the interests of playing down melodramatic suspense and heightening comic and satiric values is reminiscent of Marston's use of the disguise plot. Its use of characters with burlesque names in Claridiana and Rogero, of burlesque elements in Mendoza's wooing of Lady Lentulus, and of a dance in which pairs of characters converse in turn are all met earlier in Marston's satirical comedies. Moreover, simply the general quality of racy outrageousness to be met in scenes like those in which Claridiana and Rogero demand death for a crime they did not commit rather than admit themselves cuckolds is far more suggestive of Marston than anything to be found in the Isabella line of action. Small's comment that the comic portions are un-Marstonian because they have no "flavor of bitterness" overlooks much of Marston's comedy in *Jack Drum, What You Will,* and *The Fawn.*[41] None of this, of course, is conclusive; moreover the presence in this line of action, too, of some few echoes of Barksted's poems and of some few Shakespearean imitations more elaborate than a seasoned dramatist would probably have included suggests that Barksted may have also had some part in working up this action. Nonetheless, the conclusion supported by the evidence is that Marston's part in the play centered largely in the comic action. It seems highly probable that he designed it and even probable that he wrote much of it.

This distribution of labor has still other evidence to recommend it. The structure of *The Insatiate Countess* as a whole suggests that the tragic and comic actions were at one stage of the play's composition quite separate. Although they are fairly well integrated in the first few scenes, they are never thereafter successfully assimilated to each other. After the first few scenes the tragic action is laid in Pavia, the comic

---

[41] "Authorship," pp. 277–278.

in Venice. Moreover, the play ends in an extraordinary way for a Renaissance play with two separate scenes of judgment. Finally, the comic action is never carried to completion in that the complications concerning Mendoza are never resolved. Koeppel and Ernst have attempted to explain this last circumstance by the argument that Barksted finished a play that Marston had started, but did not know the source that Marston was using.[42] It is only barely possible, however, that Barksted did not know the sources for both plots in Painter.[43] In the light of the clumsiness of plotting in the tragic action, far more feasible is that he was content to take Marston's comic action as he found it and to finish it off as quickly as he could. Perhaps he tired of the job of integrating the two actions: certainly there is much more evidence of effort of this kind at the beginning than at the end of the play. If so, he may have wished toward the end of his labors simply to patch together Marston's part of the play as best he could and, consequently, did not see through all the complications that Marston had actuated. The play's inconclusive and disjointed plot, at least, favors such a theory.

But obviously all of this is highly speculative, and obviously all such attempts must remain so until we substantially increase our knowledge about this play. Given the evidence available, it seems reasonable to conclude that Marston designed and worked up the comic action to a point very near completion and then Barksted finished it. Marston may also have had a hand in the tragic action, it is true, but we have no evidence that he did and considerable to indicate that he did not.

Date of Composition: Marston's contribution to *The Insatiate Countess* was probably made between July of 1606 and June of 1608. Up to March 1606 he had been busy with other plays, most recently *Sophonisba*. On June 8, 1608, on the other hand, he was imprisoned, and soon afterwards he began disengaging himself from the theatre by selling his share in Blackfriars to Robert Keysar. During the period from March 1606 to June 1608 he probably worked on only two other pieces, *The City Pageant,* which Nichols reports was written in twelve

[42] Koeppel, *Quellen-Studien,* p. 31, n. 2, and Ernst, *Marstons Tragödie,* p. 66.
[43] These sources are the twenty-fourth and twenty-sixth novels in Tome II of William Painter's *Palace of Pleasure.*

days at the end of July 1606,[44] and *The Ashby Entertainment,* which was presented in August of 1607; Chambers' theory that he also worked on a play that got him in trouble in 1608 does not seem strong.[45] If we can conclude that *The Entertainment* rules out the period from July 1606 to August 1607, at any rate, it seems likely that he wrote his part of *The Insatiate Countess* between August 1607 and June 1608.

Despite Barksted's association with children's companies (the King's Revels, *ca.* 1607–1609, and the Queen's Revels, 1609–1613), his publication of *Mirrha* in 1607 suggests that he was old enough by that year to have undertaken his part in this play. If, as the facts indicate, the play was prepared for a production at Whitefriars, however, it is not likely that it was finished before 1607, since that is the earliest possible year for the activation of that theatre.[46] If, as the evidence suggests, Barksted finished a play in part begun by Marston, moreover, he probably did not finish his work on it until 1608 at the earliest. Taking 1608 as the earliest limit for the play, then, we might conclude from the publication of *Hiren* in 1611 that by 1610 Barksted had finished the play and returned to writing poetry. This would give us the years 1608–1610 for his part in the play. Actually, it is safer to conclude that he could have finished the play any time between 1608 and 1613. The first edition of 1613 supplies the only reliable terminal date.

[44] John Nichols, *The Progresses, Processions, and Magnificent Festivities of King James the First* (London, 1828), II, 68.

[45] *Stage,* II, 53, 54.   [46] Chambers, *Stage,* II, 66.

The Occasional Pieces

City Pageant

The title of this pageant indicates that it was one of the entertainments offered to King James and his guest the King of Denmark as they toured London on July 31, 1606. Since Nichols refers to only one pageant for that day and since Howes's description of it is remarkably like this one, it is safe to assume that this was the "most stately Pageant" presented at Little Conduit in the course of the tour.[1] The pageant consists of some seventy lines of Latin dialogue delivered by the Recorder of the City (Sir Henry Montague) and allegorical figures named Concordia, Londinum, and Neptunus. The "Stage Direction" describes an allegorical scene representing the "Island of Great Britain, supported on the one side by Neptune, with the force of ships; on the other, Vulcan with the power of iron, and the commodities of tin, lead, and other minerals." Concord, "supported by Piety, and Policy," descends to the island to the accompaniment of the Tritons' music and mermaids' singing, after which the characters deliver their speeches of welcome. Nichols' remark that the "workmen and plotters" of the

---

[1] Nichols, *Progresses*, II, 68, 87. See also Harrison, *Jacobean Journals*, p. 327

pageant had only twelve days in which to prepare it indicates that Marston worked on it in the last two weeks of July.[2] The British Museum manuscript (Royal Mss. 18A, xxxi) is signed with Marston's name.

The Ashby Entertainment

The occasion for this "entertainment" was the visit paid to Lord and Lady Huntington at Ashby-de-la-Zouch in Leicester by Lady Huntington's mother, the Dowager Countess of Derby. It is dated by a fragment from it now in the British Museum (Sloane 848, F9), bearing the date August 1607. The entertainment has two parts: the first an elaborate greeting for the Countess as she approached the house through the park, the second a still more elaborate Masque that was presented in the "great chamber." The whole comprises an intricate and extravagant compliment to the Countess, complete with songs, dancing, and descents in machines. Marston's name is signed to the introductory poem in the Bridgewater manuscript, and, if Bullen is correct, the "epilogue" and the corrections in dark ink are in his handwriting.[3]

The Mountebank's Masque

Despite the interest in this vigorous, if rather disjointed, masque, there are good reasons for doubting that Marston wrote it. It appears to have been produced shortly before it was performed at court on February 16, 1617/1618,[4] by which time Marston had long since given up writing. Moreover, although it abounds in the wit and sophistication of writing from the Inns of Court world (it was performed at Gray's Inn), it contains nothing of thought or expression that is particularly suggestive of Marston.

Bullen has included it in his edition only because J. P. Collier had reprinted it from a manuscript that he claimed had Marston's name penciled on it in a Renaissance hand. But that manuscript (presumably owned by the Duke of Devonshire) has been lost, and the other two manuscripts of the masque contain no reference to Marston.[5] If we

---

[2] *Progresses,* II, 68.   [3] *Works,* III, 385.
[4] See Nichols, *Progresses,* III, 466.
[5] See Nichols, *Progresses,* III, 466, and British Museum Add. Ms. 5956.

assume a deception on Collier's part, it might be argued that he was prompted to it by the passage dealing with Amoroso and his behavior at the feast of Venus Cytherea. In *The Fawn* Marston had ridiculed Sir Amoroso Debile-Dosso in his appearance at the Parliament of Cupid. But the name was too common a designation for a ladies' man at the time to establish a convincing link.

Selected Bibliography

Alden, Raymond M. *The Rise of Formal Satire in England under Classical Influence.* Philadelphia, 1899.

Allen, Morse S. *The Satire of John Marston.* Columbus, Ohio, 1920.

Aronstein, P. "John Marston als Dramatiker," *Englische Studien,* XX (1895), 28–79.

à Wood, Anthony. *Athenae Oxoniensis,* ed. Philip Bliss. 4 vols. London, 1813.

Axelrad, A. José. *Un Malcontent Elizabéthain: John Marston (1576–1634).* Paris, 1955.

Bachrach, A. G. H. "The Great Chain of Acting," *Neophilologus,* XXXIII (1949), 160–172.

Barksted, William. *The Poems of William Barksted (Unique or Very Rare Books, III),* ed. Rev. Alexander B. Grosart. Manchester, 1876.

Barnfield, Richard. *Poems. 1594–1598 (English Scholar's Library, III),* ed. Edward Arber. Birmingham, 1882.

Becker, Paul. *Das Verhältnis von John Marston's "What You Will" zu Plautus' "Amphitruo" und Sforza D'Oddi's "I Morti Vivi."* Halle, 1904.

Besig, Emma M. S., ed. *"Histrio-Mastix; or The Player Whipt"* (unpublished Master's thesis, Cornell University, 1929).

Bethell, S. L. "Shakespeare's Actors," *RES*, N.S. I (1950), 193–205.

Brereton, J. Le Gay. *Elizabethan Drama: Notes and Studies.* Sydney, 1909.

Brettle, R. E. "John Marston, Dramatist, Some New Facts about His Life," *MLR*, XXII (1927), 7–14.

——. "Marston Born in Oxfordshire," *MLR*, XXII (1927), 317–319.

——. "John Marston, Dramatist, at Oxford," *RES*, III (1927), 398–405.

——. "The 'poet Marston' Letter to G. Clifton, 1607," *RES*, IV (1928), 212–214.

Brustein, Robert S. "Italianate Court Satire and The Plays of John Marston" (unpublished Ph.D. diss., Columbia University, 1957).

Campbell, Oscar James. *Comicall Satyre and Shakespeare's Troilus and Cressida.* San Marino, Calif., 1938.

Chambers, E. K. *The Elizabethan Stage.* 4 vols. Oxford, 1923.

Chapman, George. *The Plays and Poems of George Chapman*, ed. Thomas Marc Parrott. 2 vols. London, 1914.

——. *The Poems of George Chapman*, ed. Phyllis Brooks Bartlett. New York, 1941.

Collier, John Payne. *The Poetical Decameron.* 2 vols. Edinburgh, 1820.

Croll, Morris W. "'Attic Prose' in the Seventeenth Century," *SP*, XVIII (1921), 79–128.

——. "Muret and the History of 'Attic' Prose," *PMLA*, XXXIX (1924), 254–309.

Cross, K. Gustav. "The Authorship of Lust's Dominion," *SP*, LV (1958), 39–61.

Curtis, Ford Elmore. "John Marston: His Life and Works" (unpublished Ph.D. diss., Cornell University, 1932).

Davies, Sir John. *The Complete Poems of Sir John Davies.* 2 vols. London, 1876.

Deighton, Kenneth. *Marston's Works: Conjectural Readings.* London, 1893.

d'Oddi, Sforza. *I Morti Vivi.* Florence, 1608.

du Vair, Guillaume. *The Moral Philosophie of the Stoicks* (1598), tr. Thomas James, ed. Rudolf Kirk. New Brunswick, N.J., 1951.

Epictetus. *The Discourses as Reported by Arrian, The Manual, and*

Fragments, tr. and ed. W. A. Oldfather. 2 vols. New York, 1926–1928.

Ernst, Friedrich. *John Marstons Tragödie The Insatiate Countess.* Königsberg, 1913.

Finkelpearl, Philip Joseph. "The Works of John Marston: A Critical Study" (unpublished Ph.D. diss., Harvard University, 1954).

Fleay, F. G. "Shakespeare and Marston," *Shakespeariana,* I (1884), 103–106, 136–140.

Florio, John. *Queen Anna's New World of Words, Or Dictionarie of the Italian and English Tongues.* . . . London, 1611.

Freeburg, Victor Oscar. *Disguise Plots in Elizabethan Drama.* New York, 1915.

Freedman, Lila Hermann. "Satiric Personae: A Study of Point of View in Formal Verse Satire in the English Renaissance from Wyatt to Marston" (unpublished Ph.D. diss., University of Wisconsin, 1955).

Greg, W. W. "Notes on Old Books," *Library,* II (1922), 49–57.

Grosart, Alexander B., ed. *The Complete Poems of Joseph Hall* (*Unique or Very Rare Books,* IX). Manchester, 1879.

Hall, Joseph. *The Collected Poems of Joseph Hall,* ed. Arnold Davenport. Liverpool, 1949.

Harbage, Alfred. "Elizabethan Actors," *PMLA,* LIV (1939), 685–708.

——. *Shakespeare and the Rival Traditions.* New York, 1952.

Herz, E. *Englische Schauspieler und englisches Schauspiel zur Zeit Shakespeares in Deutschland.* Hamburg, 1903.

Hillebrand, Harold Newcomb. *The Child Actors* (*University of Illinois Studies,* XI). Urbana, Ill., 1926.

Inge, William Ralph. *Christian Mysticism.* London, 1899.

J. C. "Notices on Old English Comedies, No. 1, *Eastward Hoe,*" *Blackwood's Edinburgh Magazine,* X (1821), 127–136.

Jackson, James L. "Sources of the Sub-plot of Marston's *The Dutch Courtezan,*" *PQ,* XXXI (1952), 223–224.

Jonson, Ben. *Ben Jonson,* ed. C. H. Herford and Percy and Evelyn Simpson. 11 vols. Oxford, 1925–1952.

Joseph, B. L. *Elizabethan Acting.* London, 1951.

Kernan, Alvin. "John Marston's Play *Histrio-Mastix,*" *MLQ,* XIX (1958), 134–140.

——. *The Cankered Muse: Satire of the English Renaissance.* New Haven, 1959.

Koeppel, Emil. *Quellen-Studien zu den Dramen Ben Jonson's, John*

Marston's, und Beaumont's und Fletcher's. Erlangen and Leipzig, 1895.

Langbaine, Gerard. *An Account of the English Dramatick Poets.* Oxford, 1691.

Lipsius, Justus. *Two Bookes of Constancie* (1594), tr. Sir John Stradling, ed. Rudolf Kirk. New Brunswick, N.J., 1939.

Lodge, Thomas. *The Works of Thomas Lodge* (Hunterian Club Edition). 4 vols. London, 1878.

Lucas, F. L., ed. *The Complete Works of John Webster.* 4 vols. London, 1927.

Lust's Dominion; or, The Lascivious Queen, ed. J. Le Gay Brereton (*Materials for the Study of the Old English Drama,* V). Louvain, 1931.

Marston, John. *The Workes of John Marston,* ed. William Sheares. London, 1633.

——. *The Insatiate Countess, A Tragi-Comedy.* London, 1820.

——. *The Works of John Marston,* ed. A. H. Bullen. 3 vols. London, 1887.

——. *The Scourge of Villainy,* ed. G. B. Harrison (*Bodley Head Quartos,* XIII). London, 1925.

——. *The Plays of John Marston,* ed. H. Harvey Wood. 3 vols. London, 1934–1939.

O'Connor, John J. "Chief Source of Marston's *Dutch Courtezan,*" SP, LIV (1957), 509–515.

Pellegrini, Giuliano. *Il Teatro di John Marston.* Pisa, 1952.

Penniman, Josiah H. *The War of the Theatres.* Philadelphia, 1897.

Peter, John. *Complaint and Satire in Early English Literature.* Oxford, 1956.

Randolph, M. C. "Thomas Drant's Definition of Satire," *NQ,* CLXXX (1941), 416–418.

——. "The Medical Concept in English Renaissance Satiric Theory: Its Possible Relations and Implications," *SP,* XXXVIII (1941), 125–157.

——. "The Structural Design of the Formal Verse Satire," *PQ,* XXI (1942), 368–384.

Rowlands, Samuel. *The Works of Samuel Rowlands* (Hunterian Club Edition). 3 vols. London, 1880.

Saunders, Jason Lewis. *Justus Lipsius, The Philosophy of Renaissance Stoicism.* New York, 1955.

Sharpe, Robert Boies. *The Real War of the Theatres.* Boston, 1935.

Simpson, Richard, ed. *The School of Shakespeare.* 2 vols. London, 1878.

Small, R. A. "The Authorship and Date of *The Insatiate Countess*," *Harvard Studies and Notes in Philology and Literature,* V (1896), 277–282.

——. *The Stage-Quarrel between Ben Jonson and the So-Called Poetasters.* Breslau, 1899.

Smith, Hallett. *Elizabethan Poetry: A Study of Conventions, Meaning, and Expression.* Cambridge, Mass., 1952.

Spencer, Theodore. "The Elizabethan Malcontent," *J. Q. Adams Memorial Studies,* pp. 523–535. Washington, 1948.

Stein, Arnold. "The Second English Satirist," *MLR,* XXXVIII (1943), 273–278.

——. "Donne's Harshness and the Elizabethan Tradition," *SP,* XLI (1944), 390–409.

——. "Donne's Obscurity and the Elizabethan Tradition," *ELH,* XIII (1946), 98–118.

Stoll, Elmer Edgar. *John Webster.* Boston, 1905.

——. "Shakespere, Marston and the Malcontent Type," *MP,* III (1906), 281–303.

Thorndike, Ashley H. "The Relations of *Hamlet* to Contemporary Revenge Plays," *PMLA,* XVII (1902), 125–220.

A Transcript of the Registers of the Company of Stationers of London 1544–1640, ed. Edward Arber. 6 vols. London, 1876.

Ure, Peter. "John Marston's *Sophonisba:* A Reconsideration," *Durham University Journal,* N.S. X, no. 3 (1949), 81–90.

——. "A Note on 'Opinion' in Daniel, Greville and Chapman," *MLR,* XLVI (1951), 331–338.

Waith, Eugene M. *The Pattern of Tragicomedy in Beaumont and Fletcher.* New Haven, 1952.

Wallace, C. W. *The Children of the Chapel at Blackfriars 1597–1603* (*University of Nebraska Studies,* VIII). [Lincoln, Neb.], 1908.

Weever, John. *Epigrammes in the Oldest Cut and Newest Fashion* (1599), ed. R. B. McKerrow. London, 1911.

Whipple, T. K. *Martial and the English Epigram from Sir Thomas Wyatt to Ben Jonson.* Berkeley, Calif., 1925.

Williamson, George. "Strong Lines," *English Studies,* XVIII (1936), 152–159.

——. *The Senecan Amble: A Study in Prose from Bacon to Collier.* London, 1948.

Wood, Henry. "Shakespeare Burlesqued by two Fellow-Dramatists," *American Journal of Philology,* XVI (1895), 273–299.

Zanta, Léontine. *La Renaissance du Stoïcisme au XVIe Siècle.* Paris, 1914.

Index

Acting, Elizabethan, 106-110
  see also Burlesque *and* Child actors
Act of the Common Council of 1574, 89
Adelphi, The, 204n
Affectionate Shepherd, The, 12
All Fools, 204n
Amorists, 18-21, 123, 139, 140, 166, 183, 210
  see also Satiric types
Antipodes, The, 108
Antonio and Mellida, 14, 73, 86, 105, 110, 121, 129-143, 146, 148, 149, 154, 157, 159-160, 167, 172, 179, 188, 237, 260-261
Antonio's Revenge, 72, 113, 147-156, 160, 179, 182, 186, 188, 197, 241, 242, 261
Aquinas, St. Thomas, 60
Armin, Robert, 108, 200
Ashby Entertainment, The, 62, 240, 275, 277
À Wood, Anthony, 4, 22

Bacon, Sir Francis, 43, 52, 53, 64
Barksted, William, 270-275
Barnfield, Richard, 11-12

Blackfriars:
  plays of, 90-91, 181, 251-252, 263, 265, 266, 267
  theatre in, 88, 89, 90-91, 217, 265, 268
  see also Private theatres
Blurt, Master Constable, 112
Boaistuau, Pierre, 57
Boccaccio, Giovanni, 204
Boy Bishop, 98, 103
Breton, Nicholas, 217
Brome, Richard, 108
Bullock, Christopher, 230n
Burbage, Richard, 108
Burbage-Henslowe rivalry, 88
Burlesque, 14, 18-19, 103-104, 110, 111, 112, 113, 121, 122, 123, 126, 132, 139, 140, 142, 143, 148, 153, 170, 193, 201, 211, 226, 235, 246, 273
  see also Acting, Child actors, *and* Public companies

Carew, Thomas, 43
Castiglione, Baldassare, 140
Chapman, George, 10, 43, 113, 204n, 218, 267

285

Characterization, 47-48, 105, 111-112, 118, 122-127, 136, 139-142, 153-154, 166-174, 186-197, 225-227, 234, 236-238, 244, 246
  see also Satiric types
Chester, Sir Robert, 61
Chettle,. Harry, 257
Child actors, 95-96
  acting styles of, 98-110, 113, 118, 123, 130, 141, 153, 170-171, 187, 193, 211-212, 226, 238-239, 244-245
  history of, 96-100, 114-115, 211
  public companies' use of, 96-97
  repertories of, 99, 100-103
  revival of, 81-82, 88-89, 100-101
  see also Acting, Burlesque, *and* Private companies
Children of Blackfriars, 110
Children of Paul's, 97-98
Children of the Chapel Royal, 97
Cicero, 43, 54
City Pageant, The, 240, 274-275, 276-277
Clifton, Sir Henry, 114
"Comicall satyre," 144, 159
Commedia dell' arte, 124, 127, 238
Commission of November 7, 1606, 115
Commission of September 13, 1601, 115
Common Conditions, 121
"Commonplace," 40
Contention between Liberality and Prodigality, The, 81
Conversations with Drummond, 94, 221
Cornwallis, Sir William, 63
Criticism of Marston, 2
Cynthia's Revels, 81, 94, 104, 145, 159, 263

Dances, 98, 100, 127, 130, 142, 176, 200, 244, 273
Davies, Sir John, 12
Day, John, 258
Decameron, 204
Dekker, Thomas, 94, 257, 258
De la Broderie, Ambassador, 247
De la Primaudaye, Pierre, 57
Democritus, 27, 28
Derby, Countess of, 277
Detraction, 65-66, 70, 86
Digby, Sir Everard, 268
Discourses of Epictetus, 56
Disguise, 231, 235

Disguise plot, 156, 166, 178-181, 209, 214-216, 249, 264, 273
  see also Disguise, Duke-in-disguise plot, *Fawn, Malcontent,* and *What You Will*
D'Oddi, Sforza, 160, 161, 163
Donne, John, 12, 19, 26, 38, 46, 50n
Drant, Thomas, 25
Duke-in-disguise plot, 180-181, 212
Dumb show, 153
Dutch Courtezan, The, 218, 219, 220, 221, 222, 223, 228-240, 267, 268
Du Vair, Guillaume, 54, 56, 57, 59, 61, 63, 66, 72, 75

Eastward Ho, 218, 219, 220, 221, 222, 223-228, 232, 240, 248, 267, 268-269
Effeminacy, 71
Encomium of Lady Pecunia, The, 12
Epicoene, 115
Epictetus, 27, 28, 55, 56, 58, 59, 61, 72, 75, 76, 137, 168n, 202
Epicurean, 172
Epithalamium Made at Lincoln's Inn, 12
Evans, Henry, 100, 217
Every Man In His Humour, 144n
Every Man Out of His Humour, 87, 94, 144n, 145, 146, 159, 252, 255

Falstaff, 170
Family of Love, The, 103
Fantasticalness, 170
Farce, 232, 233
Faunus and Melliflora, 12
Fawn, The, 90, 112, 179, 201-216, 234, 240, 266-268
Field, Nathan, 114, 115
Fig for Momus, A, 10, 51
Florio's Montaigne, 58, 268
Foundation of Rhetoric, The, 40

Garden of Eloquence, The, 40
Gascoigne, George, 47
Gentleman Usher, The, 104, 112
Globe theatre, 199, 200, 265, 266
Greene, Robert, 121
Greville, Fulke, 53
Guilpin, Everard, 8, 13, 30, 63
Gulling Sonnets, 12
Gyles, Nathaniel, 100, 115

Hall, Joseph, 65, 92
  attitude toward satire, 30-32
  Marston's attacks on, 9n, 10, 34, 36n
  Marston's quarrel with, 35-36
  see also *Virgidemiarum*
Hamlet, 147
Harvey-Nashe controversy, 35
Harward, Simon, 83
Haughton, William, 258
I Henry IV, 170
Henslowe, Philip, 252, 256-259
Heroic tragedy, 243
Hiren, or The Fair Greek, 271
Histriomastix, 81, 82-88, 91, 94, 95, 97, 115-116, 117, 136, 143, 144, 251-255
Hooker, Richard, 52-53
Horace, 47n
Huntingdon, Lord and Lady, 277

Imitative structure, 117-118, 129, 132, 143, 146-147, 157-159
  see also Satiricomic form
Inns of Court, 6-7, 58, 89, 144n, 277
Insatiate Countess, The, 240, 246-247, 270-275
Interlude-Morality, 98, 99, 115, 244-245
Italian locale, 138, 169

Jack Drum's Entertainment, 81, 94, 103, 117, 118-129, 131, 132, 134, 136, 138, 142, 145, 157, 159, 172, 188, 240, 252, 259-260
James I, 221, 240, 247, 269, 276
James, Thomas, 54, 57, 63
I Jeronimo, 110
Jonson, Ben, 8, 11, 74n, 81, 87, 94, 95, 144-146, 157, 159, 217, 218, 222, 223, 224, 227, 251, 252, 256, 257, 259, 262, 263, 265, 267
Juvenal, 25, 27, 38, 47n, 181, 202

Kempe, Will, 200, 259
Keysar, Robert, 100, 247
King's Men, 110

Lake, Sir Thomas, 247
Libertinism, 53
Lipsius, Justus, 54, 56, 57, 59, 60, 63, 66, 68, 69, 72, 75
Literary genres, 30
  epigram, 13
  mock complaint, 12, 17

mock dedication, 18, 130
mock encomium, 12
mock epithalamium, 12
  renaissance attitudes toward, 8-14
  see also Satire, Renaissance
Lodge, Thomas, 10, 47, 51, 83
Lovers-in-distress burlesques, 121, 122, 125, 128, 142-143, 147, 159-160, 249
  see also *Antonio and Mellida, Jack Drum's Entertainment, and* Lovers-in-distress plays
Lovers-in-distress plays, 140, 146, 162
Love's Martyr, 61
Love's Metamorphosis, 81
Lust's Dominion, 257-259
Lycosthène, Conrad, 57
Lyly, John, 98, 99-100

Machiavellian villain, 148, 186-187, 244
Maid's Metamorphosis, The, 81, 103
Malcontent, The, 94, 110, 156, 179, 181-201, 203, 209, 213, 215, 217, 234, 240, 264-266, 270
Malcontent type, 187, 188
Manual of Epictetus, 56
Marlowe, Christopher, 257, 258
Marot, Clement, 83
Marprelate Controversy, 98, 103
Marston, John:
  attitude toward rhyme, 15, 45-46
  attitude toward satire, 32-34
  biographical information about, 5-6, 58, 80, 217-218, 240, 247-248
  quarrel with Hall, 35-36
  reputation of, 4, 248
  see also Criticism of Marston; Neo-Stoicism, Marston's version of; Satiricomic form; Seriocomic view; *and* Value system
Masque, 245, 246
May Day, 112
Measure for Measure, 179
Melodrama, 126, 140, 180, 182, 184, 190, 194, 230, 232, 239, 273
Merry Devil of Edmonton, The, 123
Merry Wives of Windsor, The, 167
Metamorphosis of Pygmalion's Image and Certain Satires, The, 17, 58
  contents and organization of, 37, 42
  date of, 37
  see also Verse satires
Meung, Jean de, 83

Middleton, Thomas, 179
Minturno, Antonio Sebastian, 27
Mirrha The Mother of Adonis, 271, 272
Mistaken identity, 175
Montague, Sir Henry, 276
Montaigne, Michel de, 52, 53, 57, 58
    see also Florio's Montaigne
Montreux, Nicholas de, 230
Moral Philosophie of the Stoicks, The, 54
Morti Vivi, I, 160-167, 174, 179
Mountebank's Masque, The, 277-278
Mucedorus, 92, 121
Munday, Anthony, 95
Muret, Antoine, 54
Music, 100, 200, 244, 258
    see also Songs
Mysticism, 59-60

Nashe, Thomas, 98
Neo-Platonism, Renaissance, 59-60
Neo-Stoicism, Renaissance, 14, 56-57,
    66-72, 84, 90, 249
    background of, 52-54
    dramatic expressions of, 61, 72-73,
        128-129, 132, 134-138, 148-152,
        154, 193, 214, 241, 254, 272
    Marston's version of, 51, 58-74, 118,
        148-152, 249-250
    stylistic aims of, 53
    teacher-philosopher persona of, 27, 29
    translations, 54n
    see also Detraction, Opinion, Serio-
        comic view, Stoicism, *and* Syn-
        deresis
No Whipping, Nor Tripping, 217

Opinion, 14, 18, 63-65, 69, 70, 71, 78,
    86, 128, 135, 158, 176, 188, 216,
    222, 238
Oratory, 107
Order of Conflagration, 80, 81
Orlando Furioso, 121
Ostler, William, 115
Ovid's Banquet of Sense, 10

Painter, William, 274
Parody, 14
Pavy, Salmon, 114
Peacham, Henry, 40
Pembroke's company, 95
Persius, 25, 50n, 202
Phantasiae, 55
Philotas, 113
Phoenix, The, 179

Physiologia, 60
Plutarch, 54
Poetaster, The, 94, 115, 145, 222, 262,
    263
Poetomachia, 74n, 85, 88, 94, 157, 263,
    265, 266
Polonius, 201
*Premier livre des bergeries de Juliette,
    Le*, 230
Private companies, 199-200
Private theatres, 89, 110, 113-114, 159
Privy Council's Order of 1597, 89
Prose romances, 121
Public companies, 199-200
    burlesques of, 91-92, 106-113, 116,
        122, 131, 187
    intelligentsia's view of, 92-93
Pudsey, Edward, 259
Puritans, 27, 52, 71n, 238
Puttenham, George, 26, 40
"Pygmalion's Image," 14-22, 35, 89-90,
    143

Quintilian, 40

Rainolde, Richard, 40
Raleigh, Sir Walter, 52, 53
Ramus, Peter, 52
2 Return From Parnassus, 72n, 74n, 94
Revenge play, 147, 148, 152, 154, 156,
    182, 198
Robert II, King of Scots, 256-257
Rowlands, Samuel, 9

St. Paul's:
    plays of, 90-91, 251-252, 255, 263,
        265, 267
    theatre in, 88, 89, 90-91, 255, 263n
Satire, Renaissance, 3, 23-34
    background of, 6-8, 21-22
    derivation of "satyre," 25
    harshness and obscurity of, 31-34
    medical analogy to, 27
    persona of, 26-27
    purpose of, 26
    Renaissance assumptions about, 24, 79
    Stoicism's kinship to, 75-77
    writers of, 6-7, 13, 15, 27, 42-43
    see also "Commonplace" *and* Verse
        satires
Satiricomic form, 23, 41, 86-87, 116, 121,
    126, 131, 136, 138-139, 142-143,
    146-147, 155, 157-160, 166, 176-
    178, 180-181, 193-194, 198-199,

Satiricomic form (*cont.*) 209, 214-216, 224-227, 234, 239-240, 246, 247, 249-250

Satiric types, 47-49, 70, 124, 133-134, 136, 139, 146, 154, 166-169, 174, 190-192, 209-210, 215-216, 237-238

Satiromastix, 94, 263

Scourge of Villainy, The, 65
contents and organization of, 38-42
date of, 37
see also Verse satires

Seneca, 6, 54, 55, 57, 58, 72, 75, 126, 141, 150, 152

Sentimental comedy, 199

Seriocomic view, 50-51, 77-78, 156, 177-178, 216, 227, 234, 239-240, 241, 249-250

Shakespeare, 3, 64, 94, 95, 133, 170, 259, 271, 272, 273

Sharpham, Edward, 248, 270

Sheares, William, 270

Sir Clyomon and Sir Clamydes, 92, 121

Songs, 98, 100, 127, 130, 142, 153, 176, 200, 245
see also Music

Sophonisba, 61, 62, 73, 240, 241-246, 267, 269-270

Sources, Marston's use of, 162-168, 174, 204, 230, 242, 274

Spanish Tragedy, The, 110, 147, 148

Stoicism, classical, 54-55, 59-60, 62-63, 68, 149, 155, 242, 243
dramatic expressions of, 72-73, 151, 241, 245-246, 272
teacher-philosopher persona of, 75-76
translations, 54n, 57n

Stradling, Sir John, 57, 63

Stuttering, 176

Swan theatre, 89

Synderesis, 39, 59-60, 67-68, 253

Terence, 204n

Thomas, Valentine, 268

Tiberius von Ferrara und Annabella von Mompelgart, 268

Tragedy, 113, 147, 155, 241, 244

Turk, The, 113

Two Gentlemen of Verona, 167

Underwood, John, 115

Value system, 221-222

Verbal style, 42-46, 128, 153, 177, 215, 245, 253, 258, 262, 269, 272

Verse satires, 143
imagery of, 66-72
persona of, 2-3, 26-30, 32, 43, 77-78, 118, 124, 125, 137, 146, 149, 154, 156, 171-172, 215, 249
use of controlling thesis in, 46-48
use of *exempla* in, 49-50
use of semidramatic devices in, 49
use of structural digression in, 39-41
see also Metamorphosis of Pygmalion's Image, Satiric types, and *Scourge of Villainy*

Virgidemiarum, 26, 36, 46, 47

Volpone, 103

War of the theatres, 85, 88
see also Poetomachia

Webster, John, 181, 264

Weever, John, 4, 8, 10, 12

Westward Ho, 219

What You Will, 94, 157-178, 180, 194, 198, 214, 237, 262-264, 265-266

Whipper of The Satyre, The, 217

Whipping of The Satyre, The, 217

Whitefriars, 271, 275

Wilkes, John, 247

Wilkes, Mary, 247

Wisdom of Dr. Doddipole, The, 81, 103

Witchcraft, 244

Woman's Revenge, A, 230n